Displacements

Parallax Re-visions of Culture and Society
Stephen G. Nichols, Gerald Prince, and Wendy Steiner
SERIES EDITORS

Displacements

Women, Tradition, Literatures in French

EDITED BY

Joan DeJean & Nancy K. Miller

THE JOHNS HOPKINS UNIVERSITY PRESS
Baltimore & London

The Johns Hopkins University Press
701 West 40th Street, Baltimore, Maryland 21211
The Johns Hopkins Press Ltd., London

Library of Congress Cataloging-in-Publication Data

Displacements : women, tradition, literatures in French / edited by Joan DeJean and
     Nancy K. Miller.
          p. cm. — (Parallax : re-visions of culture and society)
     Includes bibliographical references.
     ISBN 0-8018-4070-8. — ISBN 0-8018-4071-6 (pbk.)
     1. French literature—Women authors—History and criticism.   2. Women and
literature—France.   I. DeJean, Joan E.   II. Miller, Nancy K., 1941- .   III. Series:
Parallax (Baltimore, Md.)
PQ149.D57   1991
840.9'9287—dc20   90-38542
                                                                                              CIP

Contents

Editors' Preface

The central concern of this volume, canon formation, has begun to be evoked as though it were only a passing intellectual fad. True, for the last half-dozen years—in my memory, the September 1983 *Critical Inquiry* issue on *Canons* serves as an inaugural moment—the word *canon* has been unavoidable on the critical scene, to the point that colleagues have begun to announce that this will soon be a dead issue, yet another scholarly fashion that has seen its day. This prediction seems premature. For this is one area of academic concern in which the impact of our discussions can be assessed through such vital signs as curricular reforms, new editions of previously unavailable works, and revised demarcations for literary history. These signs suggest that scholars, especially those of us who are teachers of French, still have a long way to go before we can feel equipped to carry out what I take to be the objective of the current preoccupation with canon transformation, in the words of Henry Louis Gates, Jr., "to prepare our students for their roles as citizens of a world culture . . . rather than . . . as guardians of the last frontier outpost of white male Western culture."[1]

For teachers of French, the distance separating us from that goal is even greater than for our colleagues in English. In the 1970s, while French was virtually the universal language of literary theory, French studies were a major influence on the American university scene. In the 1980s, however, that situation has been reversed: the direction of French studies has largely been determined by developments in English and American Studies. As a result of this influence, we are experiencing a kind of continental drift: French literature seems well on the way to acquiring a different history in this country from its official version in France.

This development is already beginning to exert subtle pressures on us in our role as teachers. Most concretely, to judge from recent conferences and publications, the lists of works vital to the current thinking about French literature on this side of the Atlantic is becoming more and more different from the curriculum promoted by the formidable French educational establishment. This continental drift creates no insurmountable obstacles for us in our scholarly lives, since we have already developed our independent publication channels. However, in our pedagogical lives we still live as colonials, dependent on the mother country for essential resources: the reading lists for courses on French taught in America are determined in large part by the selection of works available in the collections—from Classiques Larousse to Garnier-Flammarion—edited for French schoolchildren.

The effects of continental drift are nowhere more visible than in the area of feminist criticism. For some time now feminist criticism has not been a force to be reckoned with in France: feminism, even the movement widely known here as French feminism, is far more important in this country than in France. In fact, on this side of the Atlantic no force has exerted more pressure on the traditional canon of French literature than feminist criticism. Inspired by the so-called American feminism, teachers of French have revised reading lists to include women writers and have developed new courses on both the graduate and the undergraduate level that foreground women's writing. However, because French feminism has had no involvement with the tradition of French women's writing, for most of these efforts professors are heavily dependent on photocopies: the only two publishers with any titles by women writers beyond the most obvious ones such as *La Princesse de Clèves*—Editions des Femmes and Desjonquères—produce editions that are so expensive by the time they reach bookstores here that they cannot be used for any but the most limited audience. How long will it be before we have the French equivalent of *The Norton Anthology of Literature by Women: The Tradition in English,* the kind of indispensable pedagogical tool that, by eliminating the financial burden for the student and the research burden for the professor, makes it possible to integrate women's writing throughout the curriculum?

It was this sense of the lack of concrete gains that originally motivated us to organize this collection. We wanted to focus attention on the gap between wide popularity, even among an intellectual audience, and official disregard within the educational establishment that is a recurrent feature of the history of the reception of French women's writing in France, rather than merely a phenomenon in twentieth-century America. We wanted, for instance, to stress the example of the broad readership won at different historical moments by works by women writers that did not succeed in gaining recognition by the French Academy, either as subjects of critical commentary or as pedagogical models for schoolchildren. We also wanted to examine labels, from realism to surrealism, commonly adopted in critical or pedagogical analysis, in order to determine why such generally accepted markers of literary history have worked against the canonization of women's writing. Finally, we hoped to launch an investigation of key moments of canon formation, periods during which French literature was shaped into a program in response to a perceived need for a more clearly defined pedagogical structure. The articles that follow attempt to understand both the concrete historical factors and the ideological motivations leading to the exclusion of the women writers who merited inclusion in influential literary histories and pedagogical manuals produced by the French educational establishment and exported wherever French is taught.

The primary goal of this collection of essays is to explore the possibilities for a form of *practical criticism* that would help bring our pedagogy in line with the scholarship currently being produced in America. There are those who argue that the very notion of a canon is already obsolete. However, for those of us teaching French in America today, this argument seems a theoretical luxury we can ill afford. If we do not work to create new options, then we will be forced to live with those created by and for teachers of French in France, to continue to live in cultural marginality, influenced by our native critical tradition but dependent on a foreign cultural patrimony.

J.D.

> Tradition: fr. L *tradition-, traditio* action of handing over, teaching, tradition—more at *TREASON*
> —Webster's Third New International Dictionary

What is passed on in the teaching of a national tradition? what betrayed in the handing over of a body of writing from one generation to the next? The essays in this volume point to some of the moves that historically have come to institute a *politics of poetics* across the social text. Of course, on the face of things, at least, these

moves may seem merely idiosyncratic, more a "gentlemen's agree-
ment," as Lillian Robinson puts it in "Treason Our Text," than a
wholesale project of calculated restrictions and targeted repres-
sions. But as Robinson then goes on to argue: "a gentleman is
inescapably—that is, by definition—a member of a privileged class
and of the male sex. From this perspective, it is probably quite accurate to think of the canon as an entirely gentlemanly artifact, considering how few works by nonmembers of that class and sex make
it into the informal agglomeration of course syllabi, anthologies,
and widely commented-upon 'standard authors' that constitutes the
canon as it is generally understood."[2]

As a first step in this interrogation of canon making, we have
chosen to focus on the exclusionary politics regulating the transmission of French literature; notably, we have wanted to open the question of the exclusion by gender: women writers who are not included
in the dominant culture's imaginary, its conscious and unconscious
zones of self-representation. To be sure, these are not the only
grounds for exclusion from the gentlemen's club. If we think of the
canon as a complex social field of intersections and interventions,
the cross-hatching lines of class and race, of national "identity"
itself—the clusters of differences subsumed under the territorializa-
tion of the Hexagon—also need careful siting and remapping. In this
sense, while the elimination of women's writing from the cultural
record has been our organizing concern here, the question it points
to—how can we understand the process by which the cultural
record is constructed?—continues to occupy the horizon.

The question of canon formation and, especially in the case of
women's writing, canon *de*-formation—the gestures of selection by
which the authorial and reading practices, as well as the social "pref-
erences" of a given cultural moment are erased, forgotten, and rewritten as a transcendent literary history—is, as Jane Tompkins has
shown for American literature, always a matter of local history.
Thus the essays in the first part of this volume, "Making Canons in
France: Histories of the Classic," uncover the ways in which the
ideologies of gender, art, and national identity collaborate and col-
lide in different moments of French history. The essays interrogate
the categories and vocabularies of literary history itself—period,
genre, value, masterpiece, classic, major, minor, etcetera—all of
which have been at work in the displacement of women's writing from
its contexts, and the erasure of its effects from most accounts of the
cultural record. From this perspective, it is the legacy of individual

gentlemanly choices of critics and novelists—Boileau, Abbé Batteux, Sainte-Beuve, Taine, Balzac, Laclos, Etiemble, among others—that over time has come to constitute the collective object we know as "French literature."

Despite the typically canonized exceptions of the literary manuals—the *named* inclusions of Marie de France, Marguerite de Navarre, Christine de Pizan, Labé, Lafayette, Sévigné, Staël, Sand, Desbordes-Valmore, Colette—the inherited tradition of French culture, on the whole, remains a narrative of men's writing.[3] The second group of essays, "Canons and Contexts: Production, Reception, Revision," challenging the primacy of this gendered *déjà lu*, looks at literary genres and modes in which women's participation has been both forgotten and underread: the uncanonic *canso*, literary criticism, theater in the eighteenth century, lyric poetry in the nineteenth, avant-garde writing. These essays reopen the question of margin and center, gender and genre, within a familiar tradition's self-representation of its history and values. The revisions they articulate point to the crucial role played by social forces in the assignment of places in the national repertory.

In the third part, "Canons and Other Voices: Relocating French Literature," the essays and interviews point in two directions and signal the etymological intimacies of tradition and treason flagged above in the epigraph: on the one hand, the perpetuation in critical discourse and pedagogical enactments of the historical maneuvers of exclusion and repetition; on the other, an attention to the risk involved in drawing the borders of national and sexual identity; and of the danger of desires for inclusion unself-conscious about their own repetitions and exclusions: the "invisibilization" of other subjectivities.

These texts put pressure on the terms in which we originally conceived the project itself: can the use of "French" literature as a concept fail to impose the old political hierarchies of gender and geography, fail to reenact the colonization of those voices characterized in their diversity by accents and consigned to silence? The voices recorded here articulate a powerful resistance to any moves of reappropriation: they have insisted—in French—upon their own dislocations in every sense of the word—their relations to other continents, and the distance of islands—especially in regard to canonical regimes.

It is this sense of movement and shifting emphases that we want to mark in the title *Displacements*.

Finally, we have to ask, Is this enterprise, with its outsiders' gaze on French literature, merely an "American" preoccupation that confuses the posterity of writing with the petty tyrannies of the syllabus? An academic question about a foreign language?

Dear Friend [Colette replies to Julien Benda's questionnaire on French writers, *Mercure de France*, 1911],
Your letter arrives too late for me to answer you on the question of Latin: I have no Latin. You ask if Latin helps, as you put it, in the "formation of a French writer" . . . I've no idea. I've never thought about that. It's warm here, I'm enjoying myself, I should be working and I'm not—in a word, everything is for the best.

In the issue of the journal *Critical Inquiry* devoted to the subject of the canon (September 1983), guest editor Robert von Hallberg remarks:

A canon is commonly seen as what other people, once powerful, have made and what should now be opened up, demystified, or eliminated altogether. Rarely does one hear a critic, especially a professor, confess to dreams of potency, perhaps because now that canons are recognized as the expression of social and political power, intellectuals are, by virtue of a consensus as to their adversarial role, almost required to view these aspirations skeptically. (iii)

By virtue of their *particular* adversarial role in intellectual scenes, at an angle or radical asymmetry to the dominant structures of social and political life, feminist critics may view the requirement of skepticism otherwise. More important for feminist professors, perhaps, than a worry about recuperation (occupying the center of power interests) is, I think, the requirement from *within* feminist practice to place next to the ambitious—potent—fantasy of canon transformation in which women's writing would come to complicate the national topographics and expand its limits, a certain equally productive anxiety about the adequacy of its own maps: the old treasons of new traditions.

N.K.M.

Notes

1. Henry Louis Gates, "Whose Canon Is It, Anyway?" *New York Times Book Review*, 26 Feb. 1989.

2. Lillian Robinson, "Treason Our Text: Feminist Challenges to the Literary Canon," in *The New Feminist Criticism: Essays on Women, Literature, and Theory*, ed. Elaine Showalter (New York: Pantheon Books, 1985), 106.

3. The canonical status of all writers since World War II is of course less stable than that of earlier periods (regardless of the fluctuations that historically obtain there). Plausibly, Beauvoir, Sarraute, Duras, and Yourcenar (the first female "immortal") will find their places in the record.

I Making Canons in France

Histories of the Classic

1   ANN R. JONES AND NANCY J. VICKERS

Canon, Rule, and the Restoration Renaissance

In 1818, as France engaged in the problematic enterprise of re-creating monarchy in a form faithful to selected revolutionary principles, the state could scarcely neglect symbolic gestures. Thus in Paris the ceremonial restoration of a sixteenth-century king—the recasting and reinstallation of an equestrian statue of Henri IV—substituted an assertion of monarchic continuity for a painful memory of zealous eradication. Henri's example communicated a message to the weary veterans of the Revolution and the empire: order could follow civil chaos, and, as a consequence, calm could return to the nation. Then, and only then, literature might disentangle itself long enough from politics to reproduce a noble, classical style, a style possible only within an advanced, peaceful civilization.[1] Thus nineteenth-century "old historicists," not unlike their sixteenth-century predecessors, excavated the past in search of the present. The labels with which they delineated periodicity—"Renaissance," "Restoration"—were figures for repetition.

Like the project of restoring the monarchy to post-Revolutionary France, the project of restoring the Renaissance was fraught with contradictions. Literary historians of the period described the sixteenth century as "catholic and protestant, republican and monarchist"; its riches were deemed "new by being old"; it "progressed" toward truth ("Rapport," 773–75). Repeatedly, and often illogically, such writers conflated the language of atemporal verities with that of relentless advances. Consider, for example, the multiple contradictions enacted here through personification: "such is the 'esprit français'; such the literature and the liberty to whom he gave birth [qu'il a enfantées]. Two immortal sisters, they walk in harmony toward world empire; but they find a fatherland everywhere they go, because they are neither prejudiced nor egotistically nationalistic; they are neither from one century nor one country" ("Rapport," 773; Saint-Marc Girardin, 113–14). French literature and liberty, equally at home at all times and in all places, nonetheless keep walking; they are national, but the term *national* signifies "universal." Literary values are eternal, but literature changes as a result of political, religious, and moral causes.

Returning to the Renaissance, then, constitutes returning to a source that is at once embedded in time and liberated from it. For a long while critics, as if "blinded by the splendor" of the seventeenth and eighteenth centuries, saw "nothing in the more or less obscure times that preceded them"; but now they interrogate origins, look for sources, and, "most of all . . . exhume the monuments of our distant history, to restore them, to study them, to understand them" ("Rapport," 772–74). To the 1820s, the restored Renaissance reveals itself to be a moment of passage and transition in a progress toward maturity, a time "when everything takes shape, but nothing is finished" (Chasles, 27).[2] It is a child prematurely born or an adolescent: "But [the French] genius had scarcely emerged from his infancy and had entered that age which, for nations as for individuals, is made up of those trials and crises upon which the destiny of a whole lifetime depends" ("Rapport," 774–76).

Official exhumations of the monuments of Renaissance culture extended well beyond the restoration of Henri IV to his "rightful" place. Indeed, the French Academy repeatedly proposed Renaissance topics for its annual prize competitions. In 1821 and 1822, for example, a "truly national" and tellingly self-reflexive subject was announced for the poetry prize: "the *restoration* of letters and art under François I" (emphasis ours) (*Recueil des discours*, 687–88, 695–96). In 1828, the eloquence prize shed its own history of generating discourse either in praise of God or of the "numerous and brilliant elite" of great men selected, we are told, not by the Academy but rather by the "nation herself"; this subject matter having been "exhausted," a problem of literary history imposed itself—"the advance and progress of French language and literature from the beginning of the sixteenth century to 1610" ("Rapport," 773). Thus a complex, varied, and remote body of texts assumed the reified shape of a "history," of a canonical formation invested in the political priorities and assumptions of the moment that created it.

Seven essays were submitted, but two (those by Philarète Chasles and Saint-Marc Girardin) won the judges' approbation. For they stressed a common denominator: the persistence and triumph of the old "esprit français" as it "struggled" against Petrarchism and pedantry to achieve the grandeur and majesty of the Classical Age ("Rapport," 780). That "esprit" would, of course, run amuck in the Enlightenment (be led astray by "irreligion and democracy") until, "tired of its error," it would finally settle into the Restoration and determine with "wise boldness" the measure of liberty suited to the 1820s (Chasles, 34; Saint-Marc Girardin, 110–11). The desire to locate a principle of continuity, no matter how chaotic the circumstances, singularly marks the choices of the contest judges. The "renascent" France of the Restoration constructs a reassuring, albeit distant, mirror in the gestating nation-state of the Renaissance: if the business of the present remains unfinished, it nonetheless contains the promise of the future.

Charles Augustin Sainte-Beuve's unfinished contribution to that Academy contest, however, never reached the judges' desks. He became so absorbed in his study of sixteenth-century poets that he lost interest in meeting the deadline. But the results of his research, eleven chapters of the *Tableau historique et critique de la poésie française et du théâtre français au XVIe siècle,* were published in *Le Globe,* the liberal journal for which he had begun writing in 1826. Rewritten, the book was published as a whole in 1828 and again, augmented, in 1843 and 1876. Ironically, his version of the Renaissance turned out to be far more influential than those that won the prize: his canon of significant writers and his judgments of their work became the basis for a century of subsequent literary histories, whether they repeated or refuted the *Tableau.*[3]

Sainte-Beuve's Tableau Historique: *Criticism as the Rule of Law and Order*

Sainte-Beuve's enthusiasm for Romantic poetry and for Victor Hugo as its leader shaped his first revision of the *Tableau* (1828). Known for its celebration of Ronsard, whom Sainte-Beuve praised as a great innovator, his history casts the court poet and the Pléiade as analogues to Hugo and the Cénacle. In his conclusion, Sainte-Beuve reads in the Renaissance an experimental daring that prefigures Romantic renewals of French culture: "The style of our age will be less correct, less savant, freer and more risk-taking [than the sixteenth century] . . . ; it has already recaptured the insouciance and unexpectedness lacking in the monarchical etiquette of the age that followed. . . . In poetry as in politics, we are a young, recently liberated people; who knows where our ascent will take us? . . . The lost lyre has been found; totally unexpected preludes have been heard from it."[4]

But the *Tableau* is far less revolutionary in practice than this critical flight suggests. The monarchical project of the Restoration was more significant to Sainte-Beuve, even as a young man (he was only twenty-four in 1828), then any radical movement in politics or poetry. Indeed, an aesthetic of the age of Louis XIV consistently informs Sainte-Beuve's criteria for cultural greatness.[5] Monarchy fascinates him: he begins his *Tableau* with a long love poem by King Charles d'Orléans, whom he praises for his "decent gallantry" (10); every poet ranked as "major" is defined in relation to a royal patron. Marot, he writes, learned his playful delicacy and good taste at the court of François I; Henri II's interest in the arts opened the way for Du Bellay's literary theory; Ronsard's fame as "prince of poets" meant the admiration of rulers including Charles IX, Marguerite de Valois, and Mary Stuart (64); Malherbe's power to impose new stylistic norms depended on Henri IV's interest in poetic forms (66).

Whatever historical realism this royalist bias may inscribe, it must be stressed that it excludes individual writers, as well as literary groups, outside the court. And, as a consequence, virtually all women writers are erased. Ladies-in-waiting at court, unlike the rare, exemplarily educated queen, did not write; their role was to attract homage from courtier-poets rather than to compose poetry of their own. But throughout the sixteenth century women poets did perform their work far from court, and in coteries composed mainly of professional men. Humanists and publishers predominated in Lyon, where Louise Labé and Pernette Du Guillet took part in salons; lawyers and judges visiting from Paris joined a later literary circle in Poitiers, in which Madeleine and Catherine des Roches recited the poems they later published as a joint mother-daughter enterprise. Anne Tullone (Mâcon) and Nicole Estienne (Rouen) also wrote in provincial centers. It was not the court, on which Sainte-Beuve fixated, but rather the city that stimulated the literary production of women.

Sainte-Beuve dismisses such urban groups in passages that reveal the class hierarchy underlying his understanding of "true" Romantic, and thus of "true" Renaissance, poetry as the expression of unmediated emotion. Setting "genius" against "science," in an opposition that would have made no sense in the sixteenth century, he concludes that the scholars and humanists who took part in urban literary and philosophical discussions could not possibly be "true" poets; their concern with the techniques of the professions revealed their inauthenticity: "one did poetry as one did medicine, law, theology, or history; and every literate man could be listed among the poets. . . . But what can we find today in the rhymes of the printer Etienne Dolet, the lawyer Thomas Sebillet . . . ? Wasn't it enough for Pelletier du Mans to be at once a doctor, grammarian and geometer?" (39) Not surprisingly, Sainte-Beuve's notion of lyric as an emanation of feeling rather than of intellect leads him to banish Maurice Scève, the most visible of the Lyonnais, from the elite of poets: "practically unreadable," he wrote poems whose erudition had no appeal for his contemporaries (44).[6] Although women could hardly be accused of professional deformation, they gained no advantage on that account in Sainte-Beuve's judgments. He makes no mention whatsoever of Du Guillet; he criticizes Labé, like Scève, as overlearned. In her *Débat de Folie et d'Amour,* the speeches of the gods are too long and too full of citations; La Fontaine improved on her version by shortening it to a succinct fable (42). Labé's poems, Sainte-Beuve thinks, are few and "insignificant." Taming the striking eroticism of her sonnets, he alludes instead to "the sweetness and purity of her feelings and expression," but even such "sweetness" is qualified by the way in which he identifies and locates her by class and gender. In a single phrase, for example, he marks her social position (through use of her nickname, derived from her husband's artisan status) as well as her problematic literary position (through allusion to her model, Petrarch): "la Belle Cordière soupirait non loin de la patrie de Laure" (42).

The association of Labé with Laura, moreover, not only links her to an *object* of poetry but also to an Italy that Sainte-Beuve imagines as a threat to the naïve freshness and evolving good taste that he defines as the virtues of middle sixteenth-century French poetry. In contrast to Marot's tempering of the *vieil esprit gaulois,* the writing, like the behavior, of groups far from the court supposedly coarsened what was already "primitive" in medieval culture: "outside the court, in the depth of the provinces, especially in those foreign to the center because of their close links to Italy, such as Anjou and Poitou, the wildest merriment [la jovialité la plus effrénée] sustained its traditions and maintained its greedy feasts" (42). This dismissal of unruly regions, such as Rabelais's Poitiers and Labé's Lyon, characteristically implicates Italy as the grotesque Other.[7] Sainte-Beuve retrospectively defines Renaissance genius as consisting of purity of language and delicacy of sentiment. Both must be protected from corruption by foreign influences from which he presumes the sixteenth-century French court was in essence free. But what Renaissance court could Sainte-Beuve have in mind? François I surrounded himself with Italian artists; Catherine de' Medici was the wife of Henri II, the mother of Charles IX and Henri III. The culturally heterogeneous courts of early modern France seem wishfully reconstructed to conform to a tidier paradigm—the triumphantly centralized national court of the Sun King.

In 1850, in a note for an article on criticism under the Empire, Sainte-Beuve wrote, "Criticism is what puts order into Letters. The rule [règne] of criticism is the rule of proper order in literature. After political crises, after revolutions which have overturned everything, criticism has inherited a tutelary power; [thus it] accomplishes its task and the restoration of proper morality."[8] The task of the critic, as the police of literary law and order, is embedded in a timeless tradition of corrective and stabilizing assessments of literary merit: playing Malherbe to the Restoration, Boileau to the Second Empire, Sainte-Beuve lays claim to a sacred responsibility to preserve the values of the elite, even (or especially) in the aftermath of political rebellion. This view of the critic's role governs an essay written the same year, "What Is a Classic?" Sainte-Beuve opens with a passage from the late-Roman grammarian Aulus Gellius, who uses the word *classicus* to denote a citizen belonging to the highest rank of taxpayers; in Sainte-Beuve's paraphrase the term means "a writer of worth and note . . . who counts, who has solid possessions, and who is not to be confused with the crowd of proletarians."[9] Rather than questioning this conflation of economic and literary value, Sainte-Beuve takes it as proof of Roman discernment: "such an expression implies an epoch advanced enough to have already carried out a census and classification of literature" (39). Despite the fact that he is narrating metamorphoses of taste, his images endow writers whose fortunes have in fact been unsteady with enduring autonomy. Restoring the measure and taste the Middle Ages lacked, he writes, the fifteenth and sixteenth centuries enabled the great authors of antiquity to "stand out luminously" from the mass and to "group themselves harmoniously" on the two peaks of Parnassus

(39). And paradoxically, this emergence of "true" judgment of founding texts is attributed not just to the revival of classical perspectives
but to the emergence of the nation-state. It was, Sainte-Beuve suggests, the attainment of political order that made possible the "true"
judgment of a literary order—a judgment secured not through any
process of argument but through its transparent self-evidence. The
French had only to look back upon the triumphant state culture of
Louis XIV's reign to recognize "immediately what a classic was without having to reason about it" (41).

Although Sainte-Beuve takes issue with the literary-historical
strictness of the Academy's 1835 definition of a classic ("a writer
who has become a model in a particular language"), in his own definition he systematically evacuates history of any kind from canonical works. He calls, contradictorily again, for eternal verities and
moral progress. In practice, as his example proves, both these qualities are inevitably to be judged from a particular standpoint in the
present; but Sainte-Beuve suppresses the changing situations of readers and critics through a fantasy of the great writer's consistently
direct relationship to an evolving communal mind: "A true classic
. . . is a writer who has enriched the human spirit, who has genuinely increased its treasure, who has made it take a step ahead, who
has discovered an unequivocal moral truth" (42). The accumulated
antitheses in his description of classic style do not resolve the
contradiction between his defense of new forms and his demand
that thematic content be communicated in a way transparent to all
readers in all times: classic style must speak "to everyone in a style
of his own" yet be innovative—"new and ancient, easily contemporary to all epochs" (42).

Finally Sainte-Beuve, revealing the local interests that his posit-
ing of a transhistorical canon denies, explicitly links the requirement of lasting readability to political moderation. In order to be
received into the canon, the classic writer must ultimately support
the status quo; even if he goes to "extremes," it is only to achieve
equilibrium: "a classic author may have been revolutionary at a certain moment, or have seemed so, but he no longer is; he pillaged
everything around him at first, turned his constraints upside down
only in order to reestablish balance, very quickly, for the benefit of
order and beauty" [au *profit* de l'ordre et du beau] (42, emphasis
ours). Novelty, then, is acceptable in classic authors and in classic
ages only if carefully circumscribed; measure and order, the reassertion of unchanging values, are all: "the Temple of taste," says Sainte-

Beuve, needs expansion, but in the form of restoration (50). The basic ground plan must be preserved.

The architects and owners of "the Temple" are, of course, gendered: the writers Sainte-Beuve praises as "classics," and the readers with whom he identifies, are men. If, like Molière and La Fontaine, they were indifferent to the rules and models of their day, he celebrates them as *virile* free spirits: "as far as classics go, the most unexpected are still the best and the greatest; seek . . . those male geniuses truly born immortal and perpetually flourishing" (50). His ideal reader, too, is a man, a gentleman of leisure who has read widely and returns to well-known books at the end of his life. A class and even a religious decorum is implied in his closing advice to the would-be appreciator of the classics. At some point he must stop sampling new texts: "for one must choose, and the precondition of good taste, after having comprehended everything, is to stop traveling, to sit down and take a position. Nothing dulls and dims taste more than endless voyages; the spirit of poetry is not the Wandering Jew" (53). The discerning reader, then, is a settled bourgeois, ready for the refined enjoyment of the familiar that comes with age: "it is then that the word *classic* takes on its true meaning and is defined for every man of taste by an irresistible predilection and choice" (54). And the rewards that the canon guarantees to this man of taste include "a conversation at any moment, a friendship that does not deceive or leave us, and that habitual impression of serenity and affability that reconciles us, as we often need to be, with other men and with ourselves" (55).

Underlying Sainte-Beuve's definition of a canonical purpose—being "reconciled" with "other men and with ourselves"—are assumptions that both include and exclude. On the one hand, the complacency implicit in his notion of "reconciliation" serves to marginalize all literary radicals and explorers, adventurous readers as well as writers who would question and provoke rather than soothe. On the other, the man who reflects upon other men and himself has predictably little to say about women or the texts they produced. Although he logically entertains a cross-cultural perspective on, for example, epic poetry (other men), he erases genres in which women traditionally became visible, such as letter writing and the short novel. When Sainte-Beuve introduces women writers into his history of "taste," he does so to survey and correct, to enforce modest silence on too often erotic matter, to muffle sex(ts) rather than analyze texts.[10] Consider, as examples, his readings of Marguerite de Navarre and Louise Labé, the two most visible women in traditional histories of sixteenth-century French literature. For here Sainte-Beuve tellingly invokes evaluative criteria that inform the ongoing canonization of Marguerite and the alternating decanonizations and recanonizations of Labé.

Ruly and Unruly Women: Marguerite de Navarre and Louise Labé

Sainte-Beuve's focus on royalty as the center and source of culture leads him to privilege the sister of the king, the princess poet, Marguerite de Navarre. But his approval depends largely on her patronage of Clément Marot; his remarks for the most part are restricted to an enumeration of her relationships to significant men. In the *Tableau historique* his first sentence about her consists of praise for her devotion to Marot: she was "la protectrice de sa vie" (33). Sainte-Beuve dispenses with discussion of Marguerite's short stories and plays in order to conjecture about the sources for her poems, which include "several easy songs that suggest that she knew how to profit from the model and the services of her valet de chambre" (34). His implication goes beyond the claim that she was indebted to Marot as mentor or even as ghost writer; at the same time that her status as a member of the royal elite would include her in Sainte-Beuve's history, her status as a woman would exclude her.

Marot's patroness may well have been a queen, but, like any woman, she was subject to sexual conquest. In an aggressively leveling footnote, Sainte-Beuve sums up with titillating ambivalence the debate over whether Marguerite and Marot were lovers: "there is no doubt about Marguerite's elevated morals, but there are certain moments in anyone's youth" (34). From this apparently gender-neutral axiom, he moves to a second innuendo that arises from a complex of assumptions about feminine self-exposure and masculine dominance. Any woman who goes public as a writer must have questionable motives and sources: "whenever a woman writes, one is tempted to ask, smiling, who is behind her" (34). Sainte-Beuve's generalization says a great deal about the conditions under which he will admit a woman into the canon. She must serve men in one or more ways: as a patron, as a literary imitator, as a sexual partner, and so on. And her work in turn serves as a pretext for criticism that links literary and sexual relations in ways rarely invoked in analyses of men's writing.

This uneasy tension between royalist admiration and sexual suspicion persists in Sainte-Beuve's longer essay on Marguerite in a "Causerie du lundi" (1853). By this time his political views had hardened. After his break with Hugo, his disenchantment with the Saint-Simonians, and his revulsion at the Revolution of 1848, he increasingly saw the functions of the critic as the purification of taste and the protection of standards against the commercialization of contemporary literature (Fayolle, 60–77). His 1853 assessment of Marguerite arises almost entirely from his conviction that criticism should act as the watchdog of moral order. This version of Marguerite is a portrait of the ideally virtuous woman of the 1850s, combining sweet domesticity (he cites at length her letters to François I, including one in which she tenderly describes his children) and appreciation of her male contemporaries.

In her own time, Erasmus praised Marguerite for intellectual and spiritual qualities admired by the Renaissance in men as well as women: prudence "worthy even of a philosopher,"[11] moderation and piety, an invincible strength of spirit, indifference to worldly things. Sainte-Beuve, however, concentrates on her protection of protestant thinkers, an activity that implied specific intellectual and political positions in Marguerite's time that he then recasts in terms of his own. First, her alliance with Calvinists was a sign of liberal tolerance, never of radical sympathies: "she behaved like a person who, around [17]89, would have supported liberty wholeheartedly, without desiring or predicting the Revolution" (442). Second, he sees no intellectual coherence in her position; although she defended protestants in letters in which she even uses the "jargon of Calvinism," her writing generally shows engagingly "feminine" inconsistency on religious matters: "one must not expect much rigor either in her ideas or in her expression of them" (443). He discusses her *Heptaméron* (which, in a new edition, is the ostensible topic of his essay) only briefly, praising the subtlety of dialogue in the frame tale but dismissing the collection as a whole as written "without art, composition, or the sense of an ending" (449).

Then, in a move typical of the critical policing carried out by the canonical mentality as it deals with women writers, he shifts to a denunciation of the coarseness of the tales, their "licence et grossièreté" (450). The real issue for Sainte-Beuve, the quality he requires of a woman writer, is not skillful narration but verbal propriety. He takes Marguerite's anthology as proof that elegant and proper conversation evolved only in the seventeenth century; "professors" of "bon ton," such as Mlle de Scudéry, would have to spend years "preaching decorum" before the elegant discretion of middle seventeenth-century "entretiens" was attained (450). Women, according to Sainte-Beuve's moral system, are responsible for maintaining decency: "in all times, respectable women have had to listen to more things than they themselves say; but the decisive moment, the one to be noted, is the moment at which they ceased saying these unsuitable things themselves, and saying them to such an extent that they preserved them in writing without imagining that they thereby fell short of virtue" (431). Sainte-Beuve anachronistically imposes his version of the double standard by assigning a natural and transhistorical "pudeur" to women without recognizing that sexual differentiation in the Renaissance, whatever its marked hierarchies, allowed the hybridization of popular and courtly discourses even in "virtuous" women's texts.

The "license" Sainte-Beuve noticed in the *Heptaméron* has tended, until very recently, to be effaced in criticism of Marguerite's writing. Her piety and generosity as a patron—that is, her religious and "maternal" service to the men in her milieu—are foregrounded. The woman who ruled won attention as a queen, but she also had to be rewritten to represent the ruly woman: chaste, pious, a "protectrice" to the heroes of Renaissance culture. Castex and Surer, for example, in their manual designed for students preparing for their baccalau-reat, stress the "pure and moving impulses of her soul" and "the moral and religious scruples" she applied in transforming Boccaccio's material. Their brief literary commentary, moreover, is framed by her careful positioning in relation to notable men: they begin, "Marguerite of Angoulême, sister of François I, initially married the Duke of Alençon, and later the King of Navarre, Henri D'Albret, her second husband"; they conclude with a celebration of the protectress of Bonaventure des Périers and Marot; and only two intervening paragraphs discuss texts surprisingly thought to be composed by Marguerite *"herself"* (emphasis theirs).[12] Lagarde and Michard limit their evaluation to one sentence: "In his role [as 'Father of Letters'] François was seconded by his sister, Marguerite of Angoulême, duchess of Alençon, then queen of Navarre, protectress of Marot and author *herself* of the *Heptaméron*" (emphasis ours).[13]

Although in some senses subject to similar descriptive strategies, Louise Labé—"the 'belle cordière' (her husband was a ropemaker)" (Lagarde and Michard, 31)—constituted a more problematic site for judgments conflating poetics and anxiety about female sexual behavior. Hers has been a story of the unruly woman, whose writing was read—negatively and positively—as a transgression of cultural norms. Class and political interests interacted with gender ideologies in the first responses to the woman and the writer; they still do. The fixation on feminine sexual propriety helps to explain Sainte-Beuve's extremely idiosyncratic reading of Louise Labé, both in the *Tableau historique* and in a later essay written in 1862. He accepts the early myths about the poet: she fought in the battle of Perpignan, loved the aristocratic Olivier de Magny more than her artisan husband ("so unappetizing in his greasy apron"),[14] and died young, still grieving over unrequited love. In an about-face from the *Tableau*, he praises the "ingenious elegance" of Labé's *Débat de folie et d'amour*; he takes it as an example of the superiority of prose to poetry at this stage of French writing and emphasizes its conformity to his notion of feminine charm (306). His first comment on Labé's sonnets, however, is rather deprecatory: they are hard, rough, obviously constrained by rhythm and rhyme. But he then employs an axiom of Romantic aesthetics in order to save the poet: the sincerity of her feelings justifies the imperfection of her style.

What feelings, however? The striking thing about the 1862 commentary is that Sainte-Beuve selects three of Labé's most sublimated poems, repressing those in which she demands "chaleureux" kisses from her beloved, for example, or deploys her fame as a writer in a seductive appeal for his love. Clearly, the critic would make Labé into a Romantic heroine. Sainte-Beuve concedes that Labé suffers from a dubious reputation; he sums up the debate over her promiscuity by acknowledging that too much is said about her to believe that she "kept her ardors only for her poems" (101). But he reforms her by rewriting her as a pure spirit, a poet of "burning" force (311), a precursor of Romantic intensities and melancholies. His anachronism here, as in the *Tableau*, is interwoven with his androcentrism; Sainte-Beuve absorbs Labé into a masculine literary scheme that privileges *men's* Romanticism, which remains his constant point of reference. In his conclusion, he shifts his focus from Labé to a "woman poet of our days," Mlle Ackermann, the dedicator of "Stances" to Alfred de Musset. The essay ends with a line from Ackermann's poem, which Sainte-Beuve offers as an epigram worthy of the male poet's tomb: "Hélas! chanter ainsi, c'était vouloir mourir" (341). This relay of meritorious suffering from a Renaissance woman to a nineteenth-century male writer accounts for Sainte-Beuve's continuing interest in Labé: she is the pretext for praise of a youthful *hero* of Romanticism. Whatever differences exist between Musset and Labé—her manipulation of sixteenth-century rhetoric, her critique of Petrarchan conventions, her demand to be recognized as a woman poet by her contemporaries—are effaced. Her *Euvres* are rewritten as an episode in literary history that satisfies a nineteenth-century fascination with suffering "femininity" and advances the construction of literary history as the history of men writing about and for men.

Of the various threads in Sainte-Beuve's assessment of Labé, his reference to her damaged reputation had many historical precedents. There is no real proof that Labé led a life of sexual excess: her inheritance of wealth from one rich merchant and her marriage to another assign her to a socioeconomic class much above the fallen gentility or poverty from which successful courtesans fought their way to prosperity. Twentieth-century critics are fairly well agreed that attacks on Labé arose from her fellow citizens' disapproval of her participation in bourgeois literary coteries that challenged the cultural hegemony of the aristocracy. An example is an early charge against her by Philibert de Vienne, a Lyonnais nobleman who wrote, in his *Philosophe de cour* (1547), that Labé was at least less avaricious toward her "serviteurs" than a courtesan such as Lais of Corinth had been.[15] But he was never a member of Labé's circle, which was open to men of letters whether or not they were aristocrats; it may well have been his exclusion that motivated his charge about behavior of which he had no direct knowledge.

In fact, most accusations that Labé was a courtesan and an adulteress have been revealed as strategies through which men attempted to settle scores with other men. In 1552, one M. Ivard, former neighbor of Labé, was seeking a divorce in Geneva; he accused his wife of trying to poison him as a result of the dissolute life to which she had been led by "her cousin, la 'Belle Cordière.'"[16] In order to rid himself of one woman, Ivard defamed another who no longer had a powerful clansman to keep him in order (Labé's father had died in the same year). Tension between two men also produced one of the most serious attacks on Labé: Calvin described her as a "common whore" in a Latin pamphlet he wrote from Geneva in 1561 (Zamaron, 68; Berriot, 188–89). But this pamphlet was directed at Gabriel de Saconay, a liberal churchman of Lyon, where several young Genevan protestants had been burned in 1551. In order to denounce Saconay, Calvin descended to sexual insult, accusing him of frequenting brothels and employing the services of Labé, "a famous whore, that is, la 'Belle Cordière.'"[17] Caught in the crossfire of the Reformation, Labé was used again as ammunition for men's enmity and ambition. Aristocratic envy, a man's divorce suit, churchmen's polemics: such were the determinants of Labé's sexual reputation.

And critical opinion has continued to judge the writer according to myths about the woman. Léon Feugère, a contemporary of Sainte-Beuve (whom he cites admiringly in an 1860 study), typifies the conflation of sexual rumor and critical evaluation: "Louise Labé expresses the transports of passion in a language too indiscreet to be easily accepted by the modern reader."[18] Like Sainte-Beuve, Feugère censors the sonnets, leaving out the openly erotic ones in favor of those "that breathe out a tender melancholy." Even in the twentieth century, investigations into the poet's private life continue.[19] The obvious reason for this critical anxiety is a persistent critical commitment to purity in women's bodies and words. In 1955, for example, Lépold Senghor defended the poet and her texts together: "it would be impossible to find in our entire literature more chaste love poems. Truly, Louise Labé has no sense of sin, she is innocent at heart and in the flesh, she remains the greatest poetess to be born in France."[20] Robert Sabatier reverses the terms of earlier judges by praising the intensity of physical "frémissement" in the poems; indeed, he reads Labé as a magnificent masochist, citing Marie Bonapart on essential feminine painseeking.[21] Thus, even in 1975 the erotic in a woman's text remains a problem; whether it is repressed or celebrated, it still needs to be contained by selective censorship or interpretive sublimation.

Labé's reputation has been constructed through other biases as well, particularly the kind of assumption Sainte-Beuve made about Marguerite de Navarre: if a woman writes, a man must be behind her. "Cherchez l'homme": this obsession appears everywhere in commentary on Labé's *Euvres*. In 1584, about twenty years after Labé's death, Pierre de Saint-Julien asserted that her *Débat* was too witty and learned to have been composed by a "mere courtesan" and that it must therefore have been the work of Maurice Scève (Berriot, 196). Other lovers who influenced Labé as a poet have been suggested: Henri II, Marot, Olivier de Magny.[22] The arguments and counterarguments about these presumed mentors reveal very little about actual influence but a great deal about the critical desire to subordinate women's writing to men's. A recent case in point is Paul Ardouin's glossily illustrated celebration of the Ecole lyonnaise, which turns Scève into Labé's teacher.[23] Here the gender biases of influence studies contribute to the decanonization of the woman poet by denying her literary autonomy. Gender bias individualizes women's literary relationships to such an extent that they are represented as writing in thrall to a single romantic and literary model rather than responding to the conventions and vocabularies shared by male poets in their time.

Androcentric logic produces an opposite conclusion in the view that Labé was nonpareil, a unique poet untouched by the intricacies of sixteenth-century lyric theory. Sainte-Beuve's positive judgment of her arises from exactly this idea. She had nothing in common with the Pléiade, he writes: "her verses do not derive from it or show its influence, they know no other star but the Star of Venus! She belongs to no compartment or school, to no classification" (311). But the attribution of originary creativity brings problematic assumptions in its wake when a woman writer is at issue: Labé's "sincerity" has come to connote spontaneous artlessness. Max Jasinski, for example, conjectured that her poems isolated her because the Pléiade "doubtless found her work too naked, too untaught, too far beneath the high art to which they had proudly raised themselves."[24] Like Jasinski, other influential literary historians emphasize the genuineness of her feeling without quoting any of her texts. The one-line summary of her sonnets in Lagarde and Michard's literary manual demonstrates that this critical response has solidified into a cliché: "another poetess from the Lyon group must be mentioned, Louise Labé, . . . whose sonnets are remarkable for the *sincerity* of their sentiments" (31). The representation of artlessness as the gift of a woman poet apparently dispenses readers from actually examining her work.

If, on the contrary, a critic decides to take Labé seriously, to focus on her technique and form, the gesture is likely to efface her womanhood. Lawrence Harvey's respectful formalist study of Labé's sonnets was free of the obsessive dwelling on her private life endemic to earlier criticism, but his desire to rehabilitate Labé, to make her conform to the laws of the canon, blinded him to the thematic and rhetorical gendering of the poems. He downplays Labé's addresses to women and her self-representation as a woman by treating such performances as "fictions," explorations of what love might be rather than autobiographical confessions.[25] Thus he can defend Labé as a universal poet—understood as masculine. This assumption is transparent in the phrasing of his final paragraph where he argues that Labé's achievement lies outside the history of confessional literature: "it is surely clear that its true value lies elsewhere: in the poet's *mastery* of a form that is both fixed and flexible, in the expressive effect this form attains as it recreates a coherent vision of the *human* condition, and finally in this vision itself—of the Renaissance, yet *universal*—that calls up the powerful, poignant drama of *man's* yearning and striving toward an ideal that forever lures *him* on and remains, eternally, inaccessible" (Harvey, 84, emphasis ours).

We also, in contrast, now have a Labé defined entirely in terms of gender, as Woman. A canon of the quintessential female, being constructed in France and elsewhere, draws new political and theoretical concerns into the assessment of women writers. In a recent book, Evelyne Sullerot uses Labé as an instance of the Eternal Feminine: "It behooves us to listen to woman sing of the mystery of the seductive spell [man] casts over her . . . —a mystery which proves as powerful as that of the woman for the man, that eternal refrain that we have heard so often through the ages."[26] This rhapsody to heterosexual nature is expanded in Sullerot's presentation of Labé as typical of all women in all times: "Louise Labé is the perfect expression of the vision of life, the emotions, the suffering, the feminine experience, of the woman in love" (75). The romantic valorization of spontaneity reappears here; so does the Sainte-Beuvian fusion of the poet's erotic life and her written texts. Labé's eroticism is celebrated rather than muffled, but is there any change in the presumed eternal verities—that women love only men, that love entails suffering, that sexual attraction is a perpetually unknowable mystery—smuggled in under Sullerot's praise for Labé?

One of the tasks feminism has assigned itself since the 1970s is that of challenging assumptions like these. And indeed, the lessons of that labor would seem to demonstrate that the inequalities imposed by the politics of canon formation can be righted neither by arguing that writing transcends gender to achieve "universality" nor that it marks an essential, ahistorical "difference." It is not difficult to show how early historians of Renaissance literature reproduced their own moral and political biases by translating them into judgments of taste, presumably objective and therefore above analysis; it is harder to recognize the contemporary ideologies informing the construction of new canons. Perhaps the canon-building project itself should be abandoned; its history has certainly had little to offer women as writers or readers. This would, of course, require suspending the traditional categories of "value" in favor of other categories and questions. How invested are women writers in the articulations of difference—be it difference from men or difference from other women? How are they positioned at specific historical moments? How have they negotiated the constraints of race, class, and gender in relation to inherited discursive models? For new answers, new questions. Sainte-Beuve's instinctive sense of the "classic" need neither be re-membered nor regendered. Rather, its motivating suppositions and strategies require a suspicious rereading so that the corrective measures of the present not duplicate the corrective measures of the past. "Our criticisms judge us more than they judge others," noted Sainte-Beuve.[27]

Louise Labé was celebrated as a heroine of the Revolution in Lyon. In 1790 a division of the National Guard displayed her portrait on their banner, accompanied by the following motto: "You foresaw our designs, Charly, Belle Cordière; / to break our chains, you were the first to fly. / Belle Cordière, your hope was not in vain."[28] Clearly this radical canonization of Labé rewrites her as much from the perspective of the present as do her conservative decanonizations. And an analysis of the interests motivating such inclusion and exclusion constitutes a genuinely productive position for feminist critics. For such a strategy both escapes the cataloguing of eternal women worthies and exposes the historicity of literary value. Perhaps we need not only to imagine "flying beyond" canonical chains but also to interrogate the processes that forge them.

Notes

1. On the restoration of the statue of Henri IV, see Andrew George Lehmann, *Sainte-Beuve, A Portrait of the Critic, 1804–1842* (Oxford: Oxford University Press, 1962), 8–9. On Henri IV as bringing political order to France, see Saint-Marc Girardin, *Tableau de la littérature française au XVIe siècle* (Paris: Didier, 1862), 80–85. On political order as the prerequisite to classical style, see Philarète Chasles, *Etudes sur le seizième siècle en France* (Paris: Amyot, 1848), 33. See also the "Rapport de M. Raynouard, Secrétaire Perpétuel de l'Académie française, sur les concours de poésie et d'éloquence de année 1828," in the *Recueil des discours, rapports et pièces diverses lus dans les séances publiques et particulières de l'Académie française, 1820–29* (Paris: Firmin Didot, 1843), 776. References will henceforth appear in the text, as will references to any work cited more than once. All translations are ours unless otherwise indicated.

2. On the "unfinished" quality of the Renaissance, as evoked through metaphors of miscarriage in Sainte-Beuve, see François Rigolot, "Sainte-Beuve et le mythe du XVIe siècle," *L'Esprit créateur* 14 (1974): 41.

3. Lehmann (51) discusses the enduring reputation of the *Tableau*. Antoine

Compagnon stresses Sainte-Beuve's centrality as model and target for change in his study of curriculum formation, *La Troisième République des lettres de Flaubert à Proust* (Paris: Editions du Seuil, 1983), 174–81. See also Rigolot, 35–43.

4. Charles Augustin Sainte-Beuve, *Tableau historique et critique de la poésie française et du théâtre français au XVIe siècle* (Paris: Charpentier, 1843), 284.

5. Roger Fayolle offers an excellent analysis of Sainte-Beuve's political and critical trajectory in his *Sainte-Beuve et le XVIIIe siècle ou comment les révolutions arrivent* (Paris: Armand Colin, 1972).

6. Scève was raised to canonical status only in the early twentieth century when appreciation for the density of Symbolist poetry disposed critics such as Valéry Larbaud to admire him as a forerunner of Mallarmé. See Verdun Saulnier, *Maurice Scève* (Paris: Klincksieck, 1948), vol. 1, chap. 21.

7. On Italy as a feminized and feminizing threat to the "esprit français," see "Rapport," 776; Saint-Marc Girardin, 89; and Chasles, 1–5, 27. For an analysis of strategies through which the grotesque is used to banish oppositions and to consolidate cultural identity, see Peter Stallybrass and Allon White, *The Politics and Poetics of Transgression* (Ithaca, N.Y.: Cornell University Press, 1986).

8. Cited by Fayolle, 57.

9. Sainte-Beuve, "Qu'est-ce qu'un classique?" in his *Causeries du lundi*, 3d. ed. (Paris: Garnier, n.d.), 3:39. Ernst Robert Curtius cites Gellius as follows: "but it was not until very late, and then only in a single instance, that the name *classicus* appears: in Aulus Gellius (*Noctes Atticae*, XIX, 8, 15). . . . The thing to do [writes Gellius] is to follow the usage of a model author: 'some one of the old orators or poets, that is, a first class tax paying author, not a proletarian.' . . . The *proletarius*, whom Gellius mentions by way of comparison, belongs to *no* tax class." Curtius, *European Literature and the Latin Middle Ages*, trans. Willard Trask (Princeton: Princeton University Press, 1948, reprint, 1973), 249–50. Stallybrass and White comment on the passage as follows: "From the first it seems that the ranking of types of authors was modelled upon social rank according to property classifications and this interrelation was still being actively invoked in the nineteenth century. In recent times we have been inclined to forget this ancient and enduring link between social rank and the organizing of authors and works" (1–2).

10. Here we paraphrase Hélène Cixous, though in a contrasting context: "let the priests tremble, we're going to show them our sextes." Cixous, "le Rire de la Méduse," *L'Arc* 61 (1975): 47; translated at "The Laugh of the Medusa" by Keith Cohen and Paula Cohen, in *New French Feminisms*, ed. Elaine Marks and Isabelle de Courtivron (Amherst; University of Massachusetts Press, 1980), 255. A note on names: following sixteenth-century usage we call Marguerite, a noblewoman, by her first name alone. Labé, a bourgeoise, would have been known by both her first and family names.

11. Sainte-Beuve cites Erasmus's letter to Marguerite in "Marguerite, Reine de Navarre," *Causeries*, 7:441.

12. P.-G. Castex, P. Surer, and G. Becker, *Manuel des études littéraires françaises, XVIe siècle* (Paris: Hachette, 1966), 6. The defense of the *Heptaméron* as a purification of Boccaccio began as early as Ferdinand Brunetière in an essay on Marguerite in his *Histoire de la littérature française classique* (Paris: Delagrave, 1904), 175–80.

13. André Lagarde and Laurent Michard, *XVIe Siècle; Les Grands Auteurs du programme* (Paris: Bordas, 1965), 9.

14. Sainte-Beuve, "Oeuvres de Louise Labé, la belle cordière," in *Nouveaux lundis*, 4: 305.

15. Cited by Ferdinand Zamaron, *Louise Labé, dame de la franchise* (Paris: Nizet, 1968), 67. See also Karine Berriot, *Louise Labé: La Belle Rebelle et le François nouveau* (Paris: Editions du Seuil, 1985), 187.

16. For exonerating discussions of this case see Zamaron, 67–68; and Berriot, 187.

17. The Latin text is cited in Dorothy O'Connor, *Louise Labé, sa vie et son oeuvre* (Paris: Les Presses Françaises, 1926), 184.

18. Léon Feugère, *Les Femmes poètes au XVIe siècle* (Paris: Didier, 1860), 19.

19. For example, in her appendix to *Louise Labé*, O'Connor includes a list of witnesses in order to prove that Labé was a courtesan (185–89). Zamaron invokes his experience as a police inspector to draw the opposite conclusion from the same evidence (100).

20. Léopold Sédar Senghor, ed., *Anthologie des poètes du XVIe siècle* (Paris: Bibliothèque Mondiale, 1955), 13.

21. Robert Sabatier, *La Poésie du XVIe siècle* (Paris: Albin Michel, 1975), 115–16.

22. Luc van Brabant argued for Henri II and Marot in his *Louise Labé et ses aventures amoureuses avec Clément Marot et le Dauphin Henry* (Coxyde-sur-mer: Les Editions de la Belle sans sy, 1966).

23. Paul Ardouin, *Maurice Scève, Pernette du Guillet, Louise Labé: L'Amour à Lyon au temps de la Renaissance* (Paris: Nizet, 1981), 41–42.

24. Max Jasinski, *Histoire du sonnet en France* (Paris: Brugère, 1903), 66.

25. Lawrence Harvey, *The Aesthetics of the Renaissance Love Sonnet: An Essay on the Art of the Sonnet in the Poetry of Louise Labé* (Geneva: Droz, 1962), 14, 51.

26. Evelyne Sullerot, *Women on Love: Eight Centuries of Feminine Writing*, trans. Helen Lane (London: Jill Norman, 1979), 75.

27. Sainte-Beuve to Hortense Allart, 6 November 1845, in his *Correspondance générale*, ed. J. Bonnerot (Paris: Stock, 1949), 6:272; cited by Rigolot, 43.

28. Cited by Zamaron, 78. The French text reads: "Tu prédis nos desseins, Charly, Belle Cordière / Car pour briser nos fers tu volas la première. / Belle Cordière, ton espoir n'était pas vain."

2 JOAN DEJEAN

Classical Reeducation: Decanonizing the Feminine

Each age has its canon, its own peculiarly idiosyncratic vision of the literature of preceding centuries. One way of approaching the study of canons is palimpsest-style, by peeling back superimposed layers of critical judgment in search of the hierarchies and the process of inclusion/exclusion that commentators of a given period developed to package contemporary literary production and that of earlier ages for pedagogical dissemination and consumption. In the case of seventeenth-century literature, the stripping away of canonical layers would take us back to the period from the end of the seventeenth century to the middle of the eighteenth century during which two related developments transformed the meaning of *classic* in French. In the first place, modern (French) authors were placed on an equal footing with their ancient precursors as models for pedagogical instruction, becoming therefore "classic" according to the most standard usage, the primary sense of the term attested in seventeenth-century dictionaries ("author who is taught in classes, in the schools"). In the second place, selected authors of the second half of the seventeenth century (the period that baptized itself France's Golden Age) gradually became accepted as "classic" in another sense of the word, this time one particular to the French language and one included only in modern dictionaries: "that which pertains to the great authors of the seventeenth century and their period, considered as expressing an ideal" (Robert Dictionary).[1]

In the course of this semantic drift, these two meanings of *classic* are often considered synonymous; in many periods it is almost universally understood that "the great authors of the seventeenth century" are alone worthy to be taught in the schools. At the same time and as part of the same evolution of linguistic usage and pedagogical practice, the most influential women writers of the Golden Age are pronounced unworthy of membership in the class of "great authors of the seventeenth century" because the "ideal" their works express is deemed unfit to be proposed to schoolchildren as a model. However, these women writers are still proposed as models as long as the original canon of French literature, a canon, as we will see, for adult readers rather than schoolchildren, still survives (roughly until the beginning of the nineteenth century). In search of an explanation for the exclusion of women writers from classic status, I will contrast the two types of pedagogical programs available in France from the late seventeenth century until shortly after the Revolution, what I have just referred to as the canon for adults and the first canon for schoolchildren to include modern authors.

In the closing decades of the seventeenth century, French writers begin to draw up lists of their precursors and then to edit anthologies of their representative works. The best known of these is the *Recueil des plus belles pièces des poètes français,* published anonymously in 1692 and considered the work of either Fontenelle, a man of letters sympathetic to women writers, or a noted woman writer of the day, Marie-Catherine d'Aulnoy.[2] This compilation is in many ways a model for the major early tradition of anthologizing. It is devoted exclusively to French authors and almost exclusively to seventeenth-century writers. Its editor makes no claim to be a literary arbiter: all authors are included who have acquired a certain "reputation," whether or not they can be considered "great" authors. The editor makes no attempt to dictate literary taste but tries simply to give a sense of the field.

Readers today think of anthologies exclusively as works intended to introduce literature into the classroom in order to mold the taste of children. However, in France for over a century until just after the Revolution, almost all these volumes were compiled for adults who wished to keep abreast of the literary scene. The principle of inclusion on which the Fontenelle/d'Aulnoy anthology is based makes it clear that this anthology, like the dozens that imitated it throughout the eighteenth century, was destined for a particular public, the adults who frequented milieux like the salons, in which literature was a major topic of discussion, and who wished to have a sense of the range of modern literature, a subject not yet part of the curriculum at the time of their official education. These early anthologies are therefore pedagogical in a sense of the term perhaps closest to the recent usage "continuing education." In the vision of literary production they propose, the canon is made up of works read by an adult public active in the world rather than a public isolated in an educational establishment, a pedagogical role for literature promoted actively at least until the early nineteenth century. Indeed, prior to the mid eighteenth century, the only canonical status to which *French* authors could aspire was inclusion in worldly anthologies compiled for adults, a canonical status that was never officially legitimated. Only under the most exceptional circumstances did a new work become canonical in the original French sense of the term: that which is introduced into the classroom as a model for students. Prior to the mid eighteenth century, the classics, the works taught in the *collèges*, were all Greek and Latin, whereas modern works could become influential only by appealing to the worldly adult public.

The view of the literary scene found in the continuing education anthologies of the late seventeenth and early eighteenth centuries is remarkably different from the vision of that era presented in today's manuals. Perhaps the most striking difference concerns the presence of women writers. In anthologies devoted to writers in general, women writers are admitted in numbers far more important than at any time since. In addition, between the late seventeenth and the late eighteenth century, at least a dozen literary anthologies devoted exclusively to women writers were published. Before presenting the canonical revision that was the end result of the new literary pedagogy of the Enlightenment, I will consider very briefly two of these continuing education anthologies, one near the beginning of the tradition and one at its end, in order at least to suggest the magnitude of the options sacrificed to the remodeled classical ideology.

Marguerite Buffet's *Nouvelles observations sur la langue française, avec l'éloge des illustres savantes tant anciennes que modernes* (1668), one of the first such anthologies, is a fascinating critical hybrid. Buffet's volume is the clearest demonstration of the genre's goal of contributing to the continuing education of an adult public: its first half is a French grammar and a treatise on correct usage and orthography destined for a general audience and in particular female readers who had been denied formal linguistic training. These grammatical considerations are joined to a portrait gallery of literary women in which Buffet, alone of the representatives of this worldly tradition, broadens the definition of the literary to include demonstrations of the linguistic excellence she defines in her grammatical treatise, oral as well as written. She is thereby able to record accomplishments, such as conversational brilliance, otherwise excluded from the domain of literary criticism, and to privilege the particular artistic manifestations then being developed in the salons. Volumes like Buffet's—as well as those of her contemporaries Jean de La Forge, Jacquette Guillaume, and Claude de Vertron—provide information on numbers of influential seventeenth-century literary women who have been virtually lost to readers since the demise of the worldly canon after the Revolution.[3]

Early anthologies like Buffet's have none of the pedagogical qualities of the eighteenth-century compilations whose techniques we will analyze. They are often closer to collections of eulogies than to literary manuals from which a potential student of any age could obtain information on what an individual author actually wrote, much less on what that literary production was like. By the end of the worldly anthology tradition, however, editors had made great progress in the pedagogical presentation of material, clearly having learned from their predecessors (almost every such compilation contains references to precursor volumes) as much as from the rival tradition of manuals for classroom instruction. Both the most eloquent and the most pedagogical of the worldly anthologies is one of the final examples of the tradition, an enterprise that would clearly have realized the genre's potential, had it not become still another victim of the events of 1789.

The fourteen existing volumes of Louise Keralio Robert's *Collection des meilleurs ouvrages français composés par des femmes* (1786–1789) stand as a monument to the tradition's potential for growth. Furthermore, as she makes clear in the preface to volume 1, Keralio had initially planned a venture far more vast, "about 36 volumes" that would have presented a panorama of French literary history from the Middle Ages through the end of the eighteenth century, with the lion's share devoted to the "classical age" of French women's writing, the seventeenth century.[4] Had Keralio completed her anthology, she would have provided an alternate history of French literature until the Revolution, a narrative demonstrating the deficiency of any French literary history that omits the contributions of women to every period, a history challenging the adequacy of the notions of periodization then commonly accepted—many of which are still accepted today—to account for the production of women writers. But Keralio did not come close to finishing her history. After the initial five volumes devoted to the Middle Ages and the Renaissance (Christine de Pizan alone is allotted two volumes), she jumps ahead to Scudéry. She then skips over volumes 7 and 8, which she leaves blank, as she explains, in the hope of returning some day to fill in the gaps, and proceeds directly to Sévigné. It is easy to offer a historical explanation for Keralio's failure to complete the ambitious contract she initially offered her readers: the last volumes of her collection appeared in 1789, surely an inauspicious date, as Germaine de Staël would soon observe, both for feminist writing in general and for the until then largely aristocratic tradition of French women's literature in particular. No one would ever fill in the gaps in Keralio's history, although the tradition she represents was killed off by a movement that began long before 1789, and one that was hardly revolutionary in its politics.

The volumes Keralio did manage to complete are astonishingly well researched and put together and could easily be used today as the basis for a curriculum in French women's writing. Her format is highly pedagogical: biography followed by selections from major works, with an important innovation found in no other early anthology. Keralio understands that the best literary history presents an overview, a framework in which individual pieces can be situated. Thus she alternates her treatment of women authors from a given period with a history of French literature, presented in segments, from its origins (defined as the time of the Gauls), always integrating the women writers she is about to discuss in the general literary context of their day. And Keralio's volumes are the logical summation of the movement that begins with Buffet and her contemporaries. An examination of early French literary histories shows that, until the dawn of the nineteenth century, women writers were just about as likely as their male counterparts to be included in canonical compilations. However, at the same time as the editors of worldly anthologies were learning to make their case more forcefully, the countertradition was developing that would in the long run become so influential that it would succeed in establishing its program of French literary classics as the only vision possible of the early history of French literature.

No sooner had the first anthologists established the existence of a French tradition (by the early eighteenth century) than the power of the pedagogical canon began to be recognized. Historians have traced the movement whereby, from the sixteenth to the eighteenth century, the family gradually turned over to the *collège* the boy's preparation for professional life. Yet, despite the fact that the student was supposed to enter a profession directly upon leaving the *collège,* schools continued throughout the eighteenth century to rely almost exclusively on literary texts to teach all subjects. In the course of the eighteenth century, theorists began increasingly to call for a "national" education, a "uniform" education that would replace "provincial prejudices" with "homogeneous ideas of civic and religious virtue."[5] Contemporaneous with the development of the desire to standardize the teaching of Frenchness is the movement to give French authors at least equal importance in the curriculum that was to perform this new pedagogical mission. In a standardized, national educational program whose primary goal was to use the teaching of literature to form model Frenchmen, educators realized that the newly recognized French literary tradition should play a major role. Under these circumstances, pedagogical authorities initiated the process of teaching teachers how the works of literary moderns could be held up as models of Frenchness.

This project for the ideological packaging of literature took shape over the first half of the eighteenth century. Scholars gradually developed the anthology into a full-scale literary program: in 1740, for example, Goujet produced an eighteen-volume *Histoire de la littérature française* still directed at a post-*collège* public, but no longer governed by the principle of the worldly anthologics—that is, an author should be included if he or she is being talked about. On the contrary, Goujet's aim was strictly judgmental: "I want to lead my readers by the hand through our literary riches, to teach them what we have in each literary domain, to show them what they should choose and reject."[6] Goujet transforms the worldly anthology into the arm by which critics could police the reading habits of the "honnête homme" and could thereby shape both his taste and his national prejudices. Such a project would in effect be a form of reeducation, an undoing of the vision of the contemporary literary scene spread by the wordly anthologies. He concludes his "preliminary discourse" with a call for a similar effort on the part of pedagogues, who should be adapting the texts of literary moderns the better to accomplish their task of making their young charges into "good Christians" "useful to civil society" (1:xli).

Pedagogues quickly heeded his call to arms. The ancestor of the modern system of national exams, the *concours général des collèges parisiens,* at its inception in 1747 had a double prize, *amplification française* side by side with *amplification latine.* From this point on,

Parisian professors of rhetoric "categorically" demanded that French poets and orators be introduced into the curriculum and that students begin to write *in* French about French authors (Chartier et al., 199). At the very same time that the system of *concours* was being founded, the pedagogical philosophy and even the pedagogical tools that are still used today to prepare students for the national exams were given their original formulation. The abbé Batteux's companion volumes *Les Beaux Arts réduits à un seul principe* of 1746 and his *Cours de belles-lettres* of 1747 were designed to provide teachers with both what we know from Lagarde and Michard as a "*program of great* French authors" and the techniques for using these authors to teach Frenchness, most notably the reduction of works deemed masterpieces to *morceaux choisis* made pedagogical through an *explication de texte*. The canon that can be assembled on the basis of the worldly anthologies is quite different from the program for the study of seventeenth-century French literature generally proposed today. The ancestor of the manuals in which those of us currently teaching received our first ideas of the period is Batteux: the "reduced" canon he proposes is remarkably close to what, for better or for worse, we think of as the classic French canon. Batteux throws his considerable authority as holder of the chair of Greek and Latin philosophy at the Collège de France behind a program for the study of the French tradition that aims to eliminate all literature deemed dangerous to civic virtue, especially the women writers who figure so prominently in the nonpedagogical anthology tradition. Before taking up the question of women writers and the case Batteux builds against them, however, I will first discuss the strategy on which Batteux's pedagogy is founded.

For his reform, Batteux calls on pedagogues to follow the new scientific model, "to collect data as the basis for a system that reduces their findings to common principles."[7] In *Les Beaux Arts réduits*, Batteux defines the nature and the origin of the unique artistic principle he claims to have unearthed, and he also demonstrates the ideological goal of this method of literary and critical reduction. Let me outline the reasoning on which Batteux's model pedagogical system is founded. Good taste is unique: "there is only one good taste, that of nature" (1:127). There is, however, progress in the spread of good taste because the public "allows itself, without noticing it, to be taken in [*se laisser prendre*] by the examples [it encounters in literature]. . . . One shapes oneself unconsciously on that which one has seen." Since moderns have the advantage of access to a greater number of authors, it is logical that good taste has become more widespread and that modern taste provides the definitive guide to classical status. On the basis of these two rules, Batteux constructs the following scenario: there is only one "natural" taste. The great artists are those who have "exposed" the natural design in their works. An educated public is able immediately to appreciate and to "approve" this greatness and then, instinctively and without even realizing it, to form itself according to the standards proposed by the classic literary texts. Then, as a matter of course, the model aesthete becomes a model citizen: "One wishes to seem good, simple, direct; in other words, the complete citizen will be revealed" (1:145). The ideal citizen, furthermore, is also a perfect Christian, and the artistic manifestations of good taste inspire both civic virtue and Christian ideals (1:146).

Batteux's logic, which he calls "simple, straightforward," is based on a premise never clearly exposed in his initial treatise: good taste may be unique and innate, but it must also be taught, for only an educated public immediately understands great literature. The implied conclusion of Batteux's theory of universal taste and esthetic progress is that the French educational system should use its power to create the ideals and the standards of Frenchness. This service Batteux himself provides in the companion volume to his reductionist theory, in which he selects the precise examples that should be imposed upon the minds of those to be made into model Christian citizens, to mold them, without their knowledge, into the recognition of socially correct greatness. In his *Cours de belles-lettres*, he provides the outline for the teaching of literature designed to produce educated French male Christians. He gives examples from Greek, Latin, and French literature, although "of course French letters will occupy the first rank" (2:9). Both his volume's organization and his description of it are resolutely direct:

We will cover all the genres in succession, beginning with the simplest. We will give a summary presentation of the nature, the parts, and the rules of each of them; we will briefly trace its history; after which we will apply the rules to the most famous works in each genre, which will be analyzed both in terms of their content and in terms of their form. (2:9–10)

In the three volumes of his curriculum, Batteux proceeds genre by genre, giving, first, general history and principles, followed by a short biography of each author, and finally selected passages from each author's work, passages that—and this is his work's major long-term innovation—he then analyzes. In the *Cours de belles-lettres*, anthologizing is always accompanied by a demonstration for teachers of how to use literature in the classroom. The *Cours de belles-lettres* is the first example in France of the pedagogical genre we now call a literary manual.

When Batteux begins the course itself, it quickly becomes apparent that "our" taste simply singles out again and again those works that conform to "our" preconceived notions of what a work on a specific subject should say. When he sets up his presentation of La Fontaine, Batteux lays out the foundation for his method for reading literary texts, a method with a prodigious future in the French pedagogical tradition. His technique —"which presupposes real genius"— "consists in the comparison of a work with nature itself or, *that which amounts to the same thing, with the ideas that we have about what one can, and what one must say about the chosen subject*" (2:61, my emphasis). He illustrates his method with a reading of La Fontaine's "Le Chêne et le Roseau" that is a classical model for the critical/pedagogical genre today known as *explication de texte*.

Before examining the text, however, Batteux shows why it deserves to be singled out as an exemplary work: "Before reading it, let us try to see for ourselves what ideas nature would present us on this subject" (2:61). He then shows how the major elements in La Fontaine's fable correspond to "our" preestablished ideas of what they should be. In his *explication de texte*, furthermore, Batteux goes on to demonstrate that "our" expectations, when properly fulfilled, produce a work that is the perfect embodiment of all the stylistic and formal qualities previously characterized as the highest literary values. The great work, the classic, is the work that contains no surprises for the educated critic/reader and the work that conforms perfectly to the French male Christian critic's ideas of (human) nature. All "we" have to do to explicate literature properly is to articulate "our" prejudices and proclaim as classics those works that best exemplify "our" vision of what the world should be.

Thus Batteux's program reveals that the teaching of literature in France has been founded from its origin on the phenomenon that Anne-Marie Thiesse and Hélène Mathieu, in an indispensable recent study of the evolution of the canon of French literature in the nineteenth century that has been expanded and translated for this volume (see below, chap. 5), refer to as "l'histoire littéraire par les textes" ("literary history through texts"). Just as in the nineteenth-century process whose unfolding Thiesse and Mathieu retrace, in Batteux's original formulation of "l'histoire littéraire par les textes," works are initially singled out allegedly only because of their value as examples, that is, for the extent to which they lend themselves to the techniques of the *explication de texte*. Yet the overall implication of his work, and of the nineteenth-century programs that follow his example, is that literary history can be written solely on the basis of the works thus isolated.

Batteux's program is also a monument to the official exclusion from the pages of literary history of the novel, and therefore of the women writers who were until then its most illustrious practitioners. Self-styled Boileau of his age (his collected works appear in 1774 to coincide with the centenary of the publication of the *Art poétique*), Batteux continues his precursor's battle against prose fiction. Boileau, however, had at least discussed the novel, if only to dismiss it, in the *Art poétique* and in more detail in the *Dialogue des héros de roman*.[8] But even the scornful condemnations of the premier critic of the Golden Age had not succeeded in diminishing the genre's popularity in Batteux's day: seventeenth-century novels continued to be reedited throughout the eighteenth century and were given enormous coverage in the worldly anthologies, proof that they remained an essential part of the canon for adult readers that, at least until the Revolution, offered a challenge to the classic canon being developed by Goujet, Batteux, and their colleagues. Batteux's resolute avoidance of the novel could well have been a new tactic for eliminating the genre that for decades had proved stubbornly resistant to the decree denying it classic status. Since Batteux does not allude to the genre's existence, even in the volume he devotes to prose forms, it might be possible to explain his omission on the grounds that the novel was perhaps the mode least malleable to the demands of the *explication de texte*. However, this explanation is invalidated by the terms on which Batteux judges the only two women writers he chooses to include.

In the volume Batteux devotes to prose genres, he concludes with a discussion of the letter, for which his representative modern author is Sévigné. However, the goal of the *explications de texte* he performs on her epistles is to point out their defects, to prove that she is not a suitable pedagogical model. Her letters are so full of "dead time" (*longueurs*) that they frequently "languish" (4:355–56). Her arguments are "without body" (4:356). Her style, in short, is an appropriate model only for "overly tender mothers" (4:354), and it is unworthy of exemplary status because it is too "risky [*hasardé*] for anyone but her, and *especially for a man of letters*" (4:354–55, my emphasis).

This reasoning becomes even clearer in Batteux's treatment of Deshoulières, the only other woman writer he includes. (She was, in 1671, the winner of the first prize for poetry awarded by the Académie française, and she is the ideal example of the woman writer always part of the worldly adult canon, but since eliminated, following the judgment of Batteux's followers, from their canon for children.) Her pastoral poetry is judged "the most delicate," "the *softest* possible," but

unfortunately, the doctrine—the "esprit de mollesse," the "essence of flabbiness or pliancy"—that her poetry fosters is conducive to a weakening of moral fiber, and turns it into a sort of epicurianism entirely opposed, not only to Christian morality, but also to that vigor of the soul, to that *male force*, that is the foundation and the support of true integrity. (2:188, my emphasis)

Thus Deshoulières, like Sévigné, seems to have been included in the first pedagogical canon of French literature the better to justify the exclusion of women's writing in general. These token women achieve exemplary status above all as illustrations of the threat to "vigorous" male Christian standards represented by the "softening" and "languishing" tendencies of female literary models. Women writers, Batteux warns, had to be eliminated from the curriculum because they were a direct threat to Church and state.

Classicists have long been sensitive to the central role in the preservation of Greek literary texts played by the anthologies edited for schoolboys in antiquity. For example, of the forty to forty-four comedies of Aristophanes known to the ancients, we know only the eleven edited by a grammarian as "selected theater" for classes. Similarly, all that has come down to us of the vast production of Aeschylus and Sophocles are the seven plays selected for the curriculum.[9] In the case of French literature, one cannot, of course, speak of a phenomenon as dramatic as the permanent destruction of works. Nevertheless, for nearly two centuries it has been as if the works of most of the French women writers included in the early canon for adults no longer existed. Once modern writers had entered the pedagogical curriculum, within decades the anthologies for a cultivated adult public ceased to be compiled, and the other canon they had kept alive began to be forgotten. Increasingly, the modern writers who continued to be read were only those who could be promoted as French classics, that is, those who could be packaged in a national, and a nationalistic, literary program. The educators entrusted with the creation of a literary model for the exclusively male public of the *collèges* followed Batteux's lead and excluded the "dangerous," the "inimitable," as Lafayette would have it, examples of virtue provided by women writers.[10]

The terms in which Batteux eliminated women writers were frequently repeated as the original French pedagogical canon was set in place. I will cite one example from another pedagogue-critic of the day because I believe that the importance of repetition in canon formation must never be underestimated. Critics-pedagogues most often just reiterate the judgments of others. "[Villedieu's] works are little read today, and I dare say that they are still read too much, considering the danger that young men above all cannot fail to run from their reading" (Goujet, 18:138). When women writers are evoked by any of the eighteenth century's literary pedagogues, it is almost always simply to explain in summary fashion why their works should no longer be read. Often, Batteux's argument about their threat to the nation's male fiber is restated. Just as often, the pedagogue turns to the argument Boileau used, so prematurely, about Scudéry (in his *Dialogue des héros de roman*): "She is no longer read." Their pronouncements are just as premature as their master's— Villedieu, for example, continued to be reedited throughout the eighteenth century—but that is not the point. Women writers were so threatening to the ideology of the developing pedagogical canon that their elimination had to be reimposed until the new curriculum was firmly established.

Thus, in the sixteen-volume compilation that may best represent the view of the canon that the nineteenth century inherited from the eighteenth, *Lycée ou cours de littérature ancienne et moderne* (1797–1803), the Voltaire disciple and longtime journalist La Harpe uses this argument, virtually without exception, whenever he evokes a woman writer. He mentions eleven seventeenth-century women, not an unimpressive list, but, for all but Lafayette and Sévigné, the entry is limited to: "her boring novels, plays, etc. have been forgotten," or "her works are no longer read." La Harpe devotes fully half of the *Lycée*'s volumes to the literature of his own, not quite finished, century. In these eight volumes, however, he includes only four women writers: Tencin, de Beaumont, Riccoboni, Graffigny. La Harpe's compilation demonstrates that the flowering of the pedagogical tradition brought about the termination of the worldly tradition. Contrary to what you probably imagine, his *Lycée* is intended not for the formation of schoolchildren but as "a supplement to [the studies they've already done] for people of the world who don't have the time to begin new studies."[11] (The *Lycée* is, in fact, the record of La Harpe's lectures at what has been described as a worldly Sorbonne with an elegant public.) This is the first work of adult education to be a work of *reeducation:* La Harpe is trying to destroy the influence of the tradition of worldly anthologies, to make over the vision of the canon proposed for adult readers in the image of the pedagogical canon drawn up for schoolchildren. In the worldly anthology thus brought into the nationalistic line, women writers were virtual nonentities.[12]

Such consideration of canonical genealogies seems naturally to call for reflection on the process of canon formation taking place today. The critics who seem most inclined to consider the type of question — if not pronouncing on the value of a literary text, at least championing a text for inclusion in a curriculum — that was the exclusive concern of their classical precursors are for the most part those, whether feminists of the so-called American persuasion or supporters of other minority traditions, who ask that the canon be revised in order to include voices that have traditionally been excluded. The most visible contemporary canonical gestures have taken the form either of the critique of existing curricula and other pedagogical tools, or of the promotion of parallel canons to which students are to be exposed at the same time as more traditional programs. Not since the beginning of the eighteenth century have pedagogues been faced with the choice between two opposing plans for the programmatic packaging of French literature, one of which would systematically grant a place to women writers. It is hard to predict the ideological grounds on which a decision will be made this time.

It is, of course, possible that there is now room for more than one canon of French literature. Certainly the dissemination of French culture is no longer the relatively manageable phenomenon that it was the last time this canonical option was available: various centers, more or less distant from the source of French nationalism and with more or less regular transfusions of native blood (presumably, those trained at the source are more likely to share received ideas of Frenchness) now promote visions of the canon that may well become gradually more irreconcilable with that formulated by and for the French national educational system. Finally, it is even possible that new technologies might inadvertently generate a challenge to received ideas of the canonical.[13]

Consider the example of the ARTFL (*Trésor de la langue française*) data base. many American universities now subscribe to this program that allows users, for an hourly fee, to have access on their computers to a long list of works of French literature from the Middle Ages to the twentieth century. (A new list is due soon; the one I consulted includes some seventy texts from the seventeenth century alone.) The data base was constituted by the Institut national de la langue française rather than one of the branches of the Centre national de la recherche scientifique (CNRS) more directly entrusted with a pedagogical mission. Texts were selected for the ARTFL data base solely on the basis of their linguistic richness (the project's long-range goal is a new dictionary of the French language).[14] In the meantime, anyone at the subscribing institution has access to what looks to all intents and purposes like a computerized canon of French literature with nothing to indicate its lexicographic mission. For some time, I derived great satisfaction from the list, which I imagined to be some sort of subversive canon of French literature, generated in the bosom of the CNRS: the data base includes, among other texts that are since the Revolution no longer part of literary programs, a good selection of the poetry of Deshoulières (the very verse Batteux castigates as a danger to "Christian morality" and "male force"), as well as no fewer than seven works, both fairy tales and travel literature, by d'Aulnoy, the possible editor of the original worldly anthology. My satisfaction continues even now that I know that the French intend to propose these women writers as models only of linguistic variety. After all, no one will be around to instruct the ever growing ranks of American students who, far from the Hexagon, rely increasingly on computers rather than any printed source of information, that the works so readily available on their screen (when they may have been out of print for decades, if not centuries) are valuable solely for their word count. Without a critical apparatus to direct their judgment, students might even take Deshoulières for the classic author she was for generations of adult French readers. The first canon of classic French literature just may be due for a revival.

Notes

1. There is considerable confusion about the origin of this usage. I do not accept the attribution of this sense of *classic* to Voltaire. The Robert dictionary states that this usage was introduced only at the turn of the nineteenth century by Staël. If this is true, we have still another indication of Staël's sensitivity to

semantic innovation. (Time and again, I have traced the origin of terms crucial for the history of women's writing to her works.)

2. *Recueil des plus belles pièces des poètes français depuis Villon jusqu'à M. de Benserade*, 5 vols. (Paris: Barbin, 1692). Initially, the anthology was generally accepted as d'Aulnoy's. Only later is Fontenelle's name attached to it and, even though no convincing reason for the change in attribution has ever been offered, it has gained wide acceptance. G. Reed, *Claude Barbin* (Geneva: Droz, 1974), 40, n. 1. Today, the compilation is most often referred to as the Recueil Barbin, after the publisher who signs its dedicatory preface. (He was the publisher of many early women writers.)

3. Marguerite Buffet, *Nouvelles Observations sur la langue française, avec l'éloge des illustres savantes tant anciennes que modernes* (Paris: Jean Cusson, 1668); Jean de La Forge, *Le Cercle des femmes savantes* (Paris: Loyson, 1663); Jacquette Guillaume, *Les Dames illustres* (Paris: Thomas Jolly, 1665); Claude Charles Guionet, seigneur de Vertron, *La Nouvelle Pandore ou les Femmes illustres du siècle de Louis le Grand*, 2 vols. (Paris: Veuve Mazuel, 1698).

4. Louise Félicité Guinemet de Keralio Robert, *Collection des meilleurs ouvrages français composés par des femmes*, 14 vols. (Paris: Lagrange, 1786–89), 1:i–ii.

5. Roger Chartier, M.-M. Compère, and D. Julia, *L'Education en France au XVIIe et XVIIIe siècles* (Paris: PUF, 1964), 209. Subsequent references to this work will be included in parentheses in the text, a practice I follow with all works I cite more than once. All translations from the French are my own.

6. Abbé Claude Pierre Goujet, *Bibliothèque française; ou Histoire de la littérature française*, 18 vols. (Paris: Mariette, 1740–56), 1:ii.

7. I cite Abbé Chales Batteux in the four-volume 1774 reedition of his works, *Principes de la littérature* (Paris: Saillant), 1:126.

8. Lack of space prevents me from repeating any part of an argument I have already developed elsewhere: for Boileau, the novel is dangerous first and foremost because it is marked by the values of the women writers who dominated the genre's production in his day. See my *Fictions of Sappho, 1546–1937* (Chicago: University of Chicago Press, 1989), 110–14.

9. Henri Marrou, *Histoire de l'éducation dans l'antiquité* (Paris: Seuil, 1948), 225.

10. There were occasional attempts to found a pedagogical canon for schoolgirls, the most celebrated of which was drawn up at Saint-Cyr for and by the marquise de Maintenon. These curricula always make frequent use of women's writing—witness the impressive role played by Scudéry at St.-Cyr. However, given the tiny percentage of girls among the schoolchildren of the day, it is obvious that these alternate pedagogical curricula are largely merely utopian artifacts.

11. Jean-François La Harpe, *Lycée, ou cours de littérature ancienne et moderne*, 16 vols. (Paris: Lefèvre, 1816), 1:vi.

12. La Harpe's compilation was reprinted four times between 1813 and 1816 alone.

13. In an interview for this volume (chap. 14), Julia Kristeva expresses the belief that there will no longer be canons because of the influence of the media. I think rather that mass communication will revise traditional methods of canon transmission.

14. I thank Bernard Quemada and Evelyne Martin for this information.

Men's Reading, Women's Writing: Gender and the Rise of the Novel

> The latest enemy of the vitality of classic texts is
> feminism.
> —Allan Bloom, *The Closing of the American Mind*

I will begin with the matter of a footnote.

About six hundred pages into Frances [Fanny] Burney's nine-hundred-page novel, *Camilla*, the heroine receives the visit of the ebullient Mrs. Mittin. Mrs. Mittin eagerly tells Camilla the story of her getting to know Mrs. Berlinton.[1]

> I happened to be in the book shop when she came in, and asked for a book; the Peruvan Letters she called it; and it was not at home, and she looked quite vexed, for she said she had looked the catalogue up and down, and saw nothing she'd a mind to; so I thought it would be a good opportunity to oblige her, and be a way to make a prodigious genteel acquaintance besides; so I took down the name, and I found out the lady that had got the book, and I made her a visit, and I told her it was particular wanted by a lady that had a reason; so she let me have it, and I took it to my pretty lady, who was so pleased, she did not know how to thank me. (606)

Burney's 1796 novel was republished by Oxford University Press in 1983 in an edition established by Edward A. Bloom and Lillian D. Bloom. Their footnotes are abundant, authoritative in tone, and, on the face of it, carefully documented. Thus on this passage, for "book shop" they offer: "obviously a circulating library. In *The Southampton Guide* (6th ed., ca., 1801, pp. 74–75) [the story takes place in Southampton] there is a description of such a library: 'T. Baker's Library, in the High Street, contains a well chosen selection of nearly seven thousand volumes, forming a more general collection of useful and polite literature than is usually found in circulating libraries. The books are lent to read, at 15s. the year, 4s.6d. the quarter, and 5s. for the season.'"[2] As someone who rarely does this kind of research herself, I love having access to information provided with such detail. The precision of it—4s.6d. the quarter—feeds the fantasy (which I think it must remain) that one might be able to reconstruct the material contexts of a past of reading.

Despite the seduction of its details, this is not the footnote I'm after. The note in question comes (next in sequence) to explain the title of the book requested, the "Peruvan Letters": "Mrs. Mittin meant," the editors inform us, "either Charles de Secondat Montesquieu's *Persian Letters* (trans., 1722) or George Lyttleton's *Letters from a Persian in England to his Friend in Ispahan*. In her ignorance, she failed to distinguish between Persia and Peru" (949–50). The failure to distinguish between Persia and Peru, however, may not be an either/or affair. In their eagerness to identify one woman novelist's readings, *Camilla*'s editors miss another's writing: Françoise d'Issembourg d'Happencourt Graffigny's *Lettres d'une Péruvienne* (1747), which were being translated in England as the *Peruvian Letters* as late as 1782.[3]

I am, it might seem, placing a heavy burden on an academic detail: why Burney (or Lyttleton, for that matter), and not Graffigny? None the less, because the uneven inclusion of proper names in the set of common references that shape collective legacies is a symptomatic expression of broader cultural choices, I want to retain this instance of omission as the point of departure for a reflection on the vicissitudes of canon formation.

In this essay, I will be dealing more specifically with the ways in which the reading and writing practices of a given period are recorded, reformed, gendered, and forgotten. I will take as my particular focus the critical discourse that comes to place in literary history a dominant current in eighteenth-century fiction: the novels of manners that obsessively represent what Joan Kelly called "the social relation of the sexes."[4]

> Les hommes ont de ces oublis . . .
>
> —Marie-Jeanne Riccoboni,
> *Lettres de Milady Juliette Catesby*

In his wonderfully erudite and still timely study on the eighteenth-century novel, Georges May makes the observation that the "history of the French novel remains to be written." "The volume devoted to the eighteenth-century novel," he adds, "is especially lacking,"[5] and he wonders about this missing piece of literary history. Twenty-five years after the publication of May's *Le Dilemme du roman au dix-huitième siècle,* despite several excellent books on the novels of this period, the task, I think, still lies before us, if, by a history of the French novel, one has in mind a history that includes women's foundational role in its development. As a feminist critic concerned with imagining the volume devoted to the eighteenth-century novel still to be written, I find myself twenty-five years later returning to May's introduction (and the long chapter "Feminism and the Novel") for a place from which to begin again, for, among other things, a *gendered* account of authorship: men *and* women writers. Thus, in a roll call of novelists publishing between 1715 and 1761, he names (in this order): Prévost, Marivaux, Crébillon, Duclos, Tencin, Graffigny, and Riccoboni and characterizes them as the "least forgotten" writers of this period (3). The inclusion of women's names as a matter of course (even among the least forgotten) may not be taken for granted in 1963 or today.

In "Classical Reeducation: Decanonizing the Feminine" (see above, chap. 2), Joan DeJean shows how anthologies in seventeenth- (and eighteenth-) century France served as a kind of "continuing education" for adults "who wished to keep abreast of the literary scene"; anthologies were organized pedagogically not only to supply literary material, but to shape a generation's taste by supplementing its ideology. Let us turn now to what I see as a modern version of this mode, René Etiemble's collection of eighteenth-century prose fiction in the 1966 two-volume Pléiade, *Romanciers du XVIIIe siècle.*[6] I have chosen this volume precisely because, as Etiemble himself argues, the Pléiade edition constitutes a form of recognition meant to assure a posterity of reading. The Pléiade edition "of itself" confers legitimacy and provides authorizing versions of the included texts.

Of May's list, Etiemble includes only the male writers, to which he adds others. Now, Etiemble has read Georges May and concurs with his position that one needs a history of the eighteenth-century novel; that it is wrong to justify the ignorance of the general reading public who see in the novel only Balzac and Stendhal instead of Rétif, or Duclos, or Crébillon and miss the eighteenth century completely. But nowhere, in a preface and introduction both of which demonstrate an acute self-consciousness about the grounds for inclusion and exclusion at work in the anthology, and a sympathy for what he calls the "human reference" (2:xx), does the critic refer to the writers central to the production and formation of the very fictional forms he has collected for a sophisticated reading public ("aux gens cultivés", 1:8).

Etiemble explains that a reader who wants a more complete picture of the evolution of the genre ought to "reread" *other* works not included in his volumes (*not* included, because unlike his selection, these have received their own individual Pléiade "consecration"). Readers, he specifies, are to *return* to the novels of Montesquieu, Marivaux, Diderot, and Rousseau interweaving them in chronological order along with his choices if they are to have a complete picture, more than "a glance of what the French novel becomes in the eighteenth century" (1:7). Thus, despite Etiemble's awareness of the importance of women writers of this deconsidered form in the seventeenth century—he names Scudéry and Lafayette (1:7)—and his admiration for Georges May's mapping of the terrain, neither Graffigny, Tencin, nor Riccoboni, for example, figures in this "tableau" of the French novel. Why was Etiemble, who is not beyond a major saving operation in this anthology, not moved to make a case for women writers? Why Sénac de Meilhan, or Cazotte, and not Riccoboni or Tencin? Nothing indicates whether Etiemble read any of the women's novels I'm thinking of; read them and rejected them. (In an earlier critical overview of eighteenth-century prose writers, he mentions in passing Tencin's *Les Mémoires du comte de Comminges* and Graffigny's *Lettres péruviennes* [sic] without any evaluation.[7]) What concerns me here are the effects produced by his passing over women writers in silence.

To be sure, one could argue that the category of the "woman writer" was not a vivid one in 1966. Or rather that the category of "la romancière" very precisely left the question of the specificity of women's writing either moot or intact.[8] One could also more pointedly suggest that what attracts Etiemble to his corpus is the lure of identification, a form of "reading as male bonding" that Susan Winnett, in a shrewdly theorized essay on "narrative and the principle(s) of pleasure," identifies as a "homoaesthetic subtext," a set of assumptions that follow from a "legalized, entirely male circuit of desire."[9] Etiemble, for his part, seems drawn to the form of male memoir epitomized in Louvet's *Les Amours du Chevalier de Faublas*. From the list of "si j'aime le *Faublas* c'est . . ." let us retain this formulation: "It's in particular because of the slightly disreputable women who work at satisfying Faublas for the amusement of the well-endowed reader" ("C'est à cause en particulier des femmes un peu moins honnêtes qui s'emploient à combler Faublas, pour l'amusement du lecteur bien constitué" [2:xxv]). Although to be fair this invocation of the well-endowed (redblooded might be a better translation) reader is not Etiemble's *only* explanation for his textual preference, it is difficult to resist the impression that his evaluation of Crébillon, Duclos, Denon, and company is finally inseparable from a highly masculinist mode of critical pleasure (very specifically, reading as a French, relentlessly heterosexual, terminally misogynistic though always elegant and gallant male [2:xxvi]): in a word, reading *like* a man.

I want to suggest further that if Graffigny, Tencin, and Riccoboni do nòt appear on Etiemble's screen, it may also be because in addition to their status as women writers (hence their general invisibility), they specifically produce what I will call *feminist writing* on the same subjects. These fictions of dissent call into question the fulfillment of the virile subjectivities that typically structure libertine texts, by which I mean here the recollections of a man's life as organized by and narrated through his sexual experience—whether a list of encounters or the obsession of a single passion, like *Manon Lescaut*. I am prepared to argue that this particular plot of heterosexual engagement provides the basic psychosocial design of the memoir novel, one of the two dominant novelistic forms in the eighteenth century. Feminist fictions take another, harsher, and less jubilant view of the sexual and social stage of human relations; and in these novels female subjectivity is the figure, not merely the ground of representation against which the tropes of masculine performance display themselves.

In *Subject to Change* I make the claim that it is important to locate any poetics of feminist writing in relation to a historicized national and cultural production; indeed that a "poetics of location" is the only way to work against the universalizing tendencies of a monolith of "women's writing."[10] Although the individual works that I treat there range in time from *La Princesses de Clèves* (1678) to *La Vagabonde* (1910), I draw implicitly on the powerful body of eighteenth-century women's texts for my general understanding of this writing. The novels of women writers in eighteenth-century France may be characterized by what Rachel DuPlessis has called a "poetics of critique";[11] more specifically I focus on the *figuration* of dissent from the plots of the dominant tradition that marks these fictions. In these eighteenth-century novels—most dramatically, perhaps, Riccoboni's *Lettres de Mistress Fanni Butlerd* and *Histoire du Marquis de Cressy*, and Tencin's *Mémoires du Comte de Comminge*—the conventional sex/gender arrangements that underwrite masculinist stories (the complacent fantasies of the "roman-liste," for instance) are vividly undermined.[12]

In this sense, then, in order to understand the patterns of inclusion and exclusion that shape the history of the novel in France, it is not sufficient to speak simply of men's or women's writing. Retained for posterity among the eighteenth-century novels devoted to the social relations of the sexes, is, we might more usefully say, libertine and not feminist writing. Put another way, at an angle to the notion of a literature of "worldliness," we want to emphasize the differentiation of the viewpoint from which the world (and its discursive domains) is perceived, entered, and experienced.

To understand the history of the French novel, especially as it played itself out in the eighteenth-century fictions of manners which in so many ways made the nineteenth-century realist novel possible, it is crucial to perform two gestures: first to restore feminist writing to the body of fiction that becomes the novel; the second, to reread the texts retained by literary history through this supplemented and redoubled vision.

> Flaubert was writing the new novel of 1860, Proust the new novel of 1910. A writer must bear his date, knowing there are no masterpieces in eternity, only works in history; and that they survive only to the extent that they have left the past behind them and announced the future.
>
> —Alain Robbe-Grillet, *Pour un nouveau roman*

Let us consider a recent example of the old literary history; unlike the Etiemble volumes, this is not an anthology, but another legitimating instance of eighteenth-century letters, a mainstream exercise in cultural diffusion: the volumes published in 1984 by Arthaud, specifically the volumes of *Littérature française*, volume 5, *De Fénelon à Voltaire*, and volume 6, *De L'Encyclopédie aux Méditations*.[13]

The problem of inclusion and exclusion in these manuals, by which I will mean for the purposes of this essay the difference in treatment of men's and women's writing, is related to a problem of category and definition: the men appear in the table of contents of volume 6 with their names under the large headings: "Great Works,

Great Authors." Except for Staël (and she is part of an ensemble along with "Benjamin Constant et le groupe de Coppet") no women's names appear in the table of contents, or in the bibliographical sketches at the back of the book. But in both volumes the hidden bodies are there, of course, slotted into the subset of a literary historical category: the sentimental novel, in volume 5, under "Forms and Genres." Under the promising heading "Toward a New Novel," Tencin and Graffigny are located within the subheading "le roman des coeurs sensibles," the novel of (and for) feeling hearts. In volume 6 the category is called "le roman sensible" and includes two pages of critical comment on Riccoboni. Despite a certain grudging admiration for her "portraits of women" (6:214), in the end the authors of the manual find that Riccoboni's work does not meet the standards of the male model: Riccoboni, less talented than Richardson and Diderot as a novelist of everyday life, fails to create the illusion of reality through a judicious use of detail (Riccoboni "ignore le pittoresque" [6:216]). And at the end of the century, we find in a short list Krudener, Charrière, Cottin, Staël ("Staël elle-même"[!]) —as servile imitators, "who borrow from Rousseau their characters, situations, settings and the means of moving their female readers, for these women are addressing a female audience" (6:221).

Although in their analyses of the production, distribution, and consumption of books the authors of the manual rarely distinguish by gender, they note the role played by education in the formation of a reading public and the fact that women are excluded from the scenes of knowledge: with a few exceptions, they observe, women are not seen as fit for studying serious subjects: "women are granted the novel, the frivolous genre, without anyone suspecting that it is to them that the novel will owe its surprising development" (45). Unfortunately, this acknowledgment of the material conditions of literature and its paradoxical relation to women's social inferiority stops there and congeals into a commonplace. It does not take the next step to reflect upon its own categories of analysis, categories that by their language —"Great Works, Great Authors"— return women to invisibility, to the clichés of the *lectrice:* of a female reading public on the one hand, and of women writers as inferior imitators of a perfected male-authored model and novel of the feminine to boot— Richardson and Rousseau.

In their unexamined adherence to the masterpiece codes of the dominant tradition according to which they (re)construct a male genealogy, the Arthaud editors fail to see women writers, on the one hand, as the continuers of a powerful tradition of seventeenth-century women writers, and on the other, as the producers of new forms and new reading practices. I cannot stress too heavily the degree of canon *de*formation this failure of vision represents.[14]

What we need in order to write a history of the eighteenth-century novel are some new ways of thinking about what goes on in a "republic of letters," restoring its heterogeneity and reopening the question for criticism of the relations between social values and literary forms. Although in my own research I have been specifically concerned with the "cultural work" performed by women's writing[15] and with the social values defining woman's place that subtend a national literature at a given historical moment, the implications of such an emphasis in fact require a reimagination of the whole picture: the mix of writing that has been sorted out to become the narrow and fixed literary tradition we study, write about, teach, and pass on.

> There's no cause for alarm. I'm not going to talk either about the play *Cénie,* or even about the *Lettres péruviennes,* works that were somewhat appealing in their time and that are completely passé today. I'm going to talk mainly about Voltaire; Mme de Graffigny brings us into his home and helps us to discover him in a rather new or at least very natural light. (Monday, 17 June 1850)
>
> —Sainte-Beuve, *Lettres de Madame de Grafigny, ou Voltaire à Cirey*

Let us reconsider now the case of Mrs. Mittin's mistake. Graffigny's *Lettres d'une Péruvienne* is a novel that, like most women's writing in France, enjoyed tremendous popularity when it was published, and in this case even a certain posterity: thirty editions, including ten in English and Italian, until 1777, and then continuous publication until 1835. Despite its contemporary critical recognition (the "*Lettres d'une Péruvienne* were among the most widely read books in the eighteenth century" [*Littérature française,* 6:210]), the novel rarely appears in the standard accounts of eighteenth-century fiction, nor until recently has it been collected in standard editions. Unlike many female-authored novels, however, the *Lettres d'une Péruvienne,* had a reprieve of sorts. In 1967 an Italian scholar, Gianni Nicoletti, brought out a critical edition of the novel, which had not been republished since the early nineteenth century.[16] And in 1983, more important, perhaps, a paperback edition, based on Nicoletti's work, was published by Garnier Flammarion, in a collection of epistolary novels. This volume has made it possible for the first time to teach the novel as a matter of course. Will this be the case?

Despite the work's material availability, without a rethinking of the value paradigms that have overdetermined our reading habits, without a critical reflection about the act of women's writing as a type of cultural intervention, it is not at all clear that the *Lettres d'une Péruvienne* will emerge from the margins to be read alongside, for example, the Persian ones. The very fact of classifying the novel for publication as a love-letter novel ("romans d'amour par lettres") maintains the hierarchy of classifications that, as we saw in the discourse of the Arthaud manual, trivializes female authorship.

The reconstructive project of reading women's writing, then, necessarily involves textual strategies that acknowledge the peculiar status of this literature in the library: there, but in opposition to the "already read," the *déjà lu* of the canon—"underread"—"*sous lu*," cut off from the kind of historical and metacritical life that characterizes the works of dominant French literature. Learning to read women's writing entails not only a particular attentiveness to the marks of signature that I have called "overreading"; it also involves "reading in pairs" (or, in Naomi Schor's coinage, "intersextually").[17] By this I mean looking at the literature of men's and women's writing side by side to perceive at their points of intersection the differentiated lines of a "bicultural" production of the novel— Persian *and* Peruvian—more complicated than the familiar, national history of its tropes.

I want to offer now an example of the stakes of this revision and the difficulty of sorting out the values at work in such a project. In a long review essay on Fanny Burney's *Cecilia* (1784), Laclos elaborates a comparative (French and English) and gendered poetics in which he makes the claim that women are particularly well suited to novel writing because the genre requires the three skills of "observing, feeling, and depicting."[18] "[Women's] education," Laclos writes, "their existence in society, all their praiseworthy qualities, and if one must tell all, even some of their flaws, promise them successes in this career that they would, in our view, seek vainly in every other." Laclos explains that he doesn't have the time to develop his theory (readers can supply their own examples) but moves instead to situate Burney in his survey of the field: "Among the women whom one could cite as having placed themselves beside [à côté de] our best novelists [*meilleurs romanciers*], there would be few more distinguished and more surprising than the Author of the Work we are going to review" (501). What I want in my own hurried way to suggest here is that, writing literary criticism toward the end of the eighteenth century, Laclos reads women's writing through a set of clichés of femininity that leave the category of novelist masculine and originary: for Laclos the class of novelists is male. Thus, despite the high praise he has bestowed upon *Cecilia*, despite the relation of contiguity—*à côté de*—that ground his rhetoric, in the end, Laclos replaces Burney's novel within a clearly ranked and conventionally gendered hierarchy of difference: "Finally, we think that this novel must be counted among the best works in this genre, with nevertheless the exception of *Clarissa*, the novel in which one finds the most genius, *Tom Jones*, the best constructed novel, and *La Nouvelle Héloïse*, the most beautiful work ever produced under the title of the novel" (521).

In this move from metonymy (the aleatory contacts between writers) to metaphor (the fixed relations between the sexes) we have, I want to argue here, the principle of selection that guides the anthologies of literary history. Laclos had already elaborated the logic of this poetics of gender in his exchange of letters with Riccoboni. In the correspondence between Riccoboni and Laclos that followed the 1782 publication of the *Liaisons dangereuses*, to Riccoboni's critique of Laclos's representation of women—notably of the portrait of Madame de Merteuil in which, in her words, he would have "decorated vice with attractive features"—Laclos replied by inviting readers to turn to the "charming tableaux" of Riccoboni's own novels for more "gentle feelings." In his self-justification and explanation for the difference between his fictional universe and hers, Laclos, in what by then is a commonplace in eighteenth-century critical commentary, returns to the eternal nature of women and men for supporting evidence:[19] "women alone possess this precious sensibility, this easy and cheerful imagination that embellishes everything it touches, and creates objects as they should be: but . . . men, who are condemned to a harsher labor, have always acquitted themselves well when they have rendered nature exactly and faithfully!" (688). (In "Idealism in the Novel" [see chap. 4], Naomi Schor, citing the Riccoboni-Laclos exchange, makes the important argument that the mapping of idealism onto femininity, and the identification of masculinity with realism, play a crucial role in canon formation in the history of the nineteenth-century novel.)

In "Idée sur les romans" (1800)[20] Sade writes literary criticism according to the same principles, indeed proclaiming in a parenthesis women's generic superiority to men: "as if this sex, naturally more delicate, more suited to writing novels, could not in this genre lay claim to many more laurels than we" (27–28). Praising the works of Gomez, Lussan, Tencin, Graffigny, Beaumont, and Riccoboni for "honoring their sex," he names "Graffigny's *Lettres péruviennes,*" which, he goes on to assert, "will always be a model of tenderness and feeling, like [the letters] of Mylady Catesby, by Riccoboni; they will eternally serve those who only aspire to grace and lightness of style. But let us return to the century where we left it, pressed by the desire to praise the lovely women who in this genre taught men such good lessons" (28). I want to emphasize two points here: the way in which the category of the writer remains the male-universal against which the woman as writer is judged, and the self-appointed role of the male writer *as critic.* As a result, both the categories of the discussion and the positioning of the voice of critical discourse reproduce the content of the judgments.

Almost two centuries after Laclos's and Sade's closural moves of putting the woman in her place, Delon et al., we have seen, make the same gesture. In each instance the protocol that regulates the social relations between the sexes takes the place of—at the very least displaces—literary criteria. What grounds the reproduction of this discourse?

In "[Why] Are There No Great Women Critics? And What Difference Does It Make?" Susan Lanser and Evelyn Beck raise the question of the *"woman critic"* and ask what difference to the history of critical discourse her voice might make.[21] Lanser and Beck do not conclude about the judgments of women theorists, but they plausibly imagine that their poetics would constitute "a challenge to traditional generic classifications" (87). In the current absence of a history of women's critical writing (not to say a self-consciously feminist poetics), for now we can begin by turning to the prefatory moves of a woman writer who situates her work in relation to an already gendered literary history.

In the original preface to *Evelina,* Burney begins with a paragraph almost identical in its language to the beginning of Laclos's review article (499). Writing as a man, Burney, like Laclos, observes that "in the republic of letters, there is no member of such inferior rank, or who is so much disdained by his brethren of the quill, as the humble Novelist."

But in the detail of her editorial remarks she places her authorship in this fraternity somewhat differently. Despite the powerful models of Johnson's "knowledge," Rousseau's "eloquence," Richardson's "pathetic power," Fielding's "wit," and Smollett's "humour," Burney will not pursue, she explains, "the same ground which they have tracked." Unlike the other arts, where "a fine statue, or a beautiful picture, of some great master, may deservedly employ the imitative talents of young and inferior artists," "in books," she argues, "imitation cannot be shunned too sedulously; for the very perfection of a model which is frequently seen, serves but more forcibly to mark the inferiority of a copy." In her conclusion, however, she backs away from any implications of self-promotion in these poetics: "I have, therefore, only to intreat, that my own words may not pronounce my condemnation; and that what I have here ventured to say in regard to imitation, may be understood as it is meant, in a general sense, and not be imputed to an opinion of my own originality, which I have not the vanity, the folly, or the blindness to entertain" (n.p.).[22]

In the preface to her letter-novel, Graffigny, in the familiar ironic style of eighteenth-century philosophical discourse, like Burney, also raises the problem of imitation. In what I see as a similar defense of new ground, and what beyond the canonical tropes of authorial modesty I "overread" as a claim for the originality of a woman writer, she invites the public of novel readers to decipher another story. Writing as an editor-publisher of letters translated from the original, Graffigny regrets the power of prejudice that leads "us" (the French) to scorn other nations, notably the Indians, "except to the extent that their customs imitate ours, that their language resembles our idiom" (249). As feminist critics "we" might today reinterpret this utterance—"we recognize what mirrors and mimes us"—as a historical gloss on the status of women's writing in the dominant culture: the canon retains what it knows how to read, when it recognizes its own idiom.

By locating her subject of difference in writing and language in France (as opposed to the precursor's "Oriental" scene of the seraglio) and by placing her at the end of her fiction retired from the world in solitary study in the library, Graffigny stages another reading of Enlightenment categories. In the construction of her Peruvian other, Graffigny produces not so much minor fiction for "coeurs sensibles" as a minority literature of protest which of necessity demands to be read in majority context, against what we have learned to see as the monuments of the dominant culture. "The work of a woman," Myra Jehlen has argued, "—whose proposal to be a writer in itself reveals that female identity is not naturally what it has been assumed to be—may be used comparatively as an external ground for seeing the dominant literature whole."[23] The effect of reading from this point of view that "in itself" challenges the complacency of the "normative universal" is a displacement of the positionings of identity that keep the canon alive.

As a provisional answer to the question of canon formation as it might be posed in eighteenth-century French studies, then, I want to summarize the three local points I have been arguing for in this essay. First, that in the range of works that make up the packaging of "the eighteenth-century novel," the very categories that traditionally have defined this corpus serve as effectively to suppress a wide range of women's writing by narrowing its project; when, for instance, women's novels are placed in the category of the sentimental (for "coeurs sensibles") and not read, as men's writing conventionally is, as *realistic* fictions of *social* life, what results is a radical impoverishment of the complexity that characterizes literary exchanges in the eighteenth century.[24] My second point is that the exclusion of these voices of critique from a highly dialogic sociality is naturalized through a critical discourse of male bonding; flattered by the mirrors of his own representation, the masculinist critic sees himself, say, in Faublas. This narcissistic identification both emerges from and reinscribes a general ignorance of (and resistance to) female and feminist traditions of writing and rewriting that did not wait for Rousseau or Richardson to take shape. Finally, in order to register the heterogeneity of the cultural record of writing that becomes the history of the novel, we need to take another look within the period at the sites where the intersecting discourses on femininity (as the inflected term of the masculine-feminine couple) and fiction become—like the recklessly heterosexual couples of the social text they also articulate—permanently and dangerously entangled.

> I am convinced that the practice, as against the theory of feminist criticism has in many cases weakened the critical enterprise.
> —Richard Poirier, "Where Is Emerson Now That We Need Him? Or, Why Literature Can't Save Us"

In "Woman in France: Madame de Sablé," George Eliot, filled with admiration for French women writers—especially "those delightful women of France, who, from the beginning of the seventeenth to the close of the eighteenth century, formed some of the brightest threads in the web of political and literary history"—celebrates, among others, Germaine de Staël: "Madame de Staël's name still rises to the lips when we are asked to mention a woman of great intellectual power."[25] On our way to a conclusion about the place of women writers in the literature of the eighteenth century, and a revisionary strategy for teaching their works, I will just point to the case of Staël, who represents both the culmination of a great tradition of women writers in France and a challenge—never met—to the novel of the nineteenth century. What, for instance, of *Corinne*, the great feminist novel that punctures the illusions of masculine subjectivities and images the vision of a dramatically new voice and place for women writers?[26]

Etiemble, defending Sénac de Meilhan from obscurity, manages to work in a swipe at Staël (the only woman mentioned in the second volume). He uses the literary historian Albert Thibaudet to set her up. Thibaudet goes on about the merits of *L'Emigré* as "a figure of the cosmopolitan novel less decorative, but more lively, more moving and more true than *Corinne*." Etiemble comments: "That's a fair judgment of *Corinne*; still, despite Thibaudet, despite his *Histoire de la littérature française* where I cull these few lines, it's *Corinne* that is edited, glossed, taught, admired and pitied. Poor students! [Pauvres potaches]!" (2:xxvi–xxvii). Anyone who tried to find an edition of Staël's novel in a library or bookstore before its recent republication by des femmes in 1979 and the Gallimard Folio in 1985, or looked at a reading list, in this country at least, for exams or syllabi on the eighteenth- or nineteenth-century novel will be amazed by these claims. Staël's name, however, does of course have a place in the landscape of French studies: as a writer of literary theory who imaged and imagined comparative literature.

Courses on women writers, either in the form of a historical survey, or by genre and period, offer a simple, if conventional way to address the exclusions of the canon. The very gesture of reconstructing the histories of women's writing provides a standpoint from which to dismember the universal subjectivity enshrined in dominant literatures. It also establishes a ground from which to address the question of the work performed by women's writing and the value one wishes to ascribe to that work. But at the same time the establishment of such a parallel history (or curriculum) runs the risk of generating, and perhaps guarantees, an even greater indifference to the question of women's writing itself on the part of those authorizers and disseminators of cultural value, who, as we have seen, are happy enough to have a women's chapter that leaves their story intact. It may be that the pleasure of this new text requires another pedagogical politics.[27] It may also be that to produce a literary history that articulates the complexities of the cultural record, it is as important to conceive a pedagogy that leaves less already in place. This would mean among other things a commitment to the practice of a gendered poetics that rereads men's texts in the weave of women's.

The question, then, of "placing" women writers in French literature must be understood finally as a double operation. If the first move inevitably takes the form of a replacement that appears to leave the field intact, or rather, subject only to minor displacements (one in the stead of the other) that respect the original body, this must not be seen as its aim. Rather, seeing the first as immediately doubled by an interrogation of the body itself, it becomes possible to start another project altogether.

Notes

Earlier versions of this essay appeared under the title "Authorized Versions" in *French Review* 9, no. 3 (Feb. 1988) and in *Novel* (Winter and Spring 1988).

1. Frances [Fanny] Burney, *Camilla*, ed. Edward A. and Lillian D. Bloom (Oxford: Oxford University Press, 1983). All further references will appear in the text, as will references to any work cited more than once.

2. I am grateful to Rachel Brownstein for bringing this note to my attention.

3. An account of the translation history is provided by Gianni Nicoletti in his critical edition of the novel. Françoise de Graffigny, *Lettres d'une Péruvienne*, ed. Nicoletti (Bari: Adriatica Editrice, 1967).

4. Joan Kelly-Gadol, "The Social Relation of the Sexes: Methodological Implications of Women's History," *Signs* 4 (Summer 1974): 809–24. Reprinted in *Women, History, and Theory: The Essays of Joan Kelly* (Chicago: University of Chicago Press, 1984), 1–18. This is also part of the territory mapped by Peter Brooks in his *Novel of Worldliness* (Princeton: Princeton University Press, 1969).

5. Georges May, *Le Dilemme du roman au XVIIIe siècle: Etude sur les rapports du roman et de la critique (1715–1761)* (New Haven, Conn.: Yale University Press, 1963), 1.

6. René Etiemble, *Romanciers du XVIIIe siècle*, 2 vols. (Paris: Gallimard, Pléiade, 1966).

7. In *Encyclopédie de la Pléiade. Histoire des Littératures*, ed. Raymond Queneau (Paris: Gallimard, 1958), vol. 3, *Littératures françaises, connexes et marginales*, ed. René Etiemble, 849. These two titles often appear in the incorrect form Etiemble has chosen here: following Sainte-Beuve, this models Graffigny's title on Montesquieu's (deemphasizing the singular of female subjectivity: "d'une Péruvienne) and adds an *s* to Tencin's *Comminge*, succumbing to the

seduction of another "geographical" analogy that also erases a mark of difference: the old "comté de Comminges." A piece of mine on Tencin's novel was recently edited to add the *s*; and so the footnotes continue.

8. Thus in his massive *La Destinée féminine dans le roman européen du dix-huitième siècle* (Paris: Armand Colin, 1972), in the chapter called, "La Romancière," Pierre Fauchery states categorically: "In the eighteenth century, the myths of feminine destiny, of masculine creation, are for the most part accepted whole cloth by the women novelists. The latter, moreover, far from claiming their autonomy, take shelter behind the authority of the great writers of the other sex" (93).

9. Susan Winnett, "Coming Unstrung: Women, Men, and Principle(s) of Pleasure," forthcoming.

10. Nancy K. Miller, *Subject to Change: Reading Feminist Writing* (New York: Columbia University Press, 1988).

11. Rachel DuPlessis, *Writing beyond the Ending: Narrative Strategies of Twentieth-Century Women Writers* (Bloomington: Indiana University Press, 1985).

12. *Lettres de Mistress Fanni Butlerd* offers perhaps the clearest instance of a feminist critique of masculine advantage: when Alfred (Mylord Charles Alfred, Comte d'Erford) abandons the woman in love with him to move on to the next and make a fashionable marriage, the woman goes public with their story; her letters, like the narrative of *Histoire du Marquis de Cressy*, reveal the psychic and social cost to women of a socially unregulated male sexual "freedom." Both Riccoboni's *Cressy* and Tencin's *Mémoires du Comte de Comminge* rewrite the masculine suffering embodied by Des Grieux as a form of blindness and narcissism. Thus, in the end, both Comminge and Cressy are forced to witness the spectacular death of the superior woman they have failed: unlike Manon, however, Adélaïde and the marquise de Cressy are neither mythical nor enigmatic; it is instead their human complexity *as women* that the men in love with them prove unable to comprehend.

13. *Littérature française*, vol. 5, *De Fénelon à Voltaire*, ed. René Pomeau and Jean Ehrard; vol. 6, *De L'Encyclopédie aux Méditations*, ed. Michel Delon, Robert Mauzi, and Sylvain Menant (Paris: Arthaud, 1984).

14. The masterpiece model, which assumes that a work both exemplifies and transcends its historical moment, seems particularly inappropriate to the eighteenth-century novel, since its "most important" instance, Rousseau's *Nouvelle Héloïse* remains both largely unreadable and unread.

15. Jane Tompkins, *Sensational Designs: The Cultural Work of American Fiction: 1790–1860* (New York: Oxford University Press, 1985), xv.

16. Sainte-Beuve, we might say, finished Graffigny off for several generations of readers. In his caustic portrait of her in *Lettres de Madame de Grafigny ou Voltaire à Cirey* (written in 1850 and published in *Causeries du lundi* [Paris: Garnier, 1858], vol. 2) the critic, in another instance of literary criticism as male bonding, reviews Turgot's reservations about the novel's ending. Having commented enthusiastically and at length on the novel's ideas, ideas that inspired writings of his own, he concludes: "All these pages of Turgot are excellent, and I recommend reading them, as much as I can't recommend rereading [rouvrir] the *Lettres péruviennes*" (224).

17. On "overreading," see "Arachnologies: The Woman, the Text, and the

Critic," in my *Subject to Change;* on the "intersextual," Naomi Schor, "La Pérodie: Superposition dans *Lorenzaccio," Michigan Romance Studies* 1 (1982): 73–86.

18. Choderlos de Laclos, "Le Roman: Cecilia," in his *Oeuvres complètes,* ed. Maurice Allem (Paris: Gallimard, Pléiade, 1951).

19. See May's discussion (218ff.) of the coexistence of this discourse on women's special aptitude for novel writing with an undisguised misogyny.

20. Donatien-Alphonse-François Sade, "Idée sur les romans," (Paris: Palimugre, 1946).

21. Susan Lanser and Evelyn Beck, "[Why] Are There No Great Women Critics? And What Difference Does It Make?" in *The Prism of Sex: Essays in the Sociology of Knowledge,* ed. Julia A. Sherman and Evelyn Torton Beck (Madison: University of Wisconsin Press, 1979), 79–91. It is here that the much cited feminist formulation of women's "double-voiced discourse" is first articulated. "The writings of women who are struggling to define themselves but have not yet given up a patriarchal frame of reference may betray a tension so strong as to produce a virtually 'double-voiced' discourse" (86). The essay was originally presented as a paper in 1977.

22. Frances [Fanny] Burney, *Evelina, Or The History of A Young Lady's Entrance Into the World* (New York: Norton, 1965). Burney's novel is framed by an "Original Dedication: To the Authors of the Monthly and Critical Reviews," in which the authorial persona is that of a young writer without a name—the gender is implicitly one constructed on a continuity with the gentlemen of the press—and a preface.

In Riccoboni's second letter to Laclos she rejects the title of "un auteur" and denies any self-importance: "I am so barely an author that in reading a new book I would find myself quite unjust and foolish if I compared it to the trifles that issue from my pen and thought my ideas qualified to guide those of others." She writes instead as a woman, a French woman (Laclos, 689).

23. Myra Jehlen, "Archimedes and the Paradox of Feminist Criticism," *Signs* 6 (Summer 1981): 585.

24. Janet Todd's *Sensibility* (London: Methuen, 1986) provides a stimulating account of these issues as they emerge in eighteenth-century England.

25. George Eliot, "Woman in France: Madame de Sablé," *The Essays of George Eliot,* ed. Thomas Pinney (London: Routledge & Kegan Paul, 1963), 55.

26. On the relation of *Corinne* to women and the history of the French novel, see Joan DeJean's "Staël's *Corinne:* The Novel's Other Dilemma," *Stanford Literature Review* 10, no. 1 (Spring 1987): 77–88.

27. Margaret Switten and Elissa Gelfand have already conceived and taught such a course at Mount Holyoke called "Gender and the Rise of the Novel" (which I have appropriated for the subtitle of this essay) in which the notion I describe earlier as "reading in pairs" is imaginatively enacted. I am grateful to them for sharing their materials with me.

Following several introductory sessions on the beginning of the *roman* in the Middle Ages, the *querelle des femmes,* early poetics, and contemporary feminist criticism, the students of "Gender and the Rise of the Novel" read Tencin's *Comminge,* Prévost's *Manon Lescaut,* Graffigny's *Lettres d'une Péruvienne,* Rousseau's *Nouvelle Héloïse,* Diderot's *Jacques le fataliste,* Charrière's *Caliste,* Riccoboni's *Fanni Butlerd,* Laclos's *Liaisons dangereuses,* and the correspondence between Laclos and Riccoboni.

In the same spirit, one could also imagine reading Montesquieu's *Lettres persanes* or Prévost's *Histoire d'une grecque moderne* "with" *Lettres d'une Péruvienne:* the *Lettres portugaises* with the Graffigny; Duclos's *Les Confessions du comte de**** with Riccoboni's *Histoire du marquis de Cressy* or *Lettres de Milady Juliette Catesby.* Finally, to circle back to the question of *Corinne,* and as a move into questions of the nineteenth-century novel, one could reread the canonical tropes of the "psychological" novel *Adolphe* in the light of a male subjectivity brilliantly supplied by *Caliste* and *Corinne.* Switten and Gelfand's own account of the course appears in the *French Review* 61, no. 3 (February 1988): 443–53 under the title "Gender and the Rise of the Novel.

Idealism in the Novel:
Recanonizing Sand

> L'amour où le prendrons-nous? Telle femme l'irait
> chercher dans Balzac. Mieux vaudrait madame Sand. Il y
> a là du moins toujours un élan vers l'idéal.
> —Michelet, *La Femme*

> Cette querelle des réalistes et des idéalistes est fatigante
> et sans fin. Il y a de grands esprits et petits esprits, il y a
> des esprits masculins et des esprits féminins.
> —Champfleury, *Souvenirs et portraits de jeunesse*

Let me begin with an anecdote: in June 1986 I participated in a conference at Georgetown University on "The Representation of the Other." My paper dealt with the representation of men in women's writing and my examples were drawn from the fictions of several major French women writers, among them George Sand, whose novel *Indiana* I discussed in some detail. When I sat down after having delivered my talk, a fellow panelist, a respected male professor at a major ivy league institution, leaned over and whispered confidentially in my ear: "That was very nice Naomi, but you still haven't convinced me to read *Indiana*." I begin with this comical but unfunny episode because it has everything to do with the reasons that I have undertaken to write a critical study of George Sand. Boldly stated: in 1986, sixteen years after Kate Millett's *Sexual Politics*, thirty-seven years after Simone de Beauvoir's *The Second Sex*, fifty-seven years after Virginia Woolf's *A Room of One's Own*, to cite some of the landmarks of feminist criticism and theory, many if not most of my colleagues still believed that it was incumbent upon *us*—and when I say "us," I refer in general to us feminist critics, in particular to Sand scholars—to convince *them* that Sand (but also many other major women writers) is worth reading. Ours is of necessity a rhetoric of persuasion.

We may respond to this challenge in a number of ways: disbelief, derision, dismissal, deconstruction, but the question of the canon remains and it will not go away, for, as Leslie Fiedler has observed: "we all know in our hearts that literature is effectively what we teach in departments of English; or conversely, what we teach in departments of English is literature."[1] If we assume for the moment that we can simply substitute French for English—no small assumption—then the situation becomes quite clear: as long as works by Sand are not included routinely in surveys of nineteenth-century French literature, on reading lists for prelims and orals, on the program for the Agrégation, etcetera, however many colloquia we may hold on Sand, however many studies we may devote to her oeuvre, however many texts of hers we may reedit, she will remain beyond the pale of literature, in its strong institutional sense. Two possibly controversial assumptions ground that statement. First, that the task—rather, one of the tasks—of feminist criticism is to infiltrate and remodel the existing canon. My quarrel here is with the position provocatively argued by Lillian S. Robinson in her anthologized article, "Treason Our Text: Feminist Challenges to the Literary Canon." Robinson's claim is that upgrading women writers already marginally in the canon from second to first rank is a misguided feminist enterprise, as it leaves the criteria for canonization in place: "the case here consists in showing that an already recognized woman has been denied her rightful place, presumably because of the general devaluation of female efforts and subjects. . . . Obviously, no challenge is presented to the particular notions of literary quality, timelessness, universality, and other qualities that constitute the rationale for canonicity."[2] My effort here is to show that on the contrary, a reflection on the particular circumstances of a *de*canonization can produce results that exceed the case of an "already recognized woman" and do call into question the value system grounding the canon.

Second, that Sand deserves a place in the new, revised French canon of nineteenth-century literature. More precisely, Sand deserves to recover the eminent place she occupied in the old, unrevised French canon established by the Sorbonne between 1871 and 1914, during a period of intense national reaffirmation following the humiliating defeat of 1871. As Elaine Showalter has remarked: "it is a curious fact of literary history that canon formation has been particularly aggressive following wars, when nationalist feeling runs high and there is a strong wish to define a tradition."[3] The ideological constraints that presided over the formation of the French canon at the turn of the century are clearly at work in the promotion of Sand's so-called rustic fiction that went hand in hand with her canonization. It is after all as a novelist of the *terroir,* or countryside, the author of such classics of French children's literature as *Fanchon the Cricket, The Country Waif,* and the adult's favorite, *The Bag-Pipers,* that Sand was initially inscribed into the canon.[4] Somewhere around 1890 a consensus was reached regarding the canonicity of Sand's pastoral mode. Already in 1887, Emile Faguet had written: "hers was the genius of the idyll." According to him it is the works written in what he terms Sand's "third manner," the peasant idylls sited in her home region, the Berry, that are destined for immortality: "she found there her superior works, the ones that will endure, *Fadette, Le Champi, Jeanne,* and above all, *La Mare au Diable* and *les Maîtres sonneurs.*"[5] And, in an important and thoughtful assessment of Sand's literary achievement, Georges Pellissier asserts in 1890: "What will remain of George Sand are her pastorals, a few simple and touching love stories set in a natural framework. . . . She is par excellence a painter of the fields."[6] To recanonize Sand, then, cannot be merely to reinstate her earlier position and positioning; it must entail a reexamination of the premises of her earlier canonization, as well as a recognition of new ideological pressures. For if Sand is reinscribed into the canon at the turn of the twentieth century, it will almost certainly be as the exemplary feminist author of such novels as *Indiana, Valentine,* and *Lélia.*

But, above all, to recanonize Sand must involve a better understanding than we now have of the conditions of Sand's decanonization. For Sand's fall from aesthetic grace has been spectacular. Writing in 1949, Van Tieghem declares: "Sand's fictional oeuvre has singularly declined. It is difficult to imagine the glory and the esteem that surrounded her."[7] Indeed, a writer of international stature in her lifetime, Sand was widely read, admired, and imitated by such far-flung readers as Margaret Fuller, the Brontë sisters, and Fyodor Dostoevsky, as well as by the greatest of her French contemporaries. Allowing for the season in purgatory all French writers endure in the immediate aftermath of their deaths, after 1876 (the date of Sand's death), Sand's place in the pantheon of great nineteenth-century French authors, as noted above, appeared secure. In the introduction to selected passages from her writings published in 1924 in a series called *Pages Choisies des Grands Ecrivains*, the editor writes: "the century which witnessed the birth and death of George Sand is scarcely over, and already she takes her place among our classics."[8] And yet, already in 1890, Pellissier concludes his exceptionally intelligent and sympathetic assessment of her achievement, by saying: "George Sand is hardly read any longer"(243). And, by 1938, Virginia Woolf speaks of Sand, as a "half-forgotten author."[9] Unread in 1890, half-forgotten in 1938—what happened to George Sand?

The steady decline of Sand's artistic stock in the course of the twentieth century is inextricably bound up with a major remapping of the topography of the nineteenth-century French novel. For, in the critical tradition instituted and widely disseminated by the Sorbonne, Sand's works are classified under a rubric that has since disappeared, seemingly without leaving a trace: the idealist novel.

In the nineteenth century, following Kant's formulations in *The Critique of Judgment*, realism was yoked to idealism. Initially, realism appeared as idealism's binary opposite, as in G. H. Lewes's characteristic formulation: "of late years there has been a reaction against conventionalism which called itself Idealism, in favour of *detailism* which calls itself Realism."[10] Realism in the nineteenth century signified *only* in relation to idealism, so much so that to consider one term in isolation from the other is to deplete, even distort, its significance. Because the opposition between idealism and realism is viewed as an immanent mental structure, it is a commonplace of nineteenth-century literary criticism. Pellissier's account of the evolution of the novel is in this respect typical. After passing through a lyrical, then a historicist stage, the novel, he writes:

Leaving behind history for contemporary society . . . in the end divided itself, without exceeding this very framework, into two very distinct genres corresponding to two irreducible tendencies of the human spirit: some, viewing real life through their imaginations enamored of beauty, truth, happiness, produced a portrait always idealised in its very truth; the others, fortified with a wise and penetrating analysis, directed their energies at seeing reality as it is and at representing it as they had seen it. (233)[11]

And yet so massive, so crushing has been the triumph of realism that at least in the field of literature—in painting, where the opposition first arose, the story is quite different—idealism has all but vanished from our critical consciousness, taking with it the literary reputation of its most eminent French representative, George Sand.[12]

There is, then, a general recognition among Sand's posthumous promoters that her declining literary fortunes are linked to the triumph of Balzacian realism over the idealism associated with Sand's name:

For the last twelve or fifteen years her success diminished, though her talent had not flagged; it is just that fashion had shifted elsewhere. The positivist and scientific spirit has taken over literature; today a more exact imitation of things, characters more like those one encounters daily, absolutely precise descriptions recorded on the spot, in short a detailed, literal and micrographic copy of reality are what is wanted. The novel is in the hands of Balzac's successors.[13]

Consequently, all hopes for and predictions of Sand's return to favor are tied to a return to or of idealism, a turning away from a spent realism. In his 1910 *Cours de littérature,* Félix Hémon announces that that double return is imminent: "since Balzac, we have for so long savoured the humiliating pleasure of contemplating our portraits as we are, that we are seized by a violent desire to be flattered, idealized, fooled if need be about our poor human nature. And that is why favor is returning to this mixed oeuvre, within which one nevertheless asks to pick and choose."[14] My thesis, then, is this: Sand's spectacular aesthetic devaluation cannot be ascribed in any simple terms to her gender; it is not because Sand was a woman, rather because (like so many other woman authors) she is associated with a discredited and discarded representational mode, that she is no longer ranked among the canonic authors.

The question then becomes: what is the relationship if any between femininity and idealism? A brief comparison of the literary fates of "the two Georges" (Sand and Eliot) should serve to dispel at the outset any notion of the essential femininity of idealism as a literary practice. Speculating on the reasons for George Eliot's easy superiority over the other George, whom she read so admiringly and to whom she owed so much, Patricia Thomson writes: "in the long run, George Eliot has easily outdistanced the other George to whom she was indebted for so many insights and such a great enlargement of her horizons. It is not simply that the idealist, optimist and romantic has less of value to communicate than the writer with a deep and realistic sense of the irony and tragedy of life—although for modern readers this is surely a vital distinction."[15]

The difference in the literary fates of "the two Georges," while not reducible to the opposition idealism-realism, does overlap with it in interesting ways. For Eliot's poetics was, it will be recalled, explicitly antiidealist, classically realist. In chapter 17 of *Adam Bede*, entitled, "In which the story pauses a little," Eliot stops to explain why, deliberately frustrating her implied readers' desire, she chooses not, "to represent things as they never have been and never will be," not to "touch" up the world with a "tasteful pencil," not "make things better than they were."[16] She prefers instead to offend her "idealist friend" (233) by the representation of the vulgar details that inhere in the representation of the commonplace and the homely. As Eliot writes in "The Natural History of German Life," "the unreality" of the representation of the common people is a "grave evil," for it directly prevents "the extension of our sympathies" that is art's "greatest benefit": "appeals founded on generalizations and statistics require a sympathy readymade, a moral sentiment already in activity; but a piece of human life such as a great artist can give, surprises even the trivial and the selfish into that attention to what is apart from themselves, which may be called the raw material of moral sentiment."[17] For Eliot the superiority of realism over idealism is then moral; only a deidealized portrayal of the people can enable the sympathy for the Other that great art can uniquely inspire.

There are few prophets in the world; few sublimely beautiful women; few heroes. I can't afford to give all my love and reverence to such rarities: I want a great deal of those feelings for my everyday fellowmen, especially for the few in the foreground of the great multitude, whose faces I know, whose hands I touch, for whom I have to make way with kindly courtesy. . . . It is more needful that I should have a fibre of sympathy with that vulgar citizen who weighs out my sugar in a vilely assorted cravat and waistcoat, than with the handsome rascal in red scarf and green feathers. (224–25)

The opposition between Eliot's realism and Sand's idealism is, however, neither simple nor neat: as many commentators have noted, Eliot is in her own way an idealist, thus the very figure of the common working man, Adam Bede—who has been compared to Sand's Meunier d'Angibault—is itself heavily idealized, and Sand's idealism is in turn informed by some of the same moral and social imperatives that animate Eliot's realism.[18] But finally, the question of the differences between Eliot and Sand is mooted by the realization that the triumph of realism over idealism owes less to moral than to aesthetic considerations. Or rather, that the triumph of realism over idealism makes visible the interpenetration of the ethical and the aesthetic. If realism has triumphed over idealism, and Eliot and Balzac over Sand, it is in large measure because the aesthetic legacy linking referential illusion and political efficacy with the detailed representation of a blemished reality has remained with us in the age of the simulacrum. Even in those works, structuralist and post-structuralist, which have in recent years subjected the "order of mimesis" (Prendergast) to a radical critique, some of the underlying assumptions of classical realist aesthetics remain undisturbed. As Barthes observes in *S/Z*: "beauty . . . cannot be induced through catachresis other than from some great cultural model (written or pictorial): it is stated, not described. Contrariwise, ugliness can be abundantly described: it alone is 'realistic,' confronting the referent without an immediate code (whence the notion that realism, in art, is concerned solely with ugliness)."[19] To recanonize Sand must of necessity entail a critical rethinking of both the aesthetic and ethical valorization of the ugly and the consensual equation of the real with the unsightly, for as we shall see, it is on these linked assumptions that her decanonization rests.

So far we have relied on a vague and commonsense understanding of idealism to ground our discussion. If we are to advance and to avoid the pitfalls that result from an indiscriminate use of the term *idealism*, at this point some understanding of how it was used in nineteenth-century aesthetic discourse becomes necessary. It is in the French philosopher Hippolyte Taine's immensely popular and influential lectures on aesthetics, *Philosophie de l'Art*, in a section entitled "De l'Idéal dans l'Art," that we find the elements of a specifically late nineteenth-century theory of the ideal in art, and an indigenous French one, to boot. Now, admittedly there is something circular about bringing the aesthetics of one of her most ardent admirers to bear on Sand's literary practice. Indeed, it is difficult to separate Taine's theory from Sand's practice: for no one was more keenly aware of the necessity to devise a poetics of idealism specially adapted to the idealist text to allow readers with a realist horizon of expectations to read Sand with pleasure: "to take pleasure in them [Sand's fictions]," writes Taine, "we have to adopt their point of view, take an interest in the depiction of a more beautiful and better humanity" (132). Taine develops his notion of the ideal in two key chapters of his aesthetics: "The degree of importance of the character" ("Le degré d'importance du caractère") and "The degree of goodness of the character" ("Le degré de bienfaisance du caractère"). What, then, does Taine mean by *character*? Character, as he explains in the inaugural section of his aesthetics, is an essential, salient feature of an object: "This character is what the philosophers call *the essence* of things; and, because of that, they say that the purpose of art is to make manifest the essence of things. We will leave aside this word *essence* which is technical, and we shall simply say that the purpose of art is to make manifest the central character, some salient and notable quality, an important point of view, a principal manner of being of the object."[20] Despite his positivist trappings—Taine grounds his hierarchy of distinctive features in the realm of art on the notion of variability in the life sciences—in "Le degré d'importance du caractère" Taine does little but reinscribe the main tenets of neoclassical aesthetics: The notable character that is the marker of the ideal is essential, unchanging, universal. The supreme work of art is installed in what modern historians call *la longue durée;* it is built on the bedrock upon which the superficial and transitory products of the moment merely glide. As an example of such a perennial masterpiece, Taine cites l'abbé Prévost's *Manon Lescaut;* so "durable" is the "type" created by Prévost that *Manon* has been repeatedly rewritten and adapted in response to the changing times. It is here that Sand makes her first appearance in "De l'idéal dans l'art," for in her novel *Leone Leoni* she rewrites *Manon* reversing the roles.

On the basis of this section of Taine's work, it would appear difficult to make the case for Sand as an idealist author, for it cannot be claimed that Sand ever created in her own right the sort of universal type Taine has in mind. It is only when we turn to the second major section in Taine's text, "le degré de bienfaisance du caractère," that we can begin to grasp the sense in which Sand could be described as an idealist novelist. In these pages Taine establishes a new hierarchy, one ordained not by scientific principles of durability, but rather by moral principles of goodness. Following this second classificatory system, the highest-ranked works of art are not those featuring universal types, but rather those representing heroes and heroines: "all things being equal, the work which expresses a benevolent character is superior to the work which expresses a malevolent character" (*Philosophie,* 2: 289). It is according to this ethical scale of values that Sand is promoted as an artist of the ideal, for, writes Taine, along with Corneille and Richardson she undertakes deliberately ["de parti pris"] to represent "noble feelings and superior souls." Taine singles out for particular praise several of Sand's fictions, including *Mauprat* and *A Country Waif,* for their depictions of "native generosity" (*Philosophie,* 2: 295).

What Taine's lectures make apparent in a way distinct from that of a long line of theoreticians of the ideal in art, stretching all the way back to Plato, is the necessary slippage between the heightening of the essential and the promotion of the higher good that constitutes idealism in the realm of aesthetics. Only in the light of Taine's *double definition of aesthetic idealism* does Balzac's celebrated statement to Sand regarding their differences become fully intelligible. Writing of her poetics of idealization in her autobiography, *Story of My Life,* Sand attributes the following remarks to Balzac:

You seek man as he should be; I take him as he is. Believe me, we are both right. Our paths meet in the end. I love exceptional people too; I *am* one. Besides, I need them—to set off my vulgar people—and I never sacrifice them needlessly. But these vulgar people interest me more than they do you. I magnify and idealize them in reverse, in their ugliness or folly. I give their deformities frightening or grotesque proportions. That you could never do, and you do well not to gaze too closely on the beings who give you nightmares. Idealize only toward the lovely and the beautiful: that is woman's work.[21]

Initially Balzac casts his formulation of the difference between himself and Sand in terms all too familiar to generations of French *lycéens:* Balzac is to Sand as Racine is to Corneille. Theirs is but a replay of the paradigmatic French confrontation between realist and idealist writer. Almost immediately, however, Balzac undercuts this neat antithesis, arguing instead for an underlying commonality of purpose and method. In keeping with Taine's first definition of the term, both Sand and Balzac are idealist novelists; idealization is here taken to be synonymous with hyperbolization, a form of excess in writing that strains at the limits of verisimilitude. Enunciating her theory of writing earlier in the same section of her autobiography, Sand explicitly links idealization and implausibility:

According to it [this theory], the novel is a work of poetry as much as analysis. Authentic, even real, characters and situations are required, ranged about a figure who must exemplify the chief feeling or idea of the book. This figure usually represents passionate love. . . . This love must be idealized . . . the author should not fear to give it exceptional importance, unusual power, and charms and sufferings beyond the common run of human things, and even beyond the bounds of probability. (218)

The difference between Sand's and Balzac's idealizations is in the end one of quality, not quantity; it is of a thematic rather than a rhetorical order. The conflation in Sand's writing practice of hyperbolizing and meliorative idealization is what, in Taine's eyes, make her the paradigmatic idealist novelist, whereas Balzac, for all his larger than life character types, remains mired in the lower ethical spheres of realism. Seen in this unfamiliar perspective, realism appears as a lesser, even a failed idealism; it is idealism, not realism, that is the more inclusive term. The perceptible drift in this passage toward a stunning hierarchical reversal is, however, checked when in the last sentence Balzac suddenly aligns idealization with gender. Earlier we asked what was the relationship, if any, between idealism and femininity. Balzac's statement offers the elements of an answer. Idealism in the novel is a priori sex-blind; the feminization of the idealist mode of representation is brought about by aligning sexual difference with a *difference within idealism.* This alignment produces a splitting: associated with masculinity, negative idealization becomes the positively valorized term, henceforth known as realism, while positive idealization, linked up with femininity, becomes the negatively valorized term, a diminished and trivialized idealism.

The gendering of poetics inevitably results in their degeneration into stereotype. Thus, responding to a letter from the novelist Mme Riccoboni critical of his seductive portrayal of the evil Mme de Merteuil in *Les Liaisons dangereuses,* Laclos writes: "to women alone belongs this precious sensitivity, this easy and cheerful imagination which embellishes everything it touches, and creates objects as they should be, but . . . men, who are condemned to a harsher labor, have always acquitted themselves well when they have rendered nature exactly and faithfully."[22] The division of literary labor along gender lines rests on a series of highly questionable assumptions: mimesis is man's work; the faithful representation of "nature," a sort of Adamic curse visited on male writers, condemns them to a literary life of referential servitude. Women writers, congenitally unable to view the world without the benefit of rose-colored glasses, are essentially idealists. Hierarchy insinuates itself into this paradigm less through its blatant naturalization of women's weakness than through its more insidious and far-reaching assumption that aesthetic value resides in the (virile) depiction of the horrors of unembellished nature. What is at stake here is, finally, woman's relationship to truth. Thus Zola, a preeminent representative of the school of Balzac, attributes Sand's failure in her peasant novels to "her idealist temperament which prevented her from seeing *true truth* and above all from reproducing it."[23] The woman writer in rose-colored glasses stands as the necessary antithesis to that figure of the philosopher's imaginary, woman-as-truth. For the logic of misogyny is a no-win logic where whatever is connoted as feminine—for example, an excessive proximity to or distance from truth—is devalorized. Thus, the stereotypical association of women artists and the ideal is the obverse of an equally long and powerful tradition that condemns woman to the servile imitation of the nature with which she is so closely identified, that views her as congenitally incapable of transcending immanence to attain the ideal.[24] For James, whose generally sympathetic account of Sand in *French Poets and Novelists* is a tissue of sexual stereotypes, Sand's disregard for truth is doubly determined by her sex and her nationality; like the heroine in the song, the French woman writer is one who sees "la vie en rose": "Women, we are told, do not value truth for its own sake, but only for some personal use they make of it. My present criticism involves an assent to this somewhat cynical dogma. Add to this that woman, if she happens to be French, has an extraordinary taste for investing objects with a graceful drapery of her own contrivance, and it will be found that George Sand's cast of mind includes both the generic and the specific idiosyncrasy" (155). The essay concludes with an enlisting of a by now familiar color code, although in this instance the rosiness has been transferred from the lens of vision to reality itself: "George Sand's optimism, her idealism, are very beautiful, and the source of that impression of largeness, luminosity and liberality which she makes upon us. But we suspect that something even better in a novelist is the tender appreciation of actuality which makes even the application of a single coat of rose-colour seem an act of violence" (185).

Though we may today smugly mock the innocent sexism of a Laclos, a Balzac, or a James, the valorization of realism—the masculine mode—remains largely unexamined in contemporary theories of representation and the canonic hierarchies they serve to secure, for the theory of realism from Lukács to Barthes is essentially a theory of a single fictional practice, Balzac's. In other words, the ongoing critique of representation stops well short of questioning the realist paradigm (and Balzac's status as the paradigmatic realist) and its underlying sexism. Even those critics who have most acutely exposed the complicity of realism with bourgeois ideology, countering realism's claims to a specular objectivity by demonstrating the active part mimesis plays in legitimizing the apparatus of the Law, the network of disciplinary mechanisms that repress all exceptions to the norm, the sexual fix—even these critics have continued to be fascinated by the canonic figures, especially Balzac.[25] To begin to grasp the not so subtle ways in which idealism has been feminized and hence devalorized is to begin to ask what it might mean to read "otherwise," to ask specifically what poetics would have to be elaborated to take into account the Sandian text, to bring it into the pale of the readable, and, more important, the rereadable, for as James devastatingly remarks: "all the world can read George Sand once and not find it in the least hard. But it is not easy to return to her. . . . George Sand invites reperusal less than any other mind of equal eminence" (181). Once again Taine points the way when in his late essay on Sand he characterizes idealist prose in ways that interestingly renew earlier normative idealist aesthetics: "It is," he writes,

an ideal world and to maintain the illusion, the writer erases, attenuates and often sketches a general outline, instead of depicting an individual figure. He does not emphasize the detail, he scarcely indicates it in passing, he avoids going into it; he follows the great poetic line of the passion he pleads or the situation he describes, without stopping over the irregularities which would break the harmony. This summary way of painting is the property of all idealist art. (*Derniers Essais,* 132)

In this postrealist definition of idealism, idealism appears as a signifying practice of lack. Whereas prerealist idealism, by which I mean the idealism promoted and practiced before the emergence of the specifically nineteenth-century literary movement known as Realism, prescribed idealization as selection—the construction of the ideal through the combination of ideal parts abstracted from imperfect wholes—Sandian idealism is an art of deliberate erasure. For Sand was keenly aware of the link between details and realism, defining realism as a "science of details."[26] To be erased, passed over lightly, the detail must then be there to be erased; it is a case of emphasis subtracted. The idealist effect is produced by the evacuation of those very superfluous details that create the illusion of the real (Barthes). To read idealist fiction necessarily entails a painful renunciation of the pleasure of the detail and the illusion of referential plenitude it provides. Other renunciations, similarly painful (at least in my own experience), follow: for just as the idealist text eschews the redundant descriptive detail, it refuses the booby-trapped hermeneutic code that propels the classical realist text forward, even as it undoes conventions of characterization.[27]

The difficulties posed by the modern idealist novel are not, of course, unique to Sand—except insofar as her sex exacerbates them. They are notably intrinsic to the field of nineteenth-century German fiction. The great tradition of realist fiction so grandly embodied elsewhere in Europe is, as is well known, strikingly absent in the history of German prose fiction. In his chapter devoted to German literature, "Miller the Musician," Auerbach speculates at some length on the reasons why a "contemporary realism" (as opposed to the realism bound up with Historicism) failed to develop in Germany despite what he calls a "favorable aesthetic situation":

Contemporary conditions in Germany did not easily lend themselves to broad realistic treatment. The social picture was heterogeneous; the general life was conducted in the confused setting of a host of "historical territories," units which had come into existence through dynastic and political contingencies. In each of them the oppressive and at times choking atmosphere was counterbalanced by a certain pious submission and the sense of historical solidity, all of which was more conducive to speculation, introspection, contemplation, and the development of local idiosyncrasies than to coming to grips with the practical and the real in a spirit of determination and with an awareness of greater contexts and more extensive territories.[28]

Whether or not one accepts Auerbach's definition of realism and his explanation for "the problem of nineteenth-century German realism," the connection he makes between representational modes and sociopolitical circumstances is one with interesting implications for our study of Sand. We will want to ask how Sand's politics inflected her idealism: is there, for example, any connection between Sand's regionalism and her idealism? Is there a politics of idealism? Is idealism the representational mode of choice of an aristocrat with populist blood and leanings?

If in Balzac's formulation realism is but a subcategory of idealism, albeit the most prestigious, Sand's idealism must nonetheless be understood as a response to what was to become known as Balzacian realism. For, if idealism is not (any more than its opposite, detailism) an essentially female representational mode, the practice of an aesthetics of idealism was unquestionably for Sand a strategy for bodying forth her difference, and that difference is in part sexual. Feminist critics have traditionally emphasized transhistorical specificities of women's writing, but I would argue that female specificity in writing is (also) contextual, local, a microspecificity that shifts opportunistically in response to changing historical and literary historical circumstances. Writing in her autobiography of her literary beginnings, Sand makes it quite clear that to begin writing is to take one's place on a scene of competing representational modes (and all represented by men): "in those days writers wrote the oddest things. The eccentricities of the young Victor Hugo had excited the younger generation, who were bored with the threadbare ideas of the Restoration. Chateaubriand was no longer sufficiently romantic, and even the new master, Hugo, was barely romantic enough for the fierce appetites he had whetted. The brats of his own school . . . wanted to 'sink' him by outdoing him" (216).

Sand's choice of idealism was surely overdetermined—her motivations were political as well as psychological (the idealization of her dead father)—but what is significant is that it was a choice, albeit a difficult one. Traces of the difficult emergence of Sandian idealism from the matrix of Balzacian realism can be clearly made out in *Indiana,* the very novel Sand was working on at the moment of her conversations with Balzac. The celebrated double response of Sand's mentor Latouche to his star pupil's first solo novelistic venture accurately reflects the text's straddling of representational modes. After quickly scanning the opening pages of *Indiana,* Latouche is said to have exclaimed: "come now, this is a pastiche, School of Balzac! Pastiche! what do you mean by it?" However, having spent the night reading the entire novel, the very next morning Latouche saluted Sand's achievement in the following terms: "your book is a masterpiece. I stayed up all night to read it. No woman alive can sustain the insolence of a comparison with you . . . Balzac and Mérimée lie dead under *Indiana.*"[29]

The emergence of Sand's distinctive writing mode from that of her genial friend takes two forms to which I can only allude here in passing: First, the movement from the conventionally realistic inaugural section to the controversial epilogue that so spectacularly exceeds the bounds of bourgeois realism. Second, the elimination in the 1833 edition of the interventions designed to persuade the reader of the original 1832 edition of the narrator's allegiance to the main tenets of the realist credo and his rejection of competing novelistic trends, notably idealism: "The current fashion is to depict a fictional hero so ideal, so superior to the common run that he only yawns where others enjoy themselves. . . . These heroes bore you, I'm sure, because they are not like you, because in the long run lifting your head up to watch them float above you makes you dizzy. I place mine firmly on the ground and living the same life as you do."[30] And yet, the double-edged irony of this passage suggests that even within these digressions designed to guarantee the author's realist credentials and hence his legitimacy, another aesthetic is being promoted.

In what sense, then, can we speak of *Indiana* as an idealist novel? Indeed is it one at all? No less a Sand scholar than Pierre Salomon, author of a general introduction to Sand's life and works and editor of several of her novels, states categorically that *Indiana* is not an idealist novel, basing himself on the deidealized representations of the male figures, notably Raymon, the vile seductor allegedly modeled on Sand's lover, Aurélien de Sèze: "if sometimes George Sand appears to be an idealist writer, it is certainly not here. The analysis is cruel, and one may well wonder at so much harshness directed against a man once beloved."[31] If, however, we recall Sand's own definition of idealism in the novel, it becomes immediately apparent that the ideal in this novel resides in the figure of its heroine and not its hero, for it is Indiana whose passionate love story exhibits the implausible extremes Sand identifies as constitutive of the fictional ideal. And yet, as useful as is Sand's explicitation of her idealizing techniques, it does not fully account for the idealism in *Indiana*. To do so we must bring into play Taine's theory of the biaxiality of the ideal in art, for what sets Indiana apart from other sado-masochistic female protagonists in nineteenth-century French fiction, notably Emma Bovary, her most illustrious descendant, is that in her story the quest for the love ideal is inseparable from an aspiration toward an ideal world. For all her reading of silly women's novels, when Indiana fantasizes, it is not as Emma later will of the beautiful people and Paris, rather of freedom for herself and for all her fellow slaves: "A day will come when everything in my life will be changed, when I shall do good to others, when someone will love me, when I shall give my whole heart to the man who gives me his; meanwhile, I will suffer in silence and keep my love as a reward for him who shall set me free."[32]

In keeping with Taine's theory, idealism in Sand's inaugural fiction consists, then, in a distinctive concatenation of the erotic and the moral, not to say the political. Moreover, and this returns us to the question of the gender specificities of idealism, Sand's idealism bespeaks a yearning to be delivered both from the base desire for carnal possession characteristic of male sexuality and from the injustices of a man-made system of laws that enables the enslavement of both women and blacks. Balzac's feminizing of positive idealization, though wrong-headed, is finally not entirely wrong: idealism, as appropriated by Sand, signifies her refusal to reproduce mimetically and hence legitimate a social order inimical to the disenfranchized, among them women. Idealism for Sand is finally the

only alternative representational mode available to those who do
not enjoy the privileges of subjecthood in the real. To recanonize
Sand will, then, require nothing less than a reconsideration of realism as it constructs and supports the phallo- and ethnocentric
social order we so often confuse with reality. Finally, to recanonize
Sand will call for the elaboration of a poetics of the ethical.

Notes

This essay is to be the first chapter of a critical study of Sand. It was written
with the generous support of the American Council of Learned Societies, which
is hereby gratefully acknowledged. My thanks also to Sima Godfrey for bringing
the second epigraph to my attention.

1. Leslie Fiedler as quoted by Elizabeth A. Meese, "Sexual Politics and Critical Judgment," in *After Strange Texts; The Role of Theory in the Study of Literature*, ed. Gregory S. Jay and David L. Miller (Tuscaloosa: University of Alabama
Press, 1985), 86.

2. Lillian S. Robinson, "Treason Our Text: Feminist Challenges to the Literary Canon," in *The New Feminist Criticism: Essays on Women, Literature, Theory*, ed. Elaine Showalter (New York: Pantheon Books, 1985), 109.

3. Showalter, "Introduction," in *New Feminist Criticism*, 11.

4. And it is as an author of rustic fiction that she survives in those ultimate
repositories of the French canon, the *manuels* (e.g., Lagarde and Michard) destined for high-school students preparing for the *baccalauréat* examination. In a
recent survey of women as they are represented in textbooks, the author of the
section on literature notes: "her oeuvre is generally reduced to her rustic novels,
whereas her production is very diversified," in Brigitte Crabbé, Marie-Luce Del-
Fosse, Lucia Gaiardo, Ghislaine Verlaeckt, and Evelyne Wilwerth, *Les Femmes
dans les livres scolaires* (Brussels: Pierre Mardaga, 1985), 57. All translations are
mine except where otherwise noted. According to the same author (Evelyne Wilwerth) women writers are subject to two strategies of exclusion: "occultation
and reduction characterize the treatment of women's writing" (57). The contribution of Sand, as one of the two "monuments" of nineteenth-century French
literature—the other being, of course, Mme de Staël—cannot be elided, hence
the "reduction" of her immense oeuvre to her country fiction.

5. Emile Faguet, *Dix-Neuvième Siècle: Etudes littéraires* (Paris: Boivin &
Cie, 1887), 395, 398.

6. Georges Pellissier, *Le Mouvement littéraire au xixe siècle* (Paris:
Hachette, 1890), 243–44. All subsequent references are incorporated in the text,
as are references to any work cited more than once.

7. Philippe Van Tieghem, *Histoire de la littérature française* (Paris: Fauard,
1949), 468.

8. *Pages Choisies des Grands Ecrivains: George Sand*, ed. S. Rocheblave
(Paris: Armand Colin, 1924), np.

9. Virginia Woolf, *Three Guineas* (New York: HBJ Books, Harvest, 1966), 188,
n. 49.

10. G. H. Lewes, *The Principles of Literary Success in Literature* (Boston: Allyn & Bacon, 1891), 83. Lewes is in many ways a crucial figure in this realm of aesthetics: a significant interpreter and disseminator of Hegel's idealist philosophy, an insightful supporter of women novelists (Brontë, Sand, and, of course, Eliot), Lewes emerges as one of the prime theoreticians of realism/idealism in Victorian criticism. In fact, for Lewes, who espoused what one commentator has called a "modified Realism," idealism and realism were not compatible, not true opposites; for him, writes Alice Kaminsky, "idealism is simply a special kind of realism." Thus Lewes writes: "realism is . . . the basis of all Art, and its antithesis is not idealism but Falsism." Alice R. Kaminsky, *George Henry Lewes as Literary Critic* (Syracuse, N.Y.: Syracuse University Press, 1968), 45. For Lewes on Sand, see Lewes, "Balzac and George Sand," *Foreign Language Quarterly* 33 (1844): 265–98; Lewes, "George Sand's Recent Novels," *Foreign Language Quarterly* 37 (1846): 21–36.

11. Cf. Christopher Robinson, *French Literature in the Nineteenth Century* (Newton Abbot, England: David & Charles, 1978), whose survey of nineteenth-century French literature is informed by the opposition between "idealists" and "pragmatists," an eternal opposition given renewed impetus in the nineteenth century, "not only because of the crisis of values caused by the social cataclysm of the end of the previous century, but also because continued progress in the sciences undermined belief in accepted notions of reality itself" (8). Curiously, Robinson's generalization of the category of idealism to include most major developments in nineteenth-century French literature does not correspond to a reevaluation of Sand's fiction. Of the writer who was arguably the preeminent idealist of her time, he writes: "even a thinker so congenitally feeble as poor George Sand could see this [that during the July monarchy "problems of social inequality were substantially moral too"]. It is the very core of her revolt against society in those novels compounded from a jumble of absurd utopian and spiritualist theories, e.g., *Consuelo*; it underlies such ludicrous idealizations of the peasantry as *Petite Fadette* or *François le Champi*. Even in her early novels, with their grotesquely melodramatic stylizations of adultery at its most clichéd, *Indiana* or *Jacques* . . . , the moral corrosion effected by the social structure is constantly felt as a primary cause of individual inadequacy" (105–6).

12. More accurately, Sand and idealism are forever linked in the half-life of the literary manuals, where the pace of change is inscribed in the longest of *durées*; like a fossil preserved in amber, the Sandian idealist novel remained embalmed in the unscientific sample of manuals and introductions to French literature I have consulted.

13. Hippolyte Taine, *Derniers Essais de critique et d'histoire* (Paris: Hachette, 1894), 130–31. Cf. Henry James, who, in his essay on George Sand, included in his *French Poets and Novelists* (New York: Grosset & Dunlap, 1964), explicitly indebted to Taine's, also links Sand's falling out of fashion with the dissemination of realism: "During the last half of her career, her books went out of fashion among the new literary generation. 'Realism' had been invented, or rather propagated; and in the light of '*Madame Bovary*' her own facile fictions began to be regarded as the work of a sort of superior Mrs. Radcliffe" (168).

14. Félix Hémon, *Cours de littérature* (Paris: Charles Delagrave, 1910), 43. Cf. Rocheblave who explicitly links Sand's literary fortunes to a long-deferred return to the ideal: "while waiting that the public, at last done with a sad real-

ism, come back fully to idealist literature" (np). James, in his aforementioned piece, is far less sanguine about the prospects for a return to Sandian idealism, imagining instead that in a future "world . . . given over to a 'realism' that we have not as yet begun faintly to foreshadow, George Sand's novels will have, for the children of the twenty-first century, something of the same charm which Spenser's 'Fairy Queen' [*sic*] has for those of the nineteenth" (180–81). Though it may be argued, as does Katherine Hume in *Fantasy and Mimesis* (New York: Metheun, 1984), that realism was a short-lived movement and that postmodernism marks a return of the fantasy repressed by realism. The return of fantasy is not the same as the return of idealism, though there is a definite connection between the two. The Sand that has returned to favor, at least in the United States, is the feminist Sand. Sand's idealism has not been revalorized by contemporary feminist readings.

15. Patricia Thomson, *George Sand and the Victorians* (New York: Columbia University Press, 1975), 183, emphasis added.

16. George Eliot, *Adam Bede* (Harmondsworth, England: Penguin Books, 1980), 221, 222, 223.

17. George Eliot, *Essays of George Eliot,* ed. Thomas Pinney (New York: Columbia University Press, 1963), 270.

18. At the conclusion of his reading of chapter 17 of *Adam Bede*—which I read after having drafted this essay—J. Hillis Miller makes the point that the very difference Eliot seeks to promote between the arts of "irrealism" and "realism" tends finally to collapse. See J. Hillis Miller, *The Ethics of Reading* (New York: Columbia University Press, 1987), esp. 66–70, 78–80.

19. Roland Barthes, *S/Z,* trans. Richard Miller (New York: Hill & Wang, 1974), 59.

20. Hippolyte Taine, *Philosophie de l'art,* 2 vols. (Paris: Ressources, 1980), 33.

21. George Sand, *My Life,* trans. Dan Hofstadter (New York: Harper, 1980), 218. Cf. the recasting of this dialogue in the "Notice" of Sand's *Le Compagnon du Tour de France* (Grenoble: Presses Universitaires de Grenoble, 1988), 1:31–33.

22. Choderlos de Laclos, *Oeuvres complètes,* ed. Maurice Allem (Paris: Gallimard, Pléiade, 1951), 688.

23. Emile Zola, *Oeuvres complètes* (Paris: Cercle du Livre Précieux, 1968), 11:772.

24. For more on the detail-woman association, see my *Reading in Detail: Aesthetics and the Feminine* (New York: Methuen, 1987). Interestingly, in Eliot, according to Hillis Miller, the gendering of the realism/idealism paradigm is reversed: "The impulse toward falsehood is given an implicit male gender, the gender of the narrator himself [in an idiosyncratic strategic gesture Miller insists on referring to Eliot throughout as "he"] whereas the faithful representing of commonplace things is therefore implicitly female" (68). If Miller is right, then we can perhaps identify Eliot's writing as inaugurating the transvaluation of the traditionally negative association of femininity and detailism pursued by modern feminist writers and critics who have often (re)claimed the realistic representation of (female) experience as the hallmark of women's writing.

25. I am thinking here of the work of what might be thought of as the English or Cambridge school of critics (Tanner, Heath, McCabe, Prendergast) who, working in the wake of Barthes, are engaged in rethinking realism. Significantly, however scathing their critique of realism, it has remained completely

divorced from a critique of the canon. The work of Prendergast is in this respect symptomatic: while recognizing fleetingly that the laws of verisimilitude repress "feminine desire" with a particular vengeance, Prendergast's corpus is resolutely male. The surprising annexation of Nerval's *Sylvie* to the standard works in the library of realism only serves to point up the critic's blind spot; indeed, one almost suspects that *Sylvie* is appropriated in lieu of a text by a woman. The references here are to: Tony Tanner, *Adultery in the Novel* (Baltimore: Johns Hopkins University Press, 1978); Christopher Prendergast, *The Order of Mimesis* (Cambridge: Cambridge University Press, 1986); Colin McCabe, *Theoretical Essays: Film, Linguistics, Literature* (Manchester: Manchester University Press, 1985); Stephen Heath, "Realism, modernism, and 'language-consciousness,'" in *Realism in European Literature* ed. Nicholas Boyle and Martin Swales (Cambridge: Cambridge University Press, 1986), 103–22. This is perhaps (also) the place to make explicit what is implicit throughout this essay: to say that Balzac is the paradigmatic realist (or Sand the paradigmatic idealist) is not to endorse the reductionism of the canon. Balzac's representational versatility, his own practice of (Sandian) idealism are not the issue here. What is at issue here is that the same criteria of canonicity (derived from and confirmed by Balzac's realist fiction) that serve to decanonize Sand serve to decanonize Balzac's (and other writers') nonrealist fiction.

26. George Sand, "L'Education sentimentale par Gustave Flaubert," in her *Questions d'art et de littérature* (Paris: Calmann Lévy, 1878), 421.

27. On the breakdown in Sand's fiction of the difference between characters that grounds psychological realism, see my "Female Fetishism: The Case of George Sand," in *The Female Body in Western Culture: Contemporary Approaches*, ed. Susan Suleiman (Cambridge, Mass.: Harvard University Press, 1986), 363–72.

28. Erich Auerbach, *Mimesis: The Representation of Reality in Western Literature*, trans. Willard R. Trask (Princeton: Princeton University Press, 1968), 445. See also Martin Swales, "The Problem of Nineteenth-Century Realism," in *Realism in European Literature*, 68–84. Sand's well-known debt to Goethe—*Jacques*, for example rewrites the *Elective Affinities*—appears here in a new light, because for Auerbach, Goethe's aesthetic choices, his aristocratic rejection of realism decisively inflected the history of German literature. It is because Goethe is the central canonic figure of German literature and because Goethe eschewed bourgeois realism that realism failed to take hold in Germany.

29. George Sand, *Histoire de ma vie,* in her *Oeuvres autobiographiques,* (Paris: Gallimard, Pléiade, 1971), 2:173, 1342–43, n. 1. The translation is by Nancy K. Miller as it appears in "Arachnologies: The Woman, the Text, and the Critic," in her *Subject to Change: Reading Feminist Writing* (New York: Columbia University Press, 1988), 281.

30. George Sand, "Notes et Variantes," *Indiana*, ed. Béatrice Didier (Paris: Folio, 1984), 380, n. 13.

31. Pierre Salomon, *George Sand* (Paris: Hatier-Borcier, 1953), 29.

32. George Sand, *Indiana*, trans. George Burnham Ives (New York: Academy Press Limited, 1978), 46.

5   ANNE-MARIE THIESSE AND HÉLÈNE MATHIEU

The Decline of the Classical Age and the Birth of the Classics

The Evolution of Literary Programs of Study for the Agrégation *Exam since 1890*

"How should literature be studied in secondary education? What point of view should dominate? What relationship should there be between its study and the more general ends of education?" Such was the broad essay question in French literature proposed to the candidates for the *Agrégation* exam for young women in 1901. Apparently all the problems raised by the teaching of literature are evoked in this supremely pedagogical topic. Yet the essential question is not stated: *What is literature as educational material?* How is this domain of academic study called literature defined, and how is it constituted? By the *classics,* respond numerous contemporary studies on current practices in education, which go on to denounce the restriction of literature to a limited corpus of writers canonized by textbooks and rehashed in the classroom. But these classics, which function as so many landmarks in the manuals of literary history[1] used in secondary education, are themselves the product of the history of the teaching of literature. Criticism today needs a study of the social history of the concept of the classic and its application. To this end, we have researched crucial, little-exploited archival material: the programs of study in French literature for the competitive *Agrégation* exam.[2] These sources reveal, more precisely than official rulings, the manner in which literature is conceived as an object of academic knowledge to be acquired and transmitted.

From Mimetic Discourse to the Experimental Method

THE *AGGIORNAMENTO* OF THE THIRD REPUBLIC

Up until the end of the last century, candidates for the *Agrégation* exam in Letters had only to know and study the works of the seventeenth century,[3] the only works judged worthy to figure in the programs of study next to Greek and Latin texts. For the teaching of the humanities was based on rhetoric, that is, an apprenticeship in the rules of discourse and writing by the imitation of models, preferably models from antiquity. A legacy from the lower schools of the *ancien régime*, this coursework in rhetoric permitted the children of the bourgeoisie to acquire a linguistic competence indispensable in a parliamentary regime. "Our humanities courses, to be worthy of this name, must initiate our young men [*jeunes gens*] into the precepts of taste, the art of writing, its rules, and up to a certain point, literary history. On the other hand, in our form of government, and for the development of our bar, oratory studies are appropriate for a rather numerous class of citizens, and ancient rhetoric contains a wealth of precepts which are not outdated."[4] The notion of classic literature[5] thus designates a group of works fulfilling a *normative* function for written and spoken discourse, the supreme referent being Greek and Latin literature.[6] Need it be noted that this definition of classic literature canonizes works characterized by their linguistic and stylistic distance from "vulgar" language (contemporary French) and from literature created at that moment? At the same time, it sets literature apart as an ancient patrimony whose transmission to the dominant class, and to that class only, is assured by academic institutions. This double effect of teaching letters (the mastery of a *classical* language, namely of a class dialect, and the acquisition of a cultural capital redoubling in the symbolic order the power given by economic capital) was the real stake in the struggle for academic reform that occupied the first years of the Third Republic.

The defeat of 1870, the events of the Commune, and the threat of a monarchical reaction weighed heavily on the approach of the Third Republic to education; the educational system, which had hardly evolved since the *ancien régime*, found itself suddenly thrown into question. The republican bourgeoisie, which had just come to political power, found itself obliged, to strengthen its position and its legitimacy, to create a national ideological consensus, and to close the considerable technical, economic, and military gap between France and Prussia. Attacks raged against a system of education condemned for its old-fashioned character and, above all, its inability to prevent the disasters of 1870 and 1871. If the creation of free elementary schooling, which proved to be the true "ideological cement"[7] of republican France, easily resolved the debates on the education of the masses, the dominant class remained divided as to the education dispensed in secondary schools, which it reserved for its own children.[8] It was around the question of Latin (and of Greek), the cornerstone of the old system, that crystallized the controversy whose object, more or less implicit in the arguments advanced, was to know whether secondary education should have a practical, short-term end, or whether it should dispense a "liberal" culture functioning as a class marker for the social elite. These divergent views actually covered over oppositions within the dominant class: the lower middle class expected secondary education to give its children knowledge useful in the exercise of a profession; the upper middle class, rich in economic and/or social capital, and thus assured of positions for its sons, remained attached to the principle of the humanities that designated them as the legitimate heirs of the aristocracy. The debate was resolved by the creation of two orders of secondary education: classical studies and so-called "specialized" education,[9] without Latin, oriented toward modern languages, sciences, and economics: the creation of an *Agrégation* in specialized education authorized the radical difference between the two orders, of which one was, quite obviously, considered inferior.[10]

This division of secondary schooling into two orders, one of which was open to modernity while the other preserved the old system, made it possible to proceed with a certain updating of the programs of study in French literature, stopping short of global reform: the programs of study for special secondary education and the corresponding *Agrégation* exam allotted a certain place to nineteenth-century writers, while "normal" education remained devoted to classical writers.

The situation was absurd in many respects: at the beginning of the Third Republic, only a minority of high school students, who followed a devalued course of study, had access to post-Revolutionary literature, the others studying only works written under the *ancien régime*! Above all, there existed an aberrant distinction between their respective methods of teaching French literature: the study of literary history and the study of texts. Introduced sparingly in programs of study in 1840 in the form of questions on different periods of Greco-Latin and French literature, literary history, by definition, was not limited to the seventeenth century for the French domain. But insofar as the study of nonclassic works was not written into the program, the course was limited to a dry encyclopedic nomenclature, a catalogue of dates, titles, and schools, as is indicated in this program of study for the *Baccalauréat* degree in 1840: "[the candidates must be able to] cite those poets who stood out in each of the periods of French poetry, following the hierarchy of genre, indicating the dates of their birth and death, and the titles of their principal works." Manuals then appeared on the academic market that gave excerpts from those texts destined to illustrate the course of literary history. But the program continued to require knowledge only of the "great works" of the "great century" from future teachers. It was not that the university, which increasingly controlled the education of professors, was powerless to provide a more complete approach to French literature: an intense activity of research and the edition of texts was organized, in the last quarter of the century, around prestigious academics like Paris, Bédier, Huguet, or Lanson. But the weight of tradition and the conservatism inherent in a masculine and time-honored secondary education precluded the first step indispensable to any renewal in education—the updating of the knowledge required of teachers. Thus the task of renewal was left to an academic order devoid of any tradition: the secondary education of young women.

THE FEMININE PRECEDENT

Founded by the Camille Sée Law of 19 January 1880, public secondary education for young women met very explicit ideological needs: to tear the young women and future wives of the bourgeoisie away from the influence of the Church and reactionary ideas in order to win them to the Republic. "Raised in the school of superstition, [the young woman] will marry a man raised in the school of reason; she will be of the seventeenth or the middle of the eighteenth century, the man will be of the end of the eighteenth or the nineteenth,"[11] exclaimed Camille Sée to the Chamber of Deputies, entreating the state not to leave the education of women to the Church.

To the founders' minds, this women's pedagogy was not intended for any specific professional ends: it accorded a minimal place for scientific subjects (which distinguished it from the degree in the other track) and did not mention the study of ancient languages;[12] French language and literature constituted the principal subject. Thus, a pedagogy of "Modern Letters" was put into place as a parallel to the "normal" course of study for men, which was still dominated by classical humanities, and it was likewise sustained by a system of recruitment of its own professors (the creation of the Ecole de Sèvres[13] in 1881, of the *Agrégation* in the Secondary Education of Women in 1884). This women's *Agrégation* was distinguished from the men's not only by the lack of an exam in Latin or Greek; historical grammar, for women, took the place of the exercises in prosody and rhetoric imposed on male candidates. Above all, the preoccupation with training women (and women teachers) in the nineteenth century involved a very rapid widening of the programs to include contemporary works. Just nine years after the national funeral organized by the Republic for Victor Hugo, the author figured on the program for the women's *Agrégation*. Figures 5.1 and 5.2 show how the programs for the women's *Agrégation*, from 1890 on, stopped imitating the model for the men's *Agrégation* and substituted works of the nineteenth century for those of the seventeenth century. Somewhat later, and with more regularity, the men's programs followed the line of the women's programs.

At first, of course, it was above all the works of the nineteenth century that competed with those of the seventeenth, by virtue of the ideological stakes we have evoked: but insofar as the exclusivity of the "Grand Siècle" found itself under attack, works of other periods could be introduced gradually into the programs, to such an extent that in 1914 the principle that still prevails in the *Agrégation* (equal distribution of centuries) had been sketched out. It should be noted that in the same period the men's *Agrégation* accorded a place of growing importance to exams in French literature, at the expense of tests in ancient languages and literatures (see table 1).

The works included in the program were thus destined to provide testing topics for oral *explications de texte*; but, as was indicated in a note of the period, when the test in written composition in French called for knowledge of literary history, it had to be related to those works included in the program. Out of the separation that prevailed until that time between the study of texts designed for an apprenticeship in the rules of writing and an autonomous discourse of literary history, came a method of study conjugating these two elements. Thus appeared in the training of teachers what was for

FIGURE 5.1 Percentage of Seventeenth-Century Authors in *Agrégation* Programs

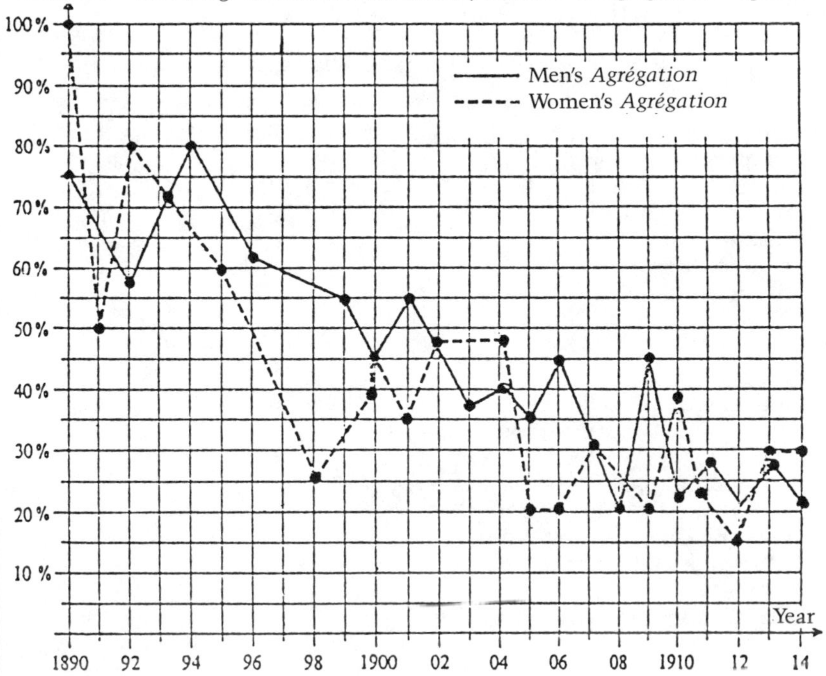

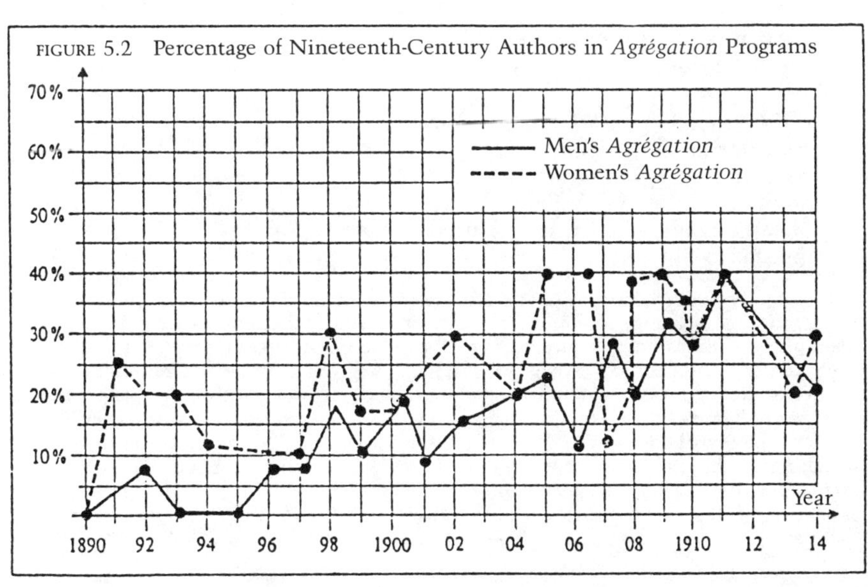

FIGURE 5.2 Percentage of Nineteenth-Century Authors in *Agrégation* Programs

TABLE 1 Distribution of Points for the Competitive Agrégation Exam

A) Agrégation in Letters (1890–1914)		
	1890 Distribution	*1908 Modification*
Written		
Essay question in French	12	15
Essay question in Latin	12	0
Grammar and prosody	10	0
Translation from Latin	10	10
Translation into Greek	10	10
Translation into Latin	—	10
Translation from Greek	—	10
Oral		
Explication[a] of a Greek text	10	10
Explication of a Latin text	10	10
Explication of a French text	10	10
Explication and commentary of a Greek or Latin text	10	0
A lesson on a topic in classical literature	10	0
A lesson on a topic taken from the program in French composition	—	10
Analysis of an Old French text	—	2.5

B) Agrégation in the Secondary Education of Women, Letters section[b]	
	Distribution
Written	
Composition on a topic of morals or education	4
Composition on a literary topic	4
Translation of a modern language	3
Oral	
Explicated reading of a French text	4
Lesson in morals	4
Exposé on a question of language or grammar	4
Explicated reading of a text in a modern language	3

[a]*Explication de texte*, or *explication française* is a formula for the written and oral presentation of a passage of literature by students, whose first efforts are guided by a questionnaire (prepared by a professor) to "help the child better understand and feel more subtly the beauty of a page of French." A given page would represent the essence of the work from which it was taken, the oeuvre of the author, the period and genre, and ultimately, the French language itself. Its goal is to "reconstitute from *the words* of the text the ideas, the sentiments, the intentions that moved the author . . . by taking on his point of view" and "to follow its development and continuity." *Extrait des Instructions du 30 septembre 1938.*

[b]An act of 31 July 1894 introduced the distinction between the sections of letters and history.

decades the official basis of literary pedagogy: *the teaching of literary history through texts.*[14]

Knowing texts, and using them as a support for literary history—the approach fulfilled quite well the requirements of positivist thought and was one of the numerous academic attempts at transposing experimental methods in the sciences into the humanities. At the same time that scientific pedagogy was the poor relation of academic programs, the scientific approach fascinated professors of literature who tried to borrow techniques used to study the living organism in order to investigate literary texts. Witness an astonishing essay question in French literature given at the competitive entry exam for the Ecole normale supérieure de jeunes filles in 1908: "Can the method that Claude Bernard described in his *Introduction à la médecine expérimentale* apply to literary studies, and if so, in what way?"

Does this mean that, under the auspices of positivist thought, a science of literature, however embryonic, appeared at the beginning of this century? Describing the method ("go to the text," analyse it) was not enough: more important was to define the corpus of texts set aside for this kind of study. Thus, if the "Grand Siècle" reigned no longer as absolute master over secondary and university programs, the term *classic author* continued to define "the author to be studied," at the cost of a slight reworking of the concept. A note to the program for secondary studies for the year 1890 reads: "The committee wondered if it was desirable to limit the choice of authors to the classics. It has decided that by the word *classic* must not be meant only authors of the seventeenth century, but also writers of the eighteenth and nineteenth centuries."[15] A concession to post-Revolutionary modernity (note the omission of the sixteenth century and the Middle Ages), this extension of the notion of the classic remained problematic, since it did not mention the criteria according to which the label of classic was to be discerned. Because the principle of selection of the classic works and authors has never been made explicit since that time, except tautologically (the classics are the "Great Writers," that is to say, the authors on the program), only a study of the de facto corpus can make possible the analysis of the principle of selection. To do this, the programs of exams and of competitions are more useful than the manuals, which reflect only imperfectly the real practices of teaching (many authors mentioned in the manuals were never actually studied). Examined over the period of a generation, the programs of literary study for the *Agrégation* give a list of the classics of a period, those writers who were the object first of university study, then of secondary study. Knowledge of those authors was judged indispensable to future professors (clearly, teachers of literature were all the more likely to lecture on authors represented on their *Agrégation*, as they would have devoted a year to their study). We have thus systematically analyzed these programs of study for two periods of twenty-five years: from 1890 to 1914 (the first period of extensive updating) and 1956 to 1980,[16] which, by comparison, allowed us to establish the invariable and the changing characteristics in the definition of classic works.[17]

The Pantheon of French Letters

THE IMMORTALS IN THE UNIVERSITY

Restricted to perhaps 10 authors until 1890, the group of the classics widened considerably between 1890 and 1914: between these two dates, 58 different authors were cited at least once on the program of study for the women's *Agrégation*, and 56 on that for men. At the time, the number of authors included in the program each year varied from 5 to 12, and the current rule (1 author per century) was not yet in use; it is thus all the more surprising to discover that the programs of study for the *Agrégation* in Letters, [18] between 1956 and 1980,[19] selected exactly the same number of authors: 62. Moreover, these three programs show the same number of authors cited at least twice in twenty-five years: 33, 33, and 32 respectively. That this number should not change is somehow strange, all the more so because twentieth-century authors were taken into account by the programs of the last twenty-five years![20] Like the Forty Immortals of the French Academy,[21] the authors of the *Agrégation* may renew themselves to some extent, but their number remains immutable. Even as in the case of the current program, which retains but 1 author per century, per year, 125 different choices (5 authors per year, over a period of twenty-five years) would have been possible, and this, among the thousand or so writers who have known some notoriety since the Middle Ages. It was thus not material imperatives that restrained the choice, but a principle of overselection of literary stars, which was carried out at the expense of more recent writers. One out of two is the approximate ratio of authors selected several times for the programs of study to the total number of writers appearing in these programs; but this figure is much less balanced for the more recent period: one-third of the nineteenth-century writers included in the men's *Agrégation* from 1890 to 1914 and only one-sixth of twentieth-century writers included in the program from 1956 to 1980 were selected at least twice. This is no doubt an indication of the difficulty in distinguishing a sure and durable set of values for the selection of modern classics, especially in the absence of any clear criteria for selection. (N.B.: living writers are barred from the programs, today as at the beginning of the century[22]). One finds this same phenomenon in the manuals, where the presentation of contemporary authors is limited to a long nomenclature, a nondescript enumeration that avoids any particular attention to highlights. Only the women's *Agrégation* at the beginning of the century rose to counter this principle because of its modern orientation. Inversely, almost all the seventeenth-century writers cited were cited many times over—time-honored tradition had canonized the classical authors of the classical century.

THE MAJOR CRITERIA FOR SELECTION

The classics selected early in the century remain, for the most part, the same works chosen today, as table 2 indicates. Of the twenty-nine writers from the sixteenth to the nineteenth centuries included more than twice in the *Agrégation* between 1956 and 1980, twenty-two were paid the same honor between 1890 and 1914. Two among them (Beaumarchais and Garnier) appeared once in the programs of the *Belle Epoque.* Five others (Marguerite de Navarre, Scarron, Flaubert, Nerval, and Baudelaire) enjoyed a slightly scandalous reputation that justified their exclusion from the programs of secondary study in the Third Republic. The criterion of morality was in fact of great importance in the selection of classic authors, and particularly when their study was being proposed to women: included four times on the men's *Agrégation* before 1914, Rabelais did not figure on the women's *Agrégation.*

In a phenomenon related to the question of morality, women writers were rarely considered worthy of study: among the literary stars on the programs under consideration, only two women appear on

TABLE 2 Authors on the *Agrégation* Programs, in Descending Order of Frequency

| 1890–1914 | | | | 1956–1980 | |
Men's Agrég.		*Women's Agrég.*		*Agrég. in Letters*	
Racine	20	Molière	13	Rabelais	4
Corneille	19	Corneille	12	Ronsard	4
Bossuet	16	Hugo	11	La Fontaine	4
Molière	16	Bossuet	10	Molière	4
La Fontaine	15	La Fontaine	10	Marivaux	4
La Bruyère	15	Racine	10	Diderot	4
Voltaire	10	Voltaire	9	Rousseau	4
Pascal	10	Rousseau	8	Montaigne	3
Rousseau	10	Montaigne	8	D'Aubigné	3
Hugo	8	Pascal	7	Racine	3
Fénelon	7	Lamartine	6	Pascal	3
Montaigne	6	Fénelon	5	Corneille	3
Vigny	5	La Bruyère	5	Voltaire	3
Chateaubriand	5	Montesquieu	5	Musset	3
Montesquieu	5	Vigny	5	Hugo	3
Marot	5	Michelet	4	Valéry	3
Du Bellay	5	Boileau	4	Garnier	2
Boileau	4	Ronsard	4	Marot	2
Sévigné (Mme De)	4	Chateaubriand	4	M. De Navarre	2
Rabelais	4	Sainte-Beuve	3	Du Bellay	2
Lamartine	4	Diderot	3	La Bruyère	2
Michelet	4	Sévigné (Mme De)	3	La Fayette (Mme De)	2
Bourdaloue	3	Leconte De Lisle	2	Scarron	2
P. L. Courier	3	Staël (M^{m3} De)	2	Montesquieu	2
La Rochefoucauld	3	Fromentin	2	Beaumarchais	2
Saint-Simon	3	Balzac	2	Vigny	2
Ronsard	3	Renan	2	Balzac	2
Régnier	3	Chénier	2	Flaubert	2
D'Aubigné	3	Marot	2	Nerval	2
Malherbe	3	D'Aubigné	2	Baudelaire	2
La Fayette (Mme De)	2	Amyot	2	Claudel	2
Marivaux	2	Du Bellay	2	Proust	2
Estienne	2	Musset	2		

each (again, a strange preservation of the number!). Mme de Lafayette, cited twice between 1890 and 1914 on the men's *Agrégation* and twice between 1956 and 1980, doubtless owes this durable favor to the exemplary character of her heroine, incarnation as she is of the values of the Eternal Feminine (depth of feeling, sacrifice of passion to duty).

The writers mentioned just once in twenty-five years on the

TABLE 3 Authors Mentioned Only Once in an *Agrégation* Program

| Century | 1890–1914 | | 1956–1980 |
	Men's Agrég.	Women's Agrég.	Agrég. in Letters
XVI	La Boétie Noël Du Fail	Montluc Vauquelin La Boétie Garnier Tristan Noël Du Fail Lemaire Des Belges M. D'Angoulême Des Perrier	Montluc Régnier
XVII	Vaugelas	Mme De La Fayette Saint-Simon Descartes	Boileau Bossuet
XVIII	Diderot D'Alembert Beaumarchais Fontenelle Saint-Evremond Lesage Vauvenargues	Vauvenargues Marivaux Rollin Mme Rolland Buffon Beaumarchais Saint-Simon	Saint-Simon Prévost (Abbé) Chénier Lesage
XIX	Sully Prudhomme Taine Musset Sainte-Beuve Dumas fils Staël (Mme De) Fromentin Balzac Renan Leconte De Lisle Stendhal Sand/Flaubert Sand	Fustel De Coulanges Taine Musset Herédia Gautier Sand	Chateaubriand Michelet Mallarmé Stendhal Verlaine Lamartine Sainte-Beuve
XX			Alain Fournier Péguy Barrès Malraux Giono Saint-John Perse Giraudoux Montherlant Eluard Camus Breton Bernanos Colette Apollinaire Gide

TABLE 4 Ratio of Authors Mentioned Twice to Total Number of Authors on *Agrégation* Programs

	Century					Total
	XVI	*XVII*	*XVIII*	*XIX*	*XX*	
Agrég. in Letters (1890–1914)	7/19	15/16	5/12	6/19	—	33/56
Women's *Agrég.* (1890–1914)	6/15	10/13	5/12	12/18	—	33/58
Agrég. in Letters (1956–1980)	8/10	8/10	6/10	7/14	3/18*	32/62
Lagarde and Michard[a]	6/9	12/28	9/27	16/46	5/139	48/239
Chassang[b]	4/32	11/53	5/47	15/80	2/179	37/391

[a]André Lagarde and Laurent Michard, *Les Grands Auteurs français du programme* (Paris: Bordas, 1962).

[b]Arsène Chassang and Charles Senninger, *Receuil de textes littéraires français* (Paris: Hachette, 1966–68).

Agrégation are indicated in table 3. Medieval authors, who were not always explicitly mentioned on older programs, were not taken into account.

Table 4 indicates the ratio of writers mentioned at least twice in the programs for the *Agrégation* to the total number of writers figuring in these same programs. The last two lines indicate an analogous ratio: the number of writers to whom a full chapter is devoted compared to the total number of writers cited, in two current manuals in use in secondary classes.

The decline of Mme de Sévigné is linked to the almost total disappearance of the epistolary genre from the program. In the same way, Mme de Staël, who had been represented only by her essays, is eliminated when that genre falls from favor. As for the introduction of Marguerite de Navarre, it is doubtless related to the rise of the novel as genre. Like the French Academy or the Pantheon of Great Men of the Nation, the group of classics remains a masculine universe that tolerates women only in the smallest numbers. It is still remarkable that the women's *Agrégation* early in this century, in spite of its innovative and modern character, did nothing to promote women's literary production, just as the current *Agrégation* (where female candidates are far more numerous than male) has contributed to a situation in which women teachers are persuaded that great literature is written by men.

Ideological and political criteria were, finally, a determining factor in the canonization of the classics, and they seem to have changed little since the beginning of the century: excluded from the programs of the Third Republic, the materialists of the eighteenth century, the revolutionary orators, and the socialists of the nineteenth century are still absent from recent programs. This ostracism is exercised even against naturalist writers like Maupassant and Zola, who were included only once in the *Agrégation* programs of the last twenty-five years (in the same period, Valéry appeared three times!).

But an enumeration of the criteria for selection of writers cannot be relevant without an examination of the principle of selection that takes into account the use for which these texts were destined.

THE TYPOLOGY OF THE CLASSIC AND ITS EVOLUTION

Table 5 gives a classification by genre and by century of all of the works chosen for the *Agrégation* in the periods under consideration. It can be observed that, although the overwhelming part played by the theater, as well as that played by poetry, hardly varies at all, the same is not the case for the novel (and the short story), which were particularly underrepresented at the beginning of the century and which now occupy first place in the programs of study. Considered "paraliterary" by scholars in 1900, even though it was clearly the major form of literary creation at the time, the novel has today acquired legitimacy, represented on the *Agrégation* by the novelists of the twentieth century, but also by those of preceding centuries (this would surely explain the rediscovery of Marguerite de Navarre). The gap between scholarly literature and living literature is thus not only chronological and purely a question of dates: a classic is a work *formally* dead (the pedagogical exploitation of the novel is simultaneous with the theoretical crisis of the genre; one can only point to the absence of forms of contemporary writing like film, which would be no less accurately placed in literary studies than theater).

According to a tendency that has hardly changed since the turn of the century, each literary form is particularly associated with one century with which it thus establishes a relationship of elective affinity: the theater belongs primarily to the seventeenth century (even if eighteenth-century theatrical works have benefited recently from a certain rehabilitation), poetry to the sixteenth and nineteenth centuries (the poetry of the seventeenth century is overrepresented on older *Agrégation* exams by the *Fables* of La Fontaine) and

TABLE 5 Breakdown by Genre of Works on the Program

A) *Agrégation in Letters (1890–1914)*

	XVI	XVII	XVIII	XIX	XX	Total
Novel	4	3	7	5	—	19 = 7.5%
Memoirs	—	3	2	2	—	7 = 2.8%
Theater	—	53	5	6	—	64 = 25.4%
Poetry	18	22	5	17	—	62 = 25%
Epistolary	—	6	8	2	—	16 = 6.3%
Essays (history, rhetoric, criticism, philosophy)	10	50	13	10	—	83 = 33%

B) *Agrégation in the Secondary Education of Women (1890–1914)*

	XVI	XVII	XVIII	XIX	XX	Total
Novel	—	4	2	7	—	13 = 6%
Memoirs	—	—	2	4	—	6 = 3%
Theater	1	33	4	4	—	41 = 19.5%
Poetry	18	19	3	25	—	66 = 31.5%
Epistolary	—	10	9	—	—	19 = 9%
Essays	9	28	14	13	—	64 = 31%

C) *Agrégation in Letters (1956–1980)*

	XVI	XVII	XVIII	XIX	XX	Total
Novel	6	4	8	5	14	37 = 32.7%
Memoirs	1	—	4	1	—	6 = 5.4%
Theater	3	10	6	2	2	23 = 19.8%
Poetry	12	5	1	15	8	41 = 33.3%
Epistolary	—	—	—	—	—	0 = 0%
Essays	3	6	5	1	1	16 = 14.9%

works of prose fiction (novel, tale, and short story) to the postclassical age. This has resulted in a representation of the *canonical form* of the three great genres and of their *classical type:* tragedy and comedy governed by the rule of the three unities, poetry by alexandrines or octosyllabic meter, and prose fiction by the psychological novel. This has simultaneously produced a perception of those works that fall outside the norms of classical form as peripheral (archaic or degenerate, according to the case). This perspective cannot be corrected with a literary history that is only the linking together of works retained as classics and thus is inclined to study, in Hegelian terms, periods of the birth, flowering, and decline of genres.

This principle of the restriction of genres to their canonical form is analogous to that which, in recent times, identifies an author with one or two privileged genres: at the turn of the century, Racine figured on the programs of the *Agrégation* as a tragedian, but also as poet, as the historiographer of Port-Royal, and as correspondent; similarly, Voltaire was studied for his tragedies, his correspondence, and his historical work as much as for his philosophical writings. The current *Agrégation* does not tolerate polygraphs and recognizes Racine only for the classical model of his tragedies and Voltaire for his articles in the *Encyclopédie* or his philosophical tales. One may wonder whether this process is not a way of eliminating, simply by not mentioning them, all the problematic aspects of a work and of a biography inscribed in a social history, reducing writers to the unique function of producers of classic texts. Literature thus finds itself defined as a set of three redundant corpuses (by century, by writer, by genre), which are equivalent and mutually illustrative: the seventeenth century is represented by Racine and classical tragedy; the eighteenth century by Voltaire and philosophical prose, and so on. By carrying this idea to its limit, it would be possible to inscribe all of classical literature on a *table* with three columns, from which any "aberrant" form would be logically eliminated. But perhaps the management of the literary patrimony for pedagogical use is working toward precisely this goal: the presentation of literature as a closed and autonomous universe, as a veritable museum of fictional works inherited from the past (and thus outmoded)?

But the corpus of classic texts and writers constituted at the turn of the century has not been preserved intact today: political and social imperatives have markedly restricted the corpus and have worked against academic conservatism (a principal target of current attacks, which see it as solely responsible for all present ills).

THE MANAGEMENT OF THE PATRIMONY

The epistolary genre, whose place on the programs of 1890–1914 was far from negligible, has completely disappeared today. At the turn of the century, it was represented not only by Mme de Sévigné, but also by Racine, Bossuet, Voltaire, Mme Roland, and others. It is also remarkable that Flaubert figured in the programs only for his correspondence with George Sand. Furthermore, examiners frequently drew material from two collections of *Lettres du XVIIe et du XVIIIe siècle*, published by Gustave Lanson, which contained letters by famous people who did not belong *stricto sensu* to the literary world (the painter Nicolas Poussin, for example). The study of epistolary texts was thus seen as an apprenticeship in the art of writing and, more precisely, in "knowing how to turn out a good letter." This was a skill required particularly of women, who, more than men, had to study correspondences (9 percent of the texts for the women's *Agrégation,* as opposed to 6 percent of the men's).[23] As for the elimination of this genre, and the teaching practices associated with it, it should be attributed less to an awareness of progress in telecommunication than to a widening in the social recruitment of secondary school students and their teachers.

The case of oratory discourse is analogous and will enable us to explore this point in greater depth. At the turn of the century, Bossuet and Bourdaloue figured regularly in the *Agrégation* programs, even though the criterion of ideological selection should have eliminated them in the years of dispute between Church and state. (If Bourdaloue did not figure in the women's *Agrégation,* was it for ideological reasons, or because the art of rhetoric was designated more particularly for men just as the epistolary art was reserved for women?) The interest of the *Agrégation* juries of the period, composed of academics who could not be suspected of clericalism, in Catholic orators can be explained as an attachment to these masters of the art of rhetoric, whose study allowed students to be able to "speak well, write well, and consequently, to read well." If the religious orators have today fallen into disuse, it is not that education has been definitively secularized—Claudel is one of the three star writers of the twentieth century on the *Agrégation.* The part of the literary patrimony that the Third Republic had inherited from the pedagogy of religious and royal middle schools has been abandoned today for reasons that have doubtless to do with the social evolution of the school public.[24] Of course, religious eloquence may well seem boring and obsolete in a country where attendance at religious services continues to decline. But the art of speaking has lost none of its importance in a world where mass media play a role of ever greater importance. And it is astonishing, even troubling, that texts in which a contemporary rhetoric is deployed are not proposed for study (political speeches, for example, or articles from the press).

The essay is another category that has been reduced in the programs. Under this general term we have assembled a diverse group of works whose common denominator is that they are not works of fiction (memoirs, relatives of fictionalized biography, were counted separately). In spite of the extensive character of the definition, this rubric has known a marked decline since the turn of the century (33 percent and 31 percent of total works in the program between 1890 and 1914, 14.9 percent between 1956 and 1980). Today, the essay means little more than Montaigne's *Essais*, Pascal's *Pensées*, or the philosophical works of Voltaire, Montesquieu, and Rousseau; however, at the turn of the century, texts as different as Vaugelas's treatise on grammar, Fromentin's writings on aesthetics, Fustel de Coulanges's historical writings, an *Histoire naturelle* by Buffon or by Michelet, critical works by Sainte-Beuve or Taine, and so on, could figure on the programs.

The question of literarity is never explicitly posed: but on the *Agrégation* exam, the domain reserved for literature is identified more and more with the totality of classic works of fiction; thus it is precisely those works that promote a better understanding of literary texts that are rejected from the program: texts of aesthetic criticism (painting, plastic arts, or cinema), historical, philosophical, or indeed, scientific works, and even works of literary criticism or linguistics![25] But the process of elimination goes still further, leading to a random division of literature.

ATOMIZED LITERATURE

Academics who, at the beginning of the twentieth century, established programs of study for the *Agrégation* did not hesitate to present literary works in the form of fragments. When they did not simply refer to a collection of selected passages (*morceaux choisis*) already in existence, they were given to making such arbitrary excerpts themselves: the candidates were thus called upon to study the *Mémoires d'Outre Tombe* from page 326 to page 353, the third and fourth parts of *La Princesse de Clèves*, or the fifth act of *Rodogune!* This principle of selecting classic pages from classic works was for the most part due to an attitude of prudence. The literature of the nineteenth and sixteenth centuries thus appeared for the first time in the programs of the women's *Agrégation* in the form of excerpts from *Morceaux choisis des auteurs français pour l'enseignement secondaire des jeunes filles* by Albert Cahen and *Morceaux choisis des auteurs français, poètes et prosateurs, des origines à nos jours* by Petit de Julleville. Current programs are indeed more respectful of the integrity of literary works (or the selections seem to be less absurd in the first place), but the effect remains the same: one novel or one play given to be studied is supposed to sum up the whole of an author's oeuvre. It is above all in secondary education that the formula of selected fragments, those great purveyors of general ideas and aphoristic summaries, reigns.

Beyond this often denounced process of reducing texts to their "essence," there is a need to question another mode of excerpting literature—division into century and genre—which is less apparent because it has been "naturalized" by practice. We have seen how the principle that prevails today in the *Agrégation* of studying one writer (represented by just some of his writings) for each century was laid out in the years 1890–1914. This truncation of literature is all the more arbitrary in that it fails to account for literary or even historical periods. The teaching of literature was, however, more or less officially founded on this principle, as much in secondary education (where each grade corresponds to the study of a century) as in the university (where professors must define themselves as specialists of one and only one century—as sixteenth-, seventeenth-, or nineteenth-century scholars). Similarly, and this was not the case at the turn of the century, current programs carry out in the choice of texts a precise balance between the three canonical genres of poetry, theater, and novel. What results is thus a recipe for the composition of classic literature: a mixture of equal parts of ingredients coming from two great categories (century and genre), the result being *normally* invariable. This principle of excerpting, inspired by an outmoded model of historical studies, owes its justification entirely to its constant and almost exclusive use in the practices of teaching and research. We have ourselves taken them up in this study; is that to say, to use the language of anthropology, that we have been victims of "indigenous categories"? Yet, on the one hand, without reinventing an original nomenclature, it would have been impossible to set forth the results of our work; on the other hand, the use of this classifiation has itself permitted us to clarify its implications (the affinity between century and genre, for example). It appeared to us as well that if the distribution of works according to this double principle of excerpting posed no difficulties for the programs of 1956–1980, such is not the case for those of 1890–1914. If "every taxonomy involves a theory,"[26] the critical usage of taxonomy reveals the theory and its historical evolution (in the progressive reduction of the concept of literarity).

The introduction of comparative literature among the tests making up the *Agrégation* exam in Modern Letters (as opposed to the *Agrégation* in *Classical* Letters) has somewhat subverted the mode of classification of classic works by bringing together works of different periods and genres. Furthermore, insofar as comparative literature calls on foreign works,[27] or those not belonging to the domain of the classic, it denounces the arbitrary and restrictive character of literary studies founded only on French classics. But the alternative adopted, which associates works different in *form* but analogous in *content,* is still problematic: the risk is to substitute for the old nomenclature an endless list of *themes* recurrent in literary works (a varied list including the fantastic as well as the political, Christian symbolism as well as the imaginary voyage, etc.). Is this not the consequence of a conception of literary education defined solely as *the study of texts* selected for their *representative* character (of a genre, a century, or a theme)?

The virulent attacks that were made against French literary education and university research in literature in the 1960s and 1970s often targeted "literary history," long identified with the chronological linking of classic works and the commentaries, just as classic, that were associated with them. The principal result of calling the discipline into question has been the abundance of new methods of textual analysis applied most often to classic works. However radical this challenge has seemed, it is no less invested in the French tradition of the discipline that greatly privileges the text over its context. Studies on the social history of literature (the history of publishing, of readership, of the status of the writer, of the discipline itself, and of its teaching) have remained outside the programs and outside the field of literary research. Currently, research in these areas is being done, but it is in general directed by historians and sociologists. What the programs of study for the *Agrégation* illustrate is the century-long tendency of the literary discipline in France to construct a landscape composed of *isolated monuments* that loom out of an ahistoric past and a social vacuum in order that they might be given over to commentary. All in all, the exhaustiveness of this catalogue of masterpieces matters little: is the essential point that the works thus removed from their context and their use in society are grouped to compose a vast still life?

Translated by Lauren Doyle-McCombs

Notes

1. *Manuel scolaire* will be translated as "manual" throughout. André Lagarde and Laurent Michard, *Les Grands Auteurs français du programme*, 6 vols. (Paris: Bordas, 1962) is typical of the modern manuals; each volume anthologizes a century of literature, which is then divided by period, by genre, or by historical movement, and presents texts by major authors, with an introduction to each division citing historical background. From the eighteenth century on, manuals have been the primary tool for the teaching of literature in French secondary schools.

2. Created in the eighteenth century, the men's *Agrégation* took the form of a national competition in 1830. The women's *Agrégation* was created in 1884. It is a competition for the recruitment of professors in secondary education, and is organized by discipline (letters, mathematics, philosophy, physics, etc.). Preparation for the exam takes place in the universities and the *écoles normales supérieures*. Those who succeed (the *agrégés*) constitute only a minority of teachers (two hundred positions per year before World War II, eight hundred in the early 1960s, two thousand today); they are considered the elite of the teaching profession. The competition is very selective, and the number of candidates is much higher than the number who actually succeed in the competition: in fact, a good number of professors in secondary education have, at some time or other, studied to take the competitive exam. (For lack of a term that might correspond to *Agrégation* in English, the French term will be retained, as will, for the same reason, the French word *Baccalauréat*. [Translator's note])

3. With the exception, however, of the historical works of Voltaire and a few texts by Montesquieu.

4. Victor Cousin, minister of public instruction, ruling of 14 July 1840. Cited by J. B. Piobetta, *Le Baccalauréat* (Paris: J. B. Baillière, 1937).

5. In this essay, *classic* refers to literature of any period that plays a role in the French pedagogical programs. *Classical* literature denotes either the literature of the seventeenth century (often referred to as the "great" century) or that of ancient Greece and Rome.

6. In a way, this acceptance of the term *classic* persists in France in the opposition Classical Letters/Modern Letters. Secondary, or "Modern," education does not require the study of ancient languages (Latin or Greek), while so-called classical education implies the study of at least Latin. Currently, the *Agrégation* in Classical Letters includes exams in French language and literature, Latin, and Greek; the *Agrégation* in Modern Letters includes tests in French language and literature, comparative literature, the translation of a living language, and the translation of Latin.

7. The expression is from J.-P. Azema and M. Winock, *La IIIe République* (Paris: Calmann-Lévy, 1971).

8. Before 1933, public secondary education was not free. There were few scholarship students: between 1892 and 1895, for example, one secondary student in eight had a scholarship, but only 0.5 percent of the children in this age group had a scholarship to study in a *lycée*. Secondary students belonged essentially to a financially comfortable social class.

9. *Enseignement spécial* is related to what we now call tracking in American education. [Translator's note]

10. The specialized education experiment was of short duration. The 1902 reform of the *Baccalauréat* eliminated it, and replaced it with a section linking science and modern languages—without Latin—to which, for the most part, "weaker students" were oriented.

11. Françoise Mayeur, *L'Education des filles en France au XIXe siècle* (Paris: Hachette, 1979), 139.

12. The young women did, in fact, immediately demand Latin courses, which were offered on an optional basis.

13. The Ecole normale supérieure de jeunes filles. See n. 2. (Translator's note)

14. Literary history through texts was for a long time the basis of literary education in secondary schools, as is demonstrated by the enormous success of the series of manuals edited by Lagarde and Michard. Violently contested in the seventies by proponents of pedagogical reform, in practice it has remained the basic reference for literary studies, even if the official programs no longer refer to it explicitly.

15. Cited by Philippe Lejeune, "L'Enseignement de la 'littérature' au lycée au siècle dernier," *Le Français aujourd'hui*, 9 February 1970.

16. This study was done in 1979, which explains the choice of dates. The programs of succeeding years did not bring about modifications likely to change the conclusions of the study. The programs indicate, as authors for the sixteenth, seventeenth, eighteenth, nineteenth, and twentieth centuries: Ronsard, Bossuet, Beaumarchais, Flaubert, Supervielle (1981); Rabelais, Corneille, Choderlos de Laclos, Verlaine, Gracq (1982); Régnier, Madame de Sévigné, Voltaire, Stendhal, Sartre (1983); Turnèbe, Pascal, Marivaux, Rimbaud, Proust (1984), Ronsard, Molière, Rousseau, Hugo, Desnos (1985).

17. This information was obtained by consulting the *Bulletin administratif de l'instruction publique* and the *Revue universitaire* for the period 1890–1914. In addition, the *Bulletin trimestiel de l'Association des Elèves de Sèvres* regularly gives the essay question in literature for the women's *Agrégation*. For the recent period, we referred to the programs that appeared in the *Bulletin officiel de l'education* as well as to the annual jury reports. The programs for men's and women's *Agrégation* exams were identical between 1956 and 1980. The system has been totally coeducational since 1976.

18. We are referring to the program in French literature common to the *Agrégation* exams in Classical Letters, Modern Letters, and Grammar.

19. We have not taken into account medieval authors, whose place in older programs was marginal and extremely variable. Even now, they have a relatively secondary role since tradition has it that they are never the object of the essay question in literature, which is the principal part of the written exam. This persistent discrimination should be studied further.

20. This study was written in 1979.

21. *Les Immortels*, once honored by election, cannot resign.

22. On the other hand, the death of a famous writer may assure his or her inscription in the programs of study for the *Agrégation*. Thus Sartre figured on the program of 1983. One exception should be noted: Julien Gracq was listed in his lifetime on the program of 1982.

23. Even the written assignments in French literature given to young women were often to be composed in an epistolary form, as in this topic given on the competitive exam at the Ecole de Sèvres in 1902: "In his comedy *La Frivolité*,

Louis de Boissy mocks the taste of French men and women for foreign literature. . . . A society woman writes to Boissy, requesting that he make a fair distinction. . . . Develop. . . ."

24. "It is doubtless not by accident that rhetoric was suppressed, as secondary education was democratized, however feebly—the study of the art of writing and speaking, however rigorously normative it may be, is 'dangerous' if it is
not strictly reserved for the use of the dominant class. . . . A dangerous kind of
knowledge, which if too widespread, would challenge the method of Lagarde
and Michard and allow people to read Chateaubriand and Senancourt, and even
newspapers, in a new way. It would also make it possible for official speeches to
be understood in a manner undesirable to the dominant class." France Vernier,
L'Ecriture et les textes (Paris: Editions Sociales, 1974), 31.

25. For several years, a double practice has dominated in French classes in
secondary schools. On the one hand, the study of classic literary texts that
teachers are supposed to know and have studied; on the other hand, exercises on
how to do a résumé and analysis of a text, which do not belong to the domain
of fictional literature, but are chosen instead from sociology, esthetics, history,
etcetera. Thus contemporary texts that have not undergone the process of selection as classics are starting to be introduced into secondary schools. The pedagogical treatment conferred on them is clearly different from that used on
literary texts—it is a question of extracting the thought independently of any
considerations of style. As if the content could be dissociated from the form.

26. P. Bourdieu, J. C. Chamboredon, and J.-C. Passeron, *Le Métier de socio-
logue* (Paris: Mouton/Bordas, 1968), 74.

27. The study of foreign works has also made an appearance in secondary
schooling, but predominantly in the penultimate year of that level. In the last
year, which is given over to studying for the *Baccalauréat* exam, French literature holds an all but exclusive place in literary studies. Students are supposed
to have knowledge of foreign literatures through modern language classes; in
practice, lack of time precludes the teaching of litérature courses. Among the
foreign authors recommended for presentation in the penultimate year (decision of 14 November 1984) are: Defoe, Jimenez, Kipling, Stevenson, Swift, de
Vasconcelos, Bradbury, Buzzati, Calvino, Carroll, Cervantes, de Queiros,
Hemingway, Poe, Pushkin, Steinbeck, Hussein, Tolstoy.

II Canons and Contexts

Production, Reception, Revision

Medieval Women and the Politics of Poetry

> You did not respond to most of my arguments about
> preferring love to wedlock, and freedom to chains.
> —Heloise to Abelard

Medieval Canon Formation and Old French Language

As a cultural phenomenon linking literacy and political power, canon formation was an eminently medieval concept.[1] For those interested in the cultural manifestations that link literacy and political power, particularly as they relate to the role of women in canon formation, medieval women, whether historical or textual, offer a fascinating case study.

Women of the period, such as those in the Langue d'oïl region of France, one of the richest centers of literary productivity in the twelfth century, disprove an assumption sometimes made in canon studies that equates textual and political representation.[2] At the moment when popular literature in the vernacular came into being, women figured prominently in certain of its manifestations, especially those, like the *lai*, the *roman*, the *fabliau*, and lyric poetry, having to do with eroticism. Women may even be said to be active and passive agents of popular literature: active as patrons and even as authors;[3] passive in their role as subjects of a courtly ethic that reflected their political disenfranchisement, and its domestic equivalent, their subordination to paternal and spousal authority.

John Guillory has pointed out that "histories of canon formation in themselves explain nothing" (504). What counts in studying literature in a particular historical context is less the literariness of language per se, its status as canonical or noncanonical, but rather "linguistic differentiation as a social fact" (504). It is in the social context of text production, particularly at the linguistic level, that is, the relationship between the language of literature and sociolects, that the question of the noncanonical becomes theoretically meaningful: "The most conspicuous aspect of the current legitimation crisis is surely the fact that the non-canonical is not that which does not appear within the field of criticism, but that which, in a given context of reading, *signifies exclusion*. The non-canonical is a newly constituted category of text production and reception" (484).

The issue here is not canon formation, then, but the nature of women's relation to literacy, and the meaning of that link. Women did write in the twelfth century and their texts were noncanonical.[4] But since all vernacular writing in the twelfth century was noncanonical, the interesting questions lie in understanding women's relationship to literary language, their success in crossing over from the discourse of the everyday world to that other language, the discourse of writing. More specifically, one needs to examine the nature of the linguistic differentiation as a social fact either in their own writing or in writing about them. "The question of reading and writing," as Guillory points out, "belongs to the whole problematic of social reproduction, because what one learns to read is always another language" (501).

Guillory formulates questions that refer primarily to literate societies where reading is the principal means of experiencing literary texts. "In fact, as is well-known, strategies of exclusion are employed historically most effectively at the level of access to literacy, a complex of social facts corresponding to all of the following questions: Who reads? What do they read? How do they read? Who writes?" (485). In the early Middle Ages, women were effectively excluded from schools per se, but not necessarily from literacy, at least not upper-class women, or women, like Heloise, the wife of Peter Abelard and later abbess of a religious order for women, who were related to highly placed ecclesiastics. More to the point, people did not have to be literate to have access to popular vernacular "literature." Early medieval society, as Brian Stock and others have shown,[5] was still mixed in its approach to literacy. Oral performance was not simply functional, but also legal and philosophical: there was thought to be something immediate and thus more certain about oral performance when compared to the abstraction of a literary text for which verification, or even contexts of meaning, were difficult to judge.[6]

Paul Zumthor has described the anthropology of oral performance as a social event, a phenomenon of collectivity.[7] So literacy pure and simple would not have functioned to marginalize women in the twelfth century. But literacy was not pure and simple at that time, nor is it (in any age) the only function of exclusion by which social factors of linguistic differentiation operate. In a preprint culture, like that of the twelfth century, exclusionary factors flowed from bilingualism, the dual language systems whereby religion and government were domains of Latin while "nonofficial" works were written in the vernacular. It is at the level of the vernacular/Latin distinction that we find the beginnings of exclusionary principles that account for the paradox of women being wisely represented in the literature of the period without having either political representation or canonical status for their texts.[8]

In the early twelfth century, vernacular literacy played a clear role of social reproduction. French was unconstrained by formal grammar, spoken by the *laicus,* or laity (a Latin term signifying exclusion from the clergy). Unlike Latin, Old French was not yet institutionalized but was defined rather by its users than by formal schools. In the mid twelfth century, Peter Helias, professor of rhetoric and grammar in Paris from 1135 to 1160, cited as a hypothetical case the possibility of establishing a French grammar.[9] The reference shows that French was recognized as an autonomous language, not yet subject to grammar as a school discipline or grammar as a key instrument of canon formation (Lusignan, 21).[10]

While some might take this as a sign that Old French had yet to submit to authoritative literacy, the reality of the vernacular dialects is somewhat more sobering: they enact social factors of linguistic differentiation associated with the processes of canon formation. The vernacular already reflected complex cultural distinctions since written textuality betrays a close interaction with Latin literacy, while espousing the unboundedness of indigenous oral cultures. Differentiation between spoken and written languages was a commonplace of the Roman imperial era, as Brian Stock reminds us:

Linguists roughly date the earliest dissimilarities between spoken and literary Latin from the second half of the third century. Not by accident, Livius Andronicus, a freed Greek slave, began composing his plays and Latin *Odusia* about the same time. Livius was an archaiser, a conscious creator of poetic diction. Later authors, while imitating Greek models less crudely, followed his example. But the emulation went far beyond language training and literature. . . . An identification was made between the correct attitude towards the classical heritage and the style of life considered appropriate for the educationally privileged sectors of society. This pattern, once established, was adapted to different linguistic situations. In the Middle Ages it drove a wedge not between Latin and Greek but between the official culture, which was in Latin, and the unofficial culture which existed in vulgar Latin or early vernaculars. (20–21)

So long as the vernacular remained primarily associated with oral folk tales, legends, and the like, there was little reason to challenge the dichotomy between Latin and Old French. But once authors begin to compose literary texts that are also written, the stage is set for a clash between the official and the unofficial, the canonic and uncanonic. Since the early ninth century, contemporary statements attest to the tension between Latin and the vernacular (Stock, 25–26). A "renaissance" associating vernacular with the written literary forms that had been the purview of the official culture could hardly fail to exacerbate motives for linguistic differentiation between Latin and Romance.

Old French "literature" competed for the cultural space where previously Latin and echoes of Greek had reigned. Where literary Old French simply translated classical texts, for example, the *Roman d'Alexandre*, the *Roman de Troie*, the *Eneas*, and so on, it could be seen as a matter of vulgarizing high culture to make it more accessible. But when it began to develop new forms, and then to reflect those new forms back onto the adaptations of classical literature (as happens in the three examples just mentioned), then one can see the tension at work. The reason why the vernacular would seek to invade the cultural space of Latin texts lies in the complex definitions of literacy. As Brian Stock notes, it was the Middle Ages that equated high culture with rationality, and, by implication, low culture with irrationality or lack of seriousness.[11]

Classical and medieval sociopolitical theories, and their religious counterparts, set great store by rationality as a key factor in controlling social behavior and maintaining political orders that relied on members' volitional acquiescence to an extent we find hard to imagine today. Canonical texts were those that, whatever else they did, encouraged a philosophical approach underlying any given subject. The maintenance of social order, perceived as a significant function of high cultural genres, made the selection and propagation of those texts a matter for serious consideration by civil and religious institutions. The reasoning continues in our own day in public and academic debates that urge a strict curricular adherence to the canon of "great books," or seek to exclude popular fiction and expressions of mass art from the curriculum.

The identification of literacy with rationality had a pronounced impact on the strategies by which twelfth-century vernacular literature responded to its marginal position vis-à-vis high culture. Poets quickly discovered that low-cultural status conferred a relative freedom on vernacular artists that they were not slow to exploit. They did so in a double movement that espoused on the one hand the rhetorical programs of high cultural literacy while often turning away from the Latin models toward indigenous forms like the Celtic myths to develop language, genres, and modes motivated by desire and sensual perception, antithetical to the teleology of rational literacy.

Toward the mid twelfth century, for example, Marie de France created a new genre, the short narrative *lai*, to which, in a further departure, she added a "Prologue," which critics since Leo Spitzer have recognized as a theoretical discourse on her innovation. The self-consciousness of her prologue already argues a preoccupation with situating her work on a hierarchically delineated cultural landscape. She raises issues that allow us to ascertain the parameters of canonic and uncanonic discourse, boundaries that appear already well established and accepted. Although we would anticipate the hierarchical relationship between Latin and the vernacular, Marie adds yet another dimension by establishing social levels within the space of the vernacular sociolect.

Whereas Latin remains an undivided unity in her schema, the vernacular splits into branches occupying different levels of a sociocultural hierarchy. Thus *romanz*, or Anglo-Norman, the dialect of the court of Henry II, to whom she dedicates the *lais*, occupies the rank just below Latin, while Breton, the original language of the lays, falls lower on the scale. Literacy, particularly writing and rational function, determine for Marie the division between Anglo-Norman and the original Breton. More specifically, oral composition of folk tales into *aventures* or stories serves to assure that the tales remain fixed in the collective folk memory:

> Des lais pensai, k'oïz aveie.
> Nu dutai pas, ben le saveie,
> Ke pur remembrance les firent
> Des aventures k'il oïrent

> Cil ki primes les comencierent
> E ki avant les enveierent.
> Plusurs en ai oï conter,
> Nes voil laissier ne oblier.
> Rimé en ai e fait ditié,
> Soventes fiez en ai veillié![12]

I remembered the lays that I had heard. / I did not doubt, indeed knew full well, / that those who first began them / and who bequeathed them to posterity / made them to record [amorous] adventures that they had heard recounted. / I have heard some of them recited, / I don't want to lose or forget them. / [So] I have rhymed and made exemplary songs of them, / many's the time I have labored far into the night over them.

The last two lines of the quotation tell us that she has packed into the reworking of the raw folk material the whole apparatus of philosophical and ethical signification that separates the literate/rational from the oral and unlearned. She devotes the bulk of her prologue to defining the work of literary composition as incorporating dimensions of wisdom (*sen*, l. 16) which will serve as a text encouraging those who come after to see ever deeper meanings.[13] She expresses much the same program of reading in the prologue to her translation of what had come down to the twelfth century as "Aesop's" Fables:

> Cil ki seivent de lettruüre,
> Devreient bien mettre cure
> Es bons livres e escriz
> E as [es]samples e as diz
> Ke li philosophe troverent
> E escritrent e remembrerent.[14]

All who are knowledgeable in letters, / should put their efforts / into good books and writings / and into [moral] examples and sayings / that the philosophers created, wrote, and recalled.

Marie articulates here a program fully in keeping with the secular and Latin literacy organized according to rational principles by Hugh of Saint Victor in his *Didascalion: On the Study of Reading* in the late 1120s. The *Didascalion* has been described as reworking Saint Augustine's *De Doctrina Christiana* and of exercising an influence in the twelfth century as far-reaching as that exercised by Cassiodorus, Isidore of Seville, and Hrabanus Maurus in their respective times.[15] It would take too long to recapitulate Hugh of Saint Victor's theories of literacy here, especially since we need only a brief idea of them to ascertain one of the poles that Marie de

France and contemporary poets were responding to in elaborating a poetics of the vernacular. Briefly, Hugh espouses a theory of the arts not simply grounded on reason, but also founded on what he calls "linguistic logic," which privileges rational control of linguistic meaning by stressing radical literality: words mean, or should mean, what they say.

Hugh links logic and rhetoric (2:18), and defines "rational" or "argumentative knowledge," also called "the Theory of Argument," as the branch of "linguistic logic" concerned "with the conceptual content of words" (2:28). In Hugh's scheme, "demonstration consists of necessary arguments and belongs to philosophers." Probable argument is the branch of linguistic logic belonging to dialecticians and rhetoricians (2:30), and that is the part that governs what the arts address. Probable argument is divided into *dialectic*, defined as "clear-sighted argument which separates true from false" and *rhetoric*, "the discipline of persuading to every suitable thing." For Hugh, each stage of the cognitive tree of the theory of argument, contains *invention*, which teaches the discovery of argument and the drawing up of lines of argumentation, and *judgment*, which teaches the judging of such arguments and lines of argumentation.

This is the schema (down to the OF form of *inventio, trover*) that Marie outlines in the prologues to the *Fables*, and the *Lais*.[16] The point is not to argue Marie's knowledge of Hugh of Saint Victor, but rather to note that she illustrates graphically the kind of interaction that occurred between Latin theory and vernacular practice, as well as the apparent deference shown by vernacular poets to Latin high culture.

Without multiplying examples we may safely conclude that Old French was in fact if not officially a fully codified and rule-governed language on the model of Latin. But it would be a mistake to think that poets of the vernacular simply acquiesced to Latin's cultural hegemony. Rather than speaking of the inferior position of the vernacular, one might more accurately describe its position as decentered in the cultural hierarchy: not on a par with Latin but rather confidently astride the canonical and the uncanonical.

The term *decentered* rather than *inferior* conveys more accurately the nuance expressed by Marie and her contemporaries that, whereas Latin may be the cultural model and foundation, and the language of the institutional sector, the vernacular is the primary vehicle for social communication. Paradoxically, the power of the vernacular derives from its uncanonic status.

Marie and her immediate precursors and successors found a ready-made vehicle for exploiting the uncanonic status of the vernacular in the requirement that institutional language, the language of cultural supremacy had to be grounded in rationality. Vernacular literature, particularly lyric poetry, the *lai*, and romance, exploited a wide range of irrational or affective behaviors in genres that simply did not exist, as such, in Latin. Canonic Latin discourse favored particular genres: philosophical dialogues, treatises, historiography, commentary, and a host of other kinds of writing associated with one branch or another of the seven liberal arts. The Latin genres all had in common a resistance to writing that encouraged sensual cognition.[17]

This means, in effect, that the whole question of generic hierarchies underlying canon formation flowed from a prior hierarchy of cognitive perception. The cognitive trinity governing perception in patristic philosophy was intellect (*nous*), reason (*logos*), and sense (*dianoia*). Rationality was predicated on the smooth interaction of these three interior faculties.[18] Cognitive faculties at some level require mediation between the inner being and the exterior world; for that purpose two other faculties were enlisted: *phantasia* (the material imagination) and *aisthesis*. Aisthesis signifies the sensuality of the material body, and coordinates in its network the five corporeal senses; *dianoia* designated the interior faculty of *sensus*, presumably that intellectual faculty that processed the material sensations conveyed to the soul by the aisthetic network.[19]

Aisthesis, in John Scottus Eriugena's ninth-century synthesis of Greek and Latin patristic thought, represents a conceptual and material function in mediating the relation of the mind-body question both as historical given (from the time of the Edenic creation) and as part of the psychophysical relation of humans to their environment. Whether through his Greek sources,[20] or by similar thinking, Eriugena seems to parallel, at least in his understanding of the importance of sense cognition for a rational apprehension of the material world, Aristotle's entelechist (use of the body as instrument) conception of the psychological image. In book 3 of *De Anima*, as Kathy Eden has pointed out in her recent book, Aristotle postulates:

two characteristic operations of the soul as motion (*kinesis*) in regard to place and judgment (*krinein*) with its related operations of thought (*noiein*) and perception (*aisthanesthai*). . . . In the course of his discussion the imagination (*phantasia*)—a power (*dunamis*) of the mind for receiving, retaining, and retrieving images—proves to be an indispensable element in both operations.

To describe the workings of this faculty Aristotle depends largely on his treatment of perception (*aisthesis*). Imagination or *phantasia* is a kind of movement activated by perception, and its images (*phantasmata*) resemble percepts (*aisthemata*), except that they lack matter. These images, moreover, enable the mind to think.[21]

For Eriugena, aisthesis represents the aggregate of the senses by which the mind makes contact with the outer world (*DDN*, 2:98–99, *PL*, 122:569C). *Phantasia* is the feeling of sensible things and thus acts as a messenger between body and soul (*DDN*, 2:99). *Phantasia* constitutes the imaging mechanism of aisthesis. These were not just philosophical categories; they motivated explanations of universal history and helped to explain canonical hierarchies that privileged rationality and associated intellect with the masculine.

In book 4 of *De Divisione Naturae*, Eriugena gives an anthropology of the Genesis story in which he synthesizes much of Greek and Latin patristic thought prior to himself, while providing an interpretation according to which inner man was created integral and undivided sexually in Paradise, but created materially as sexually divided into male and female outside Paradise after the Fall (*PL*, 122:816D–817D). Allegorically, Adam in Paradise signifies *nous* or intellect, because *nous* is masculine in Greek; Eve signifies the senses or aisthesis, because aisthesis is feminine in Greek (*PL*, 122:813B). History begins when intellect transgresses through the agency of the senses; in other words, when sensual cognition via the body asserts itself by engaging the intellect.[22] That is Eriugena's allegory of the Fall: a transgression of the intellect through the influence of the senses. "Eve's creation from Adam's rib is the introduction of sense [sensual cognition] into the unity of rational human nature."[23]

Just as universal history, in this schema, may be said to begin when sensual cognition and the body enter the scene as active partners with the intellect, so we may argue does vernacular lyric and romance narrative begin when poets, male and female, insist on engaging the literacy of rationality with a poetic politics of the body predicated on the language of desire. Vernacular (and Latin) poetry of desire places sensual cognition on equal footing with rationality making aisthesis the vehicle. What happens in the late eleventh and early twelfth centuries is that the poetic politics of aisthesis appropriates the rational structures of Latin, while admitting the possibility of desire in language and its consequences not permitted in high cultural models. In short, vernacular romance, in both its lyric and lyrico-narrative modes, anticipated in the twelfth century what Aristotle's *De Anima* (in William of Moerbeke's translation) would teach in the thirteenth: "desire is the efficient cause of movement, and desire is impossible without the imagination. And all imagination is either concerned with reasoning (*logistike*) or perception (*aisthetike*)" (Eden, 77).

Now if one views medieval literature from the viewpoint of the struggle to innovate poetic forms by combining the canonic program of rational literacy with an uncanonic politics of aisthesis, a more exciting view of the period emerges. At least a more exciting and accurate one than has been promulgated by the canon in force since the eighteenth century. That canon has tended to view medieval literature from the perspective of a hierarchy of major narrative genres: epic, chronicle, and romance. Lyric poetry has been selectively admitted according to a principle of association with male figures whose poetic talent was perceived as extraordinary because joined with high political status (the poet-princes), or because attuned to modern views of romantic or symbolic expressiveness (troubadour love poets), or virulent social critiques (e.g., Marcabru, Bertran de Born, Rutebeuf, Villon).

Inevitably, modern readers learned to view medieval vernacular literature as a primarily male phenomenon with the occasional woman writer emulating the dominant literary culture.[24] How does this view affect what Mary Jacobus calls "the nature of women's access to culture and their entry into literary discourse," one of the problems "central to feminist literary criticism"?[25] In one sense, it should help us to understand *better* the nature of women's access to medieval culture and literary discourse.

For one of the fascinating aspects of medieval women writers in France was their innovative nature. Marie de France and Christine de Pizan come immediately to mind, but in almost all instances, we find women writing in a new key, or a significantly modified one. But even when we cannot positively identify a work as being by a woman, as in the case of the anonymous lyrics of the *chansons de toile*, or spinning songs, we find the feminine inscribed as a controlling presence, a force associated with social factors in which women exercised far greater determinacy than we have been led to believe.

By way of illustration, let us look at four different areas of the Old French literary tradition: the anonymous *chanson de toile* (traditionally viewed as a women's genre), the erotic religious ode, a song by a woman troubadour, and a letter by Heloise. In each instance, we find a sense less of oppression than of self-assertion, an assumption of the right to interrogate and to act.

A Dialectics of the Unconscious: The Uncanonic Lyric

THE CHANSON DE TOILE

A well-known Old French *chanson de toile* begins:

> I. Bele Doette as fenestres se siet,
>   Lit en un livre mais au cuer ne l'en tient;
>   De son ami Doon li resovient
>   Q'en autres terres est alez tornoier.
>   *E or en ai dol!*

> Fair Doette sits at the windows
> She reads in a book without taking it in;
> She's thinking about her lover Doon
> Who has gone to the tournaments in other lands.
>   *And how it grieves me!*[26]

The song goes on to recount dramatically the return of Doon's squire, overcome by grief at having to report to his lady the death of her husband in a tourney. She responds to the blow by determining to found an abbey in which she will become a nun. But the abbey will not simply be a monument to her love for the dead Doon; more insistently it will exclude unfaithful lovers, and shelter those who have been harmed or abused in love. Already of great size, it will continue to expand to accommodate love's victims:

> VIII. Bele Doette prist s'abaiie a faire,
>   Qui mout est grande et adés serai maire;
>   Toz cels et celes vodre dedanz atraire
>   Qui por amor sevent peine et mal traire.
>   *E or en ai dol!*
> *Por uostre amor deuenrai nonne a l'eglise Saint Paul.*   (36–40)

> Fair Doette began to build her abbey
> Which is already big and soon will be bigger;
> All those men and women she would attract inside
> Who have known suffering and abuse for love.
>   *And how it grieves me!*
> *For your love I will become a nun at Saint Paul's Church.*

A good deal of sentimental nonsense has been written about this song by those who have concentrated solely on the apparently pathetic narrative of the grief-striken wife whose noble acts of self-abnegation and commemoration appeared just the reverse of the shrewish complaints of the "mal mariée."[27] Such naïve readings fail to take account of the diegetic and linguistic anomalies that abound in the text.

First, the song turns upon a juxtaposition of sensuality and religion:

> Ou est mes sires cui je doi tant amer?   (22)
> Where is my lord whom I must love so much?

> Por vostre amor vestirai je la haire
> Ne sor mon cors n'avra pelice vaire.   (28–29)
> For your love I will wear a hairshirt
> Nevermore on my body to wear gleaming furs.

> Por vos ferai une abbaïe tele   (31)
> For you I will make such an abbey

> Si nus i vient qui ait s'amor fauseie   (33)
> If anyone comes there who has been false in love

> *Por uostre amor deuenrai nonne a l'eglise Saint Paul.*   (31, 36, 41)
> For your love I will become a nun at Saint Paul's Church.

Then we must account for the multiple perspectives—some contradictory—the text uses to represent Belle Doette. Most evident are the omniscient and personal narrative viewpoints (third person and first person) unusual as a lyric combination. Doette is both third-person subject (principal actor) of the discourse *and* first-person speaking subject. The narrative ambivalence extends to her different social and domestic roles: she is secular noblewoman and, by the end of the song, a nun; she is wife, mistress, and widow. She is represented as both reader and poet (of refrain and lament); she is founder and builder of the abbey, abbess, and gatekeeper.

Finally, the song enacts two comprehensive movements: an initial rigorous separation of the masculine and feminine worlds according to the logic of historical reality, followed by a reversal of that division according to a scenario in which genders merge in an imaginative space projected from the feminine unconscious. From the first line ("Bele Doette as fenestres se siet") the woman physically constitutes the line of demarcation between masculine and feminine, as well as controlling the narrative point of view. She motivates the inner space of the chateau—the sphere of the feminine— in contradistinction to the shadowy male world beyond the windows.

At the same time, from the first stanza, we find Doette endowed with an imaginative power that transforms the inner, domestic space to include a masculine presence—a presence created according to her own erotic economy. She rejects the heroes of the book she reads, to evoke an image of her own lover, Doon. The difference between her perception and imagination and that of the male figures appears in the confrontation between Doette and the squire who returns from the "far away lands" to report his master's death.

The squire represents fact, the sequential narrative of material presence or absence. Doette, on the other hand, demonstrates a more complex and different kind of perception. *Aisthesis*, sensual perception, motivates her intention of the world. This is a form of cognition in which the sensate, inner being—the *cuer* of line 2—joins with the mind to project images of the world which are not necessarily material images.

According to the philosophical anthropology of John Scottus Eriugena, espoused by the Chartrians in the eleventh and twelfth centuries, gender should be considered rather as an accidental than as an essential category of human existence. In the original divine model, Eriugena postulated, humans were not spatial but spiritual, and thus whole rather than divided into two sexes. As we noted earlier. John the Scot held that humans had external cognate faculties, *nous* (intellect) and aisthesis (sensual perception). On the basis of grammatical gender, *nous* was seen as "a kind of male in the soul" and aisthesis as a kind of female. All humans possess this dual configuration of faculties and thus contain within themselves, as part of their essential make-up, the "masculine" and "feminine" qualities of sense and intellect. Significantly, it is the so-called feminine quality of sensual perception, aisthesis, that integrates the outer being to the inner as a kind of messenger shuttling back and forth between them (*DDN*, 2:97–98; *PL*, 122:569C–D).[28]

Aisthesis provides a dialectical matrix for cognition in a manner that incorporates diverse and contradictory impulses. It encourages a layered, multilevel narrative whose logic incorporates the emotional unconscious. It is the opposite of the straightforward matrix of *historia*, that is, narration according to an ideology of history, so characteristic of the canonic medieval genres. In short, aisthesis authorizes a poetic expression grounded in desire, a narrative of mind and body. Women authors did not discover the principle, but their literature consistently exploits it beyond the potential males found in it.

In our *chanson de toile,* the first stanza establishes the inner space of Doette's being as one where sensual perception and rationality fuse. Doette's mind and body collaborate to project a fantasy of her real lover, Doon, perceived as preferable to the subject of the book, which her inner being rejects: "Lit en un livre mais au cuer ne l'en tient" (2). In short, the imaginative space of the song is entirely given over to the mediation of the external world by Doette's inner faculty of aisthesis.

The male figure in this song is neither dominant nor powerful except as a focus of the woman's feelings. Indeed, despite traditional readings, one may argue that the dynamics of the poem turn on a progressive substitution of the feminine expressive space for masculine values. Traditional readings have failed to identify the ambivalent valence of Doette as signifier. In his edition of the poem, Constans gave the traditional explanation of Doette's name: "*Doette.* Diminutive of *Do,* nominative form of *Doon.* The wife bears the feminized form (here with the addition of a diminutive suffix) of the husband's name in accordance with old custom (and modern, outside of the large cities)."[29]

This reading is philologically and culturally correct. In terms of the textual unconscious, however, we may see another system at work. In accord with the dual-perspective structure of the poem, *Doette* may equally be seen as a diminutive of Old French *doe* signifying "dowery," and its extension *doee,* "wife." Note how this reading reverses, at least analogically, the connotation of the husband's name. "Doon" is disyllabic, but a homophonic neighbor to the OF pair *don* (masc.), *done* (fem.) "gift." Liberality on the part of the courtly seigneur, as Chrétien de Troyes and others made clear, was a disideratum. To the extent that the dowery (*doe*) of the wife (*doee*) contributed significantly to the ability of the noble husband to distribute largesse (*don*), one may posit a reciprocal homology to the *Doon > >Doette* formula: Doon:Doette::Doette:Doon. The homology conveys both the dual perspective and the reversal of dominance from masculine to feminine in the song's dynamics.

Furthermore, *doement,* the action of bringing a dowery, or the dowery itself, has, as an extension, the connotation of an endowment to establish a religious foundation church or abbey). In short, rather than a specific, historical individual, Doette signifies a universal condition of woman as a prime financial factor within the economy of a patriarchal culture. Her name may signify the feminine diminutive of her husband's, *Doon > >Doette,* but at this second level, it also figures the paradox of her condition: the dowery that constrains her to marriage in the first place, but which enables her gesture of autonomy once widowed.

The paradox of the woman's presence—as name and situation—destabilizes even the genre or tone of the song. A lament for the loss of a lover, it also celebrates a gain: the realization of her own name on her own terms. The lyrics assert Doette's power to protect her autonomy of action, an autonomy she is not about to surrender by considering remarriage.

We see this generic destabilizing at work in the linking of religion and sexuality. The pairing creates a burlesque undertone to the oxymoronic conjunction of elegy and celebration. For if the song stresses the register of grief (*dol, duel*) it also enacts the gesture of *doer* "donation," "endowment" of the abbey ostensibly as a material correlative of that grief. But *doer*, the verbal form of the seme *do-* in her name, also means "to gratify" as in the fulfillment of desire.[30] Doette implements both senses of *doer* in her "lament" in stanzas 6 and 7 where she states and reiterates her intention of founding an abbey.

The term *abbaïe* itself becomes equivocal in this context. While we have no firm evidence for an equivocal meaning attached to the concept for this early date, attestations from the thirteenth century onward, including a passage in Jean de Meun's *Roman de la Rose* and an octet from Villon's *Testament* (ll. 1551 58), link *abbey* with places of sexual indulgence. We read, for example, in a thirteenth-century song quoted by Godefroy:

> Mal et vilanie et pechié
> Fist tel pucelette
> Rendre en abiete
> Honnis soit de Dieu
> Qui me fist nonette.
> (13th c. French Song, *Somme le Roy*, ms. Troyes, f. 7a)

Evil, baseness, and shame made such a young virgin enter the abbey; may God curse the one who made me a nun.

Jean de Meun's jealous husband in Ami's discourse denounces abbeys and cloisters, and the women who inhabit them as notorious enemies of chastity in *Roman de la Rose:* "Chastity . . . certainly does not lack opponents: everywhere in cloisters and abbeys, the nuns are all her sworn enemies."[31]

Villon's passage occurs in the octets leading up to the "Ballade de Grosse Margot" with its famous refrain: "En ce bordeau ou tenons nostre estat!" ("In this whorehouse where we keep our state"). In the octets immediately preceding this ballad, Villon associates religious foundations and prostitutes. Lines 1557–58 are clearly ironic: "Si ira maint bon crestien / Voir l'abbaye ou il n'entre homme" ("There enters many a good Christian (masc.) / To visit the abbey where no male ever enters").[32] In the *Dictionnaire . . . érotique,* Pierre Guiraud comments: *"abbaye des s'offre à tous, abbaye de clunis,* 'whorehouse.'" These expressions are slang words formed by analogy with such expressions as "Monte-à-regret abbey," "the gallows," "Saint-Lasche abbey," "goldbrickers union," where the abbey stands for the "common house," "the headquarters" of the "guild" or "union." To the erotic variations we're dealing with in these cases is added a religious implication: love is a "cult," the whorehouse a "convent" in which the prostitutes are the "priestesses," the "nuns," the "novices," and the madame is the "abbess." As for the Abbey of Clunis, it is a pun on the Latin *clunis,* "buttocks" (by extension, "ass") and the famous Abbey of Cluny.[33]

EROS IN THE CLOISTER

While the specifically erotic connotations of Doette's lament may be speculative, the linking of religion and sexuality as an assertion of equal access to sensual enjoyment constitutes an important element of feminine self-expression in the early Middle Ages. A nun named Constance in the convent of le Ronceray (Angers) equates the written page with the body and reading with intercourse in a late eleventh-century letter, written in Latin to an older monk, Baudri of Bourgeuil:

> Night hateful to my study, envious of her who reads . . .
> I put the letter under my left breast—
>   they say that's nearest to the heart . . .
> At last, weary, I tried to get to sleep,
>   but love that has been wakened knows no night . . .
> I lay asleep—no, sleepless—because the page you wrote,
>   though lying on my breast, had set my womb on fire.[34]

Constance joins such eroticism to equally fervid affirmations of chastity: "I am chaste, I am chaste in manner, I wish to live chaste, O if only I might live as the bride of God!" "Custom and law guard our love, / A chaste life justifies our games."[35] Like *Belle Doette,* her rhetoric thus deploys two languages in tense balance: the erotic and the spiritual. Constance's verse letter, or *carmen,* responds to one previously written to her by Baudri. Yet she imparts to her letter a vivid eroticism wholly original, as Dronke points out. That eroticism, however, exists without contradiction as a kind of eroticism of virginity. In Constance's letter, the same themes found in Baudri become charged by her explicit use of her own body as the expressive space on which she maps the contending impulses of sexuality and chastity. Whereas Baudri treats the erotic wordplay as a literary game of outdoing Ovid—the *Heroides* are the principal subtext— Constance transforms the stakes by figuring a psychological drama in which sexuality and spirituality constitute not so much contradictions as complementary desires on a single complex continuum.

She exploits the potential of aisthesis, affective perception, for evoking images that transform the act of writing and reading into sensual terms without the material basis of the sexual act. This enables Constance to articulate her sexual desire while avoiding the material fulfillment that would destroy the equally desired countervailing pole of chastity.[36]

Constance's focus on the erotic tension of their exchange rather than on its spiritual resolution gives dramatic impact to her verse, but more importantly dialogizes the issues that Baudri raised to begin with. His song seems pale when set against Constance's. Nevertheless, Constance continually keeps the image of Baudri's letter before her. If she illustrates the graphic equivalence of the female body as an expressive space of erotic tension, she also includes Baudri.

Beginning with her first line:

> Perlegi vestram studiosa indagine cartam
> Et tetigi nuda carmina vestra manu

> I read your letter with embracing zeal
> And with my hand I have touched your naked songs

she interweaves his language and thought consistently into the fabric of her response. The first word, *Perlegi*, "I read," announces her compliance with the repeated imperative at the beginning of his letter: "Perlege . . . Perlege . . . Perlege." Her first two lines distill a series of word games from his letter into a tight response that both echoes and transforms the original. She does not imitate Baudri, but rather makes her rhetoric perform the zealous enfolding of his letter (*studiosa indagine cartam*—she recharges the equivocal word *indagine*[37] picked up from him) announced in line 1. Her rhetoric does so by conjoining their bodies and minds in the one *carmen.* Her body, like her ode, has become a representative space for both of them as she provides him with a lesson in erotico-spiritual creative writing:

> Hoc jacet in gremio dilecti schedula nostri,
>   Ecce locata meis subjacet uberibus.   (68–69)

> Here lies on my breast the record of our desire
>   There placed lying under my breasts.

THE UNCANONIC CANSO

In a secular setting where women enjoyed greater political freedom, as in the Langue d'oc region, we find examples of women turning the lyric canon of the *canso,* or love song, into a subtle dialectical instrument for suggesting the difference in the equation *canso* (song) = *cors* (body) when the poetic voice is that of a woman.

One is tempted to call the Comtessa de Dia, the earliest of the *trobairitz* or female troubadours, the René Magritte of that most canonic of all poetic forms of twelfth-century aristocratic culture, the *canso.* Like Magritte's 1928 painting, *The Treason of Images* (Ceci n'est pas une pipe"), the Comtessa's *cansos* expose the rule-governed forms of the genre, forcing us to reflect upon its (male) narcissism. At the same time, she deploys a rhetoric of sensual perception that reclaims the genre for the feminine other—reified as the love object or *domna* in the canonic examples.

Bernart de Ventadorn, the most representative troubadour of the first period, provided an *ars poetica* of the genre in a song whose first stanza reads:

> Chantars no pot gaire valer
> si d'ins dal cor no mou lo chans,
> ni chans no pot dal cor mover
> si no i es fin'amors coraus.
> Per so es mos chantars cabaus
> qu'en joi d'amor ai et enten
> la boch' e·ls olhs e·l cor e·l sen.   (1–7)[38]

There is no use in singing if the song does not spring from the heart; and the song cannot spring from the heart if there is no true love there. And so my singing is superior because I have joy in love and devote my lips and eyes and heart and mind to it.

Bernart here codifies the convention whereby poetry and love become synonymous. The song is a rhetorical mirror showing how poetic language arises from the same source, the seat of the inner

being, as the sentiment of *fin'amors*. The poet's body, fragmented
into the sense organs in the last line of the stanza, exists primarily
to create a poetry—*chantars, lo chans, chans, chantars*—whose chi-
astic symmetry will reflect its source: the poet's body.

The aggressively masculine rhyme scheme of the *coblas unison-
ans*—monorhymed stanzas—underlies the exclusion of the feminine, the ostensible coefficient of *fin'amors*. When he does mention
the woman later, she functions, like the song, as a mirror, confirm-
ing, and prolonging the poet's existence:

> C'aicel jorns me semble nadaus
> c'ab sos bels olhs espiritaus
> m'esgarda, mas so fai tan len
> c'us sols dias me dura cen.   (46–49)

The day when she looks at me with her beautiful, spiritual eyes seems like
Christmas to me; and she does it so lingeringly that one single day lasts me
a hundred.

The Comtessa, too, makes the *canso* a kind of rhetorical mirror.
Rather than the Narcissus-like mirror of solitary reflection of Bernart de Ventadorn, though, she makes a gendered mirror that
focuses on sexual division as a function of amorous misperception.
In terms of the troubadour canon, her *cansos* must ultimately be
seen as uncourtly because they expose masculine self-reflexivity—
the exclusion of the feminine viewpoint (in distinction to the views
of the feminine that abound in the canonic *canso*)—as a major
impediment to love.

One of her best-known *cansos* self-consciously incorporates
rhyme schemes based on grammatical gender to represent the philosophical differences between male and female in the love situation
defined by the genre. By playing on its gender presuppositions—
principally the expectation that the poet-speaker will be male—the
Comtessa throws these expectations into bold relief. In her song,
love and poetry are only incidentally synonymous, and so undermine the formalist assumptions of the *ars poetica* codified by Bernart de Ventadorn. For the Comtessa, the *canso* becomes an instrument of shared analysis and communication.

In *Ab ioi et ab ioven m'apais*, she uses grammatical rhymes to
assign key words from the courtly vocabulary reciprocally to herself
(the poetic *I*) and her lover. Poetry provides the matrix for her lesson,
but a poetry that analyzes the love situation in terms of both partners
rather than playing the role of a substitution for love by one of them.

> Ab ioi et ab ioven m'apais
> e iois e iovens m'apaia,
> car mos amics es lo plus gais
> per qu'ieu sui coindet' e gaia;
> e pois eu li sui veraia,
> be taing q'el me sia verais,
> c'anc de lui amar no m'estrais
> ni ai cor que m'en estraia.　　　　　　(1–8)[39]

I feed myself on pleasure and youth / and pleasure and youth feed me, / because my lover is the most gay, / that's why I am beautiful and gay; / and since I am so faithful to him, / I want him to be faithful to me, / for I can never stop loving him / nor do I have the heart to stop.

The key words occur in the grammatical rhyme, a device by which the same word can be given a masculine and feminine form. The first and last two lines of the stanza end in grammatical rhymes based on two verbs: *apaisar,* "nourish" (1–2), and *estraire,* "take away" (7–8). The middle four lines rhyme variants of adjectives having to do with physical and ethical states: *gai* (3–4), *verais* (5–6). The verb forms refer to the female speaker-poet, the active partner in the love; the adjectives ascribe the same states of reciprocity in love to both partners.

The uncanonic basis for the song derives from the identification of the speaker, the active agent in declaring love, with the feminine love object of the traditional *canso.* The Comtessa does not simply reverse the masculine-feminine roles, as Jeanroy suggested (nn. 3 and 4 above); she speaks from the marginalized position of the *domna,* or love object itself. The effect is akin to that of a speaking statue; the created object addressing its creator(s).

Line 4—"per qu'ieu sui coindet'e gaia"—provides the pivotal substitution of this song. *Coindet(a)* is the feminine diminutive of *coind, conhda.* As used here, the adjectives *coindet'e gaia* symbolize the dual status of the Comtessa. *Coinde* derived from Latin, *cognitus,* "known" which originally connoted one "who knows something."[40] The first troubadours gave it the sense of "attractive, gracious, agreeable." In the poetry of Guilhem IX and Jaufré Rudel, the term may be one of self-reference or describe the psychological effect of love on a male.[41] The implication in such cases within the context of courtly society, Glynnis Cropp argues, was the necessity, for a lover and poet "to know (*connaître*) the best way of conducting oneself agreeably, to know how (*savoir*) to please" (109). Later, with poets of Bernart de Ventadorn's generation, the two epithets, *conhd'e gai,* are used to designate qualities of the *domna.* Thereafter, the term *coinde* tends not to be used to describe the woman.

Only the Comtessa de Dai uses these marked terms simultaneously to describe the poet as lover and the woman as love object. By conflating the two roles in one, she does not simply mark her song as extra-ordinary. She also recasts the courtly lexical register of her song, marking it with ethical, psychological, and erotic descriptors that assert a feminine activism in a normally masculine code.

The noncanonical expression *coindet'e gaia* set ethical parameters for the kind of courtly knowledge *coindeta* denotes: recripocal fidelity (*Veraia/verais*). By setting a standard of fidelity herself, she urges a standard of ethical reciprocity in love. The Comtessa does not command reciprocal behavior—although as the *midons* or *domna*, seigneurial honorifics designating the lady as lord in troubadour poetry, she presumably might have done. Instead, the Comtessa's speaker uses logic: "Since I am faithful [*veraia*] to him / I certainly hold that he ought to be [subjunctive] faithful [*verais*] to me." The root *ver-* shows the similarity of principle, while the grammatical rhyme figures the difference in practice: *verais* may not be *veraia*.

Coindeta also casts the erotic register in a light of feminine insight. By her explicit affirmation of desire, the Comtessa takes the *canso* back to its prefigured form in the *vers* of Guilhem IX, the first troubadour. Lines 1–2, 7–8, identify key terms of *fin'amors* as applicable to both subject and object, male and female, the speaker and her lover.

She focuses in the first two lines on the equivocal terms *joi e joven*, which she links to the verb *apaisar*, "to nourish." The terms link inversely with the speaking voice: in line 1 they are predicates of the speaker, "I feed myself with *joi e joven*;" in line 2 they are the subjects of the verb, the speaker, its object: "*jois e jovens* feed me." The meaning of the two words ranges from unambiguously sensual complements of *amor* for Guilhem IX ("Et er totz mesclatz d'amor et de joy e de joven"), to moral qualities of human love in Guilhem's immediate successors. In the second half of the twelfth century, the terms were applied to the courtly spirit of the *domna* (419).

In the circularity of her first two lines, the Comtessa creates a usage of *joi e joven* without precedent in their doubly gendered referentiality—figuring both the motivation of the speaker as poet and the poet as *domna*—and in the evocation of their full range of meanings, sensual as well as moral. The circular rhetoric cleverly evokes the different meanings as one repeats the lines: *apaisar* has the dual meaning of "to nourish" and "to slake"; the moral connotations of *joi e joven* suggest the former meaning of *apaisar*, while the sensual connotations call up the notion of satiety. Although the moral and sexual connotations may be associated, they are not the same. Once again, the Comtessa uses the grammatical nuance of gender differentiation to suggest profound philosophical differences in the attitudes and consequences of love. She has betrayed the *canso* into expressing images of sensual interrogation never intended by the troubadours.

CONCLUSION: HELOISE AND THE ALTERITY OF
AISTHESIS

The difference of viewpoint expressed by the Comtessa's songs is not dissimilar to those we have already seen, and could find in many other examples of women's writing of the period. Such examples remind us that there was a powerful culture of women reading and writing in the Middle Ages, marginal in terms of political power, but located squarely in the mainstream of society. In an extreme form, their outlook may be summed up by Heloise's statement to Abelard—quoted with such amazement by Jean de Meun's jealous husband:

> "Se li empereres de Rome,
> souz cui doivent estre tuit home,
> me daignet valair prendre a fame
> et fere moi du monde dame,
> si vodroie je mieux, fet ele,
> et dieu a tesmoign en apele,
> estre ta putain apelee,
> que emperiz coronee."   (Lecoy, 8777–8794)

"If the emperor of Rome, to whom all men should be subject, deigned to wish to take me as his wife and make me mistress of the world, I would prefer," she said, "and I call God as my witness, to be called your whore, than to be crowned empress."

Of the women we have looked at, Heloise has the broadest scope, the most deeply philosophical outlook. She does not simply express an attitude toward marriage in her letters to Abelard. Even more than contemporary women writers, she has strongly articulated feelings about the relation of the personal to the institutional. Whether it be marriage, the religious life, or an amorous relationship, Heloise and the others question cultural assumptions, articulated in canonic texts, which do not recognize their difference of view.

Heloise will voluntarily associate herself to Abelard on condition that their bond be one of mind and body joined. That is her definition of love (*amor*) and the social bond (*amicitia*) predicated upon it. "My spirit [*animus*] was not with me, but with you; now especially if it is not with you, it is nowhere: truly it has no purpose without you."[42] Heloise here articulates the same principle of reciprocity we saw in the Comtessa; like Constance and the Comtessa, she encircles and then incorporates the male viewpoint into a more inclusive perspective. Reciprocity, the ideal of mind and body joined by *voluptas*, the principle of aisthesis, motivates her letter. Her suffering and fidelity have proved that the "carnal pleasures I delighted in with you" ("tecum carnali fruerer voluptate") (Monfrin, 117) were in fact *amor* rather than simple male libido.

Writing, for Heloise, will be to their present state of physical separation what the caress was earlier, an act of contact: "Since I am robbed of your presence, at least by offerings of your words—in ready supply with you—present me the delight of your image" (Monfrin, 116). Heloise's letters are carefully constructed rhetorical propositions adumbrating a plan for a renewal of their intercourse adapted to their changed circumstances. With great dialectical force and perceptive analysis, Heloise lays out the conditions for a union no longer based simply on physical love, although far from devoid of physical desire, as her second letter makes abundantly clear. That union must be predicated on willingness—particularly on Abelard's part—to see her as she is in body and spirit, a spirit continually dialogized by the body: "more than ever you should fear for me, now that my incontinence can no longer find in you a remedy" (letter 4, Monfrin, 117).

Heloise's frank analyses, like those of the other women writers, uncover a fundamental truth about love and its relationship to the feminine. They show the power of the noncanonical to express the essential contradiction of humans poised between "the thin ice of language and the ocean of the psyche."

Notes

1. Latin *canon* derived from Greek *kanōn* = *regula*, bore a range of connotations linking literary and linguistic rules of appropriateness to religious and political orthodoxy. "Canon" connoted "grammatical rule; metrical scheme or type; annual payment to Rome from the provinces; other forms of scheduled payments." In the early Christian community, it came to designate "lists of Biblical books or tables of rituals; rules (statute, canon) of the Christian life (especially such as are settled by a church synod or council as binding, particularly on the

secular clergy, or—later—on monks; the canon of the Mass." Alexander Souter, *A Glossary of Later Latin to 600 A.D.* (Oxford: Clarendon Press, 1949).

2. For a discussion of the fallacious equation of textual representation and political representation, see John Guillory, "Canonical and Non-Canonical: A Critique of the Current Debate," *ELH* 54 (1987): 483–527. All further references appear in the text, as do references to any work cited more than once.

3. "Des textes rassemblés par la diligente érudition de Léon Gautier et de M. E. Faral, il résulte que les 'jongleresses' étaient nombreuses; ces textes nous les montrent faisant le métier de danseuses, acrobates, chanteuses, musiciennes (c'est aussi dans ces attitudes que nous les montrent les miniatures . . . des manuscrits espagnols), mais ne nous disent pas qu'elles se soient adonnées à la composition poétique." Alfred Jeanroy, *La Poésie lyrique des troubadours* (Toulouse: Privat, 1934), 1:314.

4. "Les 'trobairitz' dont nous connaissons les noms étaient donc des 'dames,' de naissance plus ou moins relevée, tenant dans la société un rang honorable, et poétisant par goût ou pour se faire une réputation de bel esprit. La plupart ne se sont exercées que dans les genres inférieurs, n'exigeant qu'un médiocre effort (tenson, partimen, cobla). Cinq seulement se sont haussées jusqu'à la chanson; encore trois d'entre elles n'ont laissé qu'un petit nombre de vers, insignifiants par leur forme que par leur contenu; de deux seulement, la comtesse de Die et Castellosa, le legs poétique est assez considérable pour nous permettre d'apprécier leur talent, où il me paraît, je l'avoue, y avoir plus de gracieuse facilité que d'orginialité et de force." Jeanroy, 1:315. (See also n. 3.)

5. Brian Stock, *The Implications of Literacy* (Princeton: Princeton University Press, 1983), particularly chaps. 1, 5.

6. The oral component of a legal act, such as the transfer of property, involved a symbolic performance of the transfer of material possessions; "performance created the legal act. . . . Oral tradition, as a consequence, played a dual role, equally evident in the new functions for texts and in the growing emphasis on performed transfer." Stock, 45.

7. Paul Zumthor, *La Lettre et la voix: De La Littérature médiévale* (Paris: Seuil, Collection Poétique, 1987), particularly, pt. 1, chaps. 2, 3, 6.

8. I do not mean to indicate that women did not have access to Latin; as we shall see, that simply is not true. But it is the case that women in the early Middle Ages, when they wrote Latin, tended to write lighter genres of literature, rather than the full range of history, philosophy, treatises, etcetera associated with men.

9. "Et possunt huius artis species crescere, hoc est plures esse, ut si grammatica tractaretur in gallica lingua, quod possit fieri facile" ("And the number of these species of grammar may grow still more, as, for example, if one were to make a grammar of the French language, which would be easy enough"). Petrus Helias, *Summa super Priscianum*, App. 1. Quoted by Serge Lusignan, *Parler vulgairement: Les Intellectuels et la langue franqise aux XIIIe et XIVe siècles*, 2d ed. (Montreal: Les Presses de l'Université, 1987), 21. All translations are mine unless otherwise indicated.

10. Guillory explicitly links formal grammar as a school discipline to canon formation (494–504).

11. "Perhaps the most injurious consequence of medieval literacy was not in the subjects it simply omitted. *It was the notion that literacy is identical with*

rationality. By and large, literate culture in the Middle Ages assumed that it was the standard by which all cultural achievement should be measured, not only in literature itself, but also in law, philosophy, theology, and science ... In the ancient world the literary language suitable for superior discourse remained in touch with orality, even when it was written down. During the Middle Ages, when Latin was increasingly a foreign tongue employed by a minority of *clericii,* it became largely identified with written tradition. The criterion was not literacy but textuality" (Stock, 31, emphasis mine).

12. Marie de France. *Les Lais,* publiés par Jean Rychner, Les Classiques français du Moyen Age, 93 (Paris: Champion, 1966), 33–42.

13. For a bibliography and résumé of the debate over the implications of Marie's prologue, see Alfred Foulet and Karl D. Uitti, "The Prologue to the *Lais* of Marie de France: A Reconsideration," *Romance Philology* 35 (1981): 242–49.

14. Marie de France, *Fables,* ed. and trans. Harriet Spiegel (Toronto: University of Toronto Press, 1987), 1–6.

15. Hugh of Saint Victor, *The Didascalion: A Medieval Guide to the Arts,* translated from the Latin with an introduction and notes by Jerome Taylor. (New York: Columbia University Press, 1961), 7.

16. In the *Lais,* we recall, she makes a direct link between the movement of invention and judgment in Hugh's sense, and the genesis of her own project: "La philesope le saveient, / Par eus meïsmes entendeient, / Cum plus trespassereit li tens, / Plus serreient sutil de sens / E plus se savreient garder / De ceo k'i ert a trespasser. / Ki de vice se voelt defendre / Estudïer deit e entendre / A grevose ovre comencier: / Par ceo s'en puet plus esloignier / E de grant dolur delivrer. / Pur ceo començai a penser / D'aukune bone estoire faire / E de latin en romaunz traire; / Mais ne me fust guaires de pris: / Itant s'en sunt altre entremis!" (17–32) ("Philosophers knew this / and understood among themselves / [that] the more time passed / the more subtle they would be in understanding / and the more they would be able to be on guard / against what was transitory. / Whoever wishes to defend himself from vice / should study and imagine / [how] to begin a serious work: / in this way one can distance oneself [from vice] more / and deliver oneself from great pain. / For these reasons, I began to think / about making some good story / and to translate from Latin into Romance; / but this would have been of little value to me; / others had already done as much.")

17. Examples are legion and exemplified by one of the earlier ones: Augustine's famous condemnation in *Confessions* 1:13:20–22 of Virgil's celebration of Dido's passion in *Aeneid* IV. The certitude of rationality's superiority over sensual perception can be seen in Bernardus Silvestris's twelfth-century gloss on Dido's passion: "Mercury warns and censures Aeneas because he finds him ignoring useful endeavor. . . . Mercury chides Aeneas who leaves Dido and puts passion aside. Having been abandoned, Dido dies, and, burned to ashes, she passes away. For abandoned passion ceases and consumed by the heat of manliness, goes to ashes, that is to solitary thoughts." Bernardus Silvestris, *Commentary on the First Six Books of Virgil's* Aeneid, trans. Earl G. Shreiber and Thomas E. Maresca (Lincoln: University of Nebraska Press, 1979), 27.

18. One of the most extensive and influential (for the twelfth century) expositions of the cognitive faculties in relationship to the role of humans in the natural order may be found in John Scottus Eriugena's *De Divisione Naturae,* particularly books 2 and 4, in J. -P. Migne, *Patrologiae cursus completus sive Bib-*

liotheca universalis, integra, uniformis, commoda, Oeconomica, Omnium SS. Patrum, Doctorum Scriptorumque Ecclesiasticorum qui ab aevo apostolico ad Innocentii III tempora Floruerunt (Paris: Apud J.-P. Migne Editorum, 1853), vol. 122, cols. 569A–571A, 815A–D. Hereafter cited as Migne, *PL*, 122:569A–571A, etcetera.

19. John Scottus Eriugena, *Periphyseon (De Diuisione Naturae)*, Liber Secundus, ed. I. P. Sheldon-Williams (Dublin: Dublin Institute for Advanced Studies, 1972): 98–99; *PL*, 122:569BC. Sheldon-Williams's edition (which is complete only for the first three of five books) will be abbreviated, *DDN*, 2:98–99, with the reference to Migne, *PL*, 122 following.

20. Eriugena mentions Aristotle in three of the five books of *DDN*, but direct quotations have been identified as coming only from *De interpretatione*.

21. Kathy Eden, *Poetic and Legal Fiction in the Aristotelian Tradition* (Princeton: Princeton University Press, 1986), 75. The parallelism of Eriugena and Aristotle as regards aisthesis as an instrument for thinking with and through the body should be approached with caution. Eriugena, for example, conceives of an inner mental faculty quite able to think without mediating external images. On the other hand, even the limited parallelism helps us to understand how Eriugena's influence continued to remain vigorous throughout the Middle Ages during the rise of Aristotelianism, despite his censure in Paris (1210) and papal condemnation by Honorius III at Sens in 1225.

22. Eriugena, quoting Origen: "Ante nos fuit, qui per voluptatem et sensum praevaricationem ab homine memoraverit esse commissam, in specie serpentis figuram accipiens delectationis, in figura mulieris sensum, in animi mentisque typo virum constituens; quem, sensum videlicet, *aisthesis*, vocant Graeci; decepto autem sensu praevaricatricem mentem asseruit, quam Graeci *nous* vocant" (*PL*, 122:815C) ("There was one before us who claimed that sin was committed through pleasure and sense, reading the image of delight in the form of the serpent, the image of sense in the form of the woman, and establishing the man as the type of spirit (*animus*) and mind (*mens*); the which, namely sense, the Greek call *aisthesis*; he asserts that the mind becomes sinful by means of the deceived sense, the mind which the Greeks call *nous*.")

23. *PL*, 122:816B–817 in Jean Potter's summary: John the Scot, *Periphyseon: On the Division of Nature*, edited and translated by Myra L. Ulfelder, summaries by Jean Potter (Indianapolis: Bobbs-Merrill, 1976), 266.

24. "Je me figure que nos 'trobairiz,' esclaves de la tradition, incapables d'un effort d'analyse, se sont bornées à exploiter des thèmes connus, à user d'un formulaire courant, en invertissant simplement les rôles. Il n'y aurait là que des exercices littéraires, au reste non dénués de mérite. Hypothèse pour hypothèse, il me paraît plus naturel de prêter à ces femmes 'nobles et bien enseignées' une certaine paresse d'esprit, une évidente faute de goût, que ce choquant oubli de toute pudeur et de toute convenance" (Jeanroy, 1:316–17).

25. Mary Jacobus, "The Difference of View," in her *Reading Woman: Essays in Feminist Criticism* (New York: Columbia University Press, 1986), 28.

26. *Chanter M'Estuet: Songs of the Trouvères*, ed. Samuel N. Rosenberg and Hans Tischler (Bloomington: Indiana University Press, 1981), 18.

27. Gaston Paris was offended by the "Chanson de mal mariée" which presented marriage, "'comme un servage auquel la femme a le droit de se dérober, et le mari jaloux comme un ennemi contre lequel tout est permis,'

quoiqu'on n'ait rien a lui reprocher, sinon précisément d'être le mari." Paris, *Mélanges de littérature française,* 601. Quoted by Jeanroy, 2: 302.

28. For a further development of this concept, see my "Rewriting Marriage in the Middle Ages," in *The Legitimacy of the Middle Ages,* ed. S. G. Nichols, special issue of *Romanic Review* 79 (Jan. 1988): 42–62.

29. L. Constans, *Chrestomathie de l'ancien français (IXe–XVe siècles)* (Paris: Champion, 1918), 99, n. 1.

30. Godefroy's entry for *doer* gives the example: "'Veuillez que vostre mere m'ame de s'amour *doe' (Berte,* 864, Scheler)." Frédéric Godefroy, *Dictionnaire de l'ancienne langue française et de tous ses dialectes du IXe au XVe siècle,* 10 vols. (Paris: 1880–1902).

31. Guillaume de Lorris et Jean de Meun, *Le Roman de la rose,* ed. Félix Lecoy, vol. 2 (Paris: Champion, 1966) ll. 8983–91.

32. François Villon, *Le Testament,* ed. Jean Rychner and Albert Henry (Geneva: Droz, 1974), ll. 1557–58.

33. Pierre Guiraud, *Dictionnaire historique, stylistique, rhétorique, étymologique de la littérature érotique* (Paris: Payot, 1978), 120.

34. Quoted in Peter Dronke, *Women Writers of the Middle Ages: A Critical Study of Texts from Perpetua to Marguerite Porete* (Cambridge: Cambridge University Press, 1984), 88.

35. *Perlegi vestram* . . . , Letter of Constance to Baudri, 239, ll. 114–15, 122–23, in *Les Oeuvres poétiques de Baudri de Bourgueil (1046–1130),* ed. Phyllis Abrahams (Paris: Champion, 1926), 346–47.

36. Constance's technique offers a practical application of Aristotle's theory of the psychological image worked out in the third book of *De Anima,* and quoted above.

37. *Indago* possesses the connotations of the hunt, war, and philosophical introspection associated with the metaphoric language of love. *Indago* connotes encircling, closing, when hunters encircle game with nets; the surrounding of enemies in a war; and searching or examining or investigating as in philosophical reflection.

38. *The Songs of Bernart de Ventadorn,* ed. Stephen G. Nichols et al. (Chapel Hill: University of North Carolina Press, 1962), 81.

39. Gabrielle Kussler-Ratyé, "Les Chansons de la comtesse Béatrix de Dia," *Archivum Romanicum* 1 (1917): 161–82.

40. Glynnis M. Cropp, *Le Vocabulaire courtois des troubadours de l'époque classique* (Geneva: Droz, 1975), 108–9.

41. Guilhem IX: "Mout ai estat *cuendes e gais*" ("I was very pleasant and gay") ("Pos de chantar m'es pres talenz," l. 29). Jaufré Rudel: "Et quant hom ve son jauzimen / Es ben razos e d'avinen / Qu'om sia plus *coyndes e guays.*" ("And when a man sees his delight / it is right and fitting / that he be more agreeable and gay") ("Belhs m'es l'estius e·l temps floritz," ll. 5–7).

42. From Heloise's first letter to Abelard. Peter Abelard, *Historia Calamitatum,* ed. Jacques Monfrin (Paris: Vrin, 1978), 116.

The Allegory of Female Authority: Christine de Pizan and Canon Formation

As "France's first professional woman of letters," Christine de Pizan has inhabited an odd position in French literature, singularly out of context in any number of ways. As Italian born and therefore foreign, as a "professional" long before the profession was possible, and finally, as a woman, her unique marginality to the usual contextualizing grids by which one locates an authorial practice makes those frameworks all the more problematic as critical tools.[1] It is a bit of a paradox, then, to realize that the one framework in which Christine's literary practice makes the greatest sense is the canon. I say "the canon" advisedly, for Christine positioned herself with respect to the medieval list of world-class texts—names such as Plato, Aristotle, Cicero, Virgil, Ovid—with the greatest possible specificity. Because more recent candidates for the roster of famous names—such as Dante and Jean de Meun—had not yet been decided in 1405, Christine, it appears, was able to be one of the writers engaged in its formation. Christine's selection of a list of authorities in which her own work was possible and made sense did not merely happen to coincide with the canon subsequently selected by later readers; her own intervention was so aggressively spectacular and well staged that it doubtless had an impact.[2] That she herself has dropped out of the canon of French literature, or has remained a name only in the minor genres (as lyric poet), is a function of later uses of this remarkably powerful tool. In her own hands, the process of canon formation was used to position her work with carefully focused visibility.[3]

Christine's strategy had two flanks: on the one hand, to elevate an

Italian tradition within French literature, specifically by praising Dante and making of him and Boccaccio exemplary models, and on the other, to attack the authority of Jean de Meun, by criticizing him and, along with him, the misogynist tradition of *auctores.* In her attack on the misogynist authority of the *Roman de la Rose*—causing a literary controversy that subsequently evolved during the Renaissance into the more famous *querelle des femmes*—she had directly compared Dante and Jean de Meun, referring to them in significantly different terms.[4] She had written to Pierre Col:

If you wish to hear heaven and hell described in far subtler and more highly theological terms, more profitably, more poetically, and of far greater efficacy, read the book which is called *Dante,* or have it read to you for it is written masterfully in the Florentine language. There you will hear other propositions better founded, with greater subtlety, which will not displease you, and you will be able to profit far more than from your *Romance of the Rose;* it is a hundred times better written; there is no comparison.[5]

As if to underscore the contrast between their two authorities as she sees them, Christine refers to Jean's text by its title; Dante's poem she calls by Dante's name, as if text and author were one, thereby privileging Dante as an *auctor* and denigrating Jean's claim to true authority.[6] Christine's praise of Dante's Italian allegory may have been an attempt to capitalize on the powerful appeal currently felt in France for the beginnings of Italian humanism, and therefore to defend against any handicap her Italian foreignness may have been to her; hence the advice to Pierre Col to have someone explain Dante to him if he doesn't understand Italian.[7] Christine was only the second person in the history of French literature to mention Dante (her colleague at court, Philip de Mézières, has the honor of the official first). She may thus not have expected anyone to recognize the remarkably thoroughgoing use she makes of his structures in the organization of a number of her allegories—as in the *Mutacion de Fortune, Lavision,* or *Le Chemin de Long Estude,* the last title being literally a translation of Dante's homage to Virgil in the first canto of the *Commedia.* Still, her actual practice in the longer narratives in particular is to model herself on Dante's exemplary forms.[8]

Christine's attack on the *Rose*—indeed her engagement in the *Querelle de la Rose*—seems to have been quite self-consciously aimed at establishing the specific possibility of *female* authority.[9] She had closed her first letter with a distinct self-defense: "And let it not be imputed to me a folly, or arrogance, or presumption for me to dare, a mere woman, to reprehend and to criticize an author of such subtlety, whose work is acclaimed by praise, when he, a single man, has dared to undertake to defame and blame without exception an entire sex" (Hicks, 22). Her entry into the canon is thus self-consciously gendered from its inception in this polemic prose. If he speaks with the authority of a century's worth of praise, then she speaks for an entire sex.

Before going on to look at Christine's continuing attack on such misogyny as a means of clearing a space for female entry into the privileged list of texts which Jean has recently entered, it might be useful to ask just what such an antifemale discourse might be doing in Jean's—or anyone else's book. In a recent attempt to interpret the significance of medieval misogyny as a pervasive discourse that cuts across many generic boundaries, R. Howard Bloch has pinpointed its character as "a citational mode whose rhetorical thrust is to displace its own source away from anything that might be construed as personal or concessional and toward the sacred authorities whose own existence, as often as not, is the absent . . . Theophrastes."[10] Late medieval misogyny, especially as exemplified by the classic form it takes in the *Roman de la Rose,* mimics the function of the *auctores,* which, as A. J. Minnis describes it, works when "later writers . . . use extracts from [an author's] works as sententious statements or *auctoritates* . . . or employed them as literary models."[11] Jean de Meun typically defends himself against charges of obscenity and misogyny lodged by an imaginary female readership with an appeal to the *auctores:*

> And furthermore, most honorable dames,
> If you think I say things that are not true,
> Say not I lie, but search authorities
> Who've written in their books what I have said
> And shall. In no respect speak I untruth
> Unless wise men who wrote the ancient books
> Were lying, too. They all agree with me
> When manners feminine they chronicle.   (15215–24)[12]

Jean here imagines the very quarrel a female reader such as Christine would bring, and answers it with an appeal to the *auctores:* he was only following what wise men had already written in ancient books.

Other writers use this same maneuver in a similar way. It is perhaps deeply instructive of the fundamental connection between literary misogyny and the authority of the *auctores* that the character whom Chaucer uses in the *Canturbury Tales* to critique authority explicitly is the Wife of Bath: "Experience, though noon auctoritee / Were in this world, is right ynogh for me." She reasons by directly counterposing authority and experience. Even more explicitly, of course, she attacks the named tradition of misogyny, aggressively and literally going to the source and ripping pages out of the clerk Jankyn's, her last husband's, misogynist compilation. As she reasons:

> Who peyntede the leon, tel me who?
> By God! if wommen hadde writen stories,
> As clerkes han withinne hire oratories,
> They wolde han writen of men moore wikkedness
> Than al the mark of Adam may redresse.
> (Wife of Bath's Prologue, 692–96)[13]

As mesmerizing as such an authentic-sounding voice may seem, however, it is necessary to realize that the Wife here only opens up the possibility of an experientially based literature opposed to "auctorité"; Chaucer interdicts such a discourse, however, as different and original as it might be, by giving the Wife so potentially tragic a character.[14] Indeed, the most important thing Chaucer's Wife may be able to teach us is that the discursive slot in the literary system which allows for greatest resistance to authority, Chaucer has already labeled "female writer." When Dame Alice imagines the possibility of different stories, narrating female points of view, through her Chaucer himself imagines the possibility of a literature based on the decorum of actual, individual, nonscripted experience: by further labeling this radically new discursive place the "female-author position," he of course culturally undermines it. So too, not surprisingly, Alice is a figure who uses a great lot of full-blown, dirty words, made all the more wonderfully vulgar by her fake French euphemisms: she is a character whose speech Chaucer claims he merely records.[15] The discursive position of the female objector to misogyny—and more fundamentally, objector to the masculinist system of *auctores* which misogyny so paradigmatically mimics in its excess—would appear to exist as a possibility already authorized by the literary system. That such an option was available is demonstrated by Chaucer's characterization of the Wife of Bath.[16]

There are doubtless many reasons for such a persistent misogynistic context to writers' defenses against an illegitimate originality. The fundamental denial to women of social access to the institutions where the scriptoral tradition of the *auctores* were preserved (in its monachal, institutionalized scriptedness) would have made the mention of women a convenient boundary marker for any transgression over the line of traditional authority (as Boccaccio does in creating the *Decameron,* a very different generic undertaking from, for instance, the *Genealogy of the Gods*).[17] Chaucer's Wife of Bath marks the same boundary when she assumes clerks and women do not get along: "Therefore no womman of no clerk is preysed" (706). Any writer working in the vernacular, writing the mother tongue (such as Jean, Boccaccio, or Chaucer), specifically not writing in Latin (and even, as with Boccaccio's *De Mulieribus Claris,* sometimes then too), might feel particularly compelled to make a disclaimer about the position of his text in relationship to social arenas labeled marginal to canonical authority by the presence of women.[18]

Of course, these writers all knew actual women would be in their audiences and might actually have real objections to make. But the misogynist comment in the negative references to women would have functioned far more fundamentally as a code for signaling an unorthodox textual status and an experimental generic category (i.e., "original work"): the texts of social entertainment are to be judged differently from works of a more serious genre. Whatever its ultimate function in the literary system, however, it is important to realize that the misogyny of these disclaimers of intentional authority are ubiquitously present in the tradition Christine inherits.

Christine specifically attacks the *Rose* in terms of decorum; in essence, she merely steps into the place already assigned the "female objector" by the poem. She refuses to accept that Jean (now an authority himself) must only follow what his characters might plausibly say, and not what he himself might think. He himself is responsible for the immoral effects of his characters' language. Yet because she also recognizes the necessity of decorum for a given character's language, Christine objects to using vulgar terms for the sexual parts of the human body not only because such terms derogate the proper and natural function of sexuality, but most importantly because such language is most inappropriate to a character such as Lady Reason (Hicks, 13–14). In this she doubles up the argument from decorum: Lady Reason must not use vulgar terms both because of her literary status and also because of her social "gender." "Real" women don't use such language. "Too much is treated dishonorably in many parts . . . when the personage he calls Reason names the secret members plainly by name" (Hicks, 13). The problem comes up because, in telling the story of Saturn's castration by

Jupiter, Jean de Meun had made his Lady Reason use the slang term for testicles, *coilles*—for which "balls" might be a contemporary slang translation.[19] Christine's critique of Jean has drawn much criticism over the centuries, but her objection to the language of the castration story pinpoints her greatest move against Jean in the *Cité des Dames*—as well as her remarkable swerve away from the authority of her second major *auctor* in the *Cité*, Boccaccio's *De Mulieribus Claris*.[20] Her rewrite of her *auctores* goes straight to the heart of a castration anxiety that may be said to be the originary moment for the misogyny in the texts of both the *Rose* and the *De Claris*.[21] Reason's impolite language in Jean's text is the cause for which the lover dismisses Lady Reason as a figure of authority and rejects her kind of love: the lover specifically asks for "quelque cortaise parole." Thus Jean anticipates the kind of response readers like Christine would have and makes it part of his text. The canon in which Jean's text would form a major part makes "too polite" language the excluded style. The lover's foolish rejection of a word, however, motivates the rest of the plot: in rejecting Reason, the lover turns to all the other dramatis personae of the poem. A variety of interpretations is given throughout the poem to explicate the significance of Saturn's loss of his genitals; such repetition alerts us to the importance of the question to style, and to the fact that Jean's text aims to get the implications of idolatry inherent in the "polite style" understood aright.[22]

Christine finds none of the story amusing or important: but when she also objects with equal vehemence to the use of euphemism for talking about sexual intercourse, which, she argues, is just as inflammatory as the vulgar and direct terms, we see her subtly telescope Jean's stylistic differentiations into a single moral critique of Jean's behavior, as a man. "He names them by poetic but nonetheless explicit words which are a hundred times more enticing and more alluring and more sensual to those who are inclined in that way, than if he had named them by their proper names" (Hicks, 124–25).

Christine's critique of Jean de Meun's vulgarity reveals quite nicely her understanding of the poem's consideration of the proper relation between textual word and allegorical referent, although she chooses to recast her critique in terms of Jean's personal, postlapsarian moral responsibilities, thereby playing into a new conception of authorship which includes a familiarity that allows one to fault an *auctor* for perceived personal failings.[23] Even more importantly however, her moral concerns over the sexual stylistics of Jean's poem feed into her objections against the defamation of women throughout the text. Jean's defenders attempted to deflect the criticisms of misogyny by using the appeal both to authorities and to the mimetic method of drama: it was decorous for certain characters to speak profanely, and in derision of women. Christine's response is to say:

You respond . . . that Master Jean de Meun introduced characters into his book, and made each one speak fittingly, according to what pertained to him. I readily admit that the proper equipment is necessary for any particular game, but the will of the player manipulates such equipment to his own purpose. And it is clearly true (may it not displease you) that he was at fault in attributing to some of his characters functions which do not properly belong to them. (Hicks, 130)[24]

Christine's refusal to accept such an excuse, here dressed-out as the fidelity with which the verisimilar copier treats his "real" models, not only rejects claims of irresponsibility; it implicitly undermines Jean's appeal to the foundation of a scripted tradition of *auctores*. In both cases, Christine sees Jean pursuing his own purposes, for which he should be held responsible as author. For Christine to criticize misogyny is thus to criticize, at least in part, the assumptions upon which the appeal to the authority of *auctores* is based.

That Chaucer chose to model Dame Alice on La Vielle from the *Roman de la Rose*, a character against whom Christine lodges particular complaints, reveals perhaps that both writers had noses for a most alluring interstice within the literary system. Such an unruly woman has traditionally offered men a means for criticizing established authority—the Old Woman offers a similarly bawdy and outrageous freedom to Jean de Meun himself, whereby he reorganizes the tenor of Guillaume's courtly tone. So, too, men masquerade as unruly women whenever they comedically (or seriously) wish to evade the rules of the system.[25] The radical potentialities of the Wife of Bath, of course, are partly undermined by Chaucer's ultimate dismissal of her unhappy and tragic case: she is, as Robert Hanning has recently pointed out, a creation made of "recycled components from various literary traditions of anti-feminism."[26] This origin provides something of a systemic limit: "Try as she (and Chaucer) might," so Lee Patterson observes, "she remains confined within the prison house of masculine language; she brilliantly rearranges and deforms her authorities to enable them to disclose new areas of experience, but she remains dependent on them for her voice."[27] Christine's own objections to the misogynist tradition and the system of authorities it emblematizes are, not surprisingly, rather different from Chaucer's habitation of a potential discursive position through the character of the Wife of Bath, though the difference is not necessarily that Alice is a textual creature and Christine a "real" human being. If Dame Alice is made a victim of the literary system she attacks, then Christine takes care to manipulate it as fully as possible, authorizing her own practice in rewriting a tradition of literature and redefining women as they "naturally" are.

Christine's attack on misogyny begins with the subtly unorthodox opening scene of her *Cité des Dames*. Surrounded by books, Christine sits in her study, enjoying her learned tasks until she comes across a volume of antifemale vituperation, which, although itself of no authority, reminds her that there is an entire literature that attacks women. The thought disturbs her so deeply that, lamenting to God that she was ever born into a female body, she falls into a deep despondency. As she sits in her melancholy stupor, a vision breaks in upon her, of three women who have come to instruct her about the matter of woman—Reason, Rectitude (*Droit ture*), and Justice.

The three ladies have singularly chosen Christine to construct a fortified city as a place of refuge from misogynist attack; women have for too long remained vulnerable. Indeed, much like the rose, so ill-protected at the center of the garden in the *Roman de la Rose*, they have remained "exposed like a field without a surrounding hedge."[28] Christine has been chosen to construct this city specifically because of her long and continual study—"Pour la grant amour que tu as a l'inquisicion de choses vrayes par long et continual estude" (Curnow, 628). Lady Reason here virtually cites Christine's translated Dantesque title, *Le Chemin de Long Estude*. And only at this point does she finally name herself: "I am called Lady Reason; you see that you are in good hands. For the time being then, I will say no more" (Richards, 12). With Lady Reason's announcement of her identity, Christine is rewriting the famous moment of interview between Amant and Raison in the *Roman de la Rose*. She rewrites it specifically by recasting her meeting with Reason in terms of Dante's protestation in his first interview with Virgil. "Io non Enëa, io non Paulo sono" (*Inf.* 2:31–2). Christine interprets Dante's self-doubt with a reference to the doubting Saint Thomas. "I am not Saint Thomas the Apostle, who through divine grace built a rich palace in heaven for the king of India" (Richards, 15).

Then Christine introduces two more female figures of authority who will answer the arguments made by the misogynist characters in the *Rose*. After each of the three guides introduces herself (and after Justice, the third, addresses Christine directly), Reason returns to her agenda of educating Christine about the tradition of *auctores*. "Get up, daughter! Without waiting any longer, let us go the Field of Letters. There the City of Ladies will be founded on a flat and fertile plain. . . . Take the pick of your understanding and dig and clear out a ditch wherever you see the marks of my ruler, and I will help you carry away the earth on my own shoulders" (Richards, 16).

In the economy of allegorical metaphor, the clearing of the Field of Letters represents the readjustment of the canon to allow for the insertion of the *Cité* as a corrective answer to the tradition of medieval misogyny. The first basketful of dirt to be removed is formed by Christine's asking if it is because of nature that the tradition of *auctores* is misogynist: "But please tell me why and for what reason different authors have spoken against women in their books, since I already know from you that this is wrong; tell me if Nature makes man so inclined or whether they do it out of hatred" (Richards, 16).

Reason answers her, "Daughter, to give you a way of entering into the question more deeply, I will carry away this first basketful of dirt." Reason explains that, while it is not natural for men to hate women, there are, indeed, many and diverse causes of misogyny, which have moved "those authors in their books" to blame women. Some do so with a good intention—in order to warn men away from bad women or from their own lustful interests—but even these men are not to be excused, for their attacks are harmful, as Christine has already shown in her other writings. Significantly, the habit of referring to other texts in her corpus which touch the same issues establishes Christine herself as one of the authorities to which Reason can appeal. Reason explains to Christine: "So now throw aside these black, dirty, and uneven stones from your work, for they will never be fitted into the fair edifice of your City." The rubble of misogynist opinion must be cleared away before the city can be built. As part of this process Reason explains how a misogynist tradition can grow: men are moved to attack women out of the defects of their own bodies, out of jealousy, and out of a delight in slander for its own sake; more pervasively still, misogyny grows as part of a literary tradition: "Others, in order to show they have read many books, base their own writings on what they have found in books and repeat what other writers have said and cite different authors" (Richard, 18). As Bloch has suggested, the citational mode of misogyny has all the power of a self-perpetuating canon; Reason denounces those who slander women for a variety of personal reasons, but leaves for last her answer to those who attack women simply in order to write. A tradition of mindless citation, misogyny is one among many discourses which can easily lead to empty imitation. The ground for any literary endeavor would need to be cleared of such detritus. But misogyny stands as the paradigm of bad writing; as Bloch suggests, it is a discourse peculiarly marked by the mere citation of borrowed authority.

As the first stone to be placed in the newly cleared space, the legend of Semiramis seems at first glance to be an exceedingly strange choice; it is both the foundation stone of the city and the initiating structure in the architecture of Christine's text.[29] "Take the trowel of your pen and ready yourself to lay down bricks and labor diligently, for you can see here a great and large stone which I want to be the first placed as the foundation of your City" (38, my translation).

Shockingly, Christine bases her city on one of the most scandalous foundations in the field of letters: mother-son incest. While her selection of Semiramis bespeaks a resolute refusal from the outset to honor the originary set of anxieties culturally associated with mother-son incest, as in the story of Saturn's castration in the *Roman de la Rose,* the choice of this warrior queen as the first stone in the construction of the city also reveals Christine's profoundly revisionist move against Dante. If Dante is a model privileged over Jean de Meun, he is also a misogynist author whose misemphases must be corrected in order for Christine to articulate a previously missing female tradition. Thus she revises Dante specifically along lines of gender difference.

It is in the very first circle of actual hell, after the antechamber of limbo, that Dante and Virgil come upon the lustful, whirled by the black winds of desire, among whom Virgil immediately identifies Semiramis and Dido. Semiramis is summed up in a single line that is justly famous: it was she who made lust licit in her law—"che libito fe licito in sua legge" (*Inf.* 5:57). Dido killed herself, but, more to the point here, for love of Aeneas she lustfully broke faith with the ashes of her husband Sichaeus. Semiramis's and Dido's passions serve as a warning to Dante's reader of the dangers there are in reading. The question is a complicated one, but engages issues of reader involvement in the text in terms of a moral engagement that we know was important to Christine. In Semiramis and Dido (and in Francesca), Dante exemplifies the kind of reading he hopes his readers will *not* perform with his text: Authurian romance led Francesca astray, just as Virgil's Dido had led Saint Augustine astray; so Dante warns against the power that literature has to do ill, and offers the hope that his poem, led by Virgil, will have a different outcome.

More importantly for Christine, Dante's two queens, one of Babylon and one of Carthage, represent as well a complex history of the city, which is also a complicated and deeply interwoven literary history. In this twin civic and literary history lie the possible causes for Christine's deeply scandalous selection of Semiramis as the foundation stone for her imagined city. As Giuseppe Mazzotta has explained, the middle term between the Rome of Virgil and the Rome of Dante is Augustine's *Civitas Dei*.[30] So too, Christine named her own *Cité des Dames* after Augustine's *City of God*. In the *Cité* she calls him specifically "mon seigneur St. Augustin" (659), and, like Dante, Augustine is one of her central *auctores*. Not surprisingly, her selection of Semiramis as the first story is profoundly determined by her relationship to the tradition of the city left her by Augustine and Dante. In the first circle of hell, Dante and Virgil confront, in the figures of Semiramis and Dido, representatives of two versions of the city which are opposed to the imperial legitimacy of Rome. By celebrating Rome, Dante of course has radically revised Augustine. Augustine had written in *The City of God* against the pagan authority of Roman Virgil, making of Rome a version of the *civitas diaboli*, that dead and lustful city that was typified by the biblical Babylon, and was opposed to the new Jerusalem, the proper *civitas dei*. Interestingly, Augustine served the *civitas dei* in a church not far from Carthage—the city that in Virgil's *Aeneid* had stood as the antithesis of Rome. Dante reorganized Augustine's opposition between worldly Rome and heavenly Jerusalem, making Florence the demonic Babylon and reserving for an idealized imperial Rome a politically necessary place in the creation of the *civitas dei*. Resting on Rome's imperial laws, the Pax Romana had been, and continued to be, according to Dante, necessary for the creation of a true city where the Church could serve God. Dante's sense of the central importance of Rome depended, as Joan Ferrante argues, on its law—a law distinctly different from Semiramis's libidinous *legge*.[31]

Dante most obviously signals his rewrite of Augustine's rewrite of

Virgil by placing the Roman poet himself within the poem. But he also signals it by having Virgil confront the representative of Carthage, that other African city he had so tragically opposed to Rome in his epic. Augustine had most famously confessed that in his youth, a rebel to God's love, he had wept for the death of Dido, an African queen, "quia se occidit ab amore," she who had died for love. "You I did not love," he confesses to God. "Against you I committed fornication . . . but this was not what I wept for: I wept for dead Dido 'who by the sword pursued a way extreme,' meanwhile myself following a more extreme way" (cited by Mazzotta, 168n). If, as Giuseppe Mazzotta argues, Dante differs from the youthful Augustine by being able to distinguish between Dido and Aeneas, condemning Dido's passion but condoning Aeneas' transcendence of it, then Christine differs further, for she overturns Dante's distinction. She pursues what would seem to be a preconversion Augustinian reading of Dido's story and has *Droitture*, in the second section of the *Cité des Dames*, narrate the Carthaginian queen's tragic end in a grouping that includes stories of other women who have been constant in love. Dido's building of her city—her escape from her evil brother, the clever trick with the bull hide, the city's actual construction—finds a logical place in the first section of the *Cité* when Reason tells her story, along with that of Semiramis and those of other city builders. So radically different is Christine's version of the private part of Dido's life as an example of perfect constancy, however, that it will be useful to sense the tone in which Christine can so directly contradict Dante's judgment on the queen's character. *Droitture* explains:

Dido's love for Aeneas was far greater than his love for her, for even after he had given her his pledge never to take any other woman and to be hers forever, he left her even though she had restored and enriched him with property and ease, his ships refreshed, repaired, and placed in order, filled with treasure and wealth, like a woman who had spared no expense where her heart was involved. He departed at night, secretly and treacherously, without farewells and without her knowledge. This was how he repaid his hostess. (Richards, 189)

Christine's subtle resistance to the tradition of opposed cities she inherited from Augustine and Dante is persistent all along the line of its various deployments; she reorganizes it and marshalls its resonance to empower a quite specific rewriting of her carefully selected precursors in the creation of her own city. If Dido is condemned by Dante to the first circle for unfaithfulness, Christine faults Aeneas for a similar infidelity and ingratitude. So too, Christine realizes that there are two cities as well, as in Augustine's *City of God*—the Amazonian empire that failed to last, not because it was evil but because it was politically overpowered, and the one Christine is writing, her book of the city. For Christine, both Dido and Semiramis are city builders first and foremost. What Augustine and Dante condemn, Christine celebrates. If Babylon and Carthage are illicit because of their female builders, if they are opposed to the true Jerusalem or to Rome, for Christine they become original sites for an alternate tradition of civilization, all of which—Athens, Rome, Carthage, Paris—are shown to have been nurtured by women.

As a point of origin, lodged in the *Commedia*'s first architectural feature, Dante's Semiramis stands for a law opposed to the one that decrees the architecture down which Virgil and Dante scramble in the *Inferno*. Christine takes Dante's illicit "legge" and gives to it her own legitimacy, making it provide the foundation—rather literally in terms of her own architectural metaphor—for an alternate tradition of female authority. Yet if the model provided by Dante's dismissal of her "legge" helped Christine to place Semiramis *first*, it is Christine's rewrite of Boccaccio which provides the details of her narrative.[32]

That Christine thereby installs her *Cité des Dames* as a correction of the initial step in Dante's discourse of the city in the *Commedia* demonstrates the deeply resonant use to which she put the canon she constructed for herself. In the same manner she also rewrites a major moment in the history of Thebes, making an Antigone figure (Polyneices' wife, Argia) into a successful warrior who leads a female attack on the city in revenge and without the aid of Theseus (Curnow, 831; Richards, 126). Christine thereby rewrites Boccaccio's one attempt at epic in the *Teseida*, the second book of which concerns Theseus' triumphant siege of Thebes.[33] Babylon recurs throughout her text: when a famous Greek sibyl is given a Babylonian origin (Curnow, 788; Richards, 100), and when the legend of Pyramus and Thisbe is recounted from Ovid in order to demonstrate the loyalty of female passion (Curnow, 933–35; Richards, 190–92).

Such an emphasis on a rescripted tradition for a "city" founded and fostered by women, sets up a more self-consciously political construct than Jean de Meun's various gardens. The civic emphasis itself puts Christine into a proto-Renaissance Italian tradition of civic humanism, one interested in the power relations of the "polis." It may seem something of a paradox that investigation into Christine's resonant relation to the literary canon should rediscover the importance of politics in her work—and politics not only as it should be practiced in the ideal city she constructs in the text of the *Cité*, but also as it takes place in the real city.

Like Dante, she was very concerned with contemporary politics and spent a great deal of energy writing political prose; one might even say she worked as something of a propagandist for the Duke of Burgundy during the series of civil wars which swept France at the opening of the fifteenth century.[34] It had been in fact on the basis of her (very conservative) politics that she had come back into the canon in the nineteenth century, with Raimon Thomassy's study of her political writings in 1838, as well as for her poem about Joan of Arc.[35]

One of the first two to mention Dante in French literature, Christine was also one of only two poets to write about Joan of Arc during the warrior saint's lifetime. The last text to come from the pen of Christine de Pizan, the *Ditié de Jehanne D'Arc*, comprises in part Christine's warning to the city of Paris to surrender to the Maid and her king lest it be subject to serious reprisal for its disloyalty. Christine stages her celebration of the woman in terms of the resistance by a city to that woman's authority. It is, of course, actually quite sensible that Christine would address the last part of her poem to the city she had to flee because of civil war, the city where she had lived out her life as a professional writer. But the reference to the city is not only a historically logical fact; it is, when seen in terms of Christine's persistent rescripting of warrior-women's relationships to famous cities in the *Cité des Dames*, resonant literary topos.

> Oh Paris, how could you be so ill advised?
> Foolish inhabitants, you are lacking in trust!
> Do you prefer to be laid waste, Paris,
> rather than to make peace with your prince.[36]

The canon, as we know, is not merely a literary instrument, but a social one as well. Christine's access to it, as a member of a group that was in the process of picking the texts, both allowed and supported her appeal to speak from the politically central position she inhabited—from which she speaks to the city of Paris in this poem. She speaks directly to Joan of Arc—addressing her as "Tu Jehanne" (l. 169)—using the singular authority she had built for herself as female author—an authority constructed with great care out of the positions the literary system initially allowed for a woman to speak in criticism against it. In a sense, Christine began the process of canonizing Joan, by first inserting *herself* into the canon. The best way of now making Christine's *Cité des Dames* a major text in our privileged list of texts is to begin to perceive with what subtlety and savvy sensitivity she positioned that text within the canon, turning the previously silenced marginality of women into a politically central position in the medieval city just on the brink of the Renaissance.

Notes

1. *Jacqueline Cerquilini, "L'Etrangère," Revue des Langues Romanes* 92 (1988): 239–51, argues that Christine's foreignness helped cause her constitution of herself as a writing subject: "Fille de l'ailleurs devenue fils de soi-meme, c'est-à-dire s'étant constitutée en sujet de l'écriture" (244).

2. Christine de Pizan was part of a group of people who were engaged in introducing Italian authors to French readers. For instance, about the time Christine was using Boccaccio in the *Cité des Dames*, Laurent Premierfait was engaged in translating Boccaccio's works; for discussion of the shared project of introducing things Italian to French culture, see Charity Canon Willard, *Christine de Pizan: Her Life and Works, A Biography* (New York: Persea Books, 1984), 138. Further references appear in the text, as do references to any work cited more than once.

3. See John Guillory, "The Ideology of Canon-Formation: T. S. Eliot and Cleanth Brooks," *Critical Inquiry* 10 (1983): 173–98.

4. For a discussion of Christine's entry into public Parisian intellectual life with this attack on the authority of Jean de Meun, see Pierre-Yves Badel, *Le Roman de la Rose au XIVe siècle: Etude de la réception de l'oeuvre*, (Geneva: Librairie Droz, 1980), 411–46.

5. *Le Débat Sur Le Roman de la Rose*, ed. Eric Hicks (Paris: Editions Honoré Champion, 1977), 141–42; Joseph L. Baird and John R. Kane, trans., *La Querelle de la Rose: Letters and Documents*, North Carolina Studies in the Romance Languages and Literatures (Chapel Hill: Department of Romance Languages, University of North Carolina, 1978), emphasis mine.

6. For a discussion of Christine's establishment of her own authority against Jean's in the *querelle de la Rose*, see Kevin Brownlee, "The Discourse of the Self," *Romanic Review* 59 (1988): 213–21.

7. Willard (74) points out that the exchange of letters in the *Rose* controversy may itself have owed something to the Italian humanist practice of engaging in literary debates.

8. She has, for instance, Lady Justice, specifically the third figure of authority to address her in the *Cité des Dames*, call her by name. Such number play may be a reference to Beatrice's singular naming of Dante in the *Commedia* at the point of the transferral of authority between Virgil and Beatrice. Her decision to devote the third section of the *Cité* to the martyrs may owe something to Dante's practice in the *Commedia*, the third section of which is also populated by saints. All quotations of the *Cité* are from "*Le Livre de la Cité des Dames*": A Critical Edition," ed. Maureen Curnow (Diss., Vanderbilt University, 1975).

9. "La querelle lui permet de conforter sa réputation de femme de letters et

de hâter une ascension que couronne, le 23 juin 1402, une première édition de ses oeuvres complètes" Badel, 436. In 1616, Ben Jonson became the first English "author" to publish his nonposthumous collected *Works;* Christine's manuscript collection predates his by 204 years.

10. Howard Bloch, "Medieval Misogyny," *Representations* 20 (1987): 6. Bloch posits a far more general relationship between misogyny and the scandal of the fictive than would a more social historical approach. Thus: "The danger of woman . . . is that of literature itself" (20).

11. A. J. Minnis, *Medieval Theory of Authorship: Scholastic Literary Attitudes in the Later Middle Ages,* 2d ed. (Philadelphia: University of Pennsylvania Press, 1988), 10.

12. Guillaume de Lorris and Jean de Meun, *Le Roman de la Rose,* ed. Ernest Langlois 5 vols. (Paris: Librairie Ancienne Edouard Champion, 1922), vol. 4; Guillaume de Lorris and Jean de Meun, *The Romance of the Rose,* trans. Harry W. Robbins, ed. Charles W. Dunn (New York: Dutton, 1962), 320.

13. *The Works of Geoffrey Chaucer,* 2d ed., ed. F. N. Robinson (Boston: Houghton Mifflin, 1957).

14. For a defense of the Wife's discursive tactics, see Barrie Ruth Strauss, "The Subversive Discourse of the Wife of Bath: Phallocentric Discourse and the Imprisonment of Criticism," *ELH* (1988): 527–54.

15. In defense of his vulgarity Chaucer also appeals to the highest authority: "Crist spake hymself ful brode in hooly write / And wel ye woot no vileynye is it" (Gen. Prol. 741–42). For a discussion of the relationship between canon formation and "grammaticalness," or the relationship between divergent standards of correctness often registered as a difference between spoken and written language, which has bearing on the problem of Christine's objections to vulgar language, see John Guillory, "Canonical and Non-Canonical: A Critique of the Current Debate," *ELH* (1987): 483–527.

16. The texts of misogyny, as it were, carry embedded within them the twin parts of the tradition of "excuse"—both the appeal to *auctores* (as in Jean de Meun), and the newer more "verisimilar," mimetic excuse, that the writer simply copies what actual people actually say. Thus, in the *Decameron* (to which Christine refers in the *Cité*), Boccaccio also uses the "compiler's excuse" to underline, paradoxically, his own peculiarly original achievement in vernacular literature. "I could only transcribe the stories as they were actually told, which means that if the ladies who told them had told them better, I should have written them better. But even if one could assume that I was the inventor [*l'inventore*] as well as the scribe [*lo scrittore*] of these stories (which was not the case), I still insist that I would not feel ashamed if some fell short of perfection, for there is no craftsman other than God whose work is whole and faultless in every respect" (Cited in Minnis, 205).

17. Willard (45) argues that Christine's actual entry into letters was by way of the scribal workshop. She may have at first functioned as a scribe herself, just as other women copyists and illuminators were working in the newly energetic book trade of the time; Christine appears to have organized her own workshop and was used to overseeing the production of manuscripts that became the elaborate presentation copies to patrons such as the dukes of Berry and Burgundy and Queen Isabeau of Bavaria. Sandra L. Hindman, *Christine de Pizan's* Epistre Othá: *Painting and Politics at the Court of Charles VI* (Toronto: Pontifical Insti-

tute of Mediaeval Studies, 1986), 13, argues that Christine is France's first woman "publisher" as well as woman of letters and suggests that she was deeply engaged in all phases of book production, specifically providing her illuminators with detailed programs for the cycles of miniatures in manuscripts of her works (77–89).

18. In the controversy over the *Roman de la Rose,* Pierre Col, one of Christine's more persistent opponents, makes clear through his remarkably thoughtless anachronism the association of women with the vernacular: "Ovide, quant il escript *L'Art d'amours,* il escript en latin, lequel n'entendent fammes" ("When Ovid wrote the *Art of Love,* he wrote in Latin, which women did not understand") (Hicks, 105; Baird and Kane, 108).

19. Guillaume de Lorris and Jean de Meun, *Le Roman de la Rose,* ed. Félix Lecoy, vol. 1 (Paris: Champion, 1965), l. 5507.

20. For a recent attack see Sheila Delany, "'Mothers to Think Back Through': Who Are They? The Ambiguous Example of Christine de Pizan," in *Medieval Texts and Contemporary Readers,* ed. Laurie A. Finke and Martin B. Shichtman (Ithaca, N.Y.: Cornell University Press, 1987), 177–200.

21. When Lady Reason explains that Ovid turned to writing attacks on women only after he had been punished for his political and sexual transgressions by being "diffourmez de ses membres" (i.e., castrated), Christine apparently points to this origin (Curnow, 648). The argument about Ovid was, of course, conventional, but in the context of the *Cité's* rejection of the whole misogynist tradition, Christine would appear to anticipate a series of modern feminist critiques of Freudian theories about the oedipal complex and female sexuality. See, in particular, Hélène Cixous, "The Laugh of the Medusa," *Signs* 1 (1976), 875–93; and Luce Irigaray, *Speculum of the Other Woman,* trans. Gillian Gill (Ithaca, N.Y.: Cornell University Press, 1985).

22. For further discussion of the perhaps defensible tactic Jean de Meun uses and his revision of his precursors, see my "Allegory, Allegoresis, and the Deallegorization of Language: The *Roman de la Rose,* the *De planctu naturae,* and the *Parlement of Foules,*" in *Allegory, Myth, and Symbol,* ed. Morton Bloomfield (Cambridge, Mass.: Harvard University Press, 1981), 163–86.

23. Minnis's example is Boccaccio's censure of Dante (214–15).

24. See also: "Et la laidure qui la est recordee des femmes, dient pluseurs en lui excusant que c'est la Jalous qui parle, a voirement fair ainsi comme Dieu parla par la bouche Jeremie" (Hicks, 15) ("And the ugliness about women which is there recorded, many say in excusing him that it is the Jealous Husband who speaks, just as God speaks through the mouth of Jeremiah"). Jean Gerson's position is articulated at greater length and in terms of legal statute: "If someone writes notorious books and, by means of introduced characters, defames some person, whether of low or noble or illegitimate birth, the law holds such a writer to be wicked and deserving of punishment" (Baird and Kane, 80); "Aucun escripra libelles diffamatoire d'une personne, soit de petit estat ou non — soit neis mauvaise —, et soit par personnaige: les drois jugent ung tel estre a pugnir et infame" (Hicks, 72).

25. For a classic discussion of the political uses of the unruly woman in early modern France, see Natalie Zemon Davies, "Woman on Top," in her *Society and Culture in Early Modern France* (Stanford: Stanford University Press, 1977).

26. Robert W. Hanning, "'I Shal Finde it in a Maner Glose': Versions of Textual Harassment in Medieval Literature," in *Medieval Texts and Contemporary Readers,* 48.

27. Lee Patterson, "'For the Wyves love of Bathe': Feminine Rhetoric and Poetic Resolution in the *Roman de la Rose* and the *Canterbury Tales*," *Speculum* 58 (1983): 682.

28. Earl Jeffrey Richards, trans., *The Book of the City of Ladies* (New York: Persea Books, 1982), 10. All translations of the *Cité* are from this edition.

29. This architectural metaphor and its use of "stones" may resonate with textual reference to the punning on Peter's name — Pierre — the first stone upon which Christ built his church. The same pun underlies *Piers Plowman:* "Petrus, id est Christus." If this verbal play animates Christine's metaphor, it gives special weight to Psalms 118.22 (quoted in Matthew 21.42), "The stone which the builders rejected, the same is become the head of the corner" (Authorized Version), as an explanation of Semiramis's exclusion from legitimate tradition. That the stones construct a city, not a church, reveals Christine's early civic humanism as well as a strong anticlerical bent, seen directly in her explicit criticism of the imperial hierarchy after the Donation of Constantine (Curnow, 898).

30. Giuseppe Mazzotta, *Dante Poet of the Desert; History and Allegory in the Divine Comedy* (Princeton: Princeton University Press, 1979), 160–75.

31. Joan Ferrante, *The Political Vision of the Divine Comedy* (Princeton: Princeton University Press, 1984), 47–52.

32. For a discussion of the importance of the incest taboo as a means of controlling women, see Gayle Rubin, "The Traffic in Women: Notes on the Political Economy of Sex," in *Toward an Anthropology of Women*, ed. Rayna Reiter (New York: Monthly Review Press, 1975), 157–210. See also Claude Levi-Strauss, *The Elementary Structures of Kinship* (Boston: Beacon Press, 1969): "The incest prohibition is at once on the threshold of culture, in culture, and in one sense . . . culture itself" (12). Rubin objects to some of the implications of this evaluation of the identity of the taboo and of culture: "Since [Levi-Strauss] argues that the incest taboo and the result of its application constitute the origin of culture, it can be deduced that the [oppression of women] occurred with the origin of culture, and is a prerequisite of culture" (176). Rubin instead argues for the need to understand the function of a fully analyzed "sex/gender system" within the "imperatives of social systems" (182).

33. Christine had already told the entire story of Thebes, from the birth of Oedipus to Theseus's triumph over Creon in the *Mutacion de Fortune*, 4 vols., ed. Susan Solente (Paris: Editions A. J. Picard, 1959), 4:12069–13356. For Boccaccio's text, see the *Teseida*, ed. Salvatore Battaglia (Florence: Sansoni, 1938).

34. For a very critical assessment of Christine's politics, see Delany. For a more sympathetic review of Christine's conservatism, see Willard, 180–85.

35. See Willard, 222. The antimisogynist *Cité des Dames*, although it has been recently printed in a modern French version, has yet to be published in a critical edition for use in schools (i.e., in the strictest sense of the term, it is not canonical in French). The *Cité* has been published in English translation twice, once in 1521 and again in 1982.

36. Christine de Pizan, *Ditié de Jehanne D'Arc*, ed. Angus J. Kennedy and Kenneth Varty (Oxford: Society for the Study of Mediaeval Languages and Literature, 1977), 38, 49.

8 ENGLISH SHOWALTER, JR.

Writing Off the Stage:
Women Authors and
Eighteenth-Century Theater

The great playwrights of the Century of Louis XIV endowed their nation with a corpus of dramatic literature that, for a century and a half, defined literary greatness for the French. The preeminence of the Comédie française depended on more than taste and tradition, however; royal institutions ensured that the theater, the easiest genre to regulate, would also be the most secure and lucrative for writers. For simple practical reasons—the number of people involved, the need for a fixed site, the public nature of the spectacle—a clandestine stage was almost inconceivable. The theaters of the fairs and street entertainers occasionally flouted the law with a parody or political satire, but these impromptu performances could not last long. Unlike the broader publishing industry, in short, the theaters were successfully controlled by the state, and authors who wrote for the Comédie française were rewarded with performance royalties, publication privileges similar to a copyright, and memberships in the academies. Although the authors' freedom of expression was severely restricted, their other rights were better protected than in any other mode of publication.

Very few women enjoyed the economic benefits of writing for the stage, however. Barbara Mittman remarks that "the eighteenth century could claim a dozen or more women whose works were performed on the public stages of Paris—a considerable increase over the three or four that the seventeenth century had produced."[1] Mittman's figures are low for both centuries, especially the eighteenth; but simply counting authors gives a misleading impression. Most of the eighteenth-century women playwrights were in some way marginal. At least seven women wrote a play for the Italians, two for the Théâtre des variétés, and one for Nicolet's theater; by the standards of the time, these were automatically less prestigious works, regardless of their intrinsic merit. All but one of those plays, as well as works by four other women, were of one, two, or three acts, and were therefore considered minor. Finally, the majority of these authors wrote only one play that was performed in public. This small output inevitably reduces their significance as playwrights, and the regularity with which women abandoned the theater after one play points to a powerful deterrent force at work.

Although the number of women playwrights in Old Regime France was low, there were some illustrious names, and contrary to Mittman's conclusion, a tradition seems to have begun with some vigor and then died out. In the seventeenth century, Marie-Catherine de Villedieu wrote for the Comédie française in the 1660s before turning exclusively to the novel; before the end of the century she was followed by Catherine Bernard and Antoinette Deshoulières. Between 1700 and 1717, Marie-Anne Barbier had four full-length verse tragedies staged, and Madeleine de Gomez three. But it appears that constraints tightened in the eighteenth century. Barbier and Gomez openly expressed an interest in fame, and they inserted themselves with pride into a tradition of women writers, including Madeleine de Scudéry, Henriette de La Suze, and Antoinette Deshoulières *fille*, as well as her mother and the other dramatists. But from 1717 to 1749, no new plays by women were produced. In 1749 Marie-Anne Du Boccage tried to revive the sense of tradition with *Les Amazones*, but the play failed; and Françoise de Graffigny, whose *Cénie* in 1750 and *La Fille d'Aristide* in 1758 were the last full-length plays at the Comédie française by a woman until the Revolution, sounded a note of modesty and self-deprecation, both in her prefaces and in her private correspondence, and did not want to be regarded as an author or as a bluestocking.

The relative exclusion of women from this field had a far-reaching impact, even though the eighteenth-century French theater has not retained its place in the canon as the seventeenth century's has. Leading tragic dramatists like Crébillon and Voltaire would be stunned to discover that even the best of their numerous tragedies go unread and unstaged today, while "frivolous" novels and tales are studied and respected, and Marivaux is regarded as the century's great dramatist. The continuing revision of the canon has, in recent years, led to the rediscovery of several women novelists—Tencin, Riccoboni, Charrière, for example—who, like their male colleagues, took advantage of the freedom of a minor or forbidden genre to produce an original literature that is still gaining in stature. Given the scant attention now paid to the mainstream theater of numerous prolific male authors like Baculard d'Arnaud, Destouches, Gresset, Houdar de La Motte, La Chaussée, and Marmontel, it would be remarkable if, by modern standards, any of the rare women playwrights had coped more successfully with the limitations of the stage. While one or two of their plays might well claim as much right to inclusion in the recent Pléiade anthology as most of the ones chosen, the rediscovery of lost works is not the only reason for studying them. It is equally important to realize that the institutional privilege of the theater disenfranchised women in fact if not in principle and, in denying them the possibility of writing for the stage, effectively debarred them from writing for a living.

The careers of the four women—Barbier, Gomez, Du Boccage, and Graffigny—who managed at least to have a full-length play staged reveal many of the factors that enabled them to succeed where other women failed, and also many of the obstacles, enacted in regulations or simply established in custom, that only hindered them but discouraged other women entirely. All four began with close connections to the literary world, often to the theater itself. They needed the strong support of male friends, which lent plausibility to the inevitable rumor that a man was the real author. Even when her first play succeeded brilliantly, none of the women made a real career of writing for the stage, although many men of little talent managed it; Barbier's four tragedies and one comedy constitute the greatest number of plays by one woman staged at the Comédie française until George Sand's sixth was produced in 1888. But they did not lose interest in writing; they turned to another genre, or wrote plays without trying to have them produced.

For those who were writing for the income, abandoning the theater entailed a real sacrifice. In rough terms, the author of a five-act play was entitled to one-ninth of the box office receipts, as long as they did not fall below 500 *livres* for two consecutive performances. To illustrate what this might mean, Graffigny's popular play *Cénie* ran for twenty-five performances in 1750 with an average box office of 2,153 *livres*. Actual figures on her royalties are not available but must have been close to 4,000 *livres*. The first edition of her *Lettres d'une Péruvienne*, in 1747, one of the most popular novels of the century, brought her a mere 300 *livres*. Even after the success

of *Cénie,* when Malesherbes helped Graffigny reclaim her rights to
the novel from the original publisher, so that she could bring out a
revised edition with a privilege, she received only 900 *livres.*[2] The
conclusion is inescapable that social and institutional barriers to
staging a play proved a real deterrent to women. As a result, most of
the century's best-known women writers—Tencin, Riccoboni, Charrière, Du Châtelet, Madame Roland—depended for their livelihood
on some other source of income, often a husband or inherited
wealth. For women, writing was sometimes an avocation, sometimes a form of self-expression, sometimes an obsession; but it was
not a livelihood, as it was for a host of male hacks.

The present low regard for eighteenth-century theater is ironic,
for it was a theatrical age. Sociability, one of the era's most highly
prized qualities, was primarily an art of self-presentation. The literature of the time revels both in describing the art and in exposing
the artifice. Men and women played unequal roles, however, and the
theater reflects this situation both in the plays and in the fate of
women playwrights. As Laclos's Marquise de Merteuil explained
with acid precision, Valmont's bad reputation simply becomes part
of his role, even with the virtuous Présidente. He choose his own
stage and invents his own characters. For women the choices are
restricted; they must play a role scripted for them by society, and
they must never break out of it. They must behave so that they may
be taken by surprise at any time and still appear to be in character.
The least involuntary gesture, a tear, a sigh, even a private action
like the Princesse de Clèves knotting ribbons alone in her pavilion,
can betray the true self and lead to ruin.

This inequality would be handicap enough, but women's roles
demand that they be reserved, if not silent. They must not assert
even their virtue too ostentatiously; the *prudes,* who dramatize
their strict morality, and the *dévotes,* who dramatize their piety,
drew the satirists' scorn as surely as the aging coquettes and the
bluestockings. Much eighteenth-century literature is built around
the pretext that justifies the heroine's display of her virtue. In
Graffigny's last play, Aristide's daughter sells herself into bondage, a
shocking gesture, but simply the logical extension of all the dutiful
daughters who settle their fathers' debts in the bonds of marriage.
Outside literature, however, most never have the chance to confront
the world with the magnitude of their sacrifice; it is taken for
granted, or worse yet, assumed to fulfill the woman's own desire.
Graffigny's far-fetched plot, in other words, legitimates the woman's

speaking out and even acting. What she says and does, however, represents a far more routine and ordinary human reality.

Obviously, the heroine's brief empowering as a victim pushed to the limit may also symbolize a woman's coming to writing. Writing, especially for the stage, threatened a woman's reputation. Graffigny's other stage heroine, Cénie, wishes to have her confession torn from her, just as Graffigny herself wished to have her manuscript torn from her. Only in this way could she present herself to the public without seeming proud and bold. Even so, she felt constrained to write in prose rather than poetry, lest she seem too ambitious. The dilemma, or double bind, extends even to the dedication of *La Fille d'Aristide:* Graffigny must simultaneously praise her patroness, the Empress Maria Theresa, and obey an express order not to; she must present the play as a tribute while denying its worth and the Empress's need for it.

These women's plays, produced under adverse circumstances, thus merit some special attention; if read attentively they tell something of their authors' struggles. This is not to claim a distinctive mode for women's drama; Voltaire's Zaïre is surely as much a martyr to silence and a patriarchal order as any heroine of the century. It is to suggest rather that the conventional plots, stock characters, and formulaic speeches conveyed a truth to which we are no longer fully sensitive. Both male and female authors were drawn toward pathetic heroines, silenced by their own sense of honor, paralyzed by their own loyalties, victimized by their own virtue; and as the century progressed, the heroes also tended to become pathetic. In many cases, a providential ending appears to undermine even the implicit criticism of the existing political order; but it is our distance from the situation that allows us to prefer a realistically hopeless outcome or a character who revolts by cynically exploiting the social fictions. The relief of a staged happy ending did not prevent contemporary spectators from knowing how most real conflicts were resolved; and an upbeat finale did not wipe out the spectacle of suffering in the first four acts. A general rereading of eighteenth-century French theater is no doubt overdue; if women authors are privileged here, it is because their lives make it easier to sense the authentic human voice masked by a conventional discourse.

Of all the women playwrights of the century, Marie-Anne Barbier was the most outspokenly feminist. Her life is little known; born in Orléans around 1670, she frequented a literary society that included

Boursault, Pellegrin, and Bignon. By her own account, in the preface to her first play, *Arrie et Petus,* she was urged to write for the stage by Boursault, who had read some of her elegies and who knew her taste for the theater. As happened to virtually all women writers, her works were attributed to a man, Pellegrin, although the abbé de La Porte reasoned that she was neither rich nor beautiful enough to have motivated Pellegrin to sacrifice his writings to her glory, and that therefore she probably wrote them herself under his guidance. Writing just two decades later, La Porte gave the date of her death incorrectly—it was 1742—and he failed to mention that she was married and had a daughter.[3]

Barbier's first three plays are dedicated to women patrons, her prefaces take up feminist issues, and her plays always have strong female characters. In the preface to *Arrie et Petus,* she discusses the reactions to it:[4]

For the rest people found it good, maybe better than I ought to have hoped, since some took the occasion to say that a woman was incapable of doing so well. Truly I would never have imagined that what pleased about my work would count against me, or that anyone would refuse people of our sex the merit of producing good things. I realize that one could praise my play no higher than by finding it better than a woman could do, and that my vanity should be flattered. But I confess I was not insensitive to the injustice, and I could not help feeling annoyed that people wished to rob me of the most precious fruit of my labor. (xiv)

To buttress her case for women's ability to write, she cites her recent predecessors Scudéry, La Suze, the Deshoulières, and Bernard (xv).

The plot of *Arrie et Petus* sets the pattern for the other three plays; Petus and Arrie love each other, and their love is politically forbidden. Petus conspires against Claudius, is discovered, and plans to escape; but Arrie refuses, preferring an honorable suicide, to which she summons Petus in dying. In the preface to her next play, *Cornelie, mère des Gracques,* she stated some of her principles of dramatic composition:

Cornelie, daughter of Scipio Africanus, and mother of the Gracchi, was one of the most illustrious ladies of Ancient Rome. Her love of the people, her courage amid dangers, and her constance in adversity shone forth so brightly during the Tribunates of her two sons that I thought I could put nothing on the stage more glorious for our sex. . . . Nothing is more capable of producing interesting situations than love between two people whose parents are irreconcilable enemies. The conflict of love and duty produces the sort of feelings that are the soul of Tragedy. (83–84)

Like the first play, *Cornelie* ends with a suicide, and the third play, *Tomyris*, concludes with a murder, a death in combat, and two more suicides. The intransigence of all the passions, especially love, which is supremely irrational, combined with an absolute inflexibility of principles, means that no solution is ever possible, except death. The characters stall for time, but even when an accident provides a way out, honor usually prevents them from taking it. The plays, more Racinian than Corneillean, show people waiting in forlorn anguish for the inevitable to occur.

The regular repetition of Racinian despair in the early eighteenth century suggests that French audiences continued to find it a persuasive image of their condition. Some of Cornelie's lines invite contemporary application: "Force the people to be happy, what a new kind of slavery! / Already you speak the language of the Senate" (II,5); "You know the Gauls, they are an unconquered people, / Who count freedom as the supreme good" (III, 4). One might describe Barbier's heroines as theorists of passive resistance. Even in the optimistic midcentury when the tragic mode gave way to the pathetic, the passivity remained; the characters waited just as forlornly, but waiting was more often rewarded by Providence. And even as French minds were turning away from the divine order and toward the political, the plight of powerless women still served to represent man's fate, in Montesquieu's harem and Diderot's nunnery. It is perhaps no accident that Racine's greatest figures were women; in his Jansenist universe where humans struggle in a contest they are fated to lose, it is as if the tragic heroines reenact women's usual social roles writ heroically large, while the heroes, confronting an unaccustomed sense of powerlessness, appear weak, unnatural, diminished—in a word, feminized.

Barbier's final play, *La Mort de César*, exposes the exhaustion of the classical formula, all the more because Shakespeare's version of the events is so well known. In Barbier, the characters have no flaws and the political question is ignored; the story is built around love conflicts and propelled by the doubts and hesitations of the leading men. Or rather, the political conflict is transposed into the domestic and sentimental sphere; the sign of Caesar's authoritarian ambitions and the proof of their danger lie in his arbitrary treatment of the women. Antoine and Octavie, Caesar's niece, are in love, as are Brutus and Porcie, Caton's daughter; Caesar decides to marry Porcie to Antoine, Octavie to Brutus. As usual, Barbier's women hold more rigidly to their principles than the men: Octavie warns her uncle that if she marries Brutus she will no longer be free to denounce the conspiracy. One might see in this attitude a tactic of the powerless, forcing the patriarchy to self-destruct by a "work-to-rule" adherence to their subordinate status.

The most generous reading, however, cannot completely dissipate the problems in making Octavie's engagement the central issue in Caesar's assassination. The play was poorly received, and Barbier was severely criticized for taking liberties with historical facts. After its failure, Barbier wrote no more; but with five plays staged and her outspoken defense of a female tradition, she clearly could have served as a model for later women playwrights. Instead, she seems to be the last representative of the seventeenth-century "femme savante," about to succumb to social ridicule and institutional obstacles. None of her plays was revived.

Madeleine de Gomez was born Madeleine Poisson in 1684, into a theatrical family; her grandparents, parents, and brother were all actors, and her grandfather had written for the stage. The biographical dictionaries say that she married a Spanish nobleman, believing him to be rich, only to discover that he was deep in debt, and that she was thereby forced to write to earn a living. Her first play, *Habis*, was produced in 1714 and enjoyed considerable success. It was revived in 1732, an honor reserved for only 56 of the 719 new plays staged by the Comédie française between 1701 and 1774. Lancaster says that only 4 other plays of the period 1700–1715 had greater success and that *Habis* is the most successful tragedy written by a woman in France.[5]

Needless to say, Gomez was accused of having had a man write her plays for her, and she replied bluntly in the preface to *Habis:*

I am too jealous of my glory to suffer patiently that anyone take it from me or share it; and I would blush with shame to accept praise that belonged to another. If it seems surprising that a woman of my age undertook a work of this importance, people should get over their surprise by looking at the women who have immortalized their name. I can even say on behalf of my sex that the works of its mind are no longer regarded as prodigies. One cannot then, without offending the sex, deny me the merit of having made this play, alone, and without any help; and I cannot imagine that there are people bold enough to say or imply that they had a hand in the versification or the story.

The plot centers on an aging tyrant, Melgoris, king of the Cinettes, who long ago killed his grandson, Habis, because of an oracle predicting that the grandson would take his supreme power from him.

Since then, he has held his own daughter prisoner. But Habis is of course alive, and in fact the leader of Melgoris's own triumphant armies. As the play begins, Melgoris is about to marry Erixène, whose father promised her in return for Melgoris's military aid; predictably, she and Habis are in love. Rumors of Habis's return circulate. Melgoris's old fear and cruelty rise up again; his daughter, his prime minister, his bride-to-be try in turn to persuade him to forgive Habis. Finally, Habis himself, still disguised as the general Hesperus, pleads his case, and succeeds. Everything ends happily; the tyrant not only welcomes his grandson, but gives him the throne and Erixène.

Gomez does not develop the tragic potential of an obsessed character like Melgoris. Instead, she envisions him as an embodiment of authority, King and Father, and as such he is in a sense exempt from attack if not from criticism. The other characters demonstrate their virtue by their blind acquiescence in his follies and submission to his injustice. From the first scene, when Habis's mother hears rumors of his return, she expresses concern that he respect the tyrant who has kept her in jail for twenty years, caused the suicide of her husband, and attempted the murder of Habis himself: "And if to avenge himself my Son took up arms, / Whom should he strike? A King? A Father? / Whom my heart still reveres despite his mad furies" (I,1). The identity of Habis is revealed to everyone except Melgoris early on; the scene where he finally recognizes and forgives Habis is inevitable. There, too, Habis succeeds by reaffirming his absolute trust in legitimate authority; having made his case, he places his life in Melgoris's hands, stating that he prefers a virtuous death to a revolt against his king and father.

This servility pervades eighteenth-century literature, especially the French theater. The temporary errors of authority figures seldom prod the heroes to revolt or the narrators to question the political structure. Female characters were held to an even more groveling acquiescence to the unreasonable demands of their masters. Rebellion of any sort was unseemly, fit only for villains. Contemporary readers and audiences enjoyed instead the heartrending spectacle of suffering virtue, knowing that patient endurance would be rewarded in a climactic scene of recognition, forgiveness, and reconciliation. To twentieth-century readers, such texts seem to preach a foolish faith in an already moribund political order, advising the oppressed to accept their lot without challenge, imagining wisdom and benevolence in the oppressors. We prefer works that resist and thematize the excesses; self-conscious villains and calculating role players, like Versac and Valmont, Marivaux's coquettes, and Diderot's parasite, impress us as revolutionary figures whose every word questions the bases of the established order. It is not certain that we read the eighteenth century well, however, and if "revolutionary" is anything more than a critical hyperbole, the sensibility was formed by their canon, not ours. The complacent suffering of these characters, finding pride in their refusal to resist, can be as insidiously subversive as the lessons of libertine novelists or materialist philosophers. The eighteenth-century spectator did not mistake the providential ending for realism; at most it was an exhortation to those with power in the real world, but in any case it stood in ironic contrast to the situation as it had stood until the final act. The happy ending provides a release to painful tensions; without it audiences might have found the play unbearable. But they did not forget the pain they had seen, nor were they unaware of the other possible outcomes and the arbitrary thin line separating poetic justice from disaster.

Gomez's second play, *Marsidie, reine des Cimbres*, was published but not staged. The central figure is a strong heroine, who overcomes political treachery and male vacillation, but does not anticipate the magnanimity of her Roman adversary and conqueror, Marius, who sacrifices his own love for her in favor of the vanquished Gotharsis. Marsidie, however, expecting a choice between death and dishonor, has already taken poison. The unhappy conclusion is pathetic rather than tragic, an accident of timing rather than the inexorable consequence of fate and passion. It is no accident, however, that suicide is the woman's choice, or that the misfortune falls to one who resisted Rome, the archetypal symbol of virile order.

After *Marsidie*, Gomez returned to happy endings, but with little success. *Semiramis*, staged in 1716, ends with the death of the traitor Menon, whose exposure makes possible the marriage of the heroine with Ninus, the man she loves, the fulfillment of the treaty between Syria and Arabia, the reunion of Simma with his long-lost children, and the happy disposition of Ninus's rival Aretas, who is actually Semiramis's brother. *Cléarque, tryan d'Heraclée*, staged the next year, is based on a familiar hostage plot: Cléarque holds both Aristophile and her father Entigesne prisoner, threatening the old man's life as a way of forcing the daughter to accept his hand. Entigesne instructs Aristophile that she may honorably murder Cléarque before she marries him, but not afterward; if she finds herself in his power, she should commit suicide. Luckily, Leonidas shows up to assassinate the tyrant, so that this play also ends happily for everyone except the villain.

After *Cléarque,* Gomez ceased writing for the stage, but continued to turn out fiction in large quantities, her best known work being the thirty-six-part collection *Cent Nouvelles Nouvelles,* published between 1732 and 1739. Unlike Barbier, Gomez expressed no explicit feminist consciousness in her plays and gives no clue what her motives for writing were or why she abandoned the genre. Her enormous productivity would have enabled her to earn a substantial income as a novelist; like Prévost, Marivaux, and Crébillon fils, she produced multivolume works, thereby capitalizing on her popularity. According to the biographical dictionaries, she lived until 1770, but appears to have given up writing altogether after the last volume of the *Cent Nouvelles Nouvelles.*

For over thirty years after *Cléarque,* from 1717 to 1749, there were no new works by women at the Comédie française.[6] All the more understandable, then, that the flamboyant Marie-Anne Du Boccage set Parisian tongues wagging with the announcement of her tragedy *Les Amazones* in 1749. Born Marie-Anne Le Page, in 1710, a native of Rouen, Du Boccage frequented a literary society, as had Barbier; Fontenelle, Collé, Trublet, and Voltaire's correspondent Cideville were among her friends. She was said to be rich, and her husband supported her in her literary ambitions. She traveled to England in 1750 and to Italy in 1758; after 1758 she opened her salon to a group of distinguished men of letters, and continued to receive them after her widowhood in 1767, and even through the Revolutionary years, when she was impoverished. She died in 1802, in her nineties.

The title of her play proclaims a feminist awareness, and the published text includes a preface addressed "Aux Femmes." To a 1980s reader, however, the material seems disappointing. Du Boccage does not take up the defense of a female literary tradition or even of the individual woman writer's right to equal treatment. The choice of Amazons as heroines must signify an interest in female power and in radical solutions to the problems of gender relations, but the play develops conventionally. The situation might be described as a reversal of the usual hostage plot: two Amazons, Orithie, the queen, and Antiope, a princess, hold Thésée prisoner, and have fallen in love with him, in violation of Amazon law. Of course, Du Boccage was not the first to have given such power to a woman. In this instance, the debate over whether to kill Thésée or not is rendered moot by his escape. Thésée loves Antiope, and a nice loophole allows

Amazons to marry in order to save the state. Thésée generously restores Orithie to her throne and freedom, but she commits suicide out of shame and passes the crown to Ménelippe, who swears eternal enmity to Thésée.

This denial of what appears to be a happy ending is the most subversive aspect of the play. Without saying so, perhaps even without knowing it, Du Boccage follows in the course traced by Barbier and Gomez: suicide is the only possible solution for the female protagonist. Thésée's power, both as warrior and as seducer, is a mortal threat to the Amazons, however magnanimous he may appear. Du Boccage uses a double plot. The most obvious is a typical tragic passion, love conflicting with dual duties, those of friendship between two rivals in love, and those of obedience to the law. This plot reaches a conventional happy outcome: one love is rewarded, the other consoled, and a political solution is found. But the second plot, which emerges only when the first is resolved, casts the first into doubt: Orithie cannot be consoled, and no political solution can be devised in the conflict between irreconcilable opposites, Amazons and men. Orithie's destiny cannot be subsumed in a patriarchal happy ending. Her love for Thésée destroys her identity as an Amazon, but not her fidelity to the Amazon ideal. In death she assures the preservation of the ideal, and from the Amazons' perspective the marriage of Antiope to Thésée must be viewed not as a happy ending but as a sacrifice, a virgin offered to propitiate the monster.

Les Amazones met with little success. It lacks dramatic movement and Du Boccage's verse does not compensate for the static plot. If the critics recognized its subversive feminist qualities, they kept silent about them; the play did not succumb to controversy but to a lack of audience response. As happened to Graffigny after *La Fille d'Aristide,* once the failure was certain, Du Boccage's public friends gave free rein to their malice in private; Collé notes that audiences snickered, sniffled, and yawned, while Cideville wrote that "fair-minded people think she did a lot for a woman, and sensible people think that, even so, she would have done better not to release the play."

Du Boccage herself wrote to Cideville: "I do not know if I will set out again, the work is too painful. Besides the pain of the work, the trouble of putting it on stage is excessive. Monsieur Du Boccage did most of it, but at every rehearsal I made changes which exhausted me" (1 August 1749).[7] Indeed, she did not return to the theater, although she continued actively to pursue fame as an author, with her epic poem *La Colombiade* and translations from the English. She could afford to ignore the financial aspects of her career; she was working only for glory and personal satisfaction. Her motives for giving up the genre will be echoed and amplified in Graffigny's account of getting *Cénie* staged a year later. Besides the work of writing, a great deal of labor was required to bring the play to the stage. Someone had to negotiate with the actors and supervise the rehearsals; a woman could not undertake those responsibilities. The factors that served to protect the proprieties at the Comédie française functioned to enforce not only political and religious orthodoxy but gender roles as well.

Graffigny observed Du Boccage's activities with scornful interest, and refused to receive her socially, considering her too brash and brazen. Graffigny was already famous for *Lettres d'une Péruvienne,* and publishing the novel had been a delicate balancing of proper feminine modesty with the need for public exposure. When Du Boccage's tragedy was staged, Graffigny had already been working for several years on her own play, *Cénie.*[8] Much of what Graffigny says about the composition of *Cénie* could probably be said of any play: the days spent writing, listening to criticism, revising, having copies made; the moments of enthusiasm and of weariness; impatience with the actors and anxiety as the premiere approached. Some of her concerns, however, arose from her position as a woman. After Du Boccage's play was presented in the summer of 1749, the rumor circulated that Voltaire's niece, Marie Louise Denis, had also written a play for the coming season. In April 1750, Denis actually read her play to Graffigny, but lamented that Voltaire had refused to let her present it. Graffigny thought it very mediocre, and agreed with Voltaire's judgment, and perhaps they were right to condemn it; but without this censorship there might have been one more woman playwright. At the same time, Denis's play might have prevented Graffigny's from appearing; Graffigny wrote to her correspondent Devaux that she did not want to be seen as part of a trio. This is a classic dilemma for writers from a minority: if they are alone, they are treated as freaks or tokens; but if they are not alone, they are bracketed with others they dislike and do not want to resemble.

In the spring of 1749, Graffigny had written a version of *Cénie* in three acts; over the summer she expanded it to five and made other changes. Devaux asked whether she was going to versify it; she replied that prose was more decent from the pen of a woman, a belief confirmed by her friend, the former actress Jeanne Françoise Quinault. According to Graffigny, verse bespoke the pretensions of a bluestocking, whereas prose suggested only a "femme d'esprit." Nothing suggests that we should regret Graffigny's failure to versify *Cénie*; indeed, the obligation to write classical verse stultified most of the century's playwrights, and the best turned to prose. For the woman writer, prose could have been a positive sign of difference, the adoption of a more natural idiom, like the familiar letter; the history of women's writing reveals a frequent transformation of imposed genres into powerful means of self-expression. As Graffigny presents it, however, the prose form seems rather a lowering of ambition, the acceptance of a secondary achievement as the only appropriate one for a woman. Although women were arguably better off outside the mainstream because they had greater artistic freedom, it meant that they had less hope for becoming professional authors earning their own living. The costs of losing that freedom cannot be calculated.

Du Boccage confessed that her husband had had to do much of the work to bring the play to the stage. Graffigny had no husband, and so her first task was to win the patronage of a man in a position to get her play accepted. It was the prince comte de Clermont who took up the cause; he had his own private theater at Berny, where he later staged a one-act "féerie" by Graffigny. His rank as a prince of royal blood endowed him with considerable authority over the actors of the Comédie française, and his knowledge of the theater augmented his influence. First, however, Graffigny had to make additional changes to meet his criticisms. Eventually, in February 1750, Clermont got the play read, and it was soon accepted, as Graffigny heard from the author and academician Duclos in mid March. Graffigny herself could not have dealt with the troupe as men like Clermont and Duclos could. She could, and did, arrange to meet the actors socially, or ask one to come to her loge at the theater. She tried in this way, with small success, to get plays produced for numerous friends, including Devaux, Saint-Lambert, and Palissot, although after the triumph of *Cénie* she got better results. But she could not go to the actors' and actresses' dressing rooms, or hang around the theater, or besiege a key member of the troupe, or flirt with the male stars.

Du Boccage cited the fatigue of seeing a play through to production as a reason never to try again. In late May, Graffigny still thought that she would escape with no more trouble than a few social calls: "I'll go to that rehearsal at la Gaussin's and that's all. I'll have Sarrasin to dinner with Dromgold and Duclos so they can both try to get him not to treat his part so nonchalantly. I think that will be my whole job" (29 May 1750). A few days later, however, she wrote, "Ah, truly, my friend, you were right. It is no small affair to get a play acted" (1 June 1750). The tale of problems goes on for three pages, and setbacks kept occurring throughout rehearsals, virtually to the eve of the premiere. Male authors suffered the same treatment, but they were free to act on their own behalf. For Graffigny, the problems came as last-minute surprises, and the solutions depended on waiting for a suitable assistant to happen by.

Du Boccage's fatigue supplied the pretext for the rumor that sitting through all the rehearsals had developed a boil on her bottom which opened and left a hole large enough to put a finger into. The sexual innuendo in this salacious story hardly needs pointing out. The age was never kind to the author, male or female, of an unsuccessful work; with women the satire regularly took the form of reduction to the sexual body, the object of male penetration and domination. The alleged locus of Du Boccage's failure thus becomes the site of a resexualization, whose painfulness and unnaturalness serve to emphasize its punitive and stigmatizing function.

A woman author's reputation was especially vulnerable to such attacks, because women were supposed to be modest and self-effacing. Graffigny's choice of prose was an effort to minimize any semblance of self-display. She explained to Devaux in February, as Clermont was presenting the play to the actors, that she did not plan to stay anonymous, but that she hoped to give the impression that Clermont had taken the manuscript against her will. Hence she was not displeased that early rumors attributed her work to Duclos. She was extremely grateful to the actor Roseli, who caught a potentially laughable line at the last rehearsal. Despite the overwhelming popularity of the play, which drew packed houses even in the off-season, and which was so wildly applauded that people choked on the dust raised by stomping feet, when the satirist Charles Roi wrote an epigram about her,9 she wished she could withdraw the play:

I had just been devastated by learning that Roi, the vile Roi, has written a horrible epigram, not against the play but against me. They say no one wants a copy, but slanders always get around. Mlle Quinault and Duclos came and said all the reasonable things one can say about it. They calmed me for the moment but when I'm alone all I see is the horror of being the object of a horror like that one. Ah, I'll never write again, that's for sure. The good is not worth the bad. If I could do it without seeming crazy, I'd withdraw the play this minute and never show it again. I won't be at ease as long as it's playing. I'll await the end of its run like the end of a great affliction.

The vehemence of this reaction passed; not only did *Cénie* remain on the boards to the end of its summer run, but it returned in the winter season and was revived four years later. Moreover, Graffigny wrote a second play, *La Fille d'Aristide*; it was a dismal failure when it was staged in 1758, but Graffigny took the bad reviews more philosophically than Roi's satiric doggerel.

The plot of *Cénie* is complicated and implausible, although not unusual for the period. Cénie has been raised as the daughter of Dorimond and Mélisse; but she is really the daughter of her governess Orphise and an unjustly exiled nobleman. Two brothers, Méricourt and Clerval, love her; Méricourt learns the secret from Mélisse on her deathbed, and tries to use it to get Cénie (and Dorimond's fortune). Cénie of course refuses, and tells Dorimond everything; Dorimond belatedly realizes that he has been deceived by Mélisse and Méricourt, tries to repair the situation by adopting Cénie or marrying Orphise, but they are too noble to accept such charity and are on their way to a convent when the nobleman reappears, having been pardoned by a minister *ex machina*.

The heart of *Cénie* is the dilemma of women expected to remain silent yet forced to speak. The heroine's part is full of lines like: "Don't force me to blush in front of you. . . . That's what I feared the most. This fatal confession puts the final touch on your woes. Clerval, remember that you tore it from me" (III, 4); "My disastrous adventure would become the latest gossip and I would be the object of public curiosity" (IV, 1); "Courage and silence are the nobility of the unfortunate" (V, 3); "Permit me to spare you confidences which should be told only to people with hardened hearts" (V, 5). The men in *Cénie* have misgoverned, but by mistake. The women suffer unjustly, but can remain in the right only by passive submission. Eventually, truth will out, and the real natural order replaces the apparent one; then the virtuous characters are rewarded and the wicked punished.

Far from disbelieving the plot, Graffigny's contemporaries circulated rumors that *Cénie* was an anagram of *nièce*, and that the story was based on the life of Graffigny's ward, Minette de Ligniville. Graffigny denied it to Devaux, and certainly nothing in Minette's noble background resembled Cénie's story of uncertain origins and belated recognition. The play nonetheless reflects the situation of the two women in important ways, Orphise being the surrogate mother to Cénie as Graffigny was to Minette. More importantly, however, the response to the play must arise from a powerful sense on the audience's part that the emotion was genuine. The mute resignation of Cénie and Orphise translates a situation familiar to the spectators of 1750. Even as it ostensibly celebrates and rewards the virtue of silence, *Cénie* allows the women characters to speak, and itself constitutes an act of speaking out. The enthusiastic reception of the play suggests that audiences responded to that boldness far more than to the bland reassertion of conventional moral ideas.

The first thoughts of the play that became *La Fille d'Aristide* appear in Graffigny's letters while *Cénie* was just getting underway. This work, completed shortly before the author's death, erases the last distinctions between the pathetic tragedy and the tear-jerking drama of the mid-eighteenth century: like the drama, it combines a serious tone with a happy ending, and is in prose; but like the tragedies, it is set in ancient Greece, with such exotic trappings as the Athenian Senate and slaves. The public responded unfavorably and Graffigny withdrew it after four performances. As in *Cénie*, the central figure is a virtuous woman at the mercy of false impressions. Her legitimate lover goes away for a year and sends no word; he returns to find her persecuted in various ways by two old men and one young one, and of course leaps to false conclusions about her feelings. The point of the awkward and unconvincing plot is to permit the heroine, Théonise, to be suspected of indecent behavior, when in fact she has performed the supreme self-sacrifice of selling herself into slavery to pay her benefactor's fine. Needless to say, the lover rescues her and the benefactor, and everyone else repents and apologizes. In *Cénie* the women silently prepare to enter a convent; here Théonise secretly sells her freedom. The deeds finally dramatize what propriety forbids speaking: neither desire nor virtue, but the utter hopelessness of woman's situation. Self-sacrifice if not suicide is the only issue.

After Graffigny's death, no more women wrote full-length plays for the Comédie française. Some of the women novelists of the latter half of the century might well have been major playwrights under different conditions. Marie Jeanne Riccoboni had been an actress at the Théâtre italien and had written for that stage; her translations of English plays and her correspondence with Diderot about the craft of playwriting prove her continuing interest and her intelligence on the subject. Isabelle de Charrière left a large number of unpublished plays; they contain some of the liveliest dialogue and freshest scenes in the entire century. But the novel afforded a better avenue for these women's creativity, in part no doubt because of its freedom from formal rules, but also in part because the theater demanded a degree of self-promotion and managerial activity that women could not easily provide.

In one area, however, it seemed appropriate for women to hold authority and to write their own script: the education of children. Félicité de Genlis is generally credited with the invention of the genre of children's theater, and she certainly popularized it through the publication of her *Théâtre de l'éducation* (1779) and the expanded seven-volume version, *Théâtre à l'usage des jeunes personnes* (1785). In fact, Graffigny had already written a number of plays with a similar purpose, which were used in educating the Imperial children in Vienna; the titles include *Ziman et Zenise* (1749), *Les Saturnales* (1752), *Le Temple de la vertu* (1750s), and perhaps others. In the domestic sphere, a woman could assume the role of moral guide, teacher, or governess; in certain cases she could also cast the play and direct the actors. In retrospect, a children's theater seems a natural and almost inevitable response to the frustrations women encountered in the mainstream theater and the larger society it represented.

Notes

1. Barbara Mittman, "Women and the Theatre Arts," in *French Women and the Age of Enlightenment,* ed. Samia I. Spencer (Bloomington: Indiana University Press, 1984), 163.

2. See my articles *"Les Lettres d'une Péruvienne:* Composition, publication, suites," *Archives et Bibliothèques de Belgique* 54 (1983): 14–28; and "The Beginnings of Madame de Graffigny's Literary Career" in *Essays on the Age of Enlightenment in Honor of Ira O. Wade,* ed. Jean Macary (Geneva: Droz, 1977), 293–304. Claude Alasseur has detailed the economics of the Comédie française of the eighteenth century in *La Comédie française au 18e siècle, Étude économique* (Paris: Mouton, 1967).

3. Abbé Joseph de La Porte, *Histoire littéraire des femmes françoises* (Paris: Lacombe, 1769), 4: 84–93.

4. The works of the women playwrights are cited from the following source editions; the translations are my own: Françoise de Graffigny: *Oeuvres complètes,* new ed. (Paris: Briand, 1821); Marie-Anne Barbier: *Théâtre de Mademoiselle Barbier* (Paris: Briasson, 1745); Madeleine de Gomez: *Habis, tragédie*

(Paris: chez Pierre Ribou, 1714); *Marsidie, reine des Combres,* 1716, in *Le Nouveau Théâtre François* (Utrecht: Etienne Neaulme, 1733), vol. 4; *Cléarque, tyran d'Heraclée,* 1717, in *Le Nouveau Théâtre François* vol. 4; *Semiramis,* 1716, in *Le Nouveau Théâtre François* (Utrecht: Etienne Neaulme, 1737), vol. 9; Marie-Anne Du Boccage, *Recueil des oeuvres,* 2 vols. (Lyon: Frères Perisse, 1762). Subsequent references appear in the text, as do references to any work cited more than once.

5. H. Carrington Lancaster, *Sunset: A History of Parisian Drama in the Last Years of Louis XIV, 1701–1715* (Baltimore: Johns Hopkins University Press, 1945), 79.

6. Unless one counts *Thélamire,* which had a brief run in 1739. It has been attributed to a Denise Lebrun, but the attribution is dubious; it has also been attributed to a marquis de Thibouville, and had the author really been a woman, the event was unusual enough that her identity would probably have been revealed. Nothing is known of either person, in any case.

7. Cideville and Collé are quoted in Grace Gill-Mark, *Une Femme de Lettres au XVIIIe siècle: Anne-Marie Du Boccage* (Paris: Champion, 1927), 153, 154.

8. Graffigny's correspondence is almost all in the Beinecke Rare Book and Manuscript Library of Yale University and is quoted with permission. A team headed by J. A. Dainard is editing the *Correspondance complète.* Volume 1 (letters from 1695 to June 1739) was published in 1985 (Oxford: Voltaire Foundation); the introduction contains the best information about locating specific letters within the collection.

9. Roi's epigram is quoted in Georges Noël, *Une Primitive oubliée de l'école des coeurs sensibles: Madame de Graffigny* (Paris: Plon, 1913), 240. It implies that "bel esprit" is equivalent to prostitution for women no longer young and beautiful enough to earn a living from the latter.

Gender and Poetry: Charles Baudelaire and Marceline Desbordes-Valmore

> Dites "la femme souffre" et jamais "nous souffrons!"
> —Marceline Desbordes-Valmore, "A Mademoiselle A . . ."
>
> J'ai cultivé mon hystérie avec jouissance et terreur.
> —Charles Baudelaire, "Hygiène"

Marceline Desbordes-Valmore (1786–1859) is one of the very few women poets who is represented in Lagarde and Michard's six-volume anthology of French literature. But she is *not* represented in Domna Stanton's recent anthology, *The Defiant Muse: French Feminist Poems from the Middle Ages to the Present*. Thus, in contrast to many women writers who are currently receiving critical attention, she has been neither completely excluded by traditional critics nor completely embraced by feminist critics. The present essay is an attempt to demonstrate that, whether she has been applauded or condemned, it has usually been for the wrong reasons.

Orthopedic Femininity and the Other Woman

Femininity has always been an orthopedic notion (*orthopedic:* from *ortho-* "straight, correct, right"; and *paideia,* "education"). Including but not restricted to normative notions of beauty, the concept of femininity acts as a mold for shaping and controlling women's behavior. As Simone de Beauvoir points out:

As against the dispersed, contingent, and multiple existences of actual women, mythical thought opposes the Eternal Feminine, unique and changeless. If the definition provided for this concept is contradicted by the behavior of flesh-and-blood women, it is the latter who are wrong; we are told not that Femininity is a false entity, but that the women concerned are not feminine.[1]

Femininity becomes, therefore, that from which women are always in danger of deviating. Unless of course femininity is judged a liability, in which case it is that into which women are always in danger of falling. The following comments by A. Alvarez cited on the dust jacket of Sylvia Plath's first volume of poetry stand as a good example of that danger: "Miss Plath neither asks excuses for her work nor offers them. She steers clear of feminine charm, deliciousness, gentility, supersensitivity, and the act of being a poetess. She simply writes good poetry. And she does so with a seriousness that demands only that she be judged equally seriously."[2] Alvarez is not the only critic for whom femininity and seriousness have been seen as mutually exclusive.

When it comes to judging women who write poetry, indeed, the orthopedism inherent in positive or negative views of femininity seems to become all the more rigid. When they are not excluding women poets altogether, the guardians of poetic taste often enforce their views by singling out one woman writer, praising her extravagantly, and using her as a pretext to denigrate the work of *other* women.

Marceline Desbordes-Valmore seems to have had an unusual knack for finding herself in the position of privileged exception. Baudelaire offers a particularly acerbic version of the "divide and control" school of criticism in the retrospective article he wrote on the occasion of Desbordes-Valmore's death:

If ever a man desired for his wife or daughter[3] the gifts and honors of the Muse, he could not have desired them to be of a kind other than those accorded to Mme Valmore. Among the rather large population of women who have lately thrown themselves into literary activity, there are few whose works have not been, if not a source of distress for their families, or even for their lovers (for the most indecent men love decency in the beloved object), at least marred by the kind of masculine ridiculousness that, in women, takes on the proportions of monstrosity. We have known the philanthropic-woman-writer, the systematic priestess of love, the republican poetess, the poetess of the future (Saint-Simonian or Fourierist); and our eyes, in love with the beautiful, have never been able to get used to all these stuffy uglinesses, all these impious villainies (there are even poetesses of impiety), all these sacrilegious parodies of the male spirit.[4]

In an astute parenthetical turn of phrase, Baudelaire here indicates that woman's proper place is that of "beloved object," not poetic subject. Not only are women writers "monstrous" for transgressing onto male territory; transgression itself—impiety, indecency, political and theoretical assertiveness—is here designated the exclusive property of the male spirit. And the male spirit is owed the respect due a god. Like Jahwe, it suffers no images to be made of it without sacrilege. And Baudelaire was not alone. Barbey d'Aurevilly agreed:

Mme Desbordes-Valmore is not a woman of letters, being that there *are* such monsters that are now called *women of letters*. Our fathers, with their profound common sense, once called that kind of women *men of letters*, ironically confounding the two sexes in that hideous and vengeful appellation. But she, simple and too often careless [elle, la simple et trop souvent la négligée], has never played the androgynous genius. She has never posed for the *Muse*. Pose, her! What is enchanting, more than the talent shown in her verse, when there is any, is the total absence of pose.[5]

It is hard to like a woman who inspires such praise. The problem with Marceline Desbordes-Valmore is not that the misogynists excluded her but that they applauded her. What they loved was her total avoidance of monstrosity, her willingness not to impinge on male territory in any way. The avoidance of monstrosity or masculinity, the avoidance of boundary transgression or mixture, is described as the total absence of *pose*. But this amounts to saying that Marceline Desbordes-Valmore succeeded in representing orthopedic femininity as if it were nature itself. Baudelaire's essay, for example, continues:

Mme Desbordes-Valmore was a woman, always a woman, and absolutely nothing but a woman: but she was to an extraordinary extent the poetic expression of all the natural beauties of woman. Whether she is singing the langorous desires of the young girl, the mournful desolation of an abandoned Ariadne, or the warm enthusiasms of maternal love, her song always preserves the delicious accent of woman; nothing borrowed, no artificial ornament, nothing but the *eternal feminine*, as the German poet puts it. It is thus in her very sincerity that Mrs. Valmore has found her reward, that is to say a glory we think is just as secure as that of the most perfect artists. (146–47)

What is unsettling to me in this tribute is less its underlying misogyny (for which Baudelaire is justly famous: "Women are *natural*; that is, abominable", etc.) than its uncanny resemblance to a certain ideal of women's poetry that seems to have become pervasive in feminist criticism. The temptation to read poetry by women as testimony to what is specific to women ("nothing borrowed"), to observe a woman poet of the past "dance out of the looking glass of the male text into a tradition that enabled her to create her own authority"[6] is very great, and, as Jan Montefiore points out in her critique of the poetics of experience,[7] politically useful. But to the extent that any woman poet is made to stand as a *representative* woman, to the extent that poetry by a woman is seen as an unproblematic and authentic representation of her specificity *as a woman*,[8] the ideal of a women's poetry of experience comes uncomfortably close to Baudelaire's (and Barbey's) construction of Marceline Desbordes-Valmore—and indeed, of the woman poet as such—as a *sujet supposé sincère.*

Yet it was Desbordes-Valmore herself, in fact, who constructed the myth of her un-constructedness:

> Adieu, Muses! la gloire est trop peu pour mon âme;
>> L'amour sera ma seule erreur:
>> Et pour la peindre en traits de flamme,
>> Je n'ai besoin que de mon coeur.
>
>>> ("Prière aux Muses")[9]

> Farewell, Muses! fame is not enough for my soul;
>> Love will be my only error
>> And, to paint it in lines of fire,
>> All I need is my own heart.

In an autobiographical letter to Sainte-Beuve, Desbordes-Valmore describes what might be called the primal scene of her poetic practice:

At age twenty, profound sufferings obliged me to give up singing, because my voice made me cry; but music still rolled about in my fevered head, and regular measures always arranged my ideas, without my thinking about it. I was forced to write them down in order to free myself from this feverish beat, and someone told me I had written an elegy. Mr. Alibert, who was nursing my frail health, advised me to write as a cure, since he could think of no other remedy. I tried it, without having read or learned anything at all.[10]

Far from grabbing the pen out of the patriarch's hands, Desbordes-Valmore goes to great lengths to depict her birth as a writer as a kind of victimization: she couldn't help it, didn't want it, didn't know what to call it, didn't think about it, and had no qualifications for it, but, since the doctor couldn't cure her any other way, she had to take his advice. Otherwise she would have gone on being a bother. Nowhere does her "I" appear as an active, knowing, or desiring subject. Never mind that, as an actress from the age of eleven, she had memorized her share of alexandrines. She knew the kind of woman her public could allow to become a poet. As Sainte-Beuve put it, "She sang as the bird sings, as the turtledove moans, knowing nothing but the emotions of the heart, with no technique but the music of nature" (124).

The poetics of spontaneous emotion for which Desbordes-Valmore is so often praised constituted, however, an entirely conventional tenet of Romanticism. Lamartine almost echoes Sainte-Beuve's statement when he writes:

> Je chantais, mes amis, comme l'homme respire,
> Comme l'oiseau gémit, comme le vent soupire,
> Comme l'eau murmure en coulant.[11]

> I sang, my friends, as man breathes,
> As the bird moans, as the wind sighs,
> As water murmurs as it flows.

The question is: why is Desbordes-Valmore's sincerity *believed*? I will return to this question in the second part of this essay.

But there is another kind of "primal scene" in Desbordes-Valmore's letter to Sainte-Beuve which deserves comment. The autobiographical material begins:

My father gave birth to me in Douai, his native country (June 20, 1786). I was his last and only blond child. I was triumphally received and baptised because of the color of my hair, much adored in my mother. She was beautiful, like a virgin, and it was hoped that I would resemble her completely, but I only resembled her a little. If I have been loved, it has been for things other than great beauty. (99)

While this purports to be a description of biological parentage, I think it more accurately describes Desbordes-Valmore's *poetic* parentage. Father-born ("mon père *m'a mise au monde*"), she inhabits the French poetic tradition (the paternal "native land"), within which the role prescribed for women is that of *image:* the blond, virginal "great beauty." For in the canonical tradition, of course, women are not supposed to write at all. In her autobiographical letter, Desbordes-Valmore is quite explicitly situating herself as excluded from the role the canonical tradition might have assigned to her. Yet it may be perhaps paradoxically *because* she situated herself elsewhere than as the "beloved object" of traditional love poetry that she came to personify—for Sainte-Beuve, Baudelaire, Barbey, Verlaine, Hugo, Vigny, Lamartine, and many other canonical male poets—the absolute voice of the native informant from the field of the "eternal feminine."

Interestingly enough, however, the role of beautiful woman has not disappeared from Desbordes-Valmore's *oeuvre*. It is simply occupied by other women. The beautiful mother is an important presence throughout her work. Many of her poems possess a triangular structure—a female speaker, another woman, and a man. Often that other woman is a sister or confidante. But equally often she is a resented but admired rival. Yet it is sometimes hard to tell whether it is the admiration or the rivalry that a given poem is designed to express. "Aveu d'une femme," for example, begins:

> Savez-vous pourquoi, madame,
> Je refusais de vous voir:
> J'aime! et je sens qu'une femme
> Des femmes craint le pouvoir.
> Le vôtre est tout dans vos charmes,
> Qu'il faut, par force, adorer;
> L'inquiétude a des larmes:
> Je ne voulais pas pleurer.
>
> (2:381)

> Do you know why, madame,
> I refused to see you:
> I am in love! and I feel that a woman
> Fears the power of women.
> Yours is all in your charms,
> Which one must, perforce, adore;
> Uneasiness has tears:
> I did not want to weep.

This is as much a statement of identification with the position of desirer as it is of rivalry with the desired. To love is to fear the power of women. A scenario of loss of the beloved man seems inextricable from a scenario of desire for the other woman. But whose desire is it? What object takes up all the space of the poem's interest? The poem maintains a certain ambiguity to the end. Statements like "Je vis de ce qu'il éprouve," which at first sight seem to mean "My life depends on what he feels about me," can also be read to mean "I feel what he feels." The homoeroticism of many of Desbordes-Valmore's poems is definitely worthy of further study—not least in order to understand how it came to go unnoticed. This is not to make a biographical claim (although her life is interesting in its intense female attachments) but rather to suggest that Desbordes-Valmore's investment in poetry itself is in some sense homoerotic. A whole cycle of poems is addressed to a beautiful woman named Délie, who has introduced the poem's speaker to a man who was once Délie's lover.

The speaker, having duly fallen in love with him, finds that he is still in love with Délie. Is it an accident that the rival's name should be precisely that of Maurice Scève's poetic heroine? It seems quite possible that Desbordes-Valmore is here working out her role of "other woman" with respect to the French Petrarchan tradition.

This is not to say, however, that the myths that have circulated about Desbordes-Valmore's life have not depicted her as the epitome of the heterosexual Romantic heroine. As Lagarde and Michard would have it:

She conceives a burning passion for a man of letters, Henri de Latouche, a passion which will make her suffer, but which at first sustains her during her career worries and exalts her ardent soul. Echoes of that passion reverberate throughout her poetry. In 1817 she marries the actor Valmore, and leaves the theatre in 1823. Life was hard for this sensitive, passionate creature: material difficulties, suffering in love, cruel losses (four of her children died), she was spared nothing. But she found consolation in poetry.[12]

Nice fiction, of which Desbordes-Valmore is to a large extent the author, aided and abetted by various canonical overdeterminations. In reality, according to a new biography painstakingly researched by Francis Ambrière,[13] the story runs more like this: At age ten, Marceline began her theatrical career alongside her mother, Catherine, who had left her husband for another man. Financial difficulties forced Catherine and Marceline to sail to Guadeloupe, where Catherine had a rich relative. When they arrived, the relative was dead, there was a slave revolt, and Catherine soon died of yellow fever. Marceline returned to France, continued her acting career, had three lovers and two illegitimate children (who soon died), and then (in 1817) met and married Prosper Valmore. Only after that (in 1819, after the publication of her first volume of poems) did she meet Henri de Latouche, who became her lover. Four of the five children born during Marceline's marriage died before she did. Latouche believed that Ondine, the third child, was his.

Thus, the mythology of the great love followed by the reasonable marriage (which is fundamental to almost all existing studies of her poetry) is quite far from the facts of Marceline's biography, if Ambrière is correct. Just as Lamartine wrote poems to Elvire assuring her of immortality ("tu peux, tu peux mourir!") before he ever met Julie Charles, all the poetic conventions drawn upon by Desbordes-Valmore were in place before she ever met the lover who has been credited with inspiring her unique passion. And it is no accident that literary history should have recognized only Henri de

Latouche in that role: not only did her lovers have to coalesce into one great love in order for her not to appear to be a "free woman," but her visibility was reinforced by the fact that that lover was someone "we" (*hommes de lettres*) know. (Latouche was a poet and editor of the works of André Chénier, first published in 1819.) Marceline Desbordes-Valmore is thus, from the beginning, "other" than the woman depicted in the image, whether it be the image of the great beauty, the image of the unlettered songbird, or the image of the passionate, tragic, and virtuous poetess. Yet her very success in constructing an unthreatening poetics of sincerity,[14] which enabled her to maintain a place in the French poetic canon as a "romantique mineur" (Lagarde and Michard), has tended to render her unusable and invisible for feminism. As the first woman poet to "penetrate [*sic*] the 'Galerie Seghers,'"[15] she was sponsored by Jeanine Moulin, whose notoriously antifeminist anthology *La Poésie féminine*[16] stands as the antitype for Domna Stanton's anthology, *The Defiant Muse.* Stanton writes:

In an extended preface that explores the existence of a poetic tradition by French women, Mounin [*sic*] iterates the stereotypes of femininity and the clichés of feminine writing that pervade traditional literary histories. The principal preoccupations of this poetry, she claims, are conjugal and maternal happiness, and a desire for love that is couched in passive emotionalism. ... Rejecting the need for "an aggressive feminism" at the close of her preface (p. 64), just as she denies the feminism of her investigation at the outset, Mounin welcomes the absence of "all traces of antagonism between the sexes" in contemporary women's writing, and points to the future disappearance of *la poésie féminine.* In opposition to this image of women's poetry, whose disappearance can only be welcome, the present volume affirms its feminist bias. ... This project began with the determination to exclude poems that privilege *kinder, kirche, küchen,* extol conjugal bliss, passively bemoan seduction and abandonment, and seek escape into transcendent saintliness or the beauty of flora and fauna.[17]

Needless to say, it is Desbordes-Valmore's "femininity" that has led to her being excluded from an anthology of feminist poetry. Feminism too has its orthopedism.

Both applauded and condemned for that which, in her poetry, seems exemplarily, exclusively, and unprotestingly feminine, yet canny enough to have constructed that femininity out of a life that could have told a different story, Marceline Desbordes-Valmore offers her reader the chance to reexamine the relations between poetic convention and the construction of gender.

Masochism and Masculinity

It is not enough to say that the lyric has always reflected the nature of the relations between the sexes in Western culture; the lyric has surely had a central role in *constructing* those relations. Although the first love poet may well have been Sappho, the vast majority of lyrical poems of desire in the Western tradition are written by men to women. This fact gives rise to generalizations like: "In the great tradition of Petrarch and Shakespeare, the lover-poet is principally concerned with defining his own self through his desire either for the image of his beloved or for his own image mediated through her response to him" (Montefireo, 98).[18] Or the following, which identifies a consistent physiological metaphor behind descriptions of poetic creation:

This model of the pen-penis writing on the virgin page participates in a long tradition identifying the author as a male who is primary and the female as his passive creation—a secondary object lacking autonomy, endowed with often contradictory meaning but denied intentionality. Clearly this tradition excludes woman from the creation of culture, even as it reifies her as an artifact within culture.[19]

Marceline Desbordes-Valmore acknowledges the power of this tradition when she begins a poem by stating, rather matter-of-factly:

> Les femmes, je le sais, ne doivent pas écrire;
> J'écris pourtant . . . .   (2:506)

> Women, I know, are not supposed to write;
> I write, though . . . .

The poet goes on, however, to minimize the transgression by making her writing redundant with respect to what is already written "in" the lover:

> Je ne tracerai rien qui ne soit dans toi-même
> Beaucoup plus beau . . . .

> I won't trace out anything that isn't already, in you,
> Much more beautiful . . . .

Even in her less self-conscious love poems, Desbordes-Valmore seems to work out a similar rhythm of resistance and submission, initiative and self-effacement. Let us look at how it structures a fairly typical "elegy".

Son Image

Elle avait fui de mon âme offensée;
Bien loin de moi je crus l'avoir chassée:
Toute tremblante, un jour, elle arriva,
Sa douce image, et dans mon coeur rentra:
Point n'eus le temps de me mettre en colère;
Point ne savais ce qu'elle voulait faire;
Un peu trop tard mon coeur le devina.

Sans prévenir, elle dit: "Me voilà!
"Ce coeur m'attend. Par l'Amour, que j'implore,
"Comme autrefois j'y viens régner encore."
Au nom d'amour ma raison se troubla:
Je voulus fuir, et tout mon corps trembla.
Je bégayai des plaintes au perfide;
Pour me toucher[20] il prit un air timide;
Puis à mes pieds en pleurant, il tomba.
J'oubliai tout dès que l'Amour pleura.

(1:50)

That Image

It had fled from my offended soul;
Far, far from me I thought I had chased it;
All tremblingly, one day, it came along,
That dear image, and sank back into my heart.
No time to summon up my anger;
Didn't know what it was after;
A bit too late my heart realized.

Without warning, it said: "Here I am!
This heart awaits me. By Love, which I implore,
I come to reign over it once more."
At the name of love my mind was blurred
I sought to flee; my whole body trembled.
I stammered, moaning against betrayal;
He acted shy, the better to touch me;
Then, weeping, he fell at my feet.
I forgot all when Love began to weep.

The fact that all French nouns are either masculine or feminine creates a gendered drama among the figures in this poem which is obscured by the necessity of turning the image into an "it" in English. In French, the image is a "she," and remains so until she speaks. The gender of the "I" is never made grammatically clear. A number of observations come to mind here: that the object of love is feminine, as in the male lyric, so that on the grammatical level the poem conforms to the tradition even though the genders are reversed in "reality"; that the opening stanza sketches out the love relation in female-to-female terms, if "I" is to be equated with the author; or that Desbordes-Valmore is reversing the equation of femininity with passivity that is said to be traditional in the love lyric.[21] By giving "elle" the dominant role in the poem's plot, Desbordes-Valmore would seem to begin by empowering femininity.

Yet the net impression made by the poem is hardly one of empowered femininity, whatever the grammatical plot might say. The story seems, rather, one of resistance penetrated, the traditional story of a woman seduced, abandoned, and seduced again. If the "I" of the first stanza offers ineffectual resistance to a return of the offending "image," that resistance crumbles as soon as the image invokes the name of love. The speaker takes on the properties of the "elle" ("elle avait fui" / "Je voulus fuir"; "Toute tremblante, elle arriva" / "tout mon corps trembla"). The rhyme scheme with its alternation between varied feminine endings and identical masculine endings (all the masculine rhymes are verbs in the *passé simple*) foreshadows the plot of repetition and masculine return: the *passé* is not so simple. However ambivalent the speaker is toward love, she "forgets all" as soon as "he" falls on his knees and weeps. He triumphs through a show of submission; she loses her cool, her reason, and her memory.

It would seem, then, that far from presenting a picture of empowered femininity, the poem offers a story of female masochism. Before buying into the equation between femininity and masochism, however, let us look at a poem by Baudelaire:

Le Vampire

Toi qui, comme un coup de couteau,
Dans mon coeur plaintif es entrée;
Toi qui, forte comme un troupeau
De démons, vins, folle et parée,

De mon esprit humilié
Faire ton lit et ton domaine;
—Infâme à qui je suis lié
Comme le forçat à la chaîne,

Comme au jeu le joueur têtu,
Comme à la bouteille l'ivrogne,
Comme aux vermines la charogne,
—Maudite, maudite sois-tu!

J'ai prié le glaive rapide
De conquérir ma liberté,
Et j'ai dit au poison perfide
De secourir ma lacheté.

Hélas! le poison et le glaive
M'ont pris en dédain et m'ont dit:
"Tu n'es pas digne qu'on t'enlève
A ton esclavage maudit,

"Imbécile!—de son empire
Si nos efforts te délivraient,
Tes baisers ressusciteraient
Le cadavre de ton vampire!"

(1:33–34)

The Vampire

You who, sharp as a knife,
Into my plaintive heart have pierced;
You who, mighty as a troop
Of demons, came, mad and showy,

To make of my humiliated mind
Your bed and your domain;
—Vile being I am tied to
Like the convict to his chain,

Like the gambler to his game,
Like the drunkard to his drink,
Like a putrid corpse to vermin,
—Damn you, damn you, damn!

I've prayed the rapid blade
To set me free at last,
And I've asked perfidious poison
To help me in my cowardice.

Alas! the poison and the blade
Have answered with disdain:
"You are not worth saving
From your slavery and damnation,

Imbecile!—even if we tried
To free you from its empire,
Your kisses would resuscitate
The body of your vampire!"

In Baudelaire's anatomy of ambivalence, the part of phallic torturer
is played by a female figure. The "I" is not only a victim; he, like
Desbordes-Valmore's speaker, is addicted to his victimizer. If Desbordes-Valmore describes the image "entering" (*rentra* could mean
both "reentered" and "plunged") into her heart, Baudelaire describes
it (the "you") explicitly as a knife thrust. If Desbordes-Valmore
describes her submission to "le perfide" as a lapse of self-possession,
Baudelaire describes his as enslavement. Where Desbordes-Valmore

is touched, Baudelaire is vampirized. Baudelaire would seem to have raised the poetics of masochism to new heights. There is certainly no simple correlation here between femininity and passivity, masculinity and action.

The surprising thing is, there never was. A look at the Petrarchan tradition reveals that Baudelaire has not perverted a straightforward pattern, but that that pattern has never been straightforward. However true it may be to say that women are reduced to images in the Petrarchan tradition, those images are far from passive. To take only the hunting imagery suggested by Desbordes-Valmore's poem, there is little support for Mary Ellmann's contention that "the hunter is always male, the prey female."[22] This generalization appears to hold for a poem like Thomas Wyatt's "They flee from me, that sometime did me seek" (which Desbordes-Valmore's poem interestingly resembles), in that the speaker characterizes "them" as wild animals. But it is the hunter here who is passive, trying vainly to lure back his once tame prey, which has scampered off through *his* excessive gentleness. In many poems by Petrarch, Scève, or Ronsard, the male speaker presents himself as having been wounded by the image of the desired woman:

> It was the day the sun had overcast,
> In pity of his maker, his bright sheen
> When I fell prey to peril unforeseen,
> For your eyes, lady, caught and held me fast.[23]

> Your sweet poison, your grace, made me
> Idolatrous of your divine image[24]

> My lady, with love's bow in her fist
> Shot at me, to draw me to her. . . .
> Turn, she said, and hurry toward me.
> Are you fleeing my arrow, or my power?
> I am fleeing neither bow nor arrow, said I
> But the eye that has wounded my heart so deeply.[25]

> Ah! treacherous Love, give me peace or letup
> Or, taking out an arrow thicker yet,
> Cut off my life, bring on my death,
> Sweet is death, the sweeter being brief.[26]

The image of being the prey rather than the hunter, the penetrated rather than the penetrator, would seem to pervade the Petrarchan figuration *not* of femaleness but of maleness. The metaphors of desire in these poems contradict, rather than follow, the patterns that would flow from sexual physiology. This makes gender generalizations about figuration in the love lyric more complicated than any biologistic ideology would imply.[27] I would be tempted to claim that this is necessarily the case: if poetry were only a reinscription of dominant ideology, it would not need to exist.

Why is it, then, that Petrarch is not called a masochist, even though Louise Labé, using exactly the same conventions, is?[28] Why are there books published on Baudelaire's sadism but not on his masochism?[29] Why is male masochism the secret that it is lyric poetry's job to keep?

One answer, I think, has to do with rhetoric. When men employ the rhetoric of self-torture, it is *read* as rhetoric. When women employ it, it is confession. Men are read rhetorically; women, literally. Yet within the poetic tradition, it is the rhetorical, not the literal, that is taken seriously. Why should the literal be the opposite of the serious? What is the nature of the seriousness of nonliterality?

When men have described love as an experience of fragmentation, wounding, or loss of psychic intactness and control, it has been read as an analysis of "The Nature of Desire." When women have described something analogous, it has been read as an expression of "What a Woman Wants." Rhetoric, in other words, is a way of shifting the domain of a poem's meaning to a higher, less referential, more abstract and theoretical level. And this is done by universalizing, that is, by denying the presence of the sexual difference out of which the poem springs.[30] Perhaps this is why the speaker in Desbordes-Valmore's poem "Son Image" surrenders not to a man but to *Amour*, a figure for the whole rhetorical configuration of canonical love poetry. Indeed, in another poem, "Une Nuit d'hiver," *Amour* breaks the speaker's lyre and burns her verse, saying that only her silence and her tears are acceptable tributes to his power.

Yet the sexual difference on whose transcendence seriousness depends always threatens to return, which may be why "femininity" seems to be the privileged topic of male lyric poetry, or why the philosophical tradition has often viewed rhetoric itself as feminine. Disavowed femininity returns interestingly, in fact, in the very article by Baudelaire on Desbordes-Valmore with which we began. The article opens:

More than once hasn't a friend of yours, when you confided one of your tastes or passions to him, exclaimed "How strange! that's in complete disagreement with all your other passions and with your doctrine"? And you answered: "That's possible, but so be it. I like it; I like it probably precisely because of the violent contradiction my whole being finds in it."

Such is my case with respect to Mme Desbordes-Valmore. (145–46)

By beginning with the scoffing of a hypothetical friend, Baudelaire presents himself as safely in the bosom of the male homosocial literary world, from which the aesthetic of Desbordes-Valmore is as different as different can be. The distance at which she is placed by this conversation indicates that there is something transgressive or embarrassing about being caught reading her. But of course, Baudelaire has always claimed "the right to contradict oneself." He goes on, being careful to back up from every statement of admiration, and always keeping his implied male reader within reach:

If the cry, the natural sighing of an elite soul, the desperate ambition of a heart, the unexpected and unreflective [*irréfléchi*] faculties, and everything that is gratuitous and comes from God, can suffice to make a great poet, Marceline Valmore is and will always be a great poet. It is true that if you take the time to notice everything she lacks of what can be gained by work, her greatness will be singularly diminished; but at the very moment when you will feel the most irritated and disturbed by the negligence, the noise, the confusion, which you take—you, a reflective and always responsible man [*vous, homme réfléchi et toujours responsable*]—as a stance of laziness; a sudden, unexpected, unequalable beauty will spring up and carry you off irresistibly into the poetic yonder. (146)

The opposition here is between male reflectiveness and female unreflectiveness. Yet already there is a danger of being "carried off." The article continues: "Never was a poet more natural; never was a poet less artificial. No one has been able to imitate this charm because it is completely original and inborn [*natif*]" (146). The opposition glosses itself further as the artificial versus the natural; imitation versus originality; the acquired versus the inborn. There then follow the two paragraphs quoted at the beginning of the present essay: the paragraph outlining the monstrosity of all other women writers who "parody the male spirit" (monstrous because parody—imitation itself—is defined as male prerogative) and the paragraph praising Desbordes-Valmore as the personification of the woman, the whole woman, and nothing but a woman.

But more information about what is being disavowed or embraced is forthcoming in the lines that follow:

That torch, which she waves before our eyes to light up the mysterious hedgerows of sentiment, or which she places, to reignite them, on our most intimate memories, erotic or filial—that torch has been lit in the depths of her own heart. Victor Hugo has expressed magnificently, as in all he has expressed, the beauties and enchantments of family life; but only in the poems of the ardent Marceline can you find that warmth of the maternal nest, of which some among the sons of woman, less ungrateful than others, have kept the delicious memory. (147)

The "homme réfléchi" has now become a son, and the eternal feminine a mother. The return to the warmth of the maternal nest is both the appeal and the danger of Desbordes-Valmore's poetry. And this can be read not only as the drama of separation/individuation from the mother which can be seen as *the* topic of Baudelaire's poetry, but also as an indication that, for Baudelaire, Marceline Desbordes-Valmore is functioning as a *poetic* mother, a *maternal* line that has no proper place in the male homosocial literary world.

But Baudelaire's presentation of the return of disavowed femininity does not stop there. For the essay ends with the following description of his experience as a reader of Desbordes-Valmore's poetry: "The walker, contemplating these stretches veiled with mourning, can feel rising to his eyes the tears of hysteria, *hysterical tears* [in English in the original]" (149). The disavowed woman in Baudelaire's text is thus his own hysterical self.

Baudelaire is here enacting male privilege as the right to play femininity. Rhetoric is the domain of male self-difference reframed as universality. If masculinity establishes, explores, and interests itself as that which is constantly differing from itself, it arises out of the replacement of sexual difference by self-difference. But this does not mean that the replacement can simply be reversed: masculine privilege is enforced precisely by male femininity. How can the search for that which is different from male self-difference be sure that it is not already framed within male self-difference? To be differently empowered does not have to mean: to be empowered *as* different.

The encounter between Baudelaire and Desbordes-Valmore has not solved the riddle of gender and poetry. But it has perhaps brought us to the point where a different kind of reading might begin.

Notes

1. Simone de Beauvoir, *The Second Sex*, trans. H. M. Parshley (New York: Knopf, 1953), 237. Quoted in Elizabeth Spelman, *Inessential Woman* (Boston: Beacon Press, 1988), 69. Spelman's book is an eloquent critique of the functioning of white middle class heterosexual orthopedism in feminist thought.

2. Sylvia Plath, *The Colossus and Other Poems* (New York: Knopf, 1962).

3. The phrase "pour sa femme ou sa fille" is reminiscent of the opening sentence of Baudelaire's "project de préface," drawn up at the time of the trial of *Les*

Fleurs du mal: "Ce n'est pas pour mes femmes, mes filles ou mes soeurs que ce livre a été écrit." Desbordes-Valmore's work can be read as precisely the kind of poetry Baudelaire thought he was *not* writing. His essay about her begins by describing her poetry as being the exact opposite of all his other passions and of his doctrine. It is as though he was afraid of being contaminated by a resemblance.

4. Charles Baudelaire, "Réflexions sur quelques-uns de mes contemporains: Marceline Desbordes-Valmore," *Oeuvres complètes* (Paris: Pleiade, 1976), 2:146. Subsequent references are incorporated into the text, as are references to works cited more than once. All translations are mine unless otherwise indicated.

5. J. Barbey d'Aurevilly, *Les Oeuvres et les hommes* (Paris: Amyot, 1862), 145–46.

6. Sandra M. Gilbert and Susan Gubar, *The Madwoman in the Attic: The Woman Writer and the Nineteenth-Century Literary Imagination* (New Haven, Conn.: Yale University Press, 1979), 71.

7. Jan Montefiore, *Feminism and Poetry* (London: Pandora, 1987). Montefiore critiques the feminist aesthetic, which she summarizes as follows: "Poetry is, primarily, the stuff of experience rendered into speech; a woman's poems are the authentic speech of her life and being" (3). It is interesting that neither she nor I have found a quotable example of this aesthetic that is simplistic enough to stand as a target of our critique, even though traces of it seem to be everywhere. Whether it be Adrienne Rich, Gilber and Gubar, Audre Lorde, or Judy Grahn, the theorists of the poetic truth of women's experience seem to break out in cultural suspicion at the approach of excessive generalization, even their own.

8. This is the quarrel I would have with a book like the very interesting *Women's Ways of Knowing* by Mary Field Belenky, Blythe McVicker Clinchy, Nancy Rule Goldberger, and Jill Mattuck Tarule (New York: Basic Books, 1986). The book results from a series of extensive interviews with 135 women. "Before asking a woman to participate," write the authors, "we told her that we were interested in her experience—*and in women's experience*—because it had so often been excluded as people sought to understand human development. We told her that we wanted to hear what was important about life and learning *from her point of view*" (11. First emphasis mine; second emphasis the authors'). It seems to me that by telling a woman that *her* point of view is that of *a woman*, the interviewers are inviting women to process their experience through their (culturally constructed) notions of what women's experience might be, thus potentially reproducing rather than questioning the orthopedism the study is designed to combat.

9. *Les Oeuvres poétiques de Marceline Desbordes-Valmore,* ed. M. Bertrand (Grenoble: Presses Universitaires de Grenoble, 1973), 1:49.

10. Quoted in C.-A. Sainte-Beuve, *Portraits contemporains*, t. 2 (Paris: Michel Levy, 1869), 100–101.

11. Alphonse de Lamartine, "Le Poète mourant," *Oeuvres poétiques complètes*, ed. Marius-François Guyard (Paris: Pléiade, 1963), 147.

12. André Lagarde and Laurent Michard, *XIXe Siècle* (Paris: Bordas, 1969), 282. It is interesting to note that the two poems chosen by Lagarde and Michard to represent Desbordes-Valmore's poetry are poems addressed to paternal figures, an address relatively rare in her *oeuvre*. One of the poems, indeed, is cut in half: the maternal half is omitted.

13. Francis Ambrière, *Le Siècle des Valmore* (Paris: Seuil, 1987). In this huge two-volume biography, Ambrière displays a fascinatingly complex attitude toward his subject. On the one hand, he has devoted thirty years of his life to researching her every move and word. On the other hand, he is capable of saying things like "Comme la plupart des femmes, Marceline avait une invincible propension à mépriser les règlements" (1: 419). Or consider the incredible poignancy and blindness of taking the patriarch's point of view in describing Antoine-Félix Desbordes (Marceline's father), his daughters, and their children: "Son ainée, Cécile, venait de donner à Antoine-Félix le premier des dix-huit petits-enfants que ses trois filles mirent au monde, à raison de six pour chacune. Sur les dix-huit, douze moururent en bas age, tous, sauf un, enfants naturels" (1:113). By entitling the biography *Le Siècle des Valmore*, Ambrière elides the very name of his subject. Interestingly, his afterword presents another case of the disappearing female name: "Mais par-dessus tout je suis heureux de reconnaître ce que je dois à celle qui entre très exactement pour moitié dans la longue recherche préparatoire d'où mon livre est issu. Elle s'appelait Madeleine Fargeaud quand Jean Pommier m'a présenté à elle au printemps 1955. . . . Elle s'appelle aujourd'hui Madeleine Ambrière" (2: 429). Needless to say, she who did half the research does not get half the credit on the book's title page.

14. There was, however, one person who *was* threatened by the sincerity of her poetry: Prosper Valmore. When he questioned her about the great lost love depicted in her poems, she replied, "Those poems, which weighed so heavily on your heart, now infuse mine with regret for having written them. . . . They are impressions often observed in other women who suffered around me. I said to myself 'I would feel such-and-such in her place' and I made solitary music. God knows!" *Lettres de Marceline Desbordes à Prosper Valmore*, ed. Boyer D'Agen (Paris: Editions de la Sirène, 1924), 34.

15. Jeanine Moulin, *Marceline Desbordes-Valmore*, Poètes d'aujourd'hui (Paris: Seghers, 1955), 9.

16. Jeanine Moulin, *La Poésie féminine*, 2 vols. (Paris: Seghers, 1963–66).

17. Domna Stanton, *The Defiant Muse: French Feminist Poems from the Middle Ages to the Present* (New York: Feminist Press, 1986), xvii–xviii.

18. It is curious that Montefiore here has decided to treat Shakespeare's sonnets as unambiguously heterosexual.

19. Susan Gubar, "'The Blank Page' and the Issues of Female Creativity," in *Writing and Sexual Difference*, ed. Elizabeth Abel (Chicago: University of Chicago Press, 1980), 77.

20. A note about theories of overdetermination: When I first read this poem, I noted the verb *toucher* (which occurs with great frequency in Desbordes-Valmore's love poetry) and thought it might be a sign of the presence of Henri de Latouche as coded countersignature. If Ambrière's chronology is correct, however, Desbordes-Valmore had not yet met Latouche when she wrote this and other "touch" poems. Interestingly, though, a poem written in 1822 (thus, after their meeting) begins: "J'étais à toi avant de t'avoir vu. / Ma vie, en se formant, fut promise à la tienne; / *Ton nom* m'en avertit par un trouble imprévu . . . " If something is overdetermined here, it would seem to be the choice of lover: it is not that the word *toucher* occurs because it is the lover's name but that the lover is loved because his name is already so central to the poetry.

21. Cf. Montefiore: "The lady of the mirror-lyrics, who is the 'passive and

glorified instrument of the lover's desire, reflecting what she does not truly possess,' corresponds to Irigaray's contention that woman exists in masculine discourse only as an Other passively reflecting a masculine ego-ideal" (111–12). The internal quotation is from Frederick Goldin, *The Mirror of Narcissus* (Ithaca, N.Y.: Cornell University Press, 1964).

22. Mary Ellmann. *Thinking about Women* (New York: Harcourt Brace Jovanovich, 1968), 8–9.

23. Petrarch, Sonnet 3, *Selected Sonnets, Odes, and Letters,* trans. Thomas G. Bergin (Arlington Heights, Ill.: AHM Publishing Corporation, 1966), 20.

24. Maurice Scève, Délie #III, in *Les Poètes du XVIe siècle,* ed. Marc Alyn (Paris: J'ai lu, 1962), 122.

25. Scève, Délie #V, in Alyn, 123.

26. Pierre de Ronsard, *Amours de Cassandre,* XI, in Alyn, 311.

27. In her brilliant article on Petrarch's use of the myth of Actaeon ("Diana Described: Scattered Woman and Scattered Rhyme" in *Writing and Sexual Difference*), Nancy J. Vickers emphasizes the ways in which the description of beauty is a form of dismemberment. Her reading is meant to counteract the view of the idealization of Laura as a positive and benign attitude. If she might be said to be describing the unavowed sadism of idealization, what I am doing here is emphasizing the unavowed masochism inherent in the image of the hunter dismembered by his own desire.

28. See Robert Sabatier, *La Poésie du XVIe siècle* (Paris: Albin Michel, 1975): "S'agit-il de ce que Marie Bonaparte étudiant la sexualité féminine appelle 'le masochisme féminin essentiel'? En lisant les sonnets, on peut glaner une ample moisson de mots exprimant la blessure: maux, menaces, ruines, combats, crier, cruelle, sanglots, cruauté, duretés, tourment, plaie, douleur, martyre" (115–16).

29. Cf. George Blin, *Le Sadisme de Baudelaire* (Paris: Corti, 1948).

30. Cf. Adrienne Rich: "I had been taught that poetry should be 'universal,' which meant, of course, nonfemale." *On Lies, Secrets, and Silence* (New York: Norton, 1979), 44.

A Double Margin: Reflections on Women Writers and the Avant-Garde in France

To say the word *avant-garde* today is to risk falling into a conceptual and terminological quagmire. Is *avant-garde* synonymous with, or to be subtly distinguished from, the experimental, the bohemian, the modern, the modern*ist*, the postmodern? Is it a historical category or a transhistorical one? A purely aesthetic category or a philosophical/political/existential one? Is it still to be taken seriously, or does it "conjure up comical associations of aging youth?"[1] In short, does the word have specific content or has it become so vague and general as to be virtually useless?

With that bow to confusion, I shall proceed as if *I* knew what I meant when I say "avant-garde." And I shall take as a starting point a set of propositions that appear sufficiently obvious to warrant no detailed demonstration. There have existed avant-garde movements in French art and thought. Although they can be traced at least as far back as Romanticism, they came fully into their own in the early years of this century and found what was perhaps their fullest elaboration in the Surrealist movement between 1924 and 1939. The *Tel Quel* group and its allies of the 1960s and early 1970s, as well as various feminist groups after 1968, associated with specific journals and theoretical positions regarding women and "the feminine," also constituted genuine artistic and cultural avant-gardes (*pace* Peter Bürger).[2] The hallmark of these movements was a *collective project* (more or less explicitly defined and often shifting over time) that linked artistic experimentation and a critique of outmoded artistic practices with an ideological critique of bourgeois thought and a desire for social change, so that the activity of writing could also be seen as a genuine intervention in the social, cultural, and possibly even the political arena. Finally, although most of the participants in the later movements are still alive and writing in France today, the movements themselves are now dispersed and have not been replaced.

To be sure, qualifications and additions are possible (should the *nouveaux romanciers* be considered an avant-garde movement, and if not, why not? Same question for existentialism). The point I wish to make is that there has existed, at least since Surrealism, a strong and almost continuous current in French literary and artistic practice and thought, based on the double exigency to "be absolutely modern" (Rimbaud) and to change, if not the world (Marx), at least—as a first step—the way we think about the world. Furthermore, this recurrent tendency has expressed itself with remarkable consistency, privileging certain concepts (hererogeneity, play, marginality, transgression, the unconscious, eroticism, excess) and mounting heavy attacks on others (representation, the unitary subject, unitary meaning, linear narrative, the realist novel, paternal authority, Truth with a capital *T*). Alice Jardine has argued that perhaps the most important thread of continuity, subtending all of the above oppositions, has been the "putting into discourse of 'woman'": "We might say that what is generally referred to as modernity is precisely . . . the perhaps historically unprecedented exploration of the female, differently maternal body."[3] One has but to think of the Surrealists' celebration of *amour fou* (or, in the case of Bataille, *amour obscène*) in poetry and narrative, and their obsessive preoccupation with the female body in painting and photography; of Alain Robbe-Grillet's and other *nouveaux romanciers'* combination of a thematics of erotic violence with a poetics of antirealist transgression; of Phillippe Sollers's attempts to wed Joycean wordplay to erotic exhibitionism (especially in *Paradis*, his last work of the *Tel Quel* period); of Julia Kristeva's theory of the maternal/semiotic and Jacques Derrida's concept of "invagination"; and of contemporary women writers' exploration/ inscription of the female body, whether as maternal *jouissance* or as the *jouissance* of female lovers, to assent to Jardine's daring generalization.

One question, of course, is whether the "putting into discourse of 'woman'" by a woman writer is comparable, in its meaning and effects, to its putting into discourse by a male writer. Another important question, which has preoccupied many feminist theorists and which Jardine rightly emphasizes at the outset of her book, concerns the problematic relationship between "woman" as discursive entity, or metaphor, and *women* as biologically and culturally gendered human beings. "It is always a bit of a shock to the feminist critic," writes Jardine, "when she recognizes that the repeated and infinitely expanded 'feminine' . . . often has very little, if anything, to do with women" (35). And putting the dilemma even more sharply: "To refuse 'woman' or the 'feminine' as cultural and libidinal constructions (as in men's 'feminity'), is, ironically, to return to metaphysical—anatomical—definitions of sexual identity. To accept a metaphorization, a semiosis of woman, on the other hand, means risking once again the absence of women as subjects in the struggle of modernity" (37). As Jardine points out, the dilemma is especially acute for those American feminist critics who are torn between the heady attractions of (largely French) theory and the no less significant appeal of (largely American) empirical and historical study, where the material situation and the gender of an author are never a matter of indifference. Nancy Miller, who has often and forcefully argued for the materialist view even while admitting the elegant attractions of French theory, summed up the dilemma in another way a few years ago when she asked, half jokingly: "Can we imagine, or should we, a position that speaks in tropes and walks in sensible shoes?"[4]

I would like to take up Miller's challenge by reflecting on a particularly powerful trope associated both with women and with avant-gardes: that of the margin. If, as this trope suggests, culture is "like" a space to be mapped or a printed page, then the place of women, and of avant-garde movements, has traditionally been situated away from the center, "on the fringe," in the margins. One difference is that avant-garde movements have willfully chosen their marginal position—the better to launch attacks at the center—whereas women have more often than not been relegated to that position: far from the altar as from the marketplace, those centers where cultural subjects invent and enact their symbolic and material rites.

It has become increasingly clear that the relegating of *women* to the margins of culture is not unrelated to the place accorded to "Woman" by the cultural imaginary: "Woman, in the political vocabulary, will be the name for whatever undoes the whole."[5] In other vocabularies, *woman* has been the name of the hole that threatens the fullness of the subject, the wild zone that threatens the constructions of reason, the dark continent that threatens the regions of light. What strikes me as new, however, is that the "putting into discourse of 'woman'" in modern French thought has gone hand in hand with a revaluation and revalorization of the marginal spaces with which "she" has been traditionally identified. It is because of that reversal that the complicated relations, at the margins of culture, between women writers and the avant-garde in France must particularly occupy our attention.

In *Les Parleuses*, the series of conversations between Marguerite Duras and Xavière Gauthier published in 1974, the talk turns at one point to why Duras is not really known by the reading public. Gauthier remarks that people know her name, but few seem to have read her texts—perhaps because they are afraid? Duras replies that very probably things will change after her death, but that indeed "I attract misogyny in a particular way." Gauthier (who often speaks more volubly than Duras in these conversations) then observes: "That doesn't surprise me. Precisely because I think that they are totally revolutionary books, totally avant-garde, both from a usual revolutionary point of view and from a woman's point of view, and most people aren't there yet." To which Duras responds: "Yes, it's something doubly intolerable" ("une double insupportabilité").[6]

Doubly intolerable because "totally revolutionary, totally avant-garde," Duras's work (by 1974 she had published among other works the trilogy comprising *Le Ravissement de Lol V. Stein*, *Le Vice-Consul*, and *L'Amour*, and directed *India Song*) is here seen as the quintessence of the marginal. The fact that ten years later, with the publication of *L'Amant*, she would become an international bestselling author does not alter the logic of that characterization (although it did of course alter Duras's own situation[7]): the avant-garde woman writer is doubly intolerable, seen from the center, because her writing escapes not one but two sets of expectations/categorizations; it corresponds neither to the "usual revolutionary point of view" nor to the "woman's point of view." Gauthier does not explain what she means here by the "woman's point of view"—I would guess that she alludes to a certain view of women's writing which does not include experimentation with language. As for the "usual revolutionary" point of view, it seems to refer to an overtly political kind of writing which adopts an oppositional stance to society. Duras tells Gauthier that in her works there is no "refusal" or "putting into question" of society, because "to put society into question is still to acknowledge it. . . . I mean the people who do that, who write about the refusal of society, harbor within them a kind of nostalgia. They are, I am certain, much less separated from it than I am" (62). Her own position is one of total separation, total estrangement. So far out that it escapes the social order altogether? In any case, so far out as to be elsewhere. *L'existence est ailleurs.*

The sudden appearance of the last sentence in the above paragraph, produced as my free association to the word "elsewhere," itself a gloss on Duras's words, suggests to me a curious filiation; for the sentence is the famous concluding sentence of the first Surrealist Manifesto. Breton, declaring the foundation of a radically new movement, states that (his/its) existence is elsewhere; Duras, who calls her works "totally revolutionary, totally avant-garde," declares that she is elsewhere. In one reading of the trope of marginality, "woman," "woman's writing" and "avant-garde" become metaphors for each other. That is one reason why Rosalind Krauss, for example, can write about Surrealist photography that in its practice "woman and photograph become figures for each other's condition: ambivalent, blurred, indistinct, and lacking in, to use Edward Weston's word, 'authority.'"[8]

The opposition Krauss establishes between what she calls "Straight Photography," metonymically represented by Edward Weston and implicitly coded as male ("grounded in the sharply focused image, its resolution a figure of the unity of what the spectator sees, a wholeness that in turn founds the spectator himself as a unified subject") and Surrealist photography, which she explicitly codes as female (blurring all boundaries and threatening the spectator of straight photography to the point that he finds it "unbearable"—which translates exactly into *insupportable,* as used by Duras) is a move that signals Krauss's allegiance to contemporary French thought. It allows her to valorize Surrealist photography as the (metaphorically) "feminine" Other of straight photography; but it is also a move that leads to a significant (symptomatic?) slippage in terminology and conceptualization. Woman, Krauss states, is "the obsessional subject" of Surrealist photography—but in fact, as the illustrations to her essay amply document, woman, or rather the female body, is the obsessional *object* of Surrealist photographic experimentation.[9] Krauss's brilliant discussion of Surrealist "optical assaults on the body" (70) elides the difference between the subject who is agent of the assault (and who is almost invariably a male photographer) and the object that is the target of the "active aggressive assault on reality" (65), this object being also almost invariably the female body.

To call woman the obsessional *subject* of Surrealist photography is, then, misleading in a particularly interesting way, for it suggests, or rather confirms, that the figural substitution of "woman" or "the feminine" for avant-garde practice (the two being united by their common marginality in relation to "straight" or "mainstream" culture) may end up by eliding precisely the question of the female subject; and eliding, as well, the question of history. For if Surrealism, to stick to that example, is studied historically, then the absence of female subjects of Surrealist practice becomes a problem one *cannot* avoid. And I would claim that it is only by working through the problem historically that one can make progress on theoretical ground as well.

Before turning my discourse down the historical path, however, I want to emphasize a more positive and empowering aspect of the "woman"/avant-garde/marginality trope for female subjects. As the remarks by Duras I quoted earlier suggested, there is a way in which the sense of being "doubly marginal" and therefore "totally avant-garde" provides the female subject with a kind of centrality, *in her own eyes.* In a system in which the marginal, the avant-garde, the subversive, all that disturbs and "undoes the whole" is endowed with positive value, a woman artist who can identify those concepts with her own practice and metaphorically with her own femininity can find in them a source of strength and self-legitimation. Perhaps no one has done this more successfully than Hélène Cixous. Her famous essay, "The Laugh of the Medusa" (1975), is the closest thing to an avant-garde manifesto written from an explicitly feminist perspective. True to the genre of the manifesto, it is written by an "I" who represents a group ("us," in this case women); it alternates in tone between the aggressive (when addressing the hostile "straight" reader) and the hortatory (when addressing the other members of the group), and it suggests a program that implies both a revolutionary practice of writing and the disruption of existing cultural and social institutions and ideologies. What distinguishes Cixous's manifesto from its forerunners (Marinetti's Futurist manifestoes, Tzara's Dada manifestoes, Breton's Surrealist manifestoes) is that Cixous explicitly equates the radically new, subversive text with the "feminine text": "A feminine text cannot fail to be more than subversive. It is volcanic; as it is written it brings about an upheaval of the old property crust, carrier of masculine investments . . . in order to smash everything, to shatter the framework of institutions, to blow up the law, to break up the 'truth' with laughter."[10] Although the "feminine text" that is here projected (not *defined*, but projected into the future as an "écriture à venir"—this too being the hallmark of the manifesto as genre)[11] is not to be restricted to writers who are women, women are nevertheless in a privileged position to practice it: "thanks to their history, women today know (how to do and want) what men will be able to conceive of only much later" (258).

Cixous's metaphorical equation of "the feminine" with the hyperbolically marginal allows her to envisage *women* as the primary subjects of avant-garde practice. In this she differs not only from Krauss (for whom "the feminine" remains a metaphor, applied to work by male artists), but also from Kristeva; for although Kristeva leaves ample space for the maternal/semiotic in her theory of the avant-garde subject, that subject remains of necessity male. Not only are all of her exemplary avant-garde writers male, from Lautréamont and Mallarmé through Joyce, Artaud, Bataille, and Sollers, but she has even discussed, at various times, why in terms of her theory it is virtually impossible for a woman to achieve a similar status. In order to be truly innovative, one has to be able to risk giving up "la légitimation paternelle"; but if women take that risk, what awaits them more often than not is madness or suicide.[12] For the male subject, the negativity involved in giving up paternal legitimation is compensated for by a positive maternal support, and the two coexist in a dynamic balance. For the woman writer, there seems to be no viable alternative to either total paternal identification (which involves the absence of negativity, the conformism of the dutiful daughter) or else a regression to the "archaic mother," which involves yet another conformism equally incapable of producing true artistic innovation—the conformism of those who claim that "it's good because it was done by women" (Kristeva, "Unes Femmes," 24).

Even as I am writing these remarks, however, I realize that they are in some profound sense not pertinent. It is misleading to use the present tense in discussing either Kristeva's or Cixous's theoretical reflections on "écriture féminine" and its possible or impossible intersections with innovation and avant-garde practice. Those reflections are historically situated in the 1970s, at a time when there existed a strong if already splintered women's movement in France, together with an equally strong current of philosophical and literary theorizing about modernity. Today, as we have reached the 1990s, my sense is that the collective dynamism is gone and there remain only individual efforts, among women as in the French literary and intellectual arena generally. The music has stopped and the dancing is over, at least for a while. This may be the time, therefore, to put on our sensible shoes and take a walk around some real margins in the imaginary garden of the French avant-garde.

From the point of view of one who walks in sensible shoes, it is clear that there is no such thing as *the* avant-garde; there are only specific avant-garde movements, situated in a particular time and place. If we want to talk about the real marginalization of women in relation to "the avant-garde" (by real marginalization, I mean the exclusion of women from the centers of male avant-garde activity and/or their exclusion from the historical and critical accounts of that activity), we must look at individual cases in their historical and national specificity.

I propose to look at a case that has been much examined by feminist critics of late, in France and in the United States: that of Surrealism. The feminist exploration of Surrealism has proceeded along two tracks, which we might designate, following Elaine Showalter's well-known categorizations, as feminist critique (the rereading of male authors from a feminist perspective) and gynocriticsm (the rediscovery of hitherto "invisible" or undervalued women writers and their work). The pioneering work of feminist critique of Surrealism was Xavière Gauthier's *Surréalisme et sexualité* (1971). Polemical in its effect even though analytical in tone, Gauthier's detailed study of Surrealist poetry and painting sought to show, and to explain in chiefly psychoanalytic terms, "the misogyny of the compact group of male Surrealists."[13] Whether they idealized the female body and their love of it, as they did in their poetry, or whether they attacked it and dismembered it, as they did in their paintings, the male Surrealists, according to Gauthier's analysis, were essentially using the woman to work out their rebellion against the Father.

Gauthier's book appeared a year after Kate Millett's *Sexual Politics;* like Millet's work, it was important because it *posed as a problem* the subject position of male artists in relation to the objects of their representations, women. In recent years, we have seen more nuanced attempts to explore this problem, especially in the field of Surrealist visual art;[14] but there is certainly room for further reflection on the subject position of Surrealism.

As for the gynocritical work, it began with the necessary task of gathering information: who were the women writers and artists associated with Surrealism, and what did they accomplish? The 1977 volume of the review *Obliques*, devoted to *La Femme Surréal-*

iste, was the first attempt to present a catalogue of "Surrealist women," in alphabetical order, complete with photographs, bibliographies, and brief excerpts or reproductions of their work as well as some interviews and interpretive essays. In 1982, Lea Vergine's *L'Autre Moitié de l'avant-garde,* which sought to document the lives and work of women artists associated with all the major European avant-garde movements between 1910 and 1940, included eighteen women under the heading "Surréalisme;" some of them had also figured among the thirty-six women listed in *La Femme Surréaliste,* while others had not. These two books are precious reference works, but clearly they were only a first step: neither one made any claim to exhaustiveness, nor did they attempt to draw any general conclusions about the participation of women in the Surrealist movement and their contribution to it. In the last few years, important work in that direction has been accomplished by (among others) Whitney Chadwick, Jacqueline Chénieux-Gendron, and Gloria Feman Orenstein.[15] As a result, it is now becoming possible to engage in a more systematic reflection on the place (and placing) of women in Surrealism.

In what follows, I want to develop the two lines of thought suggested above. If indeed the subject position of Surrealism was male, what difficulties did that imply for the artistic practice of "Surrealist women," especially of women writers? And what exactly was the historical position of women artists and writers in the development of the Surrealist movement?

THE SURREALIST SUBJECT

Since nothing is more instructive than a good example, I shall begin by offering two. The first is a paragraph from an essay by Louis Aragon, one of the founding members of the Surrealist group, published in 1924. He is writing here about the newly established Centre des recherches surréalistes (also known as La Centrale surréaliste), which functioned in its first months as a rallying point for all those wishing to participate in the Surrealist project:

We hung a woman on the ceiling of an empty room, and every day receive visits from anxious men bearing heavy secrets. That is how we came to know Georges Bessière, like a blow of the fist. We are working at a task enigmatic to ourselves, in front of a volume of Fantomas, fastened to the wall by forks. The visitors, born under remote stars or next door, are helping to elaborate this formidable machine for killing what is in order to accomplish what is not. At number 15, Rue de Grenelle, we have opened a romantic Inn for unclassifiable ideas and continuing revolts. All that still remains of hope in this despairing universe will turn its last, raving glances toward our pathetic stall. *It is a question of formulating a new declaration of the rights of man.*[16]

The second example is from an essay by a historian of Surrealism, Robert Short, published in 1976 in an influential volume:

The criterion that the Surrealists apply to a work of art is its susceptibility to provoke a real change in those who encounter it, to call forth an affective response similar in quality to that evoked by the sight of the woman one loves.[17]

Although these texts are very different, one thing they have in common is that the author does not seem to be aware of all that he is saying. Aragon begins by talking about a woman hung on a ceiling and ends by proclaiming the Surrealist project as a desire for "a new declaration of the rights of man"—apparently unaware that the word *man* in his last sentence asks to be interpreted in its gender-specific sense, especially after all the talk about blows of the fist and machines for killing what is. Robert Short begins by talking about the Surrealists' conception of art and ends by evoking "the woman one loves"—apparently unaware that not all spectators of art are heterosexual males. In a word, both the founding Surrealist and the later historian are writing from an exclusively male subject position, and are unproblematically assigning that position to the Surrealist subject in general. They do this, I would guess, in all innocence, with no malevolent intent: theirs is not the provocation of the self-conscious misogynist, but the ordinary sexism of the man who will reply, when you point it out to him, that he hadn't noticed there were no women in the room.

But in fact, as Aragon tells us, there was a woman in the Surrealist room—her only peculiarity being that she was not made of flesh and blood. The woman in question was a life-size reclining nude figure, armless and headless (was she the inspiration for Max Ernst's first collage novel, *La Femme Cent Têtes?*), suspended from the ceiling of the Centrale. Her function was evidently to inspire the "anxious men" who came there to unburden themselves of their secrets. Did any anxious women come to unburden themselves of theirs? How might the floating lady have functioned for them?

Aragon does not mention any living women in the room; but a famous photograph by Man Ray, "La Centrale Suréaliste en 1924," documents the presence of two living women: Simone Breton and Mick Soupault, wives of the Surrealists André and Philippe. In the standard version of the photograph, the image has been cut off at the top, leaving only the feet of the headless lady visible in the upper left corner (fig. 10.1). There exists another version, however, which shows the entire figure, occupying the upper third of the photograph (fig. 10.2); below her, standing and seated in two uneven rows, are twelve men and the two women. The men, dressed in dark suits, white shirts, and ties, are writers and artists: Charles Baron, Raymond Queneau, Pierre Naville, André Breton (sporting a monocle), Jacques-André Boiffard, Giorgio de Chirico, Roger Vitrac, Paul Eluard, Philippe Soupault, Robert Desnos, Louis Aragon, and Max Morise. They look for the most part formal, solemn, almost grim, as befits an official group portrait. The two women look different, both from them and from each other: Mick Soupault, demurely dressed, is smiling slightly, like a good and tolerant wife; Simone Breton (whom Breton was to divorce a few years later, when he met his next *amour fou*) is resting her head sideways on her arm—one eye is covered by her dark hair, while the other looks at the camera with a burning stare. She is the only one who looks openly provocative, almost shocking: in one version, her legs are crossed, exposing a bit of bare flesh above her knee-high stocking (fig. 10.1).

Why do I dwell on this image? Because I think that it points up, as clearly, and more graphically than Aragon's text, the degree to which the subject position of Surrealism, as it was elaborated at the very inception of the movement, was male. The photograph also makes explicit what is only implied in Aragon's text: the problematic position of actual women who might wish to integrate themselves as subjects into the male script. I read Simone Breton and Mick Soupault in the photograph as female subjects—but as alienated subjects who have adapted themselves to the male vision of "woman," in what Luce Irigaray calls the masquerade.[18] Together, they figure the two poles of femininity between which male desire hovers: the chaste asexual wife/mother and the burning-eyed whore. Needless to say, I know nothing about the real personalities of Simone Breton and Mick Soupault—my remarks refer to their image in the photograph, which can itself be considered as the construction of a male subject. The photograph fascinates me because it lends itself so beautifully to be read as an emblem: above, the imaginary faceless woman on whom the Surrealist male artist can project his fantasies—fantasies that then become externalized, transformed, elaborated into works, poems, stories, paintings, photographs; below, two flesh and blood women who produced no works,

FIGURE 10.1 Man Ray, *The Surrealist "Central,"* 1924.

FIGURE 10.2 Man Ray, *The Surrealist "Central,"* 1924.

but who *embody* aspects of the imaginary woman hanging from the ceiling.

How much meaning can one extract from a single image or a single text? More examples are needed—for instance, another "official" group portrait, a photomontage published in 1929 in *La Révolution Surréaliste* and often reproduced since then (fig. 10.3). The montage consists of the photograph of a painting by Magritte, framed by the portraits of sixteen Surrealists with their eyes closed; the painting represents a female nude, standing in a pose reminiscent of Botticelli's *Venus*, frontally exposed; above and below her, as part of the painting, is the inscription: "Je ne vois pas la   cachée dans la forêt," ("I do not see the   hidden in the forest"), the image of the woman filling in the hole left between the words.[19] The Surrealists, all male, who frame her, adopt the position of the "Je," not seeing; at the same time, she is given *to be seen* by the spectator, who sees both the woman and the Surrealists (including Magritte, who painted her) with their eyes kept resolutely shut. This too seems to me to be an emblem of the Surrealist subject, who does not need to see the woman in order to imagine her, placing her at the center but only as an image, while any actual woman is now out of the picture altogether.

Now here is the crucial question: given the overwhelmingly male subject position of Surrealism, how did a number of women artists, who *did* produce works, manage to elaborate an imagery and a script that involved neither a masquerade of femininity nor male impersonation—which in aesthetic terms would result in purely formal imitation, the adopting of formal solutions without discovering them as a personal necessity. Luce Irigaray has touched on this problem in an essay dedicated to one of the Surrealist women whose writing has recently become known, Unica Zürn. "If woman is to put into form the *ulē* [Greek: *matter*] that she is, she must not cut herself off from it nor leave it to maternity, but succeed in creating with that primary material that she is by discovering and exposing her own morphology. Otherwise, she risks using or reusing what man has already put into forms, especially about her; risks remaking what has already been made, and losing herself in that labyrinth."[20] A woman Surrealist, in other words, cannot simply assume a subject position and take over a stock of images elaborated by the male imaginary; in order to innovate, she has to invent her own position as subject and elaborate her own set of images—different from, yet as empowering as the image of the exposed

FIGURE 10.3 Photomontage of Surrealists around a Painting by Magritte, 1929.

female body, with its endless potential for manipulation, disarticulation and rearticulation, fantasizing and projection, is for her male colleagues.

As we are coming to realize, a significant number of women artists and writers did succeed in creating their own version and vision of Surrealist practice, without merely imitating male models. Over the past ten years, there have emerged significant bodies of work produced by women who previously were either never mentioned or mentioned only in the most cursory manner in general histories of Surrealist art or of the Surrealist movement: Leonora Carrington, Dorothea Tanning, Kay Sage, Eileen Agar, Ithell Colquhoun, Toyen, Unica Zürn, Leonor Fini, Valentine Hugo—the list can be prolonged. These women were (are) primarily visual artists, but some have also produced wonderful written work—notably Leonora Carrington, who is a painter but whose short stories from the 1930s and 1940s, as well as her novel, *The Hearing Trumpet* (written around 1950) are finally finding an audience; and Unica Zürn, a graphic artist whose autobiographical texts, *Sombre Printemps* and *L'Homme-Jasmin*, written (originally in German) not long before her suicide in 1970, have acquired almost a cult status in Paris.[21] Among the women who are primarily writers, two whose names have found their way into some general studies without receiving sustained attention are Joyce Mansour (1928–1986) and Gisèle Prassinos (born in 1920).[22] One of my own favorites, better known as a film maker (*La Fiancée du pirate, Néa, Papa les p'tits bateaux*) but also the author of several books of stories and a novel, whose name appeared in *La Femme Surréaliste* but is rarely mentioned today even by critics interested in Surrealist writing by women, is Nelly Kaplan (born 1936), writing under the pen name Belen.[23]

Only a careful study of individual works and artists will allow us to answer the question of the female subject in Surrealism. In the meantime, however, one can speculate about the strategies employed by women artists and writers, both in the way they managed their lives (when and under what circumstances did a given artist become associated with the Surrealist movement? Was her work included in major exhibitions or anthologies organized by male Surrealists? Did she break with the movement, and if so, under what circumstances? What was the subsequent evolution of her artistic career?) and in the ways they situated their work within Surrealism. Since the women were generally younger and started producing later than the men who were associated with the movement, it is not unlikely that their version of Surrealist practice included a component of response to, as well as adaptation of, male Surrealist iconographies and mythologies—this being especially the case in the realm of sexuality. Here, Irigaray's notion of "mimicry," the playful or ironic counterpart of the masquerade, might provide a useful analytical category in approaching individual works. In mimicry, a woman "repeats" the male—in this case, the male Surrealist— version of "woman," but she does so in a self-conscious way that points up the citational, often ironic status of the repetition.[24]

Another specifically stylistic concept that would be useful in looking at the work of women artists is Mikhail Bakhtin's concept of "internal dialogism." The "internally dialogized" word (but this is also true of the image), Bakhtin shows, is often polemically related to another, previous word that is absent but that can be inferred from the present response to it.[25] Gloria Orenstein has suggested, relying not on Bakhtin's concept but on the anthropological concept of "muted" versus "dominant" groups, that the work of women who were personally linked—through love or marriage—to well-known male Surrealists like Max Ernst (Leonora Carrington and Dorothea Tanning), Yves Tanguy (Kay Sage), or Hans Bellmer (Unica Zürn) can be read as "a double-voiced discourse, containing both a 'dominant' and a 'muted' story."[26] In Bakhtinian terms, we can speak of the women's work as dialogically related to the men's, often with an element of internal polemic. I would suggest that such internal dialogue not only is to be found in the work of women directly involved with male Surrealists to whose work they were specifically responding, but was a general strategy adopted, in individual ways, by women wishing to insert themselves as subjects into Surrealism.

WOMEN IN THE HISTORY OF SURREALISM

Henceforth, it will be difficult for any responsible teacher or student of Surrealism not to devote some serious attention to the work of women. And if it is true that the work of women Surrealists is in internal dialogue with that of the "mainstream" male Surrealists, then our understanding of the former will necessarily influence, or even alter, our understanding of the latter. Read in the light of women artists' and writers' responses to it, the aesthetic (and political, in the broad sense) achievement of Surrealism will not necessarily be diminished, but it will look somewhat different.

At the same time, the question arises: will the discovery of a significant body of work by women oblige us to rewrite the history of the Surrealist movement? In one obvious sense, it will: the hitherto invisible women will have to be recognized.[27] In another sense, however, it won't—and to understand why, we can look at a contrasting case, that of Anglo-American modernism. The recent work of feminist scholars has shown that both the nature and the history of Anglo-American modernism began to look completely different if one takes into serious account and gives its full historical weight to the work of early women modernists like H. D., Gertrude Stein, Dorothy Richardson, and Djuna Barnes, among others. The presence of major women writers at the beginning of the modernist movement, in a literary culture that could already boast a long tradition of major writing by women, has allowed contemporary feminist critics to argue that the elimination and/or belittling of the work of women modernists (including even Virginia Woolf, who fared better than most but whose late novels were often undervalued) was very like a conspiracy perpetrated by both the male modernists and the traditional (male) historians of modernism. In the Anglo-American case, in other words, one can speak of a concerted exclusion of women's work from the modernist canon, an exclusion that Sandra Gilbert and Susan Gubar interpret as "a misogynistic reaction-formation against the rise of literary women" on the part of the male modernists whose work came to define that canon.[28]

In the case of Surrealism, one cannot make quite the same argument, especially as far as writing is concerned, because the women's work was not present in the early years of the movement, when its most significant work was produced and its "project" was elaborated. Here is an instance where the importance of historical and national specificity becomes obvious.

Let us consider some dates. The founding of the Surrealist movement in 1924 was signaled by two publications: Breton's *Manifeste du Surréalisme*, and the first issue of *La Révolution Surréaliste*, the "official" organ of the movement which continued publication through 1929; in 1930, as a result of several years of discussion and internal debate regarding the Surrealists' position vis à vis the Communist party, *La Révolution Surréaliste* was replaced by *Le Surréalisme au service de la révolution*, which continued publication (although less frequently) through 1933. In the meantime, a number of defections, exclusions and new arrivals occurred—these can be traced through the signatories of the numerous collective declarations published in the two journals. In 1932, the movement was shaken by the departure of one of its most visible and outspoken founding members, Louis Aragon, who joined the Communist party and began attacking his old comrades. After 1933, when *Le Surréalisme au service de la révolution* folded (together with any further hope for active collaboration between the Surrealists as a group and the Communists), the movement no longer had an official journal. (The journal *Minotaure,* published from 1933 to 1939, was largely open to Surrealist work, but it did not have the status of official organ, as the two earlier journals did). The movement was further weakened in 1935 by the suicide of another of its founding members, René Crevel, and by continuing attacks from the Communists. Although the Surrealists continued to publish collective statements and to proclaim an antifascist revolutionary politics, their heroic period as an avant-garde movement was coming to an end. According to Maurice Nadeau, the historian of the movement, Surrealism as a genuine avant-garde movement died around 1935. This was, of course, not a view shared by Breton and his friends. Surrealism continued to maintain itself as a movement and to organize collective manifestations in the late 1930s and throughout the war, when many of its members were in New York. After the war, it gained new adherents and staged a major international exhibition (1947), started several new journals with Breton as *Directeur,* and was not officially dispersed until 1969, three years after Breton's death. But for a long time by them, it had been no more than a surviving remnant.[29]

Historically, this is the significant fact: between 1924 and 1933, during the most dynamic and "ascendant" period of the movement, not a single woman was included as an official member. In the twelve issues of *La Révolution Surréaliste,* whose index reads like an honor roll of Surrealism (ranging from Aragon, Arp, and Artaud through Desnos, Eluard, and Ernst, to Tzara, Vaché, and Vitrac), there is *one* untitled poem by a woman, Fanny Beznos—whose biggest claim to Surrealist status is that she is mentioned in Breton's *Nadja.* A certain Madame Savitsky has a reply to the *Enquête* on suicide ("Le suicide est-il une solution?") in the first issue; a woman artist, Valentine Penrose, has a brief reply to the *Enquête sur l'amour* published in the last issue. And that's all. In the six issues of *Le Surréalisme au service de la révolution,* there are one-time appearances by three women writers (one of them being Nadejda Kroupskaia, writing about her husband Lenin—the other two are

Tzara's wife Greta Knutson, and Symone Monnerot) and visual work by three women artists, Gala Eluard, Marie-Berthe Ernst, and Valentine Hugo. Of the twenty or so major group declarations published during this period and reproduced in Nadeau's *Histoire du Surréalisme,* not a single one carries the signature of a woman. The first major document containing the signatures of women (Dora Maar, Marie-Louise Mayoux, and Méret Oppenheim) dates from 1935 ("Du Temps que les Surréalistes avaient raison").[30] After 1935, women are fairly regularly included in exhibits and group publications: in the 1930s, in addition to Hugo, Maar, and Oppenheim, we find the names of Fini, Carrington, Agar, Toyen; in the 1940s and 1950s, those of Mansour, Remedios Varo, Tanning, Kaplan, Zürn; in the 1960s, Annie Le Brun.

What conclusions can we draw from all this? First, that it is not only because of sexist bias that historians of Surrealism have tended to exclude women's work from their accounts (although sexism has played a role, since many historians mention the work of younger male Surrealists but not that of the younger women); the fact is that no women were present as active participants in the early years of the movement. Their absence can, of course, be explained as the result of an active exclusion on the part of the male Surrealists, who wanted to maintain their "men's club." But this already suggests a difference from the Anglo-American case, where women were present as active agents at the founding moment of various avant-garde projects, either as writers (H. D. and Imagism, Stein and *transition*) or as publishers and editors who promoted the work of women as well as of men.[31] It was only later that the contribution of these women was either erased from the record or else diminished. In the case of Surrealism, by contrast, women were excluded before they even got started—and this was *especially* true of writers, who even in later years remained a very small minority among women Surrealists.

The relative absence of women writers can be explained in specifically French terms, both sociological and literary. Whereas the nineteenth century in England established a significant tradition of writing by women and integrated several women writers into the major canon (Austen, the Brontës, Eliot), while the same century in the United States produced the phenomenon of bestsellerdom by women writers (who, even if they were belittled by their male colleagues, could still not be ignored), the nineteenth century in France had a quite different literary effect: there were *fewer* major women, and fewer bestsellers by women, than in the seventeenth and eighteenth centuries. Germaine de Staël and George Sand, recognized as major by their contemporaries, were eclipsed and belittled by the end of the century, remembered more for their scandalous lives than for their literary achievement. As for the blockbuster bestsellers, no woman even came close to Eugène Sue (whose popularity resembled Harriet Beecher Stowe's in the United States). If one adds to these literary considerations the social fact that France, unlike England and America, did not have a vigorous suffragette movement (French women did not get the vote until 1946), one begins to understand why early twentieth-century French women writers had less to build on, and fewer reasons for self-confidence, than their English and American counterparts. The sad fact is that with the single major exception of Colette (and perhaps Anna de Noailles, who never achieved the same degree of recognition), there were no outstanding women writers in France in the first half of this century, and certainly none who had the tenacity to construct an *oeuvre* (much less the kind of innovative, rule-breaking *oeuvre* that can be qualified as "avant-garde" and that requires the self-confidence of, say, a Gertrude Stein) until Simone de Beauvoir. Beauvoir's own achievement looms all the larger when one considers this fact; but one can also understand why, in *The Second Sex*, she lamented the absence of true audacity in women's writing (including her own).

The second conclusion one can draw from the history of Surrealism's relation to women artists and writers is that as the movement grew weaker and more embattled, it became more welcoming to women, especially young women from other countries. It is striking to note how many of the "Surrealist women" are *not* French: Carrington, Colquhoun, and Agar are English, Oppenheim Swiss, Mansour Egyptian, Fini Argentine and Italian, Kaplan Argentine, Varo Spanish, Toyen Czech, Zürn German. There were also a great many non-French male Surrealists (Ernst, Dali, Bellmer, Man Ray among them), but the *writers* of Surrealism remained overwhelmingly French. In the case of the women, the only native (more exactly, near native, born in Turkey but arriving in France as a baby) French writer in the 1930s was Gisèle Prassinos — and she was less a member of the group than a "child prodigy" they discovered and promoted.[32]

One might speculate that competition from foreign women was less threatening to the Surrealists' male egos than competition from their own. Eileen Agar suggests as much in a recent interview: "André Breton's wife [Jacqueline Lamba, Breton's second wife] was a very talented painter, he wouldn't even look at her work. But they were very nice to me, I think they were so pleased, there were so few surrealists at the time who were giving their heart and soul to it that I think they were pleased to welcome me."[33] Although no dates are mentioned, Agar seems to be referring to the mid 1930s. By then, Surrealism as a movement was on the wane (as her remarks suggest) and needed new blood. Furthermore, most of the women whom it welcomed in the 1930s were ten to fifteen years younger than the founders of the movement.[34] They therefore brought youth as well as renewal—not a small consideration for a movement that prided itself on its youthfulness. This was even more obviously the case after the war, by which time Breton and his friends were middle-aged gentlemen, more than eager to welcome young women like Joyce Mansour, Nelly Kaplan, or Annie Le Brun—especially since the young men who might have been their heirs were not about to join a moribund "avant-garde" movement. They were busy founding the new avant-gardes of the period: the rise of the *nouveau roman* and of *Tel Quel* overlaps with the last years of Surrealism.[35]

If it is clear, historically and sociologically, what women brought to Surrealism, it remains to be asked what Surrealism brought to women. In a negative perspective, one could argue that it brought them nothing, since by the time they came to it the movement's truly dynamic moment was over. Christine Brooke-Rose, writing about avant-garde literary movements in general, has ruefully noted that "women are rarely considered seriously as part of a movement when it is 'in vogue'; and they are damned with the label when it no longer is, when they can safely be considered as minor elements in it."[36] Although the history of Surrealism seems to bear out this assertion, some qualifications are necessary. It seems obvious that for the women, who came to it during the late 1930s and 1940s, and even after the war, Surrealism was able to provide both a nourishing environment, in the form of group exhibitions and publications, and a genuine source of inspiration. That may explain why some of these women, like Dorothea Tanning or Annie Le Brun, are strongly hostile to any feminist critique of Surrealism, and why Tanning has refused so far to be included in shows or publications devoted exclusively to women's work.[37] It is also true, however, that since they were not present during the founding years of the movement, it is easier to relegate them to the status of "minor elements."

The final conclusion we can draw is that if women are to be part of an avant-garde movement, they will do well to found it themselves.

Notes

1. Theodor Adorno, *Aesthetic Theory*, trans. C. Lenhardt (London: Routledge and Kegan Paul, 1984), 36.

Among the works I have found helpful in thinking about these questions are: Peter Bürger, *Theory of the Avant-Garde,* trans. Michael Shaw (Minneapolis: University of Minnesota Press, 1984); Matei Calinescu, *Five Faces of Modernity: Modernism, Avant-Garde, Decadence, Kitsch, Postmodernism* (Durham, N.C.: Duke University Press, 1987); Hal Foster, ed., *The Anti-Aesthetic: Essays on Postmodern Culture* (Port Townsend, Wash.: Bay Press, 1983); Clement Greenberg, *Art and Culture* (Boston: Beacon Press, 1961); Andreas Huyssen, *After the Great Divide: Modernism, Mass Culture, Postmodernism* (Bloomington: Indiana University Press, 1986); Rosalind Krauss, *The Originality of the Avant-Garde and Other Modernist Myths* (Cambridge, Mass.: MIT Press, 1985); Marjorie Perloff, *The Futurist Moment: Avant-Garde, Avant-Guerre, and the Language of Rupture* (Chicago: University of Chicago Press, 1986); Renato Poggioli, *The Theory of the Avant-Garde,* trans. Gerald Fitzgerald (Cambridge, Mass.: Harvard University Press, 1968); Harold Rosenberg, *The Tradition of the New* (Salem, N.H.: Ayer, 1959); Charles Russell, *Poets, Prophets, and Revolutionaries: The Literary Avant-Garde from Rimbaud through Postmodernism* (New York: Oxford University Press, 1985). See also my "Naming and Difference: Reflections on 'Modernism versus Postmodernism' in Literature," in *Approaching Postmodernism,* ed. Douwe Fokkema and Hans Bertens (Amsterdam: John Benjamins, 1986), 255–70.

2. In his influential/controversial *Theory of the Avant-Garde,* Bürger argues that the term *avant-garde* must refer only to what he calls the historical avant-gardes, embodied for him chiefly in Dada and Surrealism. According to Bürger, the European and American avant-garde movements of the 1960s are merely a "neoavant-garde, which stages for a second time the avant-gardiste break with tradition" and thereby "becomes a manifestation that is void of sense" (61). The notion that the avant-garde project could happen only once, making all other manifestations of it inauthentic "replays," sets Bürger against other theorists (notably Huyssen and Russell) who wish to see more of a continuity in the project of modernity.

3. Alice A. Jardine, *Gynesis: Configurations of Woman and Modernity* (Ithaca, N.Y.: Cornell University Press, 1985), 33–34. Hereafter cited in parentheses in the text, as are all works cited more than once.

4. Nancy K. Miller, "The Text's Heroine: A Feminist Critic and Her Fictions," *Diacritics* 12:2 (1982): 53; reprinted in *Subject to Change: Reading Feminist Writing* (New York: Columbia University Press, 1988), 76.

5. Denis Hollier, "Collages," introduction, *The College of Sociology, 1937–1939,* ed. Hollier, trans. Betty Wing (Minneapolis: University of Minnesota Press, 1988), xv.

6. Marguerite Duras and Xavière Gauthier, *Les Parleuses* (Paris: Editions de Minuit, 1974), 61; my translation, here and throughout, from the French unless otherwise stated. *Les Parleuses* has been published in English as *Woman to Woman,* trans. Katherine A. Jensen (Lincoln: University of Nebraska Press, 1987).

7. Interestingly, Duras continues to see herself as the object of misogyny and

even, somehow, as in danger of not being recognized *in France* despite her world-wide fame. See her interview with Alice Jardine below, chap. 14.

8. Rosalind Krauss, "Corpus Delicti," in R. Krauss and Jane Livingston, *L'Amour Fou: Photography and Surrealism* (New York: Abbeville Press, 1985), 95; hereafter cited in parentheses in the text.

9. It is true that the English language is partly responsible for this slippage, since *subject* can mean "subject matter," a synonym for object of representation. But a critic as theoretically sophisticated as Krauss obviously knows the other, more "Gallic" meaning of subject as agent of action.

10. Hélène Cixous, "The Laugh of the Medusa," trans. Keith Cohen and Paula Cohen, in *New French Feminisms*, ed. Elaine Marks and Isabelle de Courtivron (New York: Schocken Books, 1981), 258; hereafter cited in parentheses in the text.

11. The phrase "écriture à venir" ("writing to come") is Maurice Blanchot's; its application to avant-garde writing (specifically, to Surrealist writing) was pointed out in a lecture by Denis Hollier at the 1987 Harvard Summer Institute on the Study of Avant-Gardes, which I codirected with Alice Jardine. I thank Denis Hollier for this insight.

12. Julia Kristeva. *Des Chinoises* (Paris: Editions des Femmes, 1974), 47; and her "Unes Femmes," *Cahiers du GRIF* 12 (1975): 26. Kristeva's theory of the (male) avant-garde subject is most systematically laid out in *La Révolution du langage poétique* (Paris: Seuil, 1974); see also "Le Sujet en procès" (on Artaud), "L'Expérience et la pratique" (on Bataille), and "Polylogue" (on Sollers) in Kristeva, *Polylogue* (Paris: Seuil, 1977).

13. Xavière Gauthier, prefatory remarks to "Le Surréalisme et la sexualité" (an excerpt from her book *Surréalisme et sexualité*), in *La Femme Surréaliste*, special issue of *Obliques* 14–15 (1977): 42. See Gauthier's *Surrèalisme et sexualité* (Paris: Gallimard, Collection "Idées," 1971).

14. See, for example, Mary Ann Caws, "Ladies Shot and Painted: Female Embodiment in Surrealist Art," in *The Female Body in Western Culture: Contemporary Perspectives*, ed. Susan Rubin Suleiman (Cambridge, Mass.: Harvard University Press, 1986), 262–87; and Susan Gubar, "Representing Pornography: Feminism, Criticism, and Depictions of Female Violation," *Critical Inquiry* 13, no. 4 (1987): 712–41.

15. See Lea Vergine, *L'Autre Moitié de l'avant-garde, 1910–1940* (Paris: Editions des Femmes, 1982); Whitney Chadwick, *Women Artists and the Surrealist Movement* (Boston: Little, Brown, 1985), the first comprehensive study of Surrealist women artists, lavishly illustrated; Jacqueline Chénieux, *Le Surréalisme et le roman* (Lausanne: L'Age d'Homme, 1983), which includes serious discussion of work by Surrealist women writers; Gloria Feman Orenstein, "Reclaiming the Great Mother: A Feminist Journey to Madness and Back in Search of a Goddess Heritage," *Symposium* 36, no. 1 (1982): 45–69, which discusses work by both women writers and artists. Chénieux and Orenstein contributed to the *Obliques* issue on *La Femme Surréaliste*. Despite all this valuable work, no one has attempted until now a systematic reflection on the historical relation of women to the Surrealist movement and on its implications for French literary and cultural history, as well as for a possible theory of the avant-garde.

16. Quoted in Maurice Nadeau, *The History of Surrealism*, trans. Richard Howard (New York: Macmillan, 1965), 92; my emphasis. I have modified the

translation somewhat—notably, I have put verbs in the present tense as they were in the original, published in 1924 and explicitly referring to the "here and now."

17. Robert Short, "Dada and Surrealism," in *Modernism, 1890–1930*, ed. Malcolm Bradbury and James McFarlane (Harmondsworth, England: Penguin Books, 1976), 303.

18. See Luce Irigaray, *This Sex Which Is Not One*, trans. Catherine Porter with Carolyn Burke (Ithaca, N.Y.: Cornell University Press, 1985).

19. This painting should be compared with Magritte's famous 1926 painting, *Ceci n'est pas une pipe*, which shows a pipe accompanied by the inscription ("This is not a pipe") that gives the work its title. Although both paintings are playing with representation, they do so in diametrically opposed ways: the "reality" of the painted pipe is negated by the inscription, which highlights the difference between image and word, image and thing; the painted woman, on the contrary, is so "real" that she can *replace* the word that would be used to designate her. In the first instance, the differences between visual representation, language, and reality are emphasized; in the second, these differences are blurred—as if, where woman was concerned, the real, the imaginary, and the symbolic were interchangeable (for a male subject?).

20. Luce Irigaray, "Une Lacune natale (pour Unica Zürn)," *Le Nouveau Commerce* 62–63 (1985): 42. Irigaray's cryptic remark about "not leaving her *ulē* to maternity" would need to be commented and qualified, given that for so many contemporary women writers—including Irigaray herself—the maternal body has provided a fertile source of imagery and inspiration; one of the major texts by a woman Surrealist, Leonora Carrington's *Hearing Trumpet*, is based on a complicated playing with and valorization of the mother's body and the mother's *voice*.

21. Carrington was the only woman included in the original version of Breton's *Anthologie de l'humour noir* (1939). Her works currently in print include *The Hearing Trumpet* (San Francisco: City Lights Books, 1985), which I discuss at length in my *Subversive Intent: Gender, Politics, and the Avant-Garde* (Cambridge, Mass.: Harvard University Press, 1990); and two recent volumes that bring together her shorter works from the 1930s through the 1970s: *The House of Fear: Notes from Down Below* and *The Seventh Horse and Other Tales* (New York E. P. Dutton, 1988). Carrington is particularly interesting in that she wrote in both French and English (and even a few stories in Spanish). For works by Unica Zürn, see *L'Homme-Jasmin* (Paris: Gallimard, 1971), and *Sombre Printemps* (Paris: Belfond, 1985), with a biographical "postface" by Ruth Henry.

22. Neither Mansour nor Prassinos is included in Michael Benedikt's supposedly comprehensive anthology in English, *The Poetry of Surrealism: An Anthology* (Boston: Little Brown & Co., 1974); nor do they appear in Paul Auster's more recent bilingual anthology, *The Random House Book of Twentieth-Century French Poetry* (New York: Vintage Books, 1984). Benedikt's anthology, covering two generations of Surrealists, includes no work by women: Auster's, covering the whole century, includes one woman: Anne-Marie Albiach. In France, Gisèle Prassinos's *Les mots endormis* (Paris: Flammarion, 1967) and *Trouver sans chercher* (Paris: Flammarion, 1976), containing selections from her poetry of the 1930s as well as some later work, are in print; she also

has a number of novels and collections of stories written in a "post-Surrealist" mode. The first book-length study on her work appeared in 1988: Madeleine Cottenet-Hage, *Gisèle Prassinos ou le désir du lieu intime* (Paris: Jean-Michel Place). As of January 1989, all of Mansour's numerous books were out of print (though some can still be found in specialized bookstores). They include: *Cris* (Paris: Seghers, 1953); *Les Gisants Satisfaits* (Paris: J.-J. Pauvert, 1958); *Rapaces* (Paris: Seghers, 1960); and *Carré blanc* (Paris: Le Soleil Noir, 1965). *Rapaces* is available in a shortened bilingual edition in the United States: *Birds of Prey,* trans. Albert Herzing (Perivale Press, 1979).

23. Belen's comic, erotic novel, *Mémoires d'une liseuse de draps* (Paris: Pauvert, 1974) is currently available: her shorter fiction has recently been collected in a single volume, under her own name: Nelly Kaplan, *Le Réservoir des sens* (Paris: J.-J. Pauvert, 1988).

24. See Irigaray, *This Sex,* 76. As Irigaray suggests, mimicry may be only an "initial phase," a first strategy adopted traditionally by the oppressed. This raises the question of how one might go beyond mimicry, to other possible strategies not based on an ironic relation to a preexisting situation.

25. See M. M. Bakhtin, *The Dialogic Imagination,* ed. Michael Holquist, trans. Caryl Emerson and Michael Holquist (Austin: University of Texas Press, 1981), 282ff.

26. Gloria Feman Orenstein, "Towards a Bifocal Vision in Surrealist Aesthetics," *Trivia* 3 (Fall 1983), 72. The quoted phrase is actually from Elaine Showalter, "Feminist Criticism in the Wilderness," in *Writing and Sexual Difference,* ed. Elizabeth Abel (Chicago: University of Chicago Press, 1980).

27. Just how invisible the Surrealist women were is demonstrated by William Rubin's otherwise useful 1968 book (the catalogue of a major exhibition at the Museum of Modern Art), *Dada, Surrealism, and their Heritage* (New York: Museum of Modern Art). Among the dozens of artists mentioned by Rubin, the only woman is Méret Oppenheim, whose fur-covered teacup (1936) is perhaps the best-known Surrealist object. It has also been, almost invariably, the *only* work by Oppenheim mention or displayed in books or exhibits on Surrealism.

28. See Sandra Gilbert and Susan Gubar, "Tradition and the Female Talent," in *The Poetics of Gender,* ed. Nancy K. Miller (New York: Columbia University Press, 1986), 183–207. For an informative historical study, devoted chiefly to English and American women modernists in exile, see Shari Benstock, *Women of the Left Bank: Paris, 1900–1940* (Austin: University of Texas Press, 1986).

29. For a very useful, complete listing of Surrealist journals published in France between 1948 and 1972, see Marguerite Bonnet and Jacqueline Chénieux-Gendron, *Revues Surréalistes françaises autour d'André Breton, 1948–1972* (Millwood, N.Y.: Kraus International Publications, 1982). For an informative account of the political evolution of Surrealism, more detailed than Nadeau's through not contradicting any of his analyses, see Helena Lewis, *The Politics of Surrealism* (New York: Paragon House, 1988). It is almost touching to note that there has existed, to the late 1980s, a Surrealist Group in Chicago which published collective declarations. A leader of the group, Franklin Rosemont, has edited a selection of Breton's writings in English, with a book-length introduction that, although adulatory toward Breton and truculent toward almost everyone else, provides a good indication of a certain American strain of Surrealism.

See André Breton, *What is Surrealism? Selected Writings*, edited and introduced by Franklin Rosemont (Chicago: Monad Press, 1978)

30. Reproduced in Maurice Nadeau, *Histoire du Surréalisme* (Paris: Editions du Seuil, 1964), 422–32. A 1934 declaration, opposing the Fascist demonstrations of 6 February and calling for a united front of workers and intellectuals against Fascism, contained three women's signatures (Nadeau, 381–86). However, this was not a specifically Surrealist declaration, like "Du Temps que les Surréalistes avaient raison." I did not find women's signatures on any document prior to 1934 reproduced in Nadeau's book. The English translation of *Histoire du Surréalisme* includes many fewer documents than the original French edition.

31. On the role of women editors, see Benstock, chap. 10. Interestingly, there *were* women artists and performers participating in the early days of various Dada movements (even though they were generally ignored by later historians): Sophie Tauber and Emmy Hennings in Zurich, Hanna Höch in Berlin, among others. Could we then see French Surrealism as already a defensive reaction to the rise of "avant-garde women"? Or is it that, given the heavily literary orientation of the French movement in its early years, the relevant category here is that of *writing* and "literary women" in France, which I discuss below?

32. Prassinos's first volume of poetry and prose texts, *La Sauterelle arthritique*, was published in 1935, when she was fifteen years old, with a preface by Paul Eluard. J. H. Matthews, in his long and interesting study *The Imagery of Surrealism* (Syracuse, N.Y.: Syracuse University Press, 1977), quotes Eluard's preface but has nothing to say about Prassinos. (He does devote half a page to Mansour, however; and he subsequently published a short monograph on her work: *Joyce Mansour* [Amsterdam: Rodopi, 1985]).

33. Mary Blume, "Portrait of a Surrealist," *International Herald Tribune*, 17 August 1987.

34. Most of the first-generation male Surrealists were born around the turn of the century: Breton in 1896, Aragon in 1897, Eluard in 1895, Desnos in 1900, Ernst in 1891, Man Ray in 1890, Bellmer in 1902. Of the women, only Valentine Hugo was older (born in 1887); Toyen (1902) and Agar (1904) were around the same age. The other women who came to Surrealism before 1945 were at least a decade younger: Maar was born in 1909, Tanning in 1912, Oppenheim in 1913, Carrington in 1917, Fini in 1918, Prassinos in 1920.

35. There were, to be sure, some young male disciples—notably Jean Schuster, who became Breton's literary executor (Schuster's writings are collected in his book, *Archives 57/68* [Paris: Eric Losfeld, 1969]), and José Pierre, who is now a leading member of ACTUAL, an association devoted to collecting, preserving, and gradually publishing the archives of Surrealism. In general, the work of postwar male Surrealists strikes me (in contrast to the women's work) as oriented more toward preservation of the "archive" than toward making a major contribution to it, or better still, transforming it.

36. Christine Brooke-Rose, "Illiterations," in *Breaking the Sequence: Women's Experimental Fiction*, ed. Ellen G. Friedman and Miriam Fuchs (Princeton: Princeton University Press, 1989), 65.

37. Annie Le Brun expresses outrage and anger at the feminist critique in her collection of essays, *A Distance* (Paris: Pauvert/Carrère, 1984). Dorothea Tanning is represented only by a letter of refusal in Vergine's *L'Autre Moitié de l'avant-garde*, and is absent altogether from the issue of *Obliques* on *La Femme Surréaliste*.

III Canons and Other Voices &

Relocating French Literature

11 ELAINE MARKS

"Sapho 1900": Imaginary Renée Viviens and the Rear of the *Belle Époque*

The questions of this essay are the questions raised by those words of the title of this volume[1] situated on the far side of the colon. What is involved in the act of "placing women in French literature"? Who constitutes the group labeled women? Monique Wittig, for example, insists that lesbians are not women. And what, in 1990, is "French literature"? A rapid perusal of histories and manuals of contemporary French literature reveals that French literature is no longer the chronological, national monolith it was before 1968. Renée Vivien, an avowed lesbian, British and American by birth, and writing in French, has been "placed" by North American and French critics in the tradition of lesbian writers, a tradition that is not limited to or by national boundaries, although it has tended to be Eurocentric.

I would argue that the notion of "French literature" is so embedded in theological and nationalist discourses that changes according to gender in the canon cannot significantly address fundamental questions of culture and reading. Indeed, who is in and who is out, although of considerable importance for understanding how the canon came to be constituted in its present form, is less important than how texts are read and for what purpose. It may be more politically effective to read excluded or marginal texts not as forgotten or neglected pieces that will now take their rightful place, but rather as case histories of the ways in which prescription and proscription operate in discourses that inform literature and culture.

In the essay that follows I try to show what the proponents of a

French national literature, the proponents of a French women's literature, and the proponents of an international (Western) lesbian literature have in common; how their grounds for inclusion or exclusion in a representative body of work depend either on the critics' adhesion to certain principles of representation and narration, or on their views of the writer's sexual identity and origins.

Renée Vivien, pseudonym of Pauline Tarn, 1877–1909, was born in London, England, of an English father and an American mother and spent much of her childhood in Paris. Her father died in 1886, and she began to write verses in French in 1887 at the age of ten. The published stories of her life, those that have been written by others than herself, focus on women whom she desired successively and in some cases, simultaneously: Violette Shillito, Natalie Clifford Barney, Eveline Palmer, Hélène de Zuylen de Nyevelt, Kérimé Turkhan-Pacha, Jeanne de Bellune, Emilienne d'Alençon, Madeleine Rouveirollis; and older men who were her mentors and friends: Amédée Moullé, Charles-Brun, Eugène Vallée. Her female relationships usually involved geographical displacements: as a child between London and Paris and, later, trips to the United States (Bar Harbor and Bryn Mawr), to Mytilene on the island of Lesbos, and to the Middle East. They also involved Renée Vivien's identification with and worship of the Greek Lesbian poet Sappho, whose fragments she translated into French.

At her death in 1909—she was thirty-two years old—Renée Vivien had written approximately twenty separate volumes composed mainly of poems, but also of short stories, a novel, and a biography of Anne Boleyn. She had written a multitude of letters and an unpublished diary, part of a collection belonging to Salomon Reinach and deposited at the Bibliothèque nationale, to be made available to scholars and other readers in the year 2000. Until World War II, her life and her work received regular if discreet attention by critics interested in "littérature féminine," in the Sapphic tradition in verse and in mores, and in death-bed conversions to Catholicism. In 1951, André Billy, in his *L'Époque 1900,* coined the phrases "Sapho 1900, Sapho cent pour cent . . ."[2] implying that Renée Vivien was *the* exclusively lesbian poet of the *Belle Epoque,* and rekindled a mild interest in her biography and in her poetry. The feminist and gay liberation movements of the late 1960s and the 1970s primarily in the United States, but also in France, focusing on sociocultural contexts and subversive discourses capable of disrupting patriarchal and/or heterosexual constructions, represented Renée Vivien either as a decadent writer, an imitator of Baudelaire, politically unaware and therefore dangerous as a model; or as a conscious lesbian-feminist living within a lesbian community in Paris at the turn of the century, one of the first women writers to rewrite Western myths from an enlightened lesbian-feminist perspective. Since her early death, variously attributed to some excessive combination of alcohol, drugs, anorexia nervosa, and the desire to die, Renée Vivien has become a cult figure for a group of French male admirers, biographers, and critics such as Charles-Brun (1911), Salomon Reinach (1918), Le Dantec (1930), Paul Lorenz (1977), and Jean-Paul Goujon (1986). Complete editions of her poetry were published in Paris by Lemerre in 1923–1924 and in 1934. In 1986, Régine Desforges published a new biography of Renée Vivien by Jean-Paul Goujon, *Tes Blessures sont plus douces que leurs caresses* and, in a single volume, the *Oeuvre poétique complète de Renée Vivien,* an edition with an introduction and notes by Jean-Paul Goujon.

Her writings in prose are not as easily available in French. Her one novel, *Une Femme m'apparut,* originally published in 1904 and revised in 1905, has had no other French edition. The 1904 version is available in English in a translation by Jeannette H. Foster, published in 1976 by the Naiad Press with an introduction by Gayle Rubin. *La Dame à la louve,* a collection of short stories also published originally in French in 1904, was translated into English as *The Woman of the Wolf and Other Stories* by Karla Jay and Yvonne M. Klein and published by Gay Presses of New York in 1983. Renée Vivien's biography of Anne Boleyn was published for the first time in French in 1982 by A L'Ecart.

Renée Vivien has been placed within a variety of traditions, French and comparative, including a Baudelairean tradition, a Lesbian tradition, a tradition of significant women writers "haunted" by "the person and the poetics of Sappho,"[3] and a tradition of turn-of-the-century minor French women poets. Her critics and biographers have, almost without exception, relied on a certain concept of the *Belle Epoque* as the context within which her texts were written and her life, before it was written, was lived. These stereotypical, standardized discourses *on* the *Belle Epoque* describe a period in which nature, love, and women were glorified, including the figure of the lesbian, a period of artistic innovation and feminist activity with Paris as the cultural center of the Western world. But there are other discourses *of* the *Belle Epoque,* discourses that tell of and react to the "Death of God," discourses that explicitly or implicitly often use the clichés of social Darwinism to construct anti-Semitic, nationalist, racist, and sexist theories thereby strengthening and solidifying the binary categories superior/inferior, white/black, Aryan/Jew, male/female, order/anarchy. These other discourses, from the underside of the *Belle Epoque,* are still prevalent today. Therefore, the appropriate intertexts for Renée Vivien, writer and woman, include not only Sappho, Colette, Natalie Clifford Barney, and *l'art nouveau,* but also Nietzsche, Freud, and Charles Maurras.

In 1905, the year of the rehabilitation of (Captain) Alfred Dreyfus, Charles Maurras, one of the leaders of the movement *Action française* and the principal pedagogue of right-wing ideology in France between the 1890s and 1944, published in the same volume as his *L'Avenir de l'intelligence* an essay called "Renée Vivien" as part of his *Le Romantisme féminin.*[4] In 1976, the Naiad Press published Jeannette H. Foster's translation of Renée Vivien's *A Woman Appeared to Me* with a preface by Gayle Rubin that in many ways, but not in all, is diametrically opposed to the text by Charles Maurras.[5] I would like to confront the discourse of the nationalist, monarchist, and anti-Semite with the discourse of the lesbian-feminist cultural and social analyst, and to raise through this confrontation a series of questions that relate to the placing of women writers in French literature. I will attempt to show how both Maurras and Rubin, in brilliant and provocative essays, use the available biographical and textual data to create an imaginary Renée Vivien, to pursue a genealogical illusion, a utopian vision of unity that reinforces a coherent ideological discourse from which metaphysical anguish and the enigma of sexual identity, the thematic core of Renée Vivien's poetry and prose, have been banished. I will also argue that because of the anomalous status of women writers in relation to the traditions of French literature and because of the assumptions about women that inform discourses on women writers at different historical moments, many critics seem unable to resist the power of their own ideological whims in the interpretation of women's texts.

By placing *Le Romantisme féminin* in the same volume as his *L'Avenir de l'intelligence,* Charles Maurras informs his readers that the question of women writers and the question of gender cannot be viewed in isolation. His essay on Renée Vivien is embedded in his desire to return to another France, the France of the *ancien régime,* the France of grace, of charm, and of lightness. Renée Vivien and the three other women writers he discusses—Madame de Régnier, Madame Lucie Delarue-Mardrus, and the Comtesse de Noailles—are presented individually as important, original poets and collectively as a dangerous phenomenon. The very title of the collection of four essays condemns these women writers within Maurras's system: they are either not French by birth or not French in spirit, that is to say that they are "romantic," foreign, through their adherence to a Germanic or Anglo-Saxon literary tradition; they are not working within the French classical tradition, therefore they are marginal; they are not men and therefore they are or should be feminine: resigned, sweet, and patient. What is important in this scheme is that the male/female difference cannot be separated from the French/foreign binary opposition or from the classical/Romantic opposition. These four women writers are, in essence, sexually different and racially impure. Moreover, if they manifest any sign of the "risque lesbien," they are a danger to the nation. Let us look more closely at *L'Avenir de l'intelligence* and *Auguste Comte.* These texts will assist us in placing Charles Maurras, as he places "Renée Vivien," in French letters.

But, for those Catholics who have left the faith, this form of nostalgia can become so absorbing that the apologists of their religion have developed an extremely cogent argument. Human life, they say, has only one axis without which it breaks apart and drifts. Without divine unity and its consequences—which are discipline and dogma—mental unity, moral unity, and political unity disappear at the same time; they only come together again if the first unity is reestablished. Without God, there is no longer either true or false, there are no more rules, there is no more law. Without God, a rigorous logic equates the worst folly with the most perfect reason. Without God, killing, stealing are perfectly innocent acts; there is no crime that does not become unimportant, no revolution that is not legitimate; because, without God, only the principle of free examination exists, a principle that can exclude everything but that can establish nothing. The Catholic clergy gives us the choice between its dogma, with the extreme degree of organization that accompanies it, and this absolute absence of measure and regulation which annuls or which wastes activity. God or nothing is the alternative proposal to those tempted by doubt. (*Auguste Comte,*105).

Charles Maurras, in 1905, was nostalgically in search of an order that would resurrect what he imagined to have been the Golden Age, the Garden of Eden of the *ancien régime,* the period before the French Revolution, a period in which the adjectives *French, Catholic,* and *classical* were synonymous. *L'Avenir de l'intelligence* calls for a counterrevolution, an alliance of intelligence with the old religious and philosophical traditions against those who, like Emile

Zola and the "new intellectuals," were threatening civilization. Writing toward the end of the Dreyfus Affair, Maurras brings together, in the camp of his enemies, Rousseau, Romanticism, and foreign influences, the Protestant critical spirit and the inability of Jewish intellectuals and critics to understand "nos humanités." Charles Maurras was not a believer. He was, like Auguste Comte, one of the "Catholics who have left the faith," one of the Catholics "without God." His attempt to hold on to certain moral and aesthetic values in spite of the "Death of God" explains his interest in Auguste Comte's positivism and his initial attraction to the poetry of women writers who seem to announce a return to simplicity and sincerity of feeling in their poems. Maurras's quest of unity and order refuses contradictions, banishes anarchy and hermeticism, and posits a harmony between "lettres françaises," "l'intelligence," and "le sens national." Maurras is blatantly nationalistic. France, in his texts, has already replaced the kingdom of God, and if he supports the Catholic church as the only institution capable of encouraging adherence to the old values, it is because he views the Catholic Church as a French institution. Moreover, Frenchness, for Maurras, cannot be acquired:

People say that culture is moving from right to left and that a new world is being formed. That may be. But those who have been newly promoted are also newcomers, unless they are their clients or their valets, and these foreigners, recently enriched, are terribly lacking either in seriousness and reflexion in spite of their weighty appearance, or in lightness and grace in spite of their false Parisian polish. I find their brutish minds superficial! They are so practical, so pliant that they lose the heart and soul of everything. How could these people have a genuine taste for our humanities? What can they understand about them? Understanding of that kind cannot be learned at the university. All the diplomas in the world will not make this Jewish critic who is erudite and profound appreciate that in *Bérénice* "charming places where my heart adored you" is a manner of speaking that is not banal, but simple, moving, and very beautiful (*L'Avenir de l'intelligence*, 12)

It would appear, then, that Renée Vivien, Anglo-American and Protestant, is ipso facto excluded from participating in this Frenchness. But because she is a woman, other standards apply. Maurras does not expect Renée Vivien to have "des idées philosophiques vraies," but he does expect her to have "des émotions justes" ("Renée Vivien," 165). Because her texts cannot be judged by the same criteria as those by which the texts of Baudelaire, for example, are judged, Maurras does not immediately dismiss her work. His double standard implies that women writers may be placed both in relation to "lettres francaises" and in relation to other women writers. Although Maurras seems convinced in his essentialism, convinced that Frenchness cannot be learned if one is not born into it, he is nevertheless surprised by the quality of Renée Vivien's French and by her knowledge of Latin and Greek, as well as of English literature: "Her use of the French language, whether in prose or in verse, is remarkably fluid. There is neither impropriety in the choice of words nor a false note in the harmony of sounds. She knows that the mute *e* is responsible for the charm of our language. She plays with the eleven-syllable line of verse that Verlaine considered the most accomplished of all 'Douceur de mes chants, allons vers Mitylène . . .' ['Sweetness of my songs, let us sail towards Mitylene . . .']" ("Renée Vivien," 148). Not only is Renée Vivien the faithful disciple of Baudelaire and of Verlaine, but she is often, according to Maurras, their rival.

Indeed, what is most striking about Maurras's essay on Renée Vivien is the serious attention he gives to her poetry and, at the same time, the ironic and indulgent manner in which he treats women, and particularly young women, as thinkers. His text abounds in contradictions. He focuses on two texts by Renée Vivien, "La Genèse profane" in *Brumes de fjord* (1902) and "Prophéties" in *Cendres et poussières* (1903). In both cases he compares Renée Vivien's words to those of Charles Baudelaire, and in both cases he insists on Renée Vivien's superiority and her difference. Her superiority because she is a young woman and therefore more natural and more sensual, particularly in relation to the sense of touch; and her difference because she is a woman. It is this tautological concept of absolute difference accepted by Maurras as clear and evident, as an unquestioned assumption, that his essay does not and cannot justify.

"La Genèse profane," which Maurras compares favorably to Baudelaire's "Blasphèmes," is a prose poem in twenty-one stanzas that narrates a "profane" version of *Genesis*. Jehovah, who incarnates strength, creates the sky, man, the heterosexual embrace, and the poet Homer; Satan, who incarnates cunning, creates night, woman, the caress, and the poet Sappho, the Lesbian. And while Homer told of the life and death of warriors, Psappha sang of:

Les formes fugitives de l'amour, les pâleurs et les extases, le déroulement magnifique des chevelures, le troublant parfum des roses, l'arc-en-ciel de l'Aphroditâ, l'amertume et la douceur de l'Erôs, les danses sacrées des femmes de la Crète autour de l'autel illuminé d'étoiles, le sommeil solitaire tandis que sombrent dans la nuit la lune et les Pléiades, l'immortel orgueil qui méprise la douleur et sourit dans la mort, et le charme des baisers féminins rhythmés par le flux assourdi de la mer expirant sous des murs voluptueux de Mitylène. ("Renée Vivien," 151)

The fugitive forms of love, the pallor, and the ecstasy, the magnificent unfolding of hair, the troubling perfume of roses, the rainbow of Aphrodite, the bitterness and the sweetness of Eros, the sacred dances of the women of Crete around the altar illuminated by stars, the solitary sleep while the moon and the seven sisters disappear into the night, the immortal pride that scorns pain and smiles at death, and the charm of feminine kisses rhythmically marked by the muffled beat of the sea expiring under the voluptuous walls of Mytilene.

Maurras uses this poem as an example of the "espirt général" that pervades Renée Vivien's poetry and that informs the reader about Renée Vivien's views on religion, ethics, history, and literature. He finds this poem more Baudelairean than Baudelaire's own poetry, more forceful and more blasphemous. But he also finds the poem "un peu chargé." Maurras recognizes that Renée Vivien has created her own imaginary Psappha, a Psappha Baudelaireanized, Christianized, and romanticized. What is interesting is not that praise and criticism alternate, but that there is so little precision in Maurras's comments when he is not engaged in classifying. If one recalls his emphasis in *Auguste Comte* on what is implied in a concept of a world without God, it is curious to note that when a similar theme occurs in the texts of a woman writer, it is not recognized. Seventy-one years later, Gayle Rubin treats this same theme in an apparently very different manner: "Renée Vivien read widely in myth, legend and ancient literature. She rewrote many of western culture's most cherished myths, replacing their male and heterosexual biases with female and lesbian ones. In these excerpts from 'The Profane Genesis' Vivien changes the biblical story into the creation myth of lesbian poetry" (x–xi). Maurras's essay is moving toward a particular definition of feminine difference, and Rubin's is primarily concerned with discovering ancestors for contemporary lesbian-feminism. Neither Maurras nor Rubin is prepared to read in Vivien's prose poem a Nietzschean rewriting of religious and metaphysical texts. Maurras will allow a woman poet to imitate Baudelaire but not to propose other directions. Rubin will read a lesbian poet only in terms of post-1968 lesbian-feminist consciousness.

Toward the end of his essay Maurras reveals the theory of feminine difference on which the *Belle Epoque* relied for many of its representations of women:

Nature has arranged things so that women are bound to conceive of almost everything that touches them strictly in connection with vague ideas of happiness, luck, fatality, and destiny. The future is for them an innate obsession. In vain does the wise Horace warn them that things of the future are not precisely fixed. Women think of themselves as the protectors of being. All women listen to the magnificent resonance in their very entrails of the slightest conjecture about the relationship between what is or was with what will be. A maternal instinct constructs their universe in the form of a cradle, everything must work together to receive their fruit. A superstition, without a doubt. The superstition is complete. A woman without superstition is a monster. One notes, not without pleasure, that in spite of all her devilishness, Renée Vivien did not think of making herself into a thinker. A holy man murmurs: "That is what will save her." . . . That is, at any rate, the most natural element of her profoundly feminine art. ("Renée Vivien," 166)

Maurras judges Renée Vivien's "art" on the basis of its conformity to a particular theory of the feminine. This theory depends on the absolute program laid down by nature and on a particular relationship to the future determined by a "maternal instinct." Maurras's presentation emphasizes the notion that what is natural is both inevitable and inferior. But there is no escape. Either a woman is natural and inferior, that is to say feminine and superstitious, or she is a monster, a thinker, someone who breaks the natural order. The feminine, according to Maurras, is both a constraint and an obligation. The feminine defines limits that must not be transgressed. Within these limits women poets are judged on the degree to which male critics "frissonnent" and "frémissent" in contact with their poems, the degree to which poems by women produce effects that are sensuous and powerful. As an example of this power, Maurras extracts from the poem "Prophéties" the line: "Tu te flétriras un jour, ah! mon lys!" ("One day, you will wilt, ah! my lily!"), which he reads as superior to lines on the fear of aging in the poetry of Charles Baudelaire. The difference, for Maurras, is that Baudelaire's "frémissement apparaît un simple exercice de rhétorique," whereas Renée Vivien achieves her effects "par la magie du chant" ("Renée Vivien," 167). Renée Vivien, the accomplished versifier of the opening pages of the essay, has been transformed at the end into a feminine magician, qualified by the adjective *diabolique* and replaced by the noun *perversité*. The monster is emerging.

Maurras's praise of the feminine disappears from the last chapter of *Le Romantisme féminin*, "Leur Principe commun," in which he discusses what Renée Vivien and "Mmes de Noailles, de Régnier et Mardrus" have in common. As in the essay on Renée Vivien, there is in "Leur Principe commun" a significant difference between the beginning and the end of the chapter. Maurras begins by placing the four women poets in the tradition associated with the names of Rousseau, Chateaubriand, and Hugo. "We can no longer study Romanticism without referring to Mlle Renée Vivien, Madame de Noailles, Madame de Régnier and Madame de Mardrus: by resuscitating and enlarging the scope of Romanticism, they illuminate it" (207). The rest of the chapter is subdivided into eight parts: "L'Origine étrangère," "D'étrangetés en perversions," "L'Indépendance du mot," "L'Anarchie," "Le Génie féminin," "Le Prestige d'être bien soi," "La Profanation," and "Le Dessèchement." As the titles suggest, Maurras raises questions that are not considered in the essay on Renée Vivien, questions about the dangers of Romanticism, the dangers of women forming a community of women writers, a secret little world (here, too, the resemblance with anti-Semitic rhetoric of the period is striking), and, finally, the greatest danger of all, perhaps the very definition of monster, the "risque lesbien."

Maurras's text represents Romanticism in terms of the feminine and, through a series of metaphors, concludes that these four women writers are dangerous to the human race. The first and most negative aspect of romanticism is that the authors who practice it and the ideas that have influenced them are foreign. The term *métèques indisciplinées*, which Maurras borrows from a young nationalist writer, M. Duchot, is used to identify the four women writers who benefit from the advantages of a French culture but who cannot accept "la discipline nationale." It is also used by Maurras to remind his readers that Rousseau, Germaine de Staël, and George Sand were not French: "The lack of discipline of our young *métèques* only continues a tradition that, although it was introduced in France, has nonetheless remained separate from the true tradition of French literature. One must understand the heterogeneity of Sand, of Staël, and of Rousseau or desist from censuring their heirs; for the latter are but a wave, the last wave, of that gothic invasion for which Geneva and Coppet opened the way" (*Le Romantisme Féminin*, 208). The opposition now in place is that between France, inheritor of the classical, Greek spirit and Germany, guilty of having infected, over the past one hundred and fifty years, Greece, Spain, and Italy with its mediocrity. Maurras is not at all troubled by the facts: for example, not one of the four women writers he discusses is of German descent. It is sufficient for him "que leur sang ne fût point de veine française très pure" (210). From this moment on the text takes off, as do polemical texts based on irrational premises, in a series of fanciful accusations that recall such outrageous and popular anti-Semitic texts of the *Belle Epoque* as Edouard Drumont's *La France juive* (1886). The pure and the impure designate French and non-French; the Romantic tradition, for Maurras, is, by definition, impure. Maurras reads the same "perversité sensuelle" in Baudelaire's *Fleurs du Mal* and in Renée Vivien's poems. He accuses the "Mallarmistes" of being feminine in their worship of the word, and, except for their refusal of obscurity, he finds the same glorification of the word in the writing of the four women.

But even more dangerous for Maurras than this verbal materialism is the importance given to the ego, an importance he interprets as a sign of revolt. Renée Vivien is accused of wallowing in eccentricity, in evil, in images of death, decrepitude, and illness. The same sensibility that was praised earlier in *Le Romantisme féminin* as direct and natural is now condemned; the expression of feeling has become unhealthy. But, in an unexpected shift, Maurras insists that Romanticism has always been feminine and that the male poets associated with the Romantic movement were subjected to a change of gender; they were feminized. Suddenly, it is as if Hugo, Chateaubriand, Lamartine, Michelet, Baudelaire, Verlaine had been contaminated by the feminine, a feminine that had installed itself perniciously in the very core of Romanticism.

The remainder of the essay is a diatribe against women. In support of his passion, Maurras quotes an anonymous woman philosopher who, writing for several Parisian newspapers under the pseudonym Foemina, contends that women are more subject than men to bodily discomforts, that women are governed by the maxim: I suffer, therefore I am. The insistence on egoism as the feminine trait par excellence seems to be a satisfactory explanation for Maurras as to why women were the original discoverers of the aesthetic of harmony. From "métèques" to "criminelles" to "bacchantes" and "ménades," women writers constitute, according to Maurras, a danger not only for French letters but for the entire human race. Again, the parallel with anti-Semitic rhetoric is obvious:

Today, more than one woman of distinction repeats an old paradox reformulated as a syllogism and propagated as if it were a religious or moral doctrine. Woman, they say, is uniquely capable of understanding and of receiving, of giving and returning the essence of love that her heart desires: "men are hard," "lovers are brutal. . . ." These women are being listened to.

We must not exaggerate the malignancy of the symptom furnished by our cafes or our women's clubs and certain other characteristics of American or British customs. As far as this topic is concerned, the philosopher has to trust nature, which tells him not to lack confidence in life. It is nonetheless true that a society of women is in the act of being organized, a secret little world in which man only appears as an intruder and a monster, a lecherous and comic toy, in which it is a disaster, a scandal for a young girl to become engaged, in which a marriage is announced as if it were a burial, a tie between a woman and a man as the most degrading misalliance. Under the pale grey female Apollo who illumines this world, girls and women suffice unto themselves and arrange between themselves all affairs of the heart. (*Le Romantisme Feminin*, 229–30)

The question on which Maurras ends his *Le Romantisme féminin* is whether or not the "cité de femmes," the "secret petit monde" and the "risque lesbien" it implies, is a danger to or a preserver of the naturally feminine. He presents the arguments of those to whom he refers as "superficial observers" as if they were direct quotations. He avoids giving the source of the quotations, and it is likely that these arguments are Maurras's own version of what a positive reading of these women as preservers of femininity might be. Maurras proposes two major points as counterargument. The first is that one should not exaggerate the "risque lesbien" because women are naturally fortified against lesbianism. The second is that these young women should be applauded rather than censured. Because their goal is to become ever more feminine, they do not participate in the movement of other women who are attempting to become like men and to take the place of men. These young women are, therefore, protectors of femininity; they are benefactors. Maurras's response to his confected objections is categorical. He sees the "risque lesbien" as a powerful, disruptive force, and although he persistently opposes what is natural to what is acquired, he senses that a construction of reality which is projected, repeated, and studied can take on a life of its own or become a second nature. He is aware that words produce their own reality. The bacchantes who repeat "I, I, I" must inevitably be disloyal to civilization. They do not become more feminine, but rather they join with the others in the goal of imitating men, of pretending to be like men. Even more than the female doctor or lawyer, they become like an "être insexué," they become dry. And to be dry implies to be without "charme."

What emerges from Maurras's conclusion is that women who think about their sexuality are most apt to do so in groups and that these groups are likely to be inclined toward lesbianism. The formula, then, is: it is not feminine to think *or* a woman who thinks is ipso facto a lesbian. Reading the poetry of Renée Vivien, Maurras does not recognize the marks of a thinking woman but rather the marks of a feeling woman. Examining the women writers one by one, examining the text of their lives, Maurras is struck by a lesbian presence that he can only attribute to a narcissistic concentration on the self. The real danger, then, of "romantisme féminin," is not only that it feminizes men, that it impedes clear communication, and that it relies on foreign, non-French, impure values, but that it changes the natural sexual orientation of women. The effects produced by the texts of "romantisme féminin" are powerful enough to create a second nature. Maurras, in *Le Romantisme féminin*, implicitly equates the menace of lesbianism with the menace of foreigners, Protestants, and Jews.

The key word in *Le Romantisme féminin* is the word *charme*, the same word that directs Barbey d'Aurevilly's discourse on women in his prefatory dedication of *Les Bas-bleus* (1878).[6] This undefinable "charme" can only be identified by men of exquisite feeling, thereby eliminating Jews and foreigners. It is the ability of women to seduce men. It is unrelated to literature, art, or science, and it is essential to the maintenance of a social and an aesthetic harmony. Without this "charme" that emanates from women, men's pleasure, and consequently the meaning of men's lives, evaporates. The "risque lesbien," viewed as threatening to this "charme," must be diagnosed and the monster eradicated. According to Maurras, the two domains capable of eroding this "charme" are metaphysical anguish and the investigation of sexuality. "Sapho 1900," to the dismay of her critics,[7] was concerned with both.

What is for Charles Maurras in 1905 a dangerous "secret petit monde" is for Gayle Rubin in 1976 a "lesbian renaissance." Renée Vivien is no longer a contradictory, menacing figure but the product of "one of the most remarkable lesbian oeuvres extant" (iv). Charles Maurras was defending his version of Frenchness and maleness against contamination by impure texts and persons. Gayle Rubin celebrates her version of lesbian-feminism by extolling texts and persons who represent "forerunners of the contemporary gay women's movement" (vii). For Maurras as for Rubin, Renée Vivien's texts and life are subversive. In one case the subversion is villainous; in the other it is heroic.

"Sapho 1900" is an ideal textual figure for those critics who maintain a Manichean, theological view of the world and for whom good and evil, as well as absolute presence, can be located in specific texts. Gayle Rubin welcomes narratives that attack and challenge heterosexual privilege and male bias and that can be read both as fictions and as historical documents. She writes with equal passion about Renée Vivien's texts and Renée Vivien's life. She is primarily interested in the fact that Renée Vivien was a lesbian and that lesbian history, difficult to research, is even more difficult to transmit.

Rubin reads the 1904 version of *A Woman Appeared to Me* as a "novel [that] is also a historical document, part of the archival remains of one of the most critical periods in lesbian history" (iv). In presenting historical and biographical contexts for the novel, Rubin insists on the changes in the concept of homosexuality that occurred toward the end of the nineteenth century, particularly the change from an understanding of homosexuality as a form of behavior to an understanding of homosexuality as an identity or a fixed character. She does not connect this change to the development of racial theories. During this same period, for example, to be Jewish became a question of racial as well as religious difference, a question of character. And this character, for both homosexuals and Jews, depended on theories of strict biological determinism. Rubin does not make the connections that are implicit in Maurras's text between the representation of lesbians and Jews. Her text, with its emphasis on the "specialized homosexual communities" in "nineteenth-century cities" (v), seems to glorify any evidence of lesbian society without concern for the ideological premises on which it was constructed. When Rubin writes: "The variety of lesbian society in Paris before 1910 has been charmingly described by Colette" (v), the adverb *charmingly* warns us that in spite of apparent differences there may be a significant resemblance between Maurras's fear of lesbianism and Rubin's welcoming of it.

But contemporary investigations, such as Bram Dijkstra's[8] into the connections between discourses and representations of women, lesbians, blacks, and Jews during the *Belle Epoque* must make us suspicious of any discourse that conflates difference and identity and any community that depends on this conflation for its existence. And so it is incumbent upon readers of Gayle Rubin's text to question the unqualified praise she lavishes on Renée Vivien and Natalie Clifford Barney in such phrases and sentences as: "their shared vision of a society in which women would be free and homosexuality honored"; or "searching for their own roots, they discovered Sappho and Hellenism. They endeavored to recreate a Sapphic tradition"; or "the two women declared themselves pagans, spiritual descendants of the Greeks" (ix). The search for roots and origins betrays the theoretical and ideological presence of social Darwinism and its intersections with religious discourse. We have noted Maurras's insistence on the Greek connection as the basis of the French, male, classical tradition. How curious, then, to find a Greek connection, albeit a "Sapphic tradition," honored by Rubin because it was honored by Renée Vivien and Natalie Clifford Barney. History does not necessarily imply roots, but roots always imply an origin, a source from which one traces an identity that excludes all forms of difference. There is a tendency in the first part of Rubin's essay to uphold the notion of a lesbian community based on a fundamental, "racial" difference that would be as exclusive as Maurras's French, male, Catholic community.

In the second part of her introduction, Gayle Rubin looks more closely at the text of *A Woman Appeared to Me* and the changes made by Renée Vivien in her retelling of myths and legends. Rubin is at her best in pointing out the play in the text between heterosexual and lesbian and male and female biases and the ambiguities this play creates for the reader confronted with familiar figures and symbols—such as Saint John, or snakes, or a prostitute—that no longer adhere to their usual sexual interpretation. Like Maurras in the first part of his essay on Renée Vivien's poetry, Rubin supplies the reader with intertexts and temporarily forgets or abandons ideological rhetoric in favor of precise examples from the texts and relevant anecdotes from Renée Vivien's life.[9] She shows convincingly Renée Vivien's interest in stories that deal with independent women, rebels who refuse men and male desire. Until the last sentence of the introductory essay, there is no sustained attempt, as there is the beginning of the essay, to make of Renée Vivien's texts or her life and loves a paradigm for lesbian tradition. The examples from *A Woman Appeared to Me* and from stories such as "The Veil of Vashti" or "The Eternal Slave" are quoted in their uniqueness or related, when appropriate, to other texts in nineteenth-century French literature. The same is true of Rubin's account of the amorous relations between Barney and Vivien. They are not presented as exemplary. The last sentence is, therefore, disappointing: "At the time of Barney's death, she, Renée Vivien, and the other women linked to them were already being rediscovered by a new generation of lesbian feminists searching for their ancestry" (xxix).

It would be as serious an error to consider Renée Vivien's lesbianism a danger to the human race, as Maurras ultimately does, as it would be to treat Renée Vivien as an "ancestor" for a new generation of lesbian-feminists. If she is an "ancestor," then lesbianism is a family affair, and a family, unlike a freely chosen community of associates, is a closed, imposed biological group. Lillian Faderman, in *Surpassing the Love of Men*[10] censures Renée Vivien for imitating "French decadent literature," for imitating nineteenth-century male writers who wrote about and who represented lesbians in their poetry and their fiction. Faderman's condemnation depends on the notion that there is an authentic lesbian experience, one that has been understood and transmitted by lesbian-feminists in the United States since the 1970s. Neither Rubin's lesbian family nor Faderman's authentic and inauthentic lesbian "experience" is a satisfactory reading or placing of Renée Vivien. If it is unpardonable to proscribe her because she and her texts are dangerous to humanity, it is equally unpardonable to prescribe or proscribe her because she either is or is not part of an imaginary lesbian-feminist family.

It is not Renée Vivien's place in French or in lesbian literature that it is important to determine but the multiple discursive contexts of the *Belle Epoque* that traverse her texts. This cannot be accomplished by critics eager to establish their own arbitrary categories of classification. For it is, in the long run, the desire to classify that links Maurras and Rubin and that makes it difficult for them to approach Renée Vivien's texts. There is not one of Renée Vivien's critics who has acknowledged her preoccupation with metaphysical anguish and with sexual identity. Blinded by their own rhetoric and discourse, her critics have tended to classify "Sapho 1900" in terms of a real lesbian identity rather than as a symbolic epithet. The result has been the creation of a succession of imaginary "Renée Viviens."

Notes

1. This is a reference to the subtitle of the special issue of *Yale French Studies* in which many of these essays originally appeared.

2. André Billy, *L'Epoque 1900: 1885–1905* (Paris: J. Tallandier, 1951), 227.

3. Susan Gubar, "Sapphistries," *Signs* 10 (Autumn 1984): 43–62.

4. The edition of Charles Maurras that I have used is: *L'Avenir de l'intelligence,* suivi de *Auguste Comte, Le Romantisme féminin, Mademoiselle Monk, L'Invocation à Minerve* (Paris: Flammarion, 1927). All translations from the

French are mine, unless otherwise indicated. References to works cited more than once will henceforth be given in the text.

5. Renée Vivien, *A Woman Appeared to Me*, trans. Jeannette H. Foster, with a preface by Gayle Rubin (Tallahassee, Fla.: Naiad Press, 1976).

6. J. Barbey d'Aurevilly, *Les Bas-bleus*, ed. V. Palmé (Paris: Sociéte Générale de Libraire Catholique, 1878). It is also the key word in Philippe Sollers's novel, *Femmes* (Paris: Gallimard, 1981).

7. Colette, in her 1928 portrait of Renée Vivien, incorporated in 1932 as a chapter of *Ces Plaisirs. . .*, renamed in 1941 *Le Pur et l'impur*, insists on the childish, puerile behavior of Renée Vivien and represents both her anguish and her sexuality as eccentric and unhealthy. Indeed, although her style bears little resemblance to that of Charles Maurras, Colette reproduces, through elaborate anecdotes, Maurras's ideological positions. Toward the beginning of her text, Colette refers to "the hidden tragic melancholy that throbs in the poetry of Renée Vivien" (*The Pure and the Impure*, trans. Herma Briffault [New York: Farrar, Straus & Giroux, 1978], 80). But because Colette and Renée Vivien never talked together about their writing and because Colette only occasionally saw Renée Vivien in the act of writing, Renée Vivien, the writer, is absent. Colette focuses on Renée Vivien's face, her lisp, her claustrophobic apartments, her eating and her drinking habits, and her manner of speaking about her lesbian love affairs. Colette's Renée Vivien is only incidentally a writer. She is, rather, an exemplary dark figure of the *Belle Époque* and, as Colette's definitive title suggests, corroborating Charles Maurras's conclusion, one of the impure.

8. Bram Dijkstra, *Idols of Perversity* (Oxford: Oxford University Press, 1986).

9. Gayle Rubin fails to mention that the title of the novel is a quotation from the thirtieth canto of "Purgatory" in Dante's *Divine Comedy*. The essential reversal in the text is that a woman, a Beatrice, appears not to the male narrator, Dante, but to the female narrator of *A Woman Appeared to Me*.

10. Lillian Faderman, *Surpassing the Love of Men* (New York: William Morrow & Co., 1981).

Reading Women in the Caribbean: Marie Chauvet's *Love, Anger, and Madness*

In 1968 Gallimard published *Amour, Colère, et Folie,* the fourth novel by Marie Chauvet, an "elite" member of the Port-au-Prince bourgeoisie.[1] An analysis of Duvalier's dictatorship, but more particularly, of women's place in a society crippled by color prejudice and social injustice, the book caused a scandal. Never before had a Haitian woman dared not only to question the nationalist assumptions of François Duvalier and the *noiriste* celebration of "black essence," but to take on the burden of writing in a culture that has praised and silenced women. As Jacques Barros writes, explaining the "subaltern role" of women in Haiti: "One courts women, one desires them, one does not speak to them."[2]

Chauvet's trilogy, once printed, remained in warehouses for twelve years: "Blocked by the 'conciliabules' between the Haitian and French bourgeoisie."[3] And in a country where women were to "reign" only *inside* their houses, Chauvet's husband responded to her offense of exposing the violations women experienced both inside "le domicile conjugal" and outside by buying up rights to the book. Divorce followed, and Chauvet found herself in exile in New York. Dany Laferrière, as well as other Haitian critics, has discussed how *Amour, Colère, et Folie* was deliberately ignored, or mocked in the major papers in Port-au-Prince, and Madeleine Gardiner, one of Haiti's few women literary critics, has asked a question we need to consider at the outset: "But why this voluntary omission of the writings of a woman whose whole life has been a long quest of justice, liberty, and brotherhood, all those things that seem meanwhile to be the dream of all our men of action, poets, writers, or political men?"[4] Chauvet's three narratives of power, greed, and damnation force us to reassess the place of women in the Caribbean. For in doing something extraordinary to the way women can be thought (or can think), Chauvet speaks not only to women but to those male writers who thought they had claims on the language of history, politics, and romance.

In thinking about how women write the Caribbean, I will take Haiti as ground. The problems of the Francophone Caribbean, especially—questions of assimilation, language, and identity—are most pronounced in this island, called by one nineteenth-century observer "Black France." Yet to be granted such dubious praise Haiti had always to be a somewhat overwrought mime of France; a theater of assimilation that separated those few who could copy the language and artifices of the colonizer from the majority, those who were darker and did not speak French.

In his 1887 *The English in the West Indies,* James Anthony Froude gives us Haiti: "a Paris of the gutter. . . . The boulevards are littered with the refuse of the houses and were foul as pigsties and the ladies under the parasols were picking their way along them in Parisian boots and silk dresses. I saw a *fiacre* broken down in a black pool out of which a blacker ladyship was scrambling."[5] When thinking about a King Christophe who surrounded himself—just a few years following the Haitian Revolution and the declaration of the first black republic in 1804—with a new nobility styled after the *ancien regime,* we might wonder if the urgency of affectation was not itself caused by the absoluteness of revolt.

Site of extremes, fair and foul, Parisian silks and black skin, Haiti declared its independence from France in 1804, the only example of a successful slave revolt in history. Césaire has said "Haiti represented for me the heroic and African Antilles."[6] Yet, if Haiti remains the most African of the Caribbean islands (with the largest peasant society and the most elaborated practice of vodoun), it is also excessively French. A small, educated elite copy the style, syntax, and formality of French utterance the better to separate themselves from the black, unlettered majority. In the capital of Haiti, Port-au-Prince, the 5 percent who speak and write French fluently produce plays, poems, essays, and histories more numerous than any other Caribbean island. And for many of these writers, obviously male, images of women become central to their art: the poetry especially glorifies women as muse, ripe fruit, celebrated landscape, the essence of all things Haitian.[7]

It is recognized that the fact of literature screens the existence of about 90 percent of the population, who speak Creole, who live in poverty, and who practice vodoun, the religion that could be argued (in spite of its detractors) as forming the basis of Haitian culture. Yet what happens to women in the proliferation of literary productivity? In comparison with Gaudeloupe and Martinique, in Haiti there are surprisingly few women writers. In her *Parole des femmes* (1970), Maryse Condé asks: "Pourquoi si peu d'écrivains femmes en Haïti alors que la Guadeloupe et Martinique en comptent tant, relativement parlant?"[8]

Crippled by a mystique of femininity, never close enough to the ideal of France or far enough away from the lure of Africa, bourgeois women inhabit an equivocal world. More seriously still, these women raised to be, in one observer's words, "a kind of superior domestic," did not receive the same education as men. Praised for their beauty and goodness, they had a very limited education. Taught for the most part by nuns, they were taught a pious passivity, and the emphasis was less on awakening their mind than on practicing what Barros calls a *"dressage intellectuel"* (404). So, being "upper-class" never made a woman's life easier. When the Haitian woman uses French, she carries with her the knowledge that such eloquence can circumscribe her ever more surely in ideals not of her own making, in "official" prescriptions for her behavior: respectability, luxury, service, and beauty.

When Chauvet published *La Danse sur le volcan* in 1957, her portrayal of two heroines of Saint-Domingue right before the Revolution, women had voted for the first time in Haitian history. Even then, Chauvet wanted to give a voice and a name to those women who fought for liberation, but most often remained unheard and unnamed. When Chauvet writes *Amour, Colère, et Folie,* she attempts to demonstrate how women writing in the language of the colonizer can break out of the alternating idealization and abuse, the claims of property, possession, and propriety that constitute Caribbean history. For if black men, as Fanon so eloquently suggested in *Black Skin, White Masks* (1952), "assume a culture, . . . support the weight of a civilization" when they write or speak French, black women inhabit another sex: a possession that not only threatens to transform "native" into French, but woman into man.[9] In *Bonjour et Adieu à la Négritude* (1980), the Haitian poet in exile René Depestre laments the double alienation of the black male, oppressed in terms of class and race.[10] He never mentions the woman in African or Caribbean cultures: as so often in the writings of the revolutionary *homme de culture*, she disappears in the *Griefs de l'homme noir*.[11] What happens then when the woman decides to tell her story, or to remember her native land? For the black woman is triply alienated, by class, race, and gender.

Chauvet's work should be read as a complex answer to Fanon's scathing indictment of the mulatto Martiniquaise Mayotte Capécia, whose 1948 *Je suis Martiniquaise* he condemns as the most blatant example of the assimilated *bourgeoise* who adapts to the colonial system. If Fanon has devoted his chapter "The Woman of Color and the White Man" to a critique not only of the book ("cut-rate merchandise, a sermon in praise of corruption") but of woman's desire for "lactification" ("I know a great number of girls from Martinique, students in France . . . who admitted to me . . . that they would find it impossible to marry black men"), Chauvet writes her trilogy to examine the way women are forced in between two constructs not of their own making: black nationalist and white foreigner. Here, the force of epidermal criteria determines women's status in ways Fanon could not have imagined. Oppressed by both the "civilizing" and the "barbarian" men in their midsts, they also suffer separation from other women. If male writers felt themselves torn between their native land and the *métropole*—words from France taming their heart from Senegal, to paraphrase the words of the Haitian poet Léon Laleau—women writing not only experienced Gallic conventions (French as a literary language) as a wedge between two worlds, but they also had to confront their position outside *all* forms of production, whether literary or popular. For Chauvet would not be read by the women of her class, and she *could* not be read by the Haitian peasant and working-class women.

When we read Chauvet, we begin to face some of the problems in reading Caribbean literature, especially that written by women. In societies where the language spoken or written by the few in no way resembles the language of those most often perceived as the vulgar masses, we must think about problems of representation and appropriation. This is not to say that in Anglo-European or North American society certain kinds of literariness connect more easily with the disenfranchised or uneducated, but to emphasize that the difference is one of degree.

The point is that there are two languages, two cultures, two societies in the Caribbean. There is a complete dichotomy between the way the majority of people speak and think and the official language attached to a dominant, metropolitan power. To write in the Caribbean involves the writer in a dilemma Derek Walcott was quick to recognize: to write at all was to put a "gulf" between himself and the "mass man," to find himself in a state of exile. Now, women, it could be argued, are always alienated from the dominant structures of their society, and they can use writing to analyze that deviation or to claim reintegration: either the fragmentary or the unifying vision. Chauvet has chosen to write out of her separateness. She writes as bourgeoise, locating herself emphatically outside the majority of women in her culture, unread by those of her own class, and scorned by those whose more "political" agenda demands that they speak for and with the people. Going beyond the "peasant novel," the legacy of her fellow Haitians Jacques Roumain or Jacques-Stephen Alexis, Chauvet defies mythologizing or mystification. No ritual of language or passion for change can fool her into assuming she can speak for those whom she cannot know. And more important, if it is woman in Haiti who must bear the trappings of style, who most fully inhabits the external as essence, Chauvet shows what happens when she decides to write her history. And this writing will take up that most misunderstood and paradoxical of gods in Haitian vodoun, Erzulie, as a motive for characterization.[12] Since Chauvet believes that her women bear the burden of someone else's cult of appearances and are weighed down by impositions that remain foreign to them, she must show how they become what others have made of them. Her novel, then, examines the turning of the flesh-and-blood woman into fiction, into someone else's dream. But Chauvet's legend of history does not stop here; for her two main characters—Claire in *Amour* and Rose in *Colère*—move from being passive objects into a contemporary history where women are speaking subjects. Chauvet resists the "self," the unitary transcendent self of an old expressive humanism. Her disjunction—and her revolt—is thus both more ambiguous and more disturbing than that of other women writing in the Caribbean.

Mayotte Capécia from Martinque and Simone Schwarz-Bart, Michèle Lacrosil, and Maryse Condé from Guadeloupe all write about what it means to be a woman of color in a man's world. But the struggle to write out of a complex of color (from "noire" to "brune" to "mulâtresse-blanche") is most pronounced in Chauvet's trilogy. And while Chauvet is reticent about representing the unrepresented, Simone Schwarz-Bart in her lovely *Pluie et vent sur Telumée miracle* appeals more easily to our aesthetic sensibility.

Endorsing the claims of ancestral landscape, matriarchy, and blackness, Schwarz-Bart presents the rural surround as a depository of enduring value. To celebrate what she calls "the permanence of Antillean being" (the vicissitudes of history notwithstanding) threatens to turn the particulars of society into the ideals of folklore. Chauvet, however, knows that any call to "being" or to an "essential" self, whether defined as "black," "Haitian," or "feminine," can be manipulated by ideologues. Duvalier's *noirisme*, his celebrated "Boulevard of the Ideal" or "thought uniquely Haitian" meant death for thousands (no matter their gradation of color or their class) in Haiti. Chauvet writes her trilogy to break down, subvert, and confound—even while playing to the hilt—the claims of class, race, or gender. Writing as a mulatto, what one of her characters will describe as the "color of a fart," of a "rotten coconut," Chauvet takes her stand in between the generalities so often used to glorify, divide, or mystify. And when we read Chauvet, we do have to take the time to know some facts of Haitian history. Telumée, the peasant heroine of Schwarz-Bart's moving tale of personal genealogy, finds out "what it is to be a woman." But what if a writer surrenders the idea of the subject (and the sure identity such naming implies) to the facts of history and to the sudden pulses of desire?[13]

> Unhappy me, he is the cause!
> He finds Choucoune pretty
> He speaks French, Choucoune loves him
> —Oswald Durand, "Choucoune"

In both Africa and the Caribbean, French colonization, unlike British, believed in thorough linguistic and cultural transformation: assimilationist practices permeated colonial society and determined both social relations and individual identity. What Albert Charton, inspector-general of education in French West Africa, argued in the early 1930s could also be applied to the Caribbean: "Through education, conquest and domination became a kind of moral annexation." This annexation would cost the elite of Africa and the Caribbean their past, their own specific histories. In being allowed to take on the garb of a "superior" civilization, they lost their selves in externals not of their making: having been taught the "inadequacy" of their "indigenous culture," they turned to Europe only to confront their own inferiority and self-devaluation.[14]

Although Chauvet writes in French, she makes color, the stain of blackness, inescapable, just as she will make vodoun, the mark of savagery to Western eyes, the means of characterization and drive behind the meditations of both Claire in *Amour* and Rose in *Colère*. It is not accidental that Erzulie, the Haitian *loa* (god) of love and desire, sometimes called the "Black Venus" and sometimes the "Mater Dolorosa," as well as other names, depending on who speaks, is also identified or associated with Saint Claire. I shall return to Chauvet's radical use of one of the most problematic and powerful of the vodoun gods, but at this point I want to suggest that we think of the entire trilogy as fulfilling a destiny blocked or briefly held in check by the mask of refinement, the claims of lightness, the mastery of French. One of the most extraordinary accounts of the feared workings of destiny in Saint-Domingue is Pierre de Vaissière's *Saint-Domingue (1629–1789): La Société et la vie créoles sous l'ancien régime.* "In a word, one could say that a colored population, left to itself, is fatally destined to become black again at the end of a very few generations."[15] The lapse he describes, the series of faults that first transform white into mulatto and then mulatto "to the most absolute black," can be seen as the course of Chauvet's trilogy, ending finally in the black apocalyptic of *Folie.*[16]

Claire Clamont begins her journal in 1939, five years after the U.S. occupation of Haiti, and during the regime of the mulatto Sténio Vincent. The dates do not matter, for the story is the same: blacks and mulattoes fight it out in Port-au-Prince, and the peasants continue to suffer. Under the direction of commander Calédu (in Creole the name means someone who hits or beats hard), the nationalists take power, erasing years of prejudice and elitism, which in this particular province means violating the women of "good families," the "aristos," or "white-mulattoes," also called "light-skinned" ("claires"). What begins as the most personal of memoirs ends up a chronicle of Haiti as Duvalier consolidates his totalitarian state. Calédu, "a savage negro who had terrorized us for nearly eight years," is obviously a figure for the dread tontons-macoutes, Duvalier's personal henchmen, recruited mainly from the urban poor, those whom Claire calls "armed beggars."

Claire is above all a writer. And like any good Gothic memorialist who makes sin the source of fiction, Claire claims this role from the first, revealing it to be her strength and her scourge: "I believe I can write. I believe I can think. I became arrogant. I became aware of myself. To reduce my inner life to the measure of my eye, there's my goal. The noble task [*tâche*]!" (10). But her tale is not only about forbidden desire and secret compulsion but about the impact of writing on a Haitian woman's identity. In a Cartesian meditation, Claire is saying nothing less than "I write therefore I think therefore I am." The very constitution of self, however—her concrete "prise de conscience," to use Césaire's formulation—depends upon learning to write, to be French. To acquire a language was, as Fanon wrote in *Black Skin, White Masks,* to gain a world and a lineage. The *tâche* of writing could remove the *tache* of color.

Chauvet recognizes the perils of assimilation: the more you read, the less you hear the voice of the gods, or more precisely, the songs and legends of the black majority. She knows, as does Claire, that the mulatto, most distant from the legacy of Africa, the mark of slavery, was the proof of culture in Haiti. In the nineteenth century, especially, to "rehabilitate the black race" (*améliorer la race*) meant to demonstrate that Creole (the language spoken and understood by 98 percent of the population) and vodoun (the religion of the majority) were rapidly disappearing. As the Haitian L. J. Janvier wrote in *Les Détracteurs de la race noire et de la République d'Haiti* in 1882: "The French language is the most current, the only language in use, and every peasant understands it. . . . The mores and customs, the festivals, laws, and institutions, the dress, all is French: in everything here we model ourselves on France."[17] The vessels for the necessary rehabilitation of blackness would be the mixed-blood, the sign of the slow amelioration of the genetic traits of black Africa.

Writing out of her status as "aristocrat" and her marginality as virgin spinster, Claire meditates on language, society, and race in the intimacy of her reminiscences. But her analysis of ruling-class greed (whether black or mulatto, Calédu or her father) and American intervention is effective because she so fully inhabits her bourgeois world, its narcissism and delusions. The claims of sex are never far from the mechanics of power and submission, from a world obsessed by "the Color Question," where the literate few repeat: "black women for work, mulatto for love, white for marriage." And if we think Claire's obsessive meditation on her virginity somewhat excessive, we should note that one of the most feared ghosts in Haitian folklore is the *djablesse:* a female ghost, she must live in the woods for years, as punishment for the crime of having died a virgin, before she can enter heaven.

In *Amour,* Chauvet is attempting nothing less than the literalization of American Gothic: the Protestant turning from icon to voice and the emphasis on a self-scrutiny that reveals fleshly rottenness.

The despotism of the senses is indeed convertible with the most acute revelations of consciousness; and the Haitian Chauvet presents a testimony that locates terror in the original sin of the colonial enterprise. Claire is tyrannized by a double curse: she is dark, and she is a virgin. Marginalized, she acts out two roles simultaneously. Dark huntress, she lies in wait for the object of her desire, the white Frenchman Jean Luze; pale virgin, she is sought after by the black savage Calédu. The justifications of conquest and domination are thus confounded by a woman who, in surrendering to dreams of contamination and lust, attacks the tyranny of culture and color. A female malcontent, Claire interrogates the social maiming of inherited privilege, and she scrutinizes her own mind and motives as harshly as those around her.

Claire bears the "stain" of darkness. Unlike her sisters Félicité and Annette, "ces deux mulâtresses-blanches," Claire is "the surprise that the mixed-blood had reserved to our parents" (12). The calamity of color—colonization's harshest legacy—is background to this tale of eccentric desire. At the time of Saint-Domingue's greatest prosperity, the white colonists, fearful of the increasing wealth and property of the *gens de couleur*, divided the offspring of white and black and the intermediate shades into 128 gradations. And the "mixed-blood" with 127 parts white to 1 part black was still colored. If the terror that the natural historian of the Caribbean called "primitive" could always be projected out there, somewhere on the margins, always a fault to be resisted or overcome, Claire surrenders herself to the lapse. When she sets out to destroy "the myth of the old maid, pure and without stain," she takes vengeance on her father, who bragged that no one could tell he "had a trace of black blood in his veins." If the "law of reversion"—the return of blackness—was the thing most feared in colonial Saint-Domingue *and* independent Haiti, Claire commits herself to fulfilling the *law*. Instead of trying to discharge the stain, she recollects and accepts this "corruption of blood." "Scream out if ever this manuscript falls under your eyes; call me shameless, immoral. Season with abusive epithets if that soothes you, but you will no longer intimidate me. . . . I want my revenge" (34).

It becomes clear throughout Claire's memoirs that her revenge against class and color prejudice works only because she shares with her reader things that no "lady" of the Haitian bourgeoisie had dared. "I am skilled in the theory of the perfect fuck. I know by heart certain passages of *Lady Chatterley's Lover*" (46). In her thoughts Claire analyzes the process of idealization and its effects. The foreign, exotic other in *Amour* is Jean Luze (obviously *lux*, "light"): "the beautiful Jean Luze"; "the intelligent Jean Luze. . . . haloed in mystery, in exoticism"; "his perfect diction. And his gaze" (10–11). He is secretly desired by Claire, who makes him part of her own projections of wayward desire: torn between the attractions of a white Jean Luze and the black Calédu. Claire's analysis of self and society leads not to the ideals of European civilization, but to the mean scuttling *between* black and white, between her French and colonial heritage. As Calédu begins to force his way into her dreams of Luze, she claims she does not want "to see 'clair' in myself" (81).

Enjoying her state of nonpossession (effaced like a shadow, yet able to claim, "I am the only lucid one"), Claire alternates between the illumination her name contains and the darkness descending upon Haiti. Locked in her room (Chauvet's entire trilogy takes place in a series of deepening enclosures), devouring pornographic postcards, staring hard at Jean Luze in illicit sex with his sister-in-law Annette, throwing herself down on her bed and taking Luze in her mind, Claire composes her narrative of compulsion. The terror is not only individual—not only the revelation of her needy sex, ossified by the strict and hypocritical teachings of her "elite" father ("this Parisian mulatto"), who feared the dark and vulgar in their midsts (while serving the vodoun *loa* of his black grandmother)— but collective. Her love story tells Haiti's "history of skin": "From an early age I began to suffer because of the dark color of my skin, this mahogany color inherited from a far-away grandmother and which exploded in the close circle of Whites and white-mulattoes that my parents frequented." But she adds, alluding to *noirisme* and the growing appeal of black nationalism, "Times have changed . . . history budges and fashion also, fortunately" (12).[18]

If Calédu and his men are terrifying, Claire reveals the demon underbelly to the terror. Recalling stories of cruelty against "negroes," she invokes Haiti's *epidermic fatality*. She tells of Agnès Grandupré: quarantined and dubbed "the vicious one," she is finally beaten to death by her respectable mulatto parents for associating with the black Mathurin. Claire repeats the words of Mme Cameuse, whose gossip is responsible for many of the color scandals: "Personally, I am descended in a direct line from noble French colonists who were called Cameuse" (97). The questions of class and the prejudices of color are not easily separable, and Claire spares no one the dirty legacy of injustice: "We became evil by contagion" (15).

The history Claire tells is literary as well as political. Mr. Long, the U.S. businessman who directs "Long & Co., Export Corp.," forces the peasants to violate their own lands, cutting down their trees for export to America. Chauvet makes this violation synonymous with Calédu's rape and mutilation of Dora Soubrian, with Claire's mental ravaging of Jean Luze, and finally, with Claire's appropriation of male sexuality, through her rewriting of male poetics. The ancestral lands are ravaged by the demands of capital; the mulatto women are raped by the revenge of race; and the literary ideals of love are exposed by the lust of the "femme stérile."

The excesses of black nationalism—Duvalier's promise to bring out "the biopsychological elements of the Haitian man"—were not far from the racial theories of Gobineau. And Claire's exaltations of the aesthetic—"her sisters white and rose like a lily" and the angelic Luze—perpetuate the semantic traps of colonial mastery. Since most Haitians had assimilated the symbolic treatment of women in French love poems, Claire uses some well-known tropes. Released by her own words from the glories that could be granted only if she were to remain a pretext for what transcends her—an object of desire in the minds of men—Claire takes the pen out of the hands of her male compatriots.

Much of Haitian love poetry portrays the male as warrior fighting for the conquest of his woman ("Que t'est le bouclier de tes seins / Quand ma flèche t'abat comme un vautour" [Jacques Lenoir, "Sur un toit de vent"]). In the Caribbean, erotics have often served political ends. When René Depestre writes "Eros et Révolution" in Cuba, he does hommage to militant desire. So, it is no surprise that Claire boasts of her "valor" in fighting for Jean Luze. That her conquest is of the mind (and obtains its intensity from the rigors of her denial) takes nothing away from its impact on the reader. Her nonpossession exacerbates the sensual immediacy of her assault, and by the end of her story she proves that her erotic overwhelming has political results. Here is Claire thinking about her solitary apprehension of Jean: "I harbor an unsettling vitality, even more dangerous than I understood, I am like a cunning bug that hides in the recesses of furniture. I await my prey, patiently, in order to suck his blood. For now, my prey, it's Jean Luze" (46).

It is not easy for women to read Claire. Her characteristics are so variable, and sometimes so similar to what she condemns that her preoccupations could be seen as "nonfeminist." Chauvet wants to ironize gender. As we read through Claire's conversions, we learn that we cannot always identify her with her anatomical sex.[19] Even though her sense of violation is intensified because of the position of women in her society, her own story does not easily transcend stock images of women, nor can she create alliances on the basis of gender that magically transcend differences of race and class. Claire harasses the family servant Augustine, who, she says, has never been anything but "a household slave"; and Félicité and Annette exploit their older, darker sister.

Virgin huntress and hunted roué, Claire overturns her society's stereotypes even as she adopts them. Hers is a cross-sexed *dépense.* Violette, "the prostitute of the stinking alley," is as much her prey as her beloved Jean Luze.[20] She offers herself to Luze, to Calédu, "muscled, black and naked," and to her sister Annette or to Violette: "Behind the shutters of my window, I devour Violette with my eyes. She is young. She is beautiful. She is free. She spits on us and she's right. I would love to be in her place" (49).

To desire to be in the place of another is to be possessed. Claire's account of what it means to *want* is a startling reenactment of the experience of possession in vodoun: that moment when the *loa* or god takes his or her place in the head of the devotee. The experience is not supposed to be one of domination, but of reciprocal beholding. Forced for years to behave like a "good bourgeoise," who without husband or child could no longer desire or be desired, Claire invokes her own ceremony of knowing and abandon: "I am naked, on my bed, half-soaked in sweat, palpitating with desire. . . . Here I am possessed" (49).

Chauvet uses vodoun as both explanatory force and trope in *Amour, Colère, et Folie.* To know the full extent of Chauvet's revolt, the reader must know something about vodoun. But Chauvet does not presume merely to represent a ceremony or describe a god: she knows how easily vodoun, once taken out of its concrete surround, its actual context, can be turned into folklore. She knows how easily the cultural reality of the Haitian majority can become sensational or exotic. Indeed, Erzulie, written about mostly by male ethnographers, has too often become an iconic lady offered up either to erotic fantasy or to the demands of Christian asceticism.

Claire's contradictory characteristics take their cue from Erzulie, the most ambivalent *loa* in the vodoun pantheon. Most simply presented, Erzulie is the goddess of love. She has also been called a "Black Venus," "Virgin Mary," or "Mater Dolorosa." When her roles are described, and thus circumscribed in writing, the discourse on

Erzulie has most often perpetuated masculine fantasies of woman. Split between the "good" Erzulie-Fréda and the "evil" Erzuli-gé-rouge (Erzulie with red eyes of the militant Petro nation of *loa*), between the young, beautiful ingénue "Maîtress Erzulie" and the old, stooped "Grande Erzulie," she dramatizes a cult of mystification: the splitting of women into objects to be desired or abhorred. Yet in vodoun practice, this problematic dichotomy is both disentangled and dismantled. Nowhere is the demolition so pronounced as in the subversive erotics of Erzulie-Fréda: the goddess who takes on the garb of femininity—and even speaks excellent French—in order to discard it.[21] In vodoun the culturally defined roles of men and women are assumed and then confounded: the spectacle is itself a derailing of difference, a subversive solution to the subordination of women. Christian images of weeping or wanton women and stereotypes of the "upper-class" lady, her luxury and grace, contribute to the formal qualities of Erzulie's "epiphany" in vodoun ceremony.

When moralizing Western observers see Erzulie as either Venus or Virgin Mother, they stop short of a far more complicated lineage for the Haitian goddess. For if vodoun remains a locus of feminine strength—with women and men equal in its practice—it can be so only because it reconstitutes so extremely specifically gendered stereotypes. Erzulie demands of her servitors abstention from sex on her sacred days. But Erzulie "marries" women as well as men. Everything *written* about Erzulie can be contradicted. She is, some will tell you, the *loa* of lust most often prayed to by prostitutes. A goddess served by the Haitian élite or young virgins, Erzulie is also sought after by those with homosexual tendencies.

When Chauvet takes Erzulie as a type for characterization, she endorses and repeats her extremes, her moves back and forth between refinement and savagery, sexuality and denial. Erzulie goes beyond any false dichotomizing, as she prescribes and responds to multiple and apparently incoherent directives. The indeterminacy of the goddess, whose libido wanders between women and men, enacts a fantasy of *l'amoureuse,* a play that is ever determined by precise sociocultural models. Claire's bedroom thus becomes a space of pleasure and knowledge that allows no inhibitions. Here, a woman can speak like a man, desire like a man, even while interrogating the socially prescribed codes of such behavior.

But Chauvet also gives us the Haitian love goddess in her *dé-doublement* of color: Erzulie in her two emanations is *noire* and *mulâtresse-blanche.* Her two-sidedness is captured in what Claire sees as her "dualité," exercised in her oscillating dreams of Calédu and Luze. To find sure identity in a world where pigmentation determines worth is no easy matter. Claire's color complex arises out of an ideal or image of beauty. Brought up by pale parents, she has no idea of the "dark color" of her skin until she visits her father's coffee plantation, where she is greeted by the peasant Louisor: "By God, that's quite a beautiful negress you've got there, Agronome" (113). Later, Claire hears her sister Félicité: "Why is Claire black, mama? . . . She is black and we are white" (119). Although her mother assures her that Claire's complexion is really sunburn, Claire cannot be rid of the taint of color bequeathed to her by her black ancestor. Obsessed by what others have made of her, and resubmitting herself to an image of beauty in the minds of men, Claire spends hours in front of the mirror, lamenting: "Why? Why? Why? . . . Why am I black? Why?" (120).[22]

As Claire's journal progresses, however, the mirror game changes, stressing that to repeat and submit to a spectacle of exploitation is not to be consumed by it. Instead, Chauvet allows her character to react like a woman spurned or passive in a masculine world of representations, in order to demonstrate how such mechanisms of control operate. Only then can Claire rid herself of that "second skin": "I looked at my ravaged face in the mirror. I discovered, surprise, my asymmetrical aspect: left profile, dreamy, tender; right profile, sensual, savage. Is this myself or what I see of myself?" (185). Claire sees simultaneously the romanticized elite woman and the fierce, earthy woman. In vodoun practice, Erzulie's multiple emanations, her incongruous faces, produce the continuing slippage between what might otherwise remain rigid or reductive assumptions.

At the end of this discourse on love, Claire joins "love" and "battle"—the undoubling of Erzulie—when she knifes Calédu in the back with the knife Jean had given her as "a keepsake." Although she had planned to kill herself, Claire is no Dido. She will not bless her conqueror. No matter his color or his nationality. Still holding the dagger red with blood, she pushes Jean Luze away as he embraces her. Having accomplished the deed that allows Luze and the revolutionary male "intellectuals" to liberate the prisoners (and it is implied, the entire town) from Calédu and his gang, Claire returns to her room.

How far does Chauvet intend us to take the implications of Claire's revolution? Chauvet politicizes Claire's love for the "archangel" Luze by taking the sword out of her heart and driving it into

Calédu's back. The symbol of Erzulie, drawn on the floor with flour or meal, is a heart pierced with a sword, and she is thus identified with Catholic representations of the pierced heart of "Our lady of Sorrows." No longer pierced, Claire pierces: turning her heart—the sign of feminine sentiment (ready to receive the masculine stab) into an active subjectivity, putting Luze's knife, his token of "love," where it counts.

> If, in her simplicity, she confounded the God of her
> white father with that of the vodoun cult, she loved the
> mild mother of the Crucified as much as she feared
> Erzulie-Gé-rouge, female loa of her black ancestors.
> —Adeline Moravia, *Aude et ses fantômes*

Colère begins with the appropriation of land. Property, a land of one's own, were the terms by which Haitians articulated their independence. In *Amour* peasants were forced to deforest their lands for the profit of Mr. Long and Calédu. Now Chauvet turns to the landowners, the "petite-bourgeoisie" of Turgeau, an "ultra-chic" neighborhood of Port-au-Prince. The conquest of the Normils' land is the appropriation of their history. And from the moment Chauvet announces, "The men in black have fixed stakes around the house," each member of the family responds to the assault by reconstructing a past (191).

Colonization demanded that the "master" turn color into commodity, a conversion accomplished by the denial of property (identity). Prospero takes Caliban's land in *The Tempest* by constructing a history that denies Caliban's claim to ownership: "This island's mine, by Sycorax my mother, / Which thou tak'st from me." Chauvet complicates the New World theater by particularizing the facts of control, by locating her story of dehumanization in contemporary Haiti. The "men in black" are the Calibans who claim a "natural" right to power, being able to construct (out of their internalization of the color fetish) an ethics out of a biological trait. Indeed, Duvalier's racial theories justified an authoritarian populism as particularly suitable to those of African descent. *Colère* exposes the phantasmic and duplicitous force of this tyranny. Identities are constructed and histories made, but the antagonisms themselves only perpetuate the ruses of the colonial relationship.

Perhaps the greatest horror of colonization and slavery was the conversion of person into property. Dominion over the black was extended to the bed, and the taking of black women by white men was nothing less than a ritual reenactment of the daily pattern of social dominance. For Chauvet in postindependence Haiti women were still the bodies across which political power gets confirmed. When the Normil house is quarantined in *Colère*, the inhabitants are isolated and circumscribed. First, the "devils" drive stakes into the ground to encircle the house, post a placard, "NO ENTRY," and then build a wall to separate the Normils from their land. The land becomes the site for the performance of male power, but this fable of violation and dispossession can be enacted only when that land is annexed to a woman's body. The desired body is Rose, the mulatto daughter: a virgin Rose assumes "martyrdom" in order to regain her family land.

Chauvet's exchange of Rose for land upsets the poetic idealization of earth as woman, one of most repeated tropes of Haitian literature, whether the writer be romantic lyricist or political "man of the people." Jacques Roumain in his novel *Gouverneurs de la Rosée* makes the equation between women and land that other writers (Jacques-Stephen Alexis and René Depestre, for example) will perpetuate: "The earth is like a good woman: if you mistreat her, she revolts."[23]

The name Rose, like the land Haiti, has its origins in a myth of violation. The legend of abuse begins with the flanks of a woman "brutally fertilized," as the Haitian historian Timoléon Brutus puts it, "by a slave in heat or a drunken White, a criminal escaped from Cayenne [the French colonial prison]; or a degenerate from feudal nobility in quest of riches throughout the continent." By summoning this legend, Brutus hopes to show that it is "ridiculous" to place mulatto over black or vice versa, since "the origin of everyone is common." No superiority can be claimed, or extricated, from the color and class chaos that began Haitian society. Yet although this oddly regenerative rape produces an ambiguity that levels distinctions of color and class, the "black woman" remains *singular*. In this amalgam of neutralized distinctions, she stands out as victim and martyr. Chauvet recalls the legend of "Sor Rose" or "Soeur Rose" in her own story in order to question the consequences of this envisioned matriarchy. The "ancestress" (or "l'aieule") must be ravished for the nation to be born: A woman's passivity or submission is necessary for the ideology of nation building to be effective. And her reparation—or reward for presence—is to be "mother of us all," in other words, to be socialized, historicized, or mythologized out of existence. When Chauvet names her young heroine Rose, she reveals that her violation is *always* sexualized, and that it has been accomplished not only by the black intruder, but by her mulatto family, as well as by the white colonialist who began the entire cycle of domination, cruelty, and desperation.[24]

The colonizer makes profit, assumes privilege, and practices usurpation. In Chauvet's retelling, the colonized repeat the forms of imperialism but gain nothing. Those who claim blackness and invade the earth—and penetrate the women—of their fellow Haitians play a game of power. Like *Amour, Colère* is about contamination. The impurity here is most effectively displayed by the exchange of money, and women. The novel's crucial scene that both repeats and deepens the initial violation of the land is between the lawyer, the father, Louis Normil, and his daughter Rose. Louis Normil hopes to enlist the aid of the lawyer in retrieving his land. At the end of the tense interview, a door opens and the character who will be known only as the "gorilla" enters: " a little, skinny man in a black uniform whose inordinately long bony hands hung at the end of his arms like a gorilla's paws" (227). While seeming to perpetuate racism, Chauvet discloses the reduction of human into beast by repeating the process. The man named "gorilla" bears the history of a constructed "barbarism,"[25] the most horrific projections of the colonizers and their recorders, the "natural historians" of the Americas.

The business of money demands the play of sex. The gorilla approves of Rose, and a deal is made: the money must be delivered by "this lovely young lady." Although Rose is now a commodity in the marketplace, she will actively participate in her own exchange. Her mother tells her, "Don't go, Rose, don't go," but Rose, knowing that her father's attempt to deliver the money alone has failed, decides to go on her own.[26] What follows is Rose's history of her meetings with the gorilla, every night for one month. This chapter remains one of the most disturbing memoirs by a woman in all of Caribbean fiction. Breaking out of a masculine agenda of property, possession, and propriety, Rose's monologue turns an object of consumption—rotten merchandise—into a speaking subject.[27]

By insisting on the details of the *tontons-macoutes'* brutalization of women, Chauvet recalls the particular nature of Duvalier's terror. For the first time in Haiti his militia annihilated the protection traditionally conferred by age or sex. "Duvalierist violence reversed the sexual distinction between the victims who, up to this point, gave women the advantage. Women were treated like men, often worse than men. *Femininity* became a disadvantage whereas before it had been a partial protection" (Trouillot, 178). In *Amour,* Claire dreamed of Calédu as "an enormous phallus strained in a spasm of voluptuous suffering"; and she throws herself, "both repelled and submissive" at its feet. Now, Rose realizes Claire's dream as she offers herself, spread-legged, arms crossed, to the *tonton-macoute* with black velvet hands. What is striking about Rose's account is not the repetition of brutal violation, for Claire has already told us the story of Dora Soubiran, raped and crippled by Calédu, who accompanied each blow with the cry: "Aristos, band of aristos, mulatto-aristos, I will mutilate all of you, aristos, aristos" (163). What matters here is how Rose tells her story.

What is the history that male historians never tell? How does Rose's story, though historically determined, subvert the claims of ownership and mastery? She refuses appropriation by adopting and then analyzing not only the injustice that is socially constructed—color prejudice, for example—but most important, the inequality, that survives always as a sexual prerogative. Like the savage who bore the brunt of the "discoverer's" ambiguous relation to what he had discovered, women bear the marks of postindependence history in the Caribbean. Further, the revenge against past domination, most often played out *against* the "weaker sex," is usually futile because of the internalization of racial inferiority.[28] Even though the gorilla gets his girl, he finds himself ever more dependent on his object, in a coupling that will only perpetuate the original relation of mastery and servitude.

Rose's history proceeds in a double context: her brother Paul's obsession with her "error and concupiscence" and her grandfather's chronicle of the family's male genealogy. Paul kills off his sister as irrevocably as God turned his back on Eden, or Adam on Eve: "The odor of death is already on Rose" (260). The mother alone knows how not to perpetuate the bourgeois cult of the pure, submissive body. The bond between Rose and her mother remains unspoken, but inescapable: both are recipients of justice as defined by men. The mother's first excursion outside the bounds of her home foretells Rose's story: "The mother waited until the house was asleep and with precaution left the bed where her husband slept. She put on a robe and tiptoed down the stairs. Outside a full moon meandered in the sky. . . . 'Who goes there?' a voice cried out. And a silhouette rose up, gigantic and black. . . . 'Do you want to sleep with me, mulâtresse? You want to fuck?'" (216).

While Paul dreams of revenge on the man who sullied his adored sister, the grandfather, Claude Normil, concentrates on the family claim to right and authority, passing on the stories of acquisition to his grandson, "the invalid." The grandfather recalls a heritage of African gods and blackness. The great-grandfather, he says, "like a true Haitian black, faithfully served his *loa*" (195). A peasant, he had received a small plot of land in exchange for a few animals and worked hard until he became a wealthy landowner. Chauvet makes it quite clear that Rose's bizarre coupling with the black man recalls a past obliterated and forgotten by everyone else in the family. For the invasion of the men in black is a terrible trick of history: a return of the repressed that is nevertheless fake. "Very big, very strong, and black," the great-grandfather's progeny (as would be claimed by the ideologues of *noirisme*) is none other than the skinny gorilla, who is attached not to the land but to Rose. Rose alone decides to fight for the land in the only way allowed her: "I will risk everything in order to save our lands" (206).

What does Rose risk? If a woman's identity in Haiti—at least for the upper classes—depended on what class and color she chose to make her mate, Rose's deliberate surrender to the skinny black is for her family a greater tragedy than the loss of their land. Her story, her "fall" must be explained. Chauvet, however, gives Rose the right to explanation: a woman, in recounting her violations, violates the coercive idealism of those men in her midst. Opened by the gorilla's fist, reflected in the mirrors of his bedroom, her sex sucked dry of its blood by her "vampire," she admits, "My complicity has no limits." (285). To the reductive, masculine fables of purity and impurity she opposes her chronicle of women's oppression: "Is my fate really so terrible? Surely many husbands must behave in love like this man. Vices sanctified by the marriage sacrament. . . . The stakes have delimited the infernal circle and the hands that drive them in are perhaps no less guilty than our own. We are paying for our terrible inheritance, the ancestral curse that will disappear only with our race" (291).

She thus interrogates the "heroic" history told by her grandfather, asking the questions that expose the dirty underside of privilege: "By what right do we possess our possessions? By what right are we privileged while others wallow in misery? The misery of those my peasant ancestor had surely exploited, the misery of the poor who stole from his garden and whom he lashed pitilessly, the misery of those beggars who have put on uniforms, the misery of the one who avenges himself on me for having been repelled all his life by the women he desired" (292–93).

In his *Discourse on Colonialism,* Aimé Césaire asked his reader to consider how "the colonies can serve as a safety valve for modern society." Chauvet's Rose not only answers Paul's question, "Why this punishment?" but she inhabits a role, controlled by images rooted in male mythologies of women and structured by their need to make women the repositories for their fears and desires. Chauvet appropriates the masculine projection of the turn from a "garden woman" to what Alain Corbin calls a "seminal drain."[29] Chauvet allows Rose to repeat and rewrite the coercive terminology of extremes: the production of women as figures for either paradise or hell. And yet, Chauvet's is a risky project. How does Rose's meditation and her martyrdom avoid turning into a mere adoption of the images others have made of her? To answer this question is to understand the moral exigency of Chauvet's narrative, her uncompromising confounding of untried assumptions.

In *Amour,* Claire had said, "Purity does not exist." Nowhere is the absence of purity more practiced than in the use of images. Two powerful emblems of male domination are compounded in the move from Claire to Rose, and both have been used against women. Claire, dark Sycorax, the old hag (or cannibal) with sagging breasts; and Rose, the fallen woman, giving off "an odor of death, of clotted blood and rottenness" (292). Both operate efficiently in our imagination only because we assume a purity, a truth that stands firm somewhere *outside* the contingencies of history, the petty details of economics. Chauvet takes us through the process of idealization by giving voice to the deidealized putrid body. She reanimates the corpse, the failed icon, the dirtied ideal. And when Rose talks, the rot she discovers is nothing other than the purity her lover construes.

For make no mistake about it. Rose's story is that of the Virgin, Mary Magdelene, or Saint Theresa, all moments of excess in the minds of men. And of course, Rose recalls Erzulie, the goddess cursed by the Church as whore, but whose generosity often knows no bounds. The gorilla confesses from the first, "I can only be a man with these beautiful saintly heads of your kind, the beautiful head of a conquered martyr" (284). Rose plays her role to the hilt: docile, and silent (except for her sighs), she obeys. Chauvet here conducts a rather excessive mimicry of what most Haitian married women experience daily. As Yveline Momplaisir writes, some ten years after Chauvet's trilogy: "In general, the Haitian man is narrow-

minded and it would be very difficult to change his mentality: he is
possessive; woman is his thing. And she is submissive since she's
been trained in docility since childhood."[30]

But Rose is not so much conquered as challenged to take the
words *virgin, saint, resignation, innocence,* and *candor* and rein-
vent their meaning. When the gorilla praises her as the perfect saint
with her perfect suffering, she reveals how a man's dream of perfection neatly kills off the flesh-and-blood woman: "He slept with a
cadaver. With a cadaver and he doesn't know it. That's my revenge"
(285). What Rose experiences are the rather smelly effects of idealization. The moment she returns from her first assignation, her
young invalid brother says, "You smell bad"; "You smell different
than yourself" (254). Or, as Rose recalls his words: "You no longer
smell like flowers." Rose will inhabit that bad smell so fully that
she reclaims a purity that is noncoercive and inclusive of those her
"high" society would deem corrupt. "Meanwhile, I felt somehow
purified. When I have done with this torture, I will still have more
modesty and innocence to offer him" (287).

Rose's story goes beyond some masochistic delight in abnegation
and pain. Her accommodation is heavy with irony, and in spite of
her reliance upon certain images expected of a good bourgeoise, she
breaks out of her mutilation in the excess of her responses. Let the
gorilla call her virgin; she will claim "nothing astonished me in
love" (288). She qualifies her docility, "a nauseating docility";
"Docile, too docile for a virgin. Am I virgin? Accomplice? Am I not
getting used to him, looking to him for my pleasure?" (289). Taking
herself beyond the genteel constraints of her class, she thinks, "If I
were liberated, he would surely find in me a partner worthy of him"
(290). What kind of partner would this Rose be? Her thoughts end in
a wild conversion ritual, as both partners turn into the "bestial
couple": the gorilla, "a poor dog in search of tenderness," and the virgin, "lascivious and insatiable panther!" (293).[31] Rose's articulation
of the "savage," even while suffering the guilt of her insights, not
only gives a history of women's experience in the colonial and post-
colonial Caribbean, but takes us back to the white man's greatest
fear: their virginal ladies mounted by dark Calibans. Chauvet spares
neither Rose nor the gorilla: both are victims of what they have
internalized as a racial and sexual myth.

Rose's sudden turn, the submissive virgin who becomes a lusty
panther, recalls Claire's two-faced reflection in the mirror. Again,
the liberation suggested by Rose, and its reliance on double and con-

tradictory images, threatening to disrupt the distinctions that order and control, takes its most potent source in vodoun. Chauvet achieves a complex victory, for Rose's meditation is grounded in the religion condemned as pagan and bestial by its detractors. If Erzulie, however, is "the ideal of the love bed," as Zora Neal Hurston has said, even this ideal must be de-idealized.[32] Erzulie-gé-rouge, suffering and angry, often tears at her flesh with her nails; and Rose repeats, "I will tear at my impure body with my nails and I will die" (293). Chauvet breaks through restrictive forms of female behavior by hinting that Rose, "mounted" (possessed) by Erzulie can *disfigure* the image others have made of her. The fear of women's anger obviously contributes to the power of Erzulie's 'evil' incarnation as described by mostly male ethnographers, whether Haitian or foreign. How dare she break out of the status of ideal and exquisitely feminine lady?

Both Claire and Rose, like Erzulie, the goddess of incongruous pleasures, break the laws that language bears. Not only does Chauvet attempt to recuperate the voices of a religion that promise a subversive solution to the economic or political impasse of the disenfranchised, but she seeks to find a new language for women writing in the Caribbean. In reclaiming vodoun within the pages of a novel defined by the terms of the *métropole,* she gives some clue to a sexuality that has been dependent to a large extent on men. By uncovering forbidden knowledge, she both particularizes and subverts that exclusive recognition the men called *négritude.* What Fanon had deemed a necessary plunge into "that occult zone of instability" becomes for Chauvet an experiment in how much can be uttered. For the lawbreakers Claire and Rose *everything* can be said.

Reading Chauvet requires a labor far greater than reading other French Caribbean writers. A reader must know something about Haiti. Yet the test of what matters—what must be read in the "underread"—is whether or not it can be easily digested, or more precisely, cannibalized. Indeed, Chauvet's avoidance of lyrical compromise, her refusal to write so the outsider can easily incorporate a *place* not his or her own, makes her work crucial for those readers who want to avoid "recolonizing" those writings from "outside France."

Notes

1. *Amour, Colère, et Folie* (Paris: Gallimard, 1968). All further references to this book appear in parentheses in the text, as do references to any work cited more than once. All translations are mine. Chauvet's first published work, written for the stage under the pseudonym Colibri, was *La Légende des fleurs* (Port-au-Prince: Editions Deschamps, 1950). *Fille d'Haïti* (Paris: Fasquelle Editeurs, 1954) won the *Prix de l'Alliance française* in Haiti; *La Danse sur le volcan* (Paris: Librarie Plon, 1957), a novel, based on historical documentation, of two heroines of Saint-Domingue on the eve of the Haitian Revolution, was translated into English by Salvator Attanasio as *Dance on the Volcano* (New York: William Sloan Associates, 1959); and *Fonds des nègres* (Port-au-Prince: Editions Deschamps, 1960) won the *Prix France-Antilles* in Paris.

2. Jacques Barros, *Haïti de 1804 à nos jours* (Paris: L'Harmattan, 1984), 1:404.

3. Dany Laferrière, "Marie Chauvet: *Amour, Colère, Folie*," in *Littérature Haïtienne*, ed. Jean Jonassaint, special issue of *Mot pour Mot* 11 (1983):7–10.

4. Madeleine Gardiner, *Visages de femmes: Portraits d'écrivains* (Port-au-Prince: Editions Henri Deschamps, 1981). The history of Chauvet's reception in France and Haiti needs further investigation. Only now has Editions Deschamps in Haiti begun the project of reediting her works, with the publication of *Les Rapaces* (1986), her last work written in exile in New York, where she died in 1973. See also Frank Laraque, "Violence et sexualité dans *Colère* de Marie Chauvet," *Présence haïtienne*, no. 2 (September 1975):53–56. I thank Jean Jonassaint, Colette Pratt, Betty Wilson, and Lisabeth Paravisini for sharing with me their knowledge of Chauvet.

5. James Anthony Froude, *The English in the West Indies* (London: Longmans, 1888), 343.

6. "An Interview with Aimé Césaire," addendum to his *Discourse on Colonialism*, trans. Joan Pinkham (New York: Monthly Review Press, 1972), 74.

7. On the varying representations of women in Haitian poetry see Léon-François Hoffmann, "L'Image de la femme dans la poésie haïtienne," *Présence Africaine* 34–35 (1960–61):201–15; Yves L. Auguste, "L'Amour dans la littérature haïtienne," *Présence Africaine* 60 (1966):159–71; and Maximilien Laroche, "La métaphor du guerrier dans la poésie érotique," in his *L'Image comme écho: Essais sur la littérature et la culture haïtienne* (Montreal: Editions Nouvelle Optique, 1978).

8. Maryse Condé, *La Parole des femmes: Essai sur des romancières des Antilles de langue français* (Paris: L'Harmattan, 1979), 83.

9. See Frantz Fanon, *Black Skin, White Masks*, trans. Charles Lam Markmann (New York: Grove Press, 1967), 17–18: "to speak means to be in a position to use a certain syntax, to grasp the morphology of this or that language, but it means above all to assume a culture, to support the weight of a civilization."

10. See René Depestre, *Bonjour et Adieu à la Négritude* (Paris: Editions Robert Laffont, 1980), 50: "Negritude . . . was originally the *prise de conscience* of the fact that the black proletariat is doubly alienated: on the one hand, alienated (like the white proletariat) in so far as being gifted with a work-power sold on the capitalist markets; on the other hand, in so far as having black pigment, alienated in his epidermic singularity."

11. Jacques Roumain, the poet and novelist who founded the Haitian Communist party in 1934, best known for his novel *Les Gouverneurs de la Rosée* (1944), wrote a Marxist analysis of race prejudice in the United States called *Griefs de l'homme noir* (1939).

12. For a discussion of Erzulie as the phenomenon that subverts the claims of "femininity" and Western ideals of love or beauty, see my "Caribbean Cannibals and Whores," *Raritan* 9, no. 2 (Fall 1989): 45–67.

13. On the relation of Schwarz-Bart and Chauvet to history, see Lizabeth Paravisini and Barbara Webb, "On the Threshold of Becoming: Contemporary Women Writers," *Cimarron* 1, no. 5 (Spring 1988):121–26. For a brilliant analysis of the way history articulates itself in Caribbean women's writing, and a discussion of the use and abuse of women in Chauvet's *Amour, Colère, et Folie,* see Clarisse Zimra, "W/Righting His/tory: Versions of Things Past in Contemporary Caribbean Women Writers," in *Explorations: Essays in Comparative Literature,* ed. Mototo Ueda (Lanham, Md.: University Press of America, 1986): 227–52.

14. See Albert Charton, "The Social Function of Education in French West Africa," in *Africans Learn to Be French,* ed. W. Bryant Mumford, head of the Colonial Department, University of London Institute of Education (New York: Negro Universities Press, 1970), 101, 98. This chapter documents the ideology behind French educational practice in Africa. Most of the African writers in French passed through this school system and inevitably came under the influence of this ideology, even if they later revolted against it. I am grateful to Thomas Cassirer for making this material available to me.

15. Pierre de Vaissière, *Saint-Domingue (1629–1789): La Sociéte et la vie créoles sous l'ancien régime* (Paris: 1909), 219.

16. In *Folie,* the third part of Chauvet's trilogy, the vodoun gods make their presence known. In this narrative of four "mad" poets, Chauvet writes a literary history of Haiti, while disclosing vodoun as her call to memory. Weaned from vodoun through education and an acquired *langue de culture,* Chauvet dramatizes the difficulties of growing up in a country where Mozart and merengue, the gods of Guinea and the Catholic saints coexist.

17. Cited in Laënnec Hurbon, *Le Barbare imaginaire* (Port-au-Prince: Editions Henri Deschamps, 1987), 59. In *La République d'Haïti et ses visiteurs,* Louis-Joseph Janvier writes, "La France c'est la capitale des peuples et Haïti c'est la France noire," cited in Hurbon, 62.

18. According to Michel-Rolph Trouillot, one of the most astute writers on Haiti today, Duvalier exploited the "scorn of black skin" for his totalitarian ambitions. "Noirisme," writes Trouillot, was nothing but a "political ideology": "power to the epidermic representatives of the greatest number." See Trouillot, *Les Racines historiques de l'état Duvalierien* (Port-au-Prince: Editions Deschamps, 1986), 142. See also his *Haiti: State against Nation: The Origins and Legacy of Duvalierism* (New York: Monthly Review Press, 1990).

19. Here, I refer the reader to Sarah Kofman's interview in chapter 14, below: "for me, one isn't a man or a woman: those categories are anatomical and social, and can be traced back to the metaphysical tradition that starts with Aristotle. . . . When you say to me, 'Do you write as a woman?' I cannot accept this metaphysical formulation."

20. When she describes Luze with "eyes . . . like those precious rocks hidden in a velvet case," is Chauvet reminding her readers of Baudelaire's hommage to

Jeanne Duval? Or hidden like a wily bug in the confines of her formal exterior, is Claire recalling that moment in Rimbaud's *Illuminations:* "Oh, those precious rocks that were hiding—those flowers that were already gazing."

21. Vodoun is a rite of the image, and one might see "possession" as the taking in and performance of the collective imaginary of a particular *houmfort* or cult temple. If so, then Erzulie's emanations are more easily understood as accretions or compoundings of varying visualizations or representations of women. Irigaray's explanation of *la mascarade* and *mimétisme* are particularly instructive here. For the woman—or man—possessed by Erzulie assumes a "lady's" style and posture, while uncovering the way such a spectacle exploits or consumes its participant. See Luce Irigaray, *This Sex Which Is Not One* (Ithaca, N.Y.: Cornell University Press, 1985). Irigaray's "playful crossing . . . unsettling . . . which would allow woman to rediscover the place of her 'self-affection,'" to discover her "'god'" depends upon keeping an enforced *duality* intact (77–78). Such a strategy helps us to understand how vodoun ceremony keeps the male and female in play, while suddenly undifferentiating these categories.

22. Chauvet deliberately echoes Massillon Coicou's famous "Complaintes d'esclave" in his *Poésies nationales* (Paris: imprimerie Victor Goupy et Jourdan, 1892): "Why am I negro? Oh, why am I black?"

23. Jacques Roumain, *Gouverneurs de la Rosée* (Paris: Editions Messidor, 1988), 37.

24. See Timoléon Brutus, *L'Homme d'Airain* (Port-au-Prince: Imprimerie N. A. Théodore, 1946), 120–21. Note that the derealization of woman is also necessary to the ideology of *négritude,* as Sartre retold it: "Black Orpheus" descends in order to retrieve the unretrievable "Eurydice," who remains nothing but motive for *his* voice, for *his* poetry.

25. Recall Edward Long's conclusion in *The History of Jamaica* (1774; reprint, 3 vols., New York: Arno Press, 1972), 3:365 "that the oran-outang and some races of black men are very nearly allied, is I think, more than probable."

26. Rose's father also prostitutes himself when he goes to his rich mistress, sleeps with her, and borrows the necessary five hundred dollars.

27. Her monologue completes Irigaray's elliptical sentence in *This Sex Which Is Not One:* "Commodities, as we all know, do not take themselves to market on their own, and if they could talk. . . ." (84).

28. Freud makes the intimate connection between sexuality and dreams of domination in "Sexual Abberations," *The Basic Writings of Sigmund Freud,* trans. and ed. A. A. Brill (New York: Random House, 1938), 570. "That cruelty and the sexual instinct are most intimately connected is beyond doubt taught by the history of civilization. . . . The aggression which is mixed with the sexual instinct is, according to some authors, a remnant of cannibalistic lust." In 1959, Frantz Fanon, in *A Dying Colonialism,* trans. Haakon Chevalier (New York: Grove Press, Inc., 1965), 45–46, will give Freud's assertion a history by making desire explicit in the context of the Algerian Revolution: "Whenever, in dreams having an erotic content, a European meets an Algerian woman, the specific features of his relations with the colonized society manifest themselves. These dreams evolve neither on the same erotic plane, nor at the same tempo, as those that involve a European woman. . . . Straight off, with the maximum of violence, there is possession, rape, near-murder."

29. See Alain Corbin's discussion of prostitution in nineteenth-century France

for an incisive discussion of the "stinking body" and the "infection of the social structure," "Commercial Sexuality in Nineteenth-Century France: A System of Images and Regulations," *Representations* 14 (Spring 1986): 109–220. See also his *Les Filles de Noce* (Paris: Flammarion, 1978). For Derek Walcott, the Martiniquan whore in *Another Life* gives off "that very special reek" of his native land, Saint Lucia; and V. S. Naipaul makes nearly all his women loci of projection for all that is rotten and diseased in his much despised Trinidad.

30. Yveline Momplaisir, "La Condition de la femme haïtienne," *Le Nouveau Monde* (9 July 1978), cited in Barros, 407.

31. The resuscitation and inversion of "the beauty and the beast" union is also attempted in Walcott's extraordinary "Goats and Monkeys," his meditation on *Othello* in *The Castaway and Other Poems* (1965), in his *Collected Poems: 1948–1984* (New York: Farrar, Straus & Giroux, 1986), 83–85. "Virgin and ape, maid and malevolent Moor, / their immortal coupling, still halves our world. / He is your sacrificial beast, bellowing, goaded, a black bull snarled in ribbons of its blood."

32. See Zora Neale Hurston's presentations of the luxuriant Erzulie in *Tell My Horse* (Berkeley, Calif.: Turtle Island, 1981), 143–51.

Métissage, Emancipation, and Female Textuality in Two Francophone Writers

Prospero: . . . Miranda: But how is it
That this lives in thy mind? What seest thou else
In the dark backward and abysm of time?
—William Shakespeare, *The Tempest*

. . . Mais je rêve, j'utopographe, je sais.
—Annie Leclerc, *Parole de femme*

To read a narrative that depicts the journey of a female self striving to become the subject of her own discourse, the narrator of her own story, is to witness the unfolding of an autobiographical project. To raise the question of referentiality and ask whether the text points to an individual existence beyond the pages of the book is to distort the picture. As Picasso once said about his portrait of Gertrude Stein, although she was not exactly like it, she would eventually become so. The ability to "defamiliarize" ordinary experience, forcing us to notice what we live with but ignore, has long been considered an important characteristic of art. Such is the Russian formalists' notion of *ostraneniye*, or "making strange," the Surrealists' dream of a heightened level of awareness, Nathalie Sarraute's "era of suspicion." New ways of seeing can indeed emancipate us. Literature, like all art, can show us new means of constructing the world, for it is by changing the images and structures through which we encode meaning that we can begin to develop new scripts and assign new roles to the heroines of the stories we recount in order to explain and understand our lives.

The female writer who struggles to articulate a personal vision and to verbalize the vast areas of feminine experience that have remained unexpressed, if not repressed, is engaged in an attempt to excavate those elements of the female self which have been buried under the cultural and patriarchal myths of selfhood. She perceives these myths as alienating and radically *other,* and her aim is often the retrieval of a more authentic image, one that may not be ostensibly "true" or "familiar" at first, since our ways of perceiving are so subtly conditioned by our social and historical circumstance and since our collective imagination is so overwhelmingly nonfemale. Having no literary tradition that empowers her to speak, she seeks to elaborate discursive patterns that will both reveal the "hidden face of Eve"[1] and displace the traditional distinctions of rigidly defined literary genres. Formulating a problematics of female authorship is thus an urgent task for feminist writers and one that they approach with much ambivalence.

Theorists of autobiography have traditionally assumed with Roy Pascal that we read autobiographies "not as factual truth, but as a wrestling with truth."[2] In their attempt at a selective grouping of first-person narratives, however, theorists have largely failed to "take hold of autobiography's protean forms," as Avrom Fleishman puts it.[3] And feminist critics in particular have been quick to suggest that, in the words of Nancy K. Miller, "any theoretical model *indifferent* to a problematics of genre as inflected by gender" must be regarded as suspect.[4] Since it is notoriously difficult for us as women to recognize ourselves in the images that literature and society (sometimes including our own mothers) traditionally project or uphold as models, it should not be surprising for an autobiographical narrative to proclaim itself as fiction: for the narrator's process of reflection, narration, and self-integration within language is bound to unveil patterns of self-definition (and self-dissimulation) which may seem new and strange and with which we are not always consciously familiar. The self engendered on the page allows a writer to subject ordinary experience to new scrutiny and to show that the polarity fact/fiction does not establish and constitute absolute categories of feeling and perceiving reality. The narrative text epitomizes this duality in its splitting of the subject of discourse into a narrating self and an experiencing self, which can never coincide exactly. Addressing the problematics of authorship,[5] the female narrator gets caught in a duplicitous process: she exists in the text under circumstances of alienated communication because the text is the locus of her dialogue with a tradition she tacitly aims at subverting. Describing the events that have helped her assume a given heritage, she communicates with a narratee who figures in a particular kind of relationship both with her as narrator and with their shared cultural environment. By examining the narrative structure through these constitutive relational patterns, we can elicit from the text a model of reading which does not betray its complicated and duplicitous messages. For example, Marie Cardinal dedicates her novel to the "doctor who helped [her] be born," and he is the explicit listener of her life story.[6] As such, his role is clear. But as I will discuss later, the text encodes his presence as a catalyst whose function is not only to facilitate access to the narrator's effaced, forgotten, joyful "Algerian" self but also to mediate the reader's understanding of the story being told in the book, the "histoire racontée à du papier."[7]

Marie Cardinal and Marie-Thérèse Humbert are contemporary women writers who have lived and worked in France. They present us with new ways of reading the heroine's text, new ways that they perceive as emancipatory. Their cultural backgrounds and creative roots reach far beyond the confines of France's *hexagone;* they were both born and brought up in former colonies of France (Cardinal in Algeria; Humbert in Mauritius). Finding themselves at the confluence of different cultures, they must sort out their loyalties and affiliations on a personal as well as social and political level, and their predicament is analogous to that of any woman writer who tries to come to terms with her own sexual difference in a male-dominated society. They draw heavily on their personal colonial experience but publish their works as *romans,* first-person narratives of young women who are determined to make sense of their past and to inscribe themselves within and outside of the cultures that subtend that experience. They take their readers on a journey of personal discovery where the silent other of sex, language, and culture is allowed to emerge and is given a voice. This process of discovery thus becomes the source of rebirth and reconciliation, the mode of healing the narrating self.

Both Cardinal's and Humbert's tales center on the debilitating sexual and racial stereotypes of their colonial past and the degree to which their narrators have internalized them. Indoctrinated into a blind acceptance of these values (which at the time seem the only possible course for survival), the protagonists become progressively unable to cope with "reality" as presented and depicted in the master narratives of colonization.[8] They are thus alienated from something at once internal and external to the self. It is at that precise moment of disjunction that the narrative text articulates a dialogue between two instances of the self, the "I" and the "she," the "I" of the here and now, who reconstructs the absent, past "she," the emancipation of the "I" being triggered and actualized by the voice of the "she" taking shape on the page. These two instances of the self figuratively alternate roles as narrator and narratee in the context of different narrative segments.[9] The interaction between the narrator's self-image and her interlocutors (the reconstructed "she" as well as the various other protagonists of the story in their role as [virtual] narratees)—what she focuses on and what she omits—gives dynamism to the unfolding of the narrative and elicits a particular response from the reader. As Wolfgang Iser puts it: "Effect and response arise from a dialectical relationship between showing and concealing—in other words, from the difference between what is said and what is meant."[10] The topos created by this interaction is the privileged textual space where initially unquestioned assumptions about self and other, sex and language, belief and culture can be examined in a dramatic mode: this is where autobiography acquires a meaning and a function not unlike those of fiction with its mythmaking and myth-deflating power.

The novels have numerous formal and thematic similarities and offer a critique of colonialism from two different class perspectives. In *Les Mots pour le dire* the narrator belongs to the French landowning bourgeoisie, whose stance toward the Algerian Arabs is one of benevolent paternalism laced with Catholic missionary zeal; in *A l'autre bout de moi* the narrator's family lives on the margins of the rich white settlers' world, which scorns them because their imperfect pedigree ("some Hindu great-grandmother who was all but forgotten since we carefully avoided talking about her"[11]) is not offset by any redeeming form of financial success. Despite this important class distinction, the childhoods of the protagonists benefit from a similar cultural diversity (a mothering of sorts by the natural environment and the nonwhites who are part of their daily lives, in the absence of a truly nurturing biological mother, in the presence of a flamboyant and indifferent father). They both come to identify with the non-European, Third World elements of their "alien" cultures. For Cardinal's narrator, it is the acceptance of a privileged difference that is a *métissage* of the heart and mind; for Humbert's, it is a more telling trajectory back to her "mixed-blood" origins after a murderous confrontation with subjectivity in the guise of her twin sister, the mirror image, the "monster" who steals her illusory individuality.

> J'appartiens à un pays que j'ai quitté. . . . il faut qu'une
> fois encore j'arrache, de mon pays, toutes mes racines qui
> saignent.
>
> —Colette, "Jour gris," *Les Vrilles de la vigne*

The structure of *Les Mots pour le dire* parallels Cardinal's experience of Freudian psychoanalysis. Having reached a point of dislocation and madness after resettling in Paris with her family, she decides to enter analysis. The combined influence of her church and class, along with the traumas of a difficult relationship with her rejecting mother, have made her completely *aliénée, folle* (insane—or alienated—mad). After years of analysis, she succeeds in unlocking the source of the pain, and the process of writing becomes the process of rebirth: "I must think back to find again the forgotten woman, more than forgotten, disintegrated. . . . She and I. I am she. . . . I protect her; she lavishes freedom and invention on me. . . . I have to split myself in two" (8). This is the most complete and radical sort of rebirth: "self-engendering as a verbal body,"[12] the discovery of language and its infinite possibilities, the realization, the surfacing of an enormous creative potential: "I and the words were both on the surface and clearly visible" (239); "words were boxes, they all contained living matter" (239, tr. m.). Not so much the story of an analysis as an investigation of the analogies between the dialogical analytic process and the healing, self-directed exchange that allows the unmasking of the woman, the novel belies all attempts to label it as a social document about psychoanalysis.[13] It enacts a coherent staging of that process but, in so doing, subverts it.

At the beginning of the novel, the narrator is emotionally comatose, chemically tranquilized, silent, obedient, and submissive; her body, however, is hysterically alive, constantly generating more blood, more fibroid tissue, anarchically feminine. She *is* her fibromatous uterus, and when her surgeon decides to cure her physical symptoms—constant hemorrhaging—by the "aggressive" method of hysterectomy, she knows that this would be a mutilation, an amputation of the madwoman who is a part of her and with whom she must learn to live: "I began to accept [the insane one], to love her even" (10). She escapes into the dark office of the analyst, where for the next seven years, she will come at regular intervals to lie on the couch "curled up, like a fetus in the womb"; she feels herself to be a "huge embryo pregnant with myself" (12, 13, tr. m.). The imagery she uses to describe the location of the office is particularly suited to the birthing metaphor; it is in an island of surprising calm and tranquility in the midst of Paris, at the end of a narrow cul-de-sac (2), a "ruelle en impasse" (7), just as her life is lived in an impasse, in limbo, while she undergoes analysis. She is only enduring until she can be strong enough to survive without the protection of the womblike room with its mirroring presence of the "little dark-skinned man" (2), who never judges and will remain impersonal and masked till the end of the book. In this he is the opposite of the tall, dynamic surgeon, who wears white and examines his patient in a glaringly lit room with a ceiling "white as a lie" (7).

How are we to understand this contrast between the surgeon and the analyst? Clearly, the surgeon stands for a patriarchal society intent on annihilating the disturbing signs of a feminine difference flowing out of control. But more important, in the textual context of the narrative situation he is an antimodel for the critic, whereas the analyst figures as an ideal other. The analyst's silent, invisible (she cannot see him from the couch), but very attentive presence casts him in the role of a midwife who helps the narrator pregnant with her effaced self. The text constructs him as an ideal listener-reader, one without preconceived and Procrustean notions of literary or autobiographical canon. It is in this implicit contrast between the two doctors that the narrative signals itself as a "communicational act," as Ross Chambers formulates it, and provides us with the model of reading most appropriate to the "point" it is trying to make.[14]

This is a model, needless to say, that would neither amputate the text of meaning nor fit it into a preexisting theoretical framework: here, the text figures as the female body of the writer and the critic, as the midwife of its meaning. What is being advocated is a female reappropriation of the best form of ancient Socratic *maieusis*, not surprising for a feminist author who was trained as professor of philosophy. The metaphor of "physician of the soul" is, of course, well known to readers of Augustine's *Confessions* (10:3: "medice meus intime"), in which God, the transcendental addressee, is the model of Augustine's ideal reader, the one who can help the narrator transcend his own corporeality, so that his soul may be reborn. In a reversal of this mind/body dichotomy and of the traditional quest of spiritual autobiographers for a transcendent self, Cardinal aims at rediscovering the body in its female specificity as the source of her own discursive practice.

The specular relationship created between writer and reader (or critic) in the analytical situation suggests that, for the writer as well, there is an antimodel of creativity; her inability to write without constant reference to a rigid code and pious reverence for the great masters stifles her completely:

That's what writing was for me: to put correctly into words, in accordance with the strict rules of grammar, references and information that had been given to me. In this area improvement consisted in expanding vocabulary in so far as it was possible, and learning Grevisse almost by heart. I was attached to this book, whose old-fashioned title, *Good Usage*, seemed to me to guarantee the seriousness and suitability of my passion for it. In the same way I loved saying that I read *Les Petites Filles modèles* when I was little. In Grevisse, there are many doors open to freedom and fantasy, many goodnatured winks, like little signs of collusion, meant for those who do not wish to be confirmed in the orthodoxy of a dead language and a tightly corseted grammar. I felt that these evasions were, nevertheless, not for me, but were reserved for writers. I had too much respect, even veneration, for books to imagine that I could write one. . . . Writing itself seemed to be an important act of which I was unworthy. (215, 216, tr. m.)

Such a thorough internalization of the repressive rules of the symbolic order puts the writer in the role of a surgeon operating a ruthless censorship on her own text, asphyxiating any free play of subjectivity.[15] It is not surprising that when she does start finding her own *"mots pour le dire,"* she hides herself to write and then hides her notebooks under her mattress as though this transgression of the symbolic order can be effective only if it is not subjected to the judging eye of the literary law.

This eye is also the one she sees in her hallucination (chap. 8), which terrorizes her: it is the eye behind the camera of her father, who had attempted to photograph her as a toddler while she was urinating on the ground. This experience, lived by the child as a violation of her secret desires, unleashed a formidable anger against this peeping father: "I strike him with all my strength. . . . I want to kill him!" (152). Her hatred is then promptly repressed by the shame she is made to feel for her violent impulses: "You musn't hit mama, you mustn't hit papa! It's very wicked, it's shameful! Punished, crazy! Very ugly, very naughty, crazy!" (152, tr. m.). Once the "eye" of the hallucination is exorcised she can begin to deal with her fear of being "a genuine monster" (165). This is the combined fear, as Barbara Johnson puts it, of "effecting the death of [her] own parents" and of being creatively different, free, and successful.[16] To overcome this fear, which paralyzes her writing, she has to learn to let the words flow freely, without regard for grammatical rules or objective reality: the flow of words must mimic the anarchic flow of blood and eventually replace it. Describing her apprenticeship at self-portrayal, she explains: "With pencil and paper, I let my mind wander. Not like on the couch in the cul-de-sac. The divagations in the notebooks were made up of the elements of my life which were arranged according to my fancy: going where I pleased, living out moments I had only imagined. *I was not in the yoke of truth, as in analysis.* I was conscious of being more free than I had ever been" (215, my emphasis).

The distinction between the analysis and the book we are reading is clearly established. Later on, allowing her husband to read her manuscript, she confesses with some trepidation: "I should have thought of it before; I should have stopped to consider that I was writing, that I was telling a story if only to the paper [*que je racontais une histoire à du papier* (266)]; I should have spoken about it to the doctor" (226). The freedom to write, and to write secretly, is yet another transgression, a transgression of the rules of psychoanalytic practice. But the risk she takes of being judged by Jean-Pierre, her husband, the *agrégé de grammaire*, is not a gratuitous one: the book exists in a homologous relationship to her analytic discourse, and just as analysis has changed her perception of herself, so reading her text will change Jean-Pierre's perception of his wife: "How you've changed. You intimidate me. Who are you?" (228). The invitation to read/know her anew is thus an invitation to love again after the long estrangement caused by her "illness." Sharing in the power of language to redefine reality, to name the woman who had become effaced under her social role as wife and mother, "model young wife and mother, worthy of my own mother" (219), Jean-Pierre now sees the new/old face of the narrator, the one that conveys a harmonious relationship to Mediterranean nature, where the sea, the sand, the sun, the sky are one continuous whole, interacting in their difference to allow the free play of meaning. The female is again the equal partner of the male, who needs her to assume her difference so he can become capable of a genuine act of love, an act of loving/reading. The staging of Jean-Pierre as the receptive reader par excellence can be interpreted as a *mise en abyme* of the reading process and of its effect as it is encoded in the narrative structure.[17] The power to be read on her own terms is thus inseparable, for the female writer, from a genuine "suspension of disbelief" on the part of her audience, whereas her right to be a narrator is acquired through an arduous effort at self-emancipation from the laws of preexisting and distorting master discourses (such as the literary tradition and psychoanalytic practice).

Not surprisingly, this newfound freedom results from her understanding and acceptance of the specificity of her female experience, a specificity that stretches her beyond the personal to the political and historical context of Algeria. Along with the discovery of what it means to be a woman and a victim comes the realization that her victimization as daughter coexisted with her mother's inability to assume and legitimize her own lack of sexual and maternal love and to face her own fear of sexual difference. This fear caused the mother's complicity with the repressive, paternalistic colonial order, despite her qualities of intelligence, sensuality, and integrity (see chap. 16). Although the narrator rejects her as mother, she can see the woman and relate to her as victim. Like Algeria during the war of independence, the mother's agony is the scene of a civil war between conflicting ideologies. Rather than reexamine all the values she lives by, the mother prefers to let herself go completely, to give in to the profound distress that had inhabited her psyche all along. She loses all self-respect, is drunk and incontinent, and subsequently dies. Her daughter finds her, "on the floor. She had been dead for ten or twelve hours already. She was curled up in a ball. Rigor mortis had fixed horror on her face and body" (289). It is the mother now who is the monster, the fetuslike creature whose posture mirrors that of the fetus-daughter she had unsuccessfully tried to abort; that daughter, now safely beyond her nefarious influence, can at last say, "I love you" (292), and make her peace with the past.

It is during a visit to her mother's grave that the daughter is able to recall with poetic tenderness the moments of genuine joy she had experienced when walking on the beach or gazing at the stars with her mother. Looking for shells washed ashore by the waves, looking at the stars in the warmth of the Mediterranean night, together, they had been "in contact with the cosmos" (202). Her mother knew the names of all the shells—"the mother-of-pearl shells, cowries, pointed sea snails, ear shells and the pink razor clam shells" (291)—and of all the stars—"the shepherd's star . . . the Big Dipper . . . the Charioteer . . . the Little Dipper . . . Vega . . . the Milky Way" (202, tr. m.). This naming of the universe is her most precious maternal legacy, and the daughter is able to insert herself, her book, her words into that universe. The daughter thereby erases the narrative of hatred and unsuccessful abortion which her mother had divulged to her when she was twelve. They were both standing on a sidewalk of Algiers, "the same sidewalk on which later would run the blood of enmity" (132). The recounting of these secrets had been the mother's *saloperie* (131), her villainy (105), to her daughter, and the words fell on the young daughter "like so many mutilating swords" (135). This information about the girl's gestation (that prehistoric time of her life) thwarts her feminine development. She does not start menstruating before the age of twenty. The doubly archaic revelation—reproduction as a "female problem" and excavation of her prediscursive past—is lived by the narrator as the murder of her femininity. Indeed, a story can kill, it can be what Peter Brooks calls "un acte d'agression,"[18] and to counter it, another story, more powerful in its enabling, nurturing, or life-affirming characteristics, is needed. Such are the tales and legends that the old Algerian woman Daïba tells to the children on the farm while feeding them "pastry dripping with honey" (98) and unleavened bread. Hers are mythic tales with a powerful, positive, imaginary content, "sudden flights on winged horses prancing all the way to Allah's Paradise . . . adventures of black giants who shook mountains, fountains springing up in the desert, and genies inside bottles" (98). Such was the magic of those days on the farm: contact with an archaic civilization, games with the Arab children, freedom from French reason and religion. The richness and diversity of her early experiences give the girl a strength to draw from when she is forced to leave Algeria and to cope with the psychic wounds that both her mother and the war inflicted upon her.

Talking to her dead mother in the cemetery, she recalls trips to another cemetery in Algeria, where her dead sister lies and where her mother, inconsolable over the loss of that "exceptional" child, the absent daughter who can never be replaced, used to take her. This loss is the original cause of the mother's profound and murderous contempt for the second daughter. The death of the mother, then, frees this daughter, who can simultaneously terminate her analysis and end her narrative: writing *is* symbolic matricide. Writing is the act of self-emancipation which allows the narrator to reach autonomy, despite her painful bleeding, much as Algeria won independence through its own bloodbath.

The novel contains two parallel chapters (6 and 16), which describe the Algerian tragedy and the mother's demise in much the same terms: "French Algeria lived out its agony" (87) and "During this last year of my analysis, my mother was living through her final agony" (270); "While lacerated Algeria showed her infected wounds in the full light of day, I revived a country of love and tenderness where the earth smelled of jasmine and fried food" (88) and "On the contrary, she [the mother] didn't give a damn, she exhibited herself as if she took pleasure in exposing her wounds" (280). Colonialism, like sexism, is thus degrading and abject: it is their combined forces that kill "the mother and the motherland"[19] and give the narrator the opportunity to discover what femininity really means in that context. The role of women is to be mothers of future soldiers, who will fight wars and perpetuate inequality and injustice. The only way to break the cycle is to start sharing in the power of men to make decisions that affect all of our lives, to become an active participant in society. In fact, it is her feeling of impotence in affairs of the state that provokes the narrator's major attacks of anxiety: "It seems to me that the Thing took root in me permanently when I understood that we were about to assassinate Algeria. For Algeria was my real mother" (88). The way out of the impasse is a heightened political awareness of the complicated structures of domination that amputate freedom and self-determination from people and countries.

In a direct confession of the apolitical nature of her life before she started to write, the narrator admits that she never even used to read the newspapers. She had first seen the Algerian war as a sentimental family affair of fraternal enmity. Her life had been "thirty-seven years of absolute submission. Thirty-seven years of accepting the inequality and the injustice, without flinching, without even being aware of it!" (264). But with self-integration comes a raised consciousness. The book ends on the historical marker: "*Quelques jours plus tard, c'était mai 68.*"[20] We have come full circle; the personal and the political are inseparable.

> If I'd been black that would at least have given the information I was from Africa. . . . But nobody could see me, there, for what I am back where I come from. Nobody in Paris.
>
> —Nadine Gordimer, *Burger's Daughter*

> Mi patria en el recuerdo
> y yo en París clavado
> como un blando murciélago
> —Nicolás Guillén, "Exilio," *Man-Making Words*

The year 1968 was also an important one in the history of Mauritius. It marked the island's independence from Britain, its access to the rank of country. Independence was achieved with little or no bloodshed, because none of the diverse ethnic groups could really claim original ownership of the place. The island had been uninhabited until European settlers began visiting it in the seventeenth and eighteenth centuries, and today it is peopled with the descendants of the French settlers, their black slaves, the Indian laborers who came to work the sugar-cane fields when slavery was abolished in 1835, the Chinese and Muslim shopkeepers, and the *métis* whose status varies greatly depending on the relative darkness of their skin and the size of their fortune.

Marie-Thérèse Humbert's novel *A l'autre bout de moi* is the story of these *"apatrides de la race"* (22) ("racially homeless people"), the coloreds or mixed-bloods, whose marginality is partly the result of their own inability to assume their nonwhite heritage because they have internalized the ideals of the racist colonial society. Twin sisters, Anne and Nadège, live in a house on the outskirts of the vast colonial domains of the white bourgeoisie and a short distance from the Hindu quarter. This "house on the margins, on the limits, without ties and without parentage" (17) is a metaphor for their racial and cultural contexts. Coming of age in the 1950s, the decade preceding independence, the sisters are set on a collision course, for they choose to be loyal to different traditions; Nadège gleefully accepts her *métissage:* she is chameleonlike, adventurous, imaginative, interested in Hindu culture and religion as well as popular superstitions; she is a free spirit, at once the Ariel and the Caliban of this "enchant'd isle," full of humor, impossible to define and constantly changing. She is the favored daughter of the family and she has an affair with a young Indian politician. For both reasons, she incurs the wrath of Anne, the controlled, reasonable, calculating one, whose rigid need for respectability, like that of the heroines of the romances she reads, includes romantic hopes of a bourgeois marriage. These hopes are thwarted by Nadège's pregnancy, for in Anne's world of almost-white-but-not-quite, any wrong step can be the first on the road back to further ostracism by the whites. When Nadège proudly announces her condition, Anne's murderous hatred is unleashed. She tells Nadège why she had always resented her; she shouts her contempt and her fury, disclosing her own profound distress. In an act of love for Anne, Nadège decides to obtain an (illegal) abortion and dies hemorrhaging. Her death and the police investigations that follow rob Anne of her pretensions to a purely Western life style, revealing the "air d'étrangeté" (398), the *Unheimlichkeit*, the uncanniness, of her own home and country. At the end, the impossible fusion with her twin is realized in Anne's appropriation of Nadège's place as the lover of the Indian, Aunauth Gopaul. It is interesting to note that the names of the twins, Anne-Nadège, spoken quickly with the Mauritian Creole accent, sound much like *"anamnèse,"* since consonants are softened and the *-ège* ending is always pronounced like *-èse.* Thus Anne literally figures as the "one who returns" (*ana-*) and Nadège as her "memory" (*-mnesis*), or previous self.[21]

Anne's autobiographical narrative is an attempt to return Nadège's love, Nadège's loving offer to immolate her (pro)creation. It engages Anne, the narrator, in a dialogue with Nadège and with the repressed (sister) in herself. She can begin to tell her/their story after she has allowed Nadège's voice to emerge: "But the voice which used to be Nadège's is now mine; I know it, I am certain of it" (12). The narrative is framed by a Prologue, which situates Anne and Aunauth as exiles in Paris, where they are studying at the Sorbonne. This seemingly self-imposed exile creates sufficient distance from the recent past to be the revealer of Anne's narrative impulse, the Archimedean point she needed to lift the veil of silence on that past and on her country.[22] The present reality of Paris silences her too: it is lived as a jarring hiatus from the past, and her impulse to write is a defensive one, spurred on by the desire to recreate that past and reintegrate it into a new present, to shout "Mauritius [Nadège] exists!" to people who have never paid any attention to it, been indifferent to its fate. Like her island, she feels *"abolie"* (12) ("negated") by the ignorance of others, especially since France is a spiritual motherland for the Francophones of Mauritius. Her situation as Mauritian in Paris thus triggers the memory—enacts the repetition—of an earlier trauma: her parents' inability to see her as different from Nadège. She still resents their mother's legacy of shame, hatred, bitterness, and silence: "Mother-Silence, Mother-Gloom, our marine silence" (43). And now in France, she also resents the sea of ignorance in which Mauritius floats. Like her parents' indifference, the ignorance of the *métropole* makes her feel painfully nonexistent.

Anne the protagonist can become Anne the narrator only after she has decided to return to her privileged "place of origin" and let the island tell itself through the voices of its inhabitants—all of whom have their own different stories, "life/lines," to tell her, in the form of direct or indirect discourses of which, as we shall see later, she is both the narratee and relayer. In this return to the "origins," Anne is like Augustine's narrator in the *Confessions,* who is finally whole after he has reached his resting place in God, who can then speak through him and whose words are translated textually by the weaving of scriptural verses into the narrative. Anne's autobiographical gesture is implicitly similar to the Augustinian project but covertly aims at subverting it. The narrative is divided into thirteen parts (like the *Confessions*), and as it unfolds, Anne confesses her "sins" to her sister. These are the sins of Western metaphysics: to wish desperately to *be* a unique individual, *"être à tout prix"* (419) ("to be at any cost"), and to capture one essential truth about oneself—whereas life is flux, theater, dream. Striving to occult in her the elements of a different race, her Hindu ancestry, and the qualities embodied by Nadège, she is a victim of the Western obsession with being, an obsession that shows nothing but contempt for its unassimilable opposites. Nadège, who is remarkably free of this totalizing goal, is self-assured in her difference. She has no distance, no duality: inner and outer are the same for her. Her life is lived in harmony with the passing of time, the mysteries of life. "Strangely intimate with the earth's profane mysteries and long seasonal gestations, with the winds' and the clouds' infinite wanderings" (312), she projects a persona that needs no mirror to reassure itself of its own existence:

Nadège never cared about being. . . . Never, but never, did she try to see herself elsewhere than in *the eyes of others*. She would amuse herself with these fortuitous mirrors as a child would with the changing colors of a prism, perpetually enjoying her ability to create new shades, becoming by turns intrigued, charmed, shocked or seduced by these external reflections, and thus deviating constantly from herself. There is nothing less imaginative and less true than a mirror! she used to declare contemptuously. But while she played, I would contemplate with despair my own dull shadow, lusterless compared to the shimmer of her multiple reflections; my wretched face, never quite mine because it was always too similar or too different from her own. (419, my emphasis)

Nadège is interested in Christian mysticism as well as Hindu rites. She participates every year in the Hindu festival of lights, the *Divali*, adorning their house with a small brass lantern, and the Hindu gods with colorful flowers. She is like a joyful Zarathustra; she does not need origins. Her very name also connotes nirvana, emptiness, nothingness, *nada*, Nadège. Anne, on the other hand, cannot surrender to polysemy and experiences it as a threat to her ego. She is always narcissistically searching for approval in the form of a reflection that would give her substance, ground her firmly somewhere: "Where is the place where I should live?" (122) she asks. But the reflection she finds always turns out to be illusory and elusive: "When I look in the mirror, it is you I see, you who need no mirror, you who *are* without a mirror. The image of myself that I try to capture deceives me, escapes me; it's you who are there in the mirror, only the expression of the eyes differs and the reflection that I see, my own image, looks like a bad photograph" (121).

The place where she can, and should, live, of course, is on the page, in the book that embodies these tensions in its own narrative structure, combining the self-portraits of all the characters, these *autres* who are Nadège's mirrors, her infinite dispersion. The words "my own image looks like a bad photograph" connote the scriptural phrase, *"per speculum in aenigmate"* (1 Cor. 13.12),[23] which Augustine repeatedly uses to signify his state of imperfection, which will be reversed when he reaches the "intellectual heaven." In book 12:13 of the *Confessions,* Augustine articulates his project of self-knowledge as the search for completeness and perfection. Augustine the sinner is now converted, and the book is a reflection of the man as a creature in the image of God, ready to enter "the intellectual heaven, where the intellect is privileged to know all at once, not in part only, not as if it were *looking at a confused reflection in a mirror* [*non in aenigmate, non per speculum*], but as a whole, clearly, *face to face* [*facie ad faciem*]."

Humbert's text never makes explicit reference to Augustine's *Confessions* as it does to Shakespeare's *Tempest,* for example; but it embodies in its structure an undeniable reflection of that *architexte*[24] of Western autobiographical discourse, while also reversing its messages. Humbert's text points to a negative view of mirroring, in the Western sense, as usurpation, occultation of difference. As Roland Barthes has said: "In the West, the mirror is essentially a narcissistic object: man thinks about the mirror only so as to look at himself; but it would seem that in the Orient the mirror is void; it is a symbol of the very emptiness of symbols. . . . The mirror only reflects other mirrors and this infinite reflecting is the void."[25]

It is in chapter 12 of *A l'autre bout de moi,* during the police interrogation, that Anne recalls (privately, not publicly) her confrontation with Nadège: "I had slapped her face with all my strength and rage. She took another step with her arms spread out. Then she slowly lowered them, as if in a daze. And before me, there was only her strangely distorted face, like a mask. No, I felt no pity, but once again this hideous joy, so keen that is seemed closer to pain than to pleasure; *before this unexpressive mask, at last, I had a face!"* (427, my emphasis). Anne's insults literally deface Nadège, steal her face, effecting her death as surely as the botched abortion will on the following day. It is not just the abortionist who is on trial; Anne too must account—on the page, by writing—for her inability to tolerate Nadège's polysemic difference and for her secret desire to assimilate it. She recalls how, during their altercation, Nadège had fallen down in the sand and had lain there, curled in a fetal position; she, Anne, had shouted "Fetus! Hideous fetus! Die!" (428), aiming the insult at her sister but thereby amputating herself, deprivileging otherness as radically *other* in order to co-opt it, to abort it.

I would like to suggest that what is implied (and at stake) here is the immolation of the *métis*, the Creole, as symbol, product, and (pro)creation of Western colonialism, on the altars of Western belief in the One and the Same, in a humanism that subsumes all heterogeneity. Anne the narrator sees herself as the product of this indoctrination, which resulted in a damaging self-image. In that, her predicament is analogous to that of all individuals who have internalized their society's negative view, or ignorance, of their specificity. These individuals include women in any patriarchal system, and women writers in particular, as they face the dilemmas inherent in recapturing what has been effaced or diminished. Anne's journey back to the past aims at deconstructing that indoctrination, peeling off the layers of a damaging belief in the importance of origins and rootedness.

Her journey, then, is that of her island itself at the time of its political independence from Britain. Its multiracial society was burdened by two centuries of colonization, first by the French, then by the British, whereas its survival had been ensured by the labor of the Indian and black populations who were not native either. All these diverse ethnic groups had to devise a mode of pacific coexistence that would allow the free play of influences and exchanges among different cultures. The issue, therefore, was not to define the national identity of the island (since it did not have any) but to use this geographical space, this topos, this "house without ties and without parentage" as the place where a mosaic of forms, styles, and languages could interact and survive.

Viewed from that angle, the political problematic of the island becomes the personal problematic of the woman writer. She has no specifically female tradition to build on but, in order to survive, must quilt together from the pieces of her legacy a viable whole—

viable in that it embraces a multiplicity of elements that can allow the writer to assume the past (the literary tradition) as past and therefore to reintegrate it into a radically different present,[26] making it the implicit or explicit intertext of her text, adding that past to the texture of her voice so she may begin to transform and reinterpret history. This problematic would point to a notion of the female text as *mé-tissage*, that is, the weaving of different strands of raw material and threads of various colors into one piece of fabric; female textuality as *métissage*. It would emancipate the writer from any internal or external coercion to use any one literary style or form, freeing her to enlarge, redefine, or explode the canons of our discursive practices.

Humbert's text encodes heterogeneity through this use of intertextual references to various generic and ideological models or antimodels—to Augustine and Shakespeare but also to Corneille, Racine, Baudelaire, Nietzsche, Conrad, Faulkner, Sylvia Plath, Michel Tournier, and others. Intratextually, she encodes diversity by giving her text over to a polyphonic chorus of voices who relate their own stories to us by means of her narrative. The purpose of these stories is twofold: to give a voice to the silenced ones of history and to allow Anne to become the heroine of her own tale by choosing a script for the way she will live her life from the various life stories that are recounted to her. Her situation as listener and interpreter of these stories is homologous to ours before her text, suggesting that she encodes certain models of reading appropriate to her own discourse. Without going into a detailed analysis of the many instances of situational self-reflexivity which would illustrate my point here, I would like to focus on two embedded stories ("narrational embedding") which are both narratives of abandonment.[27] Anne retells these stories in order to deal with and break away from that age-old script of female passivity. They are the stories of her own mother and of Sassita, the young Indian maid. Both women are quiet, submissive, "dead to desire as well as to revolt" (352), as Nadège will become when she too is all but abandoned by her lover, who wants to protect his political image.

Sassita was married at the age of fourteen to a fifty-six-year-old man who promptly repudiated her on their wedding night because the bedsheets had failed to become stained with blood. Dumbfounded at her bad luck and at the man's obstinate attempts to draw blood, she had rejoined her family and resigned herself to their daylong beatings as punishment for tarnishing the family's honor. She fatalistically accepted the guilt imposed on her by external circumstances. Listening to her story, Anne is filled with shame at the troubling unfairness of life and at the fatalism of the Indian woman.

The mother's story is disclosed when the sisters discover her diary after her death; they learn how disappointed she had been at their birth because they were "of a golden terracotta color" (130), not pink and blond and safely beyond their nonwhite ancestry. Also, her fear of sex and her disappointment in her husband's infidelities added to the debilitation of her young daughters. The discovery of their mother's secrets further accentuates the sisters' alienation from each other: Anne is progressively absorbed by her hopes to live a normal/respectable life, whereas Nadège gives free rein to her "blaze of vital energy" (120).

These pictures of effaced, obliterated femininity are the only paradigms or frames of reference Anne and Nadège have, their only lifelines to the status of female persons. In a reversal typical of the deployment and resolution of Humbert's narrative text, it is Nadège who is abandoned when her father threatens her lover with a political scandal (Nadège is still a minor at the time of her affair). She resigns herself to her fate as Sassita had, becoming a "tragic heroine," whereas Anne learns to dissimulate, to swerve, and to survive, thus gradually distancing herself from her role as "romantic heroine." Anne deviates from the traditional script and thereby frees herself to say her own lines, on her own stage, the island, to which she decides to return.[28]

By refusing to conform to her assigned role as dutiful daughter of a stifling tradition, Anne assumes her position as multicultural and multiracial subject of "Francophone" discourse. She makes a political choice that empowers her to remember and to speak the past, to write and break the code of silence that had been her mother's legacy. Humbert's text simultaneously repeats and revises the canon, manifesting its difference—its *Creole* difference—in her own specific use of language: her power to name "Anne/Nadège" thus seems inseparable from her ability to insert the speech of her island into the very fabric of the French language.

Notes

I thank Ronnie Scharfman and Celeste Schenck for encouraging this project. I am also indebted to Michal Peled Ginsburg, Keala Jewell, John McCumber, and

Sylvie Romanowski for their incisive comments on an earlier version of this essay. Parts of the essay were read at the Third Colloquium on Twentieth-Century Literature in French, 6–8 March 1986, at Louisiana State University.

1. I borrow the phrase from the book by Nawal El Saadawi, *The Hidden Face of Eve: Women in the Arab World* (London: Zed Press, 1980).

2. Roy Pascal, *Design and Truth in Autobiography* (London: Routledge & Kegan Paul, 1960), 75. But see also Elizabeth W. Bruss, *Autobiographical Acts: The Changing Situation of a Literary Genre* (Baltimore: Johns Hopkins University Press, 1976); James Olney, *Metaphors of Self: The Meaning of Autobiography* (Princeton: Princeton University Press, 1972); Philippe Lejeune, *Le Pacte autobiographique* (Paris: Seuil, 1975); and Lejeune, *Je est un autre* (Paris: Seuil, 1980).

3. Avrom Fleishman, *Figures of Autobiography: The Language of Self-Writing in Victorian and Modern England* (Berkeley and Los Angeles: University of California Press, 1983), 37.

4. Nancy K. Miller, "Writing Fictions: Women's Autobiography in France," in *Life/Lines: Theorizing Women's Autobiography*, ed. by Bella Brodzki and Celeste Schenck (Ithaca, N.Y.: Cornell University Press, 1988), 45–61.

5. And its anxieties, as brilliantly analyzed by Sandra M. Gilbert and Susan Gubar in *The Madwoman in the Attic: The Woman Writer and the Nineteenth-Century Literary Imagination* (New Haven, Conn.: Yale University Press, 1979), 45–92.

6. "Au docteur qui m'a aidée à naître," in Marie Cardinal, *Les Mots pour le dire* (Paris: Grasset et Fasquelle, 1975). English translation by Pat Goodheart, *The Words to Say It* (Cambridge, Mass.: VanVactor and Goodheart, 1983), is cited hereafter in the text. Occasionally, I will modify the translation and indicate "tr.m." when I do so. When necessary, reference to the French edition will be given in the text or in the corresponding notes. Permission to cite from the French and English editions was granted by Editions Grasset, Paris, and VanVactor and Goodheart, Cambridge, Mass. I gratefully acknowledge this here.

7. *Les mots pour le dire*, 266 ("the story as told to some paper"). The phrase recalls Montaigne's "mémoire de papier" and his well-known need to "parler au papier." See Michel de Montaigne, *Essais*, 3:1, in *Oeuvres complètes* (Paris: Gallimard, Pléiade, 1962), 767.

8. I use this term in the sense of Jean-François Lyotard's "grand récits" in *La Condition postmoderne: Rapport sur le savoir* (Paris: Minuit, 1979). It is translated by Geoff Bennington and Brian Massumi as *The Postmodern Condition: A Report on Knowledge* (Minneapolis: University of Minnesota Press, 1984).

9. For a comprehensive approach to narratology, or general theory of narrative, see Seymour Chatman, *Story and Discourse: Narrative Structure in Fiction and Film* (Ithaca, N.Y.: Cornell University Press, 1978).

10. Wolfgang Iser, *The Act of Reading: A Theory of Esthetic Response* (Baltimore: Johns Hopkins University Press, 1978), 45.

11. Marie-Thérèse Humbert, *A l'autre bout de moi* (Paris: Stock, 1979), 28. Hereafter all references will appear in the text, as will references to any work cited more than once. All translations will be mine. Permission to quote the work of Humbert, granted by Editions Stock, Paris, is gratefully acknowledged here.

12. Rodolphe Gasché, "Self-Engendering as a Verbal Body," *MLN* 93 (May 1978): 677–94. This study of Antonin Artaud is relevant here for two reasons: madness, language, and writing are central to Cardinal's understanding of her access to the status of subject of discourse; furthermore, the plague, Freud, Marseilles (Artaud's birthplace), and Algiers would figure as the scenes of *dédoublement* for both writers: the plague being at once a *fléau* like Cardinal's hemorrhaging and psychoanalysis, as Freud once put it.

13. See in particular Bruno Bettelheim's Preface and Afterword to the English translation; Marilyn Yalom, *Maternity, Mortality, and the Literature of Madness* (University Park: Pennsylvania State University Press, 1985), chap. 5; Elaine A. Martin, "Mothers, Madness, and the Middle Class in *The Bell Jar* and *Les Mots pour le dire*," *French-American Review* 5 (Spring 1981): 24–47; and the following reviews: Diane McWhorter, "Recovering from Insanity," *New York Times Book Review*, 1 Jan. 1984, 15; and Fernande Schulmann, "Marie Cardinal: *Les Mots pour le dire*," *Esprit* 452 (Dec. 1975): 942–43.

14. Cf. Ross Chambers, *Story and Situation: Narrative Seduction and the Power of Fiction* (Minneapolis: University of Minnesota Press, 1984), 3–15. My own critical method in this paper owes much to Ross Chambers's seminar on narrative at the University of Michigan.

15. The rules are the *règles*, the female menstrual cycle, which "may provide a near-perfect metaphor for Cardinal's dialectic . . . of subversion and conformity," according to Carolyn A. Durham in her excellent study of another work by Cardinal: "Feminism and Formalism: Dialectical Structures in Marie Cardinal's *Une Vie pour deux*," *Tulsa Studies in Women's Literature* 4 (Spring 1985): 84.

16. See Barbara Johnson, "My Monster/My Self," *Diacritics* 12 (Summer 1982): 9. In this review of Mary Shelley's *Frankenstein*, Nancy Friday's *My Mother/My Self*, and Dorothy Dinnerstein's *Mermaid and the Minotaur*, Johnson suggests that these "three books deploy a *theory* of autobiography as monstrosity" (10).

17. See Lucien Dällenbach, *Le Récit spéculaire* (Paris: Seuil, 1977): Chambers, 18–49.

19. Peter Brooks, "Constructions psychanalytiques et narratives," *Poétique* 61 (Feb. 1985): 64.

19. See Marguerite Le Clézio, "Mother and Motherland: The Daughter's Quest for Origins," *Stanford French Review* 5 (Winter 1981): 381–89. This is a study of Marie Cardinal and Jeanne Hyvrard.

20. The last chapter of the book, which consists of this single line, "A few days later it was May 68," is inexplicably missing from the English version. I take this textual "mutilation" as an ironic and unfortunate instance of the kinds of distortion that reductionist theories—psychoanalytic or otherwise—can perform on historical context. The irony, of course, lies in the fact that the narrator of *Les Mots pour le dire* sees herself as narrowly escaping a similar amputation at the hands of her surgeon, but it is also clear that just as the narrator's mother tries to abort her, certain Western theoretical traditions would rather deny (abort?) the historical realities that subtend the experiences of marginal (women) writers. Thus Bruno Bettelheim in his Preface and Afterword does not once mention the word *Algeria* and effectively succeeds in silencing that geopolitical dimension of the text.

21. I develop this point in the last chapter of my *Autobiographical Voices:*

Race, Gender, Self-Portraiture (Ithaca, N.Y.: Cornell University Press, 1989).

22. I purposely use this image—as Myra Jehlen has in "Archimedes and the Paradox of Feminist Criticism," in *The Signs Reader: Women, Gender and Scholarship,* ed. Elizabeth Abel and Emily K. Abel (Chicago: University of Chicago Press, 1983), 69–95—in order to propose that exile and marginality are perhaps the necessary preconditions for "our seeing the old world from a genuinely new perspective" (94).

23. This phrase is traditionally translated as "through a glass, darkly." I prefer to follow R. S. Pine-Coffin's rendering of it: "like a confused reflection in a mirror." Saint Augustine, *Confessions,* trans. R. S. Pine-Coffin (New York: Penguin Books, 1961), 289.

24. To use Gérard Genette's term. See his *Introduction à l'architexte* (Paris: Seuil, 1979).

25. Roland Barthes, *L'Empire des signes,* Les Sentiers de la création (Geneva: Skira, 1970), 104, my translation.

26. I am paraphrasing Peter Brooks's discussion (65) of transference in Balzac's *Le Colonel Chabert.*

27. On situational self-reflexivity and "narrational embedding," see Chambers, 18–49, 33.

28. This decision to return after having first left for Paris is set in implicit contrast to the move planned by her Uncle André, who decides to emigrate to South Africa with his family, thus getting an official seal of approval that he safely "passes" for one of pure European descent, since there is indeed "no whiter white than the South African white man" (see 449).

Exploding the Issue: "French" "Women" "Writers" and "The Canon"?

Fourteen Interviews

"How can one possibly write an article on the literary canon at the end of the twentieth century?" was our initial response to the invitation to participate in this volume. The question of literary history did not at first seem to be the most compelling one to us, in light of the postmodern sensitivity to the need to reconceptualize History. We are, of course, committed to revising the canon. Nevertheless, the epistemological assumptions upon which such an endeavor is based need to be questioned, for they are inevitably implicated in the phallocentric thought and binary logic that organized the canon in the first place. For example, it did not seem to us that *being placed in French literature,* that is, in a by definition overwhelmingly Western, white, Christian, male canon, is what those writers who have been excluded from it are struggling for *today.*

Nonetheless, it is now clear that the very work that has most convincingly elaborated postmodern, poststructuralist theory—and helped create new contexts for marginalized writers—could itself rapidly disappear if the power of institutions (and their ideologies) to (de)legitimize certain kinds of knowledge is not taken seriously. It therefore seemed important to us, particularly at that moment in time, to find a way to map some of the fields of force operating between the new topologies of knowledge and their continued dependence upon archaic structures of power. To do this, we decided to turn away from History with its third-person pronouns, past tenses, and "fixing" of narratives—and to turn toward Discourse itself with it implications of the "I" and "you," its emphasis on the "now," and its insistence on process. Despite the complicated status of interviewing (looking to the author as an authority on texts), we decided to assume the contradictions and ask questions of some of those intimately involved with these issues. In the context of this project: women writers and the literary tradition in France today.

It soon became clear, as we were deciding whom to interview for this project, that we would be forced to reproduce for ourselves the process of canon formation itself. We knew that we were beginning with and would be limited by our own knowledge, subjective preference, ideology, complicated personal and professional relationships, and a resistance to pluralism as well as to party lines. We decided that, rather than attempt to cover the field of all women writing in French today, we would focus most particularly on those women writing in Paris whose work has been perceived in the United States as "French Feminism," and we would examine the political and intellectual effects of such a representation. This group of women is comprised of both fiction and theory writers who have already had a marked impact on feminist literary theory in the United States either directly or indirectly, and whose work is located within the fields of force mentioned above.

We then proceeded to formulate six questions (five identical and one specially designed) for each writer. This is where the process became more complicated. For we wanted to make apparent in the formulation of the questions themselves our own problems with the entire problematic. We wanted to remain "in between"; to show that we were "representing" — albeit in no simple way — a desire not entirely ours. This required complex rhetorical moves on our part — moves that very often led to long pre- and post-interview explanations of our doubletalk. What was finally most interesting about this process was its chiasmatic effects.

We felt that these were American questions, translations of an American academic desire, projections having to do with a canon that is ultimately perhaps not as French as it is American (French literature in the United States). Our combined desire was to problematize this American desire. The responses of the women in France forced us, however, to acknowledge our strong (if reluctant) complicity with this American desire. We were surprised. It was hard for us to understand how so many could profess indifference to inclusion of their own work in the canon. Most of these writers, after all, are far from being widely taught in French universities.

And inclusion was not the only problem: for many of these women the word *canon* does not refer to the literary tradition, and few of them see it as an area of feminist concern.

However, the above-mentioned complicity was most certainly not one-sided. If there was a combined desire on the part of these women in France, it was to expose the "American," even "irrelevant," nature of our questions. Yet it seems to us that the strong, when not passionate, tones of these women's responses betray a reluctant acknowledgement of their oppression as women by the literary establishment and an often covert recognition that they are not, after all, indifferent to the effects of these highly theoretical matters on the destiny of their own work, especially in the United States.

The following short texts were excerpted in most cases from much longer interviews, yet the wide range of concerns still comes through. Many of those concerns were the direct result of reactions to our questions. First of all, several writers we invited to respond to our questions simply refused (including Nathalie Sarraute and Marguerite Yourcenar). Those who did respond were often interested not in answering the questions but in questioning them and then relating them to other issues that seemed more urgent to them. Is the question of the "canon" not hopelessly passé in our high-tech, media culture? What can be the meaning of a national ("French") canon in an increasingly transnational world? Why bring up "writing" (as fiction, as *écriture*) in the context of its enemies (criticism, the institution)? And, for many, there was the question of why we wanted to concentrate on the metaphysical category of "women" when the crucial field of force is occupied by the construction of sexual difference through notions of the feminine and the masculine.

If there was one theme shared by the interviewees, it was a resistance, when not violence, vis-à-vis university discourse and its tendency to ring the death knell for creative thinking and writing. Many of the writers maintain that women in the university today run the real danger of becoming more male than men—and all agree that the French university system is hopeless on both scores. Beyond that there is little "sameness" in these interviews.

By U.S. feminist standards, the attitudes expressed toward women range wildly: from (rather foreign) implications that there have been so few women in both the fictional and theoretical canon up until now because "only good work survives" or because "women just don't make good theoreticians," to (more familiar) pessimism with regard to how much things have really changed, amid warnings that women must remain vigilant.

The most remarkable aspect of these collected responses (and the aspect we ultimately felt most drawn to) is their strong resistance to the notion of the "canon" itself. For even when the writers did admit that such a thing exists, they wondered why anyone would want to be *in* it. One of the most often repeated points was that there is no *one* canon—especially in the twentieth century.

Perhaps the canon is, in fact, a myth (in the strong Barthesian sense of that word). To construct an image of one canon is to deny process—canons change continually. To construct an image of *one canon* is inevitably to become involved with the law—and the sacred. Do we want to do away with the canon or bring women into it? Either way, to fight the battle in these terms is to accept the sacred and its relationship to the law. The implication of this insight is that the primarily Anglo-American war with the canon is an (undeclared) holy war, an ecclesiastical battle. It does seem to us that these unavoidable associations for the French of the "canon" with the Church, the sacred, and the law have become naturalized in English. In speaking with these women in France, it was finally that naturalization itself which became strange, rendering our questions foreign, even to us.

We are extremely grateful to the women writers who agreed to allow us to "canon"-ize—in the musical sense of compose—their voices here.

The interviews, conducted between 8 May 1986 and 6 November 1987, eventually took on every conceivable permutation of oral/ written forms. The majority of the interviews took place in person in French. However, Claudine Herrmann, Luce Irigaray, and Michèle Montrelay wrote their texts. Jeanne Hyvrard read from a prepared text and also answered extemporaneously. Hélène Cixous, Fran- çoise Collin, and Sarah Kofman used the oral excerpts as the basis for a written text, while Monique Wittig's interview took place in English over the telephone. Excerpts from the interviews were chosen for maximum montage effect. Every writer was given the opportun- ity to review both the excerpts selected and the translations. In the end, few of the writers were satisfied with the process of limiting their comments to excerpts, which they felt decontextualized their remarks. They agreed, nonetheless, to let us publish these excerpts, given that we are coediting a collection of the interviews in their entirety entitled Shifting Scenes: Interviews on Women, Writing and Politics in Post-68 France, *for Columbia University Press.*

Interview Questions

QUESTION #1: What does it mean to you to write at the end of the twentieth century?

QUESTION #2: Is it valid/of value to write as a woman, and is it part of your writing practice today?

QUESTION #3: Many women writing today find themselves, for the first time in history, at the center of such institutions as the university and psychoanalysis. In your opinion, will this new placement of women help them to enter the twentieth-century canon, and if so, will they be in the very heart of this corpus or (still) in the footnotes?

QUESTION #4: Today we are seeing women produce literary, philosophical, and psychoanalytical theory of recognized importance, and, parallel to this, we are also seeing a new fluidity in the borderlines among disciplines and genres of writing. Will this parallelism lead only to women being welcomed alongside men, or to a definitive blurring of these categories?

QUESTION #5: Given the problematic and the politics of the categories of the canon, and given the questions we've been dealing with, do you think your oeuvre will be included in the twentieth-century canon, and if so, how will it be presented? In your opinion, what will the content of the canon be?

Chantal Chawaf[1]

QUESTION #1—It brings up the possibility and the necessity of seeking out new directions . . . of trying to verbalize areas . . . not yet inscribed in literature . . . which increase our consciousness as well as our knowledge of women, the feminine, life, and men. This would facilitate the communication and rapport between men and women. . . . One type of strategy . . . is indispensable if one wants to survive and continue to be free to create and explore: there is power and resistance in stepping aside enough to preserve an area . . . a terrain, a realm for writing the body. . . .

QUESTION #2—Obviously it is, it's like breathing. . . . It's a privilege to be a woman today . . . but a woman's identity is also a problem for her because of the experience she has of her body, of her female identity with respect to her mother, and because of her experience, actual or not, of motherhood—she doesn't have to be a mother or have children herself to experience motherhood. . . . A woman stays closer to the feminine because she identifies with her mother and therefore with the body, pregnancy, the whole world of the flesh, of affects . . . gestation, generation, of the prenatal, the preverbal, and the pregenital. . . . Ethically and metaphyiscally in women a whole current of thought opens up to life and a symbolization of the living. . . . Woman has the marvelous ability to open up a passage between language and this body which has been deprived of words . . . and limited to its organs . . . but which is in fact an immense and infinite thing.

QUESTION #3— . . . Just being a woman or of the female sex doesn't mean a woman's work will change things for women with respect to this particular cultural problem. Women who work in such institutions must have another perspective as well, one that is different from that of the institution. Unfortunately this is not the case for all the women in these systems. . . . Women do, however, need [to be in the institution], but being there requires awareness, a good deal of courage, and perhaps a combative, strategic spirit as well as diplomacy and subtlety. . . .

QUESTION #4—It seems to me that if everything went well it could change things. If it doesn't, if it puts women on one side and men on the other, then men and women haven't been communicating, then all the work on the feminine hasn't been assimilated. . . . When, however, men are interested in what a woman is working on, then something happens, and the men are transformed. . . . But there is a social barrier connected to barriers of power, self-interest, economics, and politics that needs to be shaken up; it's much harder to shake up those barriers than one individual man. . . .

QUESTION #5—For us—I'm speaking in the plural— . . . to be happy about appearing in the canons of the twentieth century . . . they would at the very least have to reflect what I have tried to do and change, and what has changed through what I have done. If it is the

kind of canon that completely co-opts your work and classifies you
as a continuation of the nineteenth century or as pastiche, then I'm
not interested in being a part of it. . . . The only chance I have of
being included is if the canon makers acknowledge both that my
work surpasses me as an individual, and that more than symbolic
work needs to be done. . . . It also depends on society and its evolution. . . . We women in addition need solidarity among ourselves; in
France at least this is far from always being the case. . . .

QUESTION #6: Do you think that it's possible to talk about the specificity of women's writing today?

—It's still too early. . . . There are not yet enough women who have
shown that they have something specific to accomplish artistically
and culturally through literature. . . . Instead of talking about specificity, I'd rather say that there are still domains into which literature
hasn't been introduced or which haven't yet been introduced into literature. It is precisely these domains that have been turned over to
hospitals, psychoanalysis, and psychiatry. They have been called
regressive, but are essentially the domains of the body, the feminine, and desire. They haven't been expressed yet and can't be, for
without . . . a language or a tongue, there is no way to symbolize
them. That remains for us to do, that is our job. . . . In the end,
though, this task goes beyond women's specificity because it can be
done by any artist or creative person, but of course as women we
have quite an experience of and closeness to the body and the
mother since regression is the return to the maternal. . . .

Hélène Cixous[2]

QUESTION #1—When I think in terms of the twentieth century, I
think in terms of the age of mass media, the age of the greatest possible threat to its opposites, by which I mean, in particular, writing
as a practice distanced from the media-imposed star system. Writing
at this point means more than what it did when I first started to
write. When I began I was pushed by a subjective total need, stem-
ming from my earliest childhood, to enter the land of writing.
There I came to the realization that writing was being threatened
from all sides by the events of the time, the violence of the age, a violence which in fact goes by the name of mass media. I understood
that writing was not only a matter of writing as meditation on the

human passions, that it was also a necessary, immediate gesture of defense of writing itself and of what it represents, which is to say a certain kind of thinking which refuses simplifications, which wants absolutely to take into account all the contradictions that make up living itself.

QUESTION #2—When I began to write I didn't ask myself any questions. The questions came to find me. I couldn't not respond, because I would have felt that I was betraying a people to which I belong. I belong to the people of women. And I belong as well to other peoples: the Jewish people, the Algerian people. I cannot not respond if one of my peoples is put in question. In short, there is a part of me that answers to the name *woman.*

QUESTION #3—This question seemed "American" to me. But all in all, I don't think that I really know the French university system. I have the feeling that women in French universities have little interest in women's problems. The majority of French university women are aligned with men. I don't think it is the women in universities who will contribute to making sure there is more room for women.

QUESTION #4—I don't believe that the borders between literary, philosophical, and psychoanalytical categories are going to suddenly disappear. On the other hand, it is obvious that neither is there any pure literature, pure philosophy, pure psychoanalysis. What interests me is the passage into literature of a portion of philosophy, the passage into philosophy of a portion of psychoanalysis, etcetera. The fact remains though that one will always be dominant.

QUESTION #5—I have nothing to say to this question. Here again is this story of the "canon" which is really an American notion. But perhaps it is your use of the singular that troubles me. In my opinion what there is in France is not "the" canon, but categorizations which are ideological and vary from one theory to another. One always attempts to code. But there is an infinite variety of codes.

QUESTION #6: From Hélène Cixous, theoretician and practitioner of *l'écriture féminine,* to Hélène Cixous, historical dramatist à la Shakespeare: this trajectory has provoked strongly opposed reactions.[3] Some see this displacing of the feminine in favor of giving man back his place at the center of the story/history as a splendid success; others are worried that in the process of this return to History the "repressed feminine," barely glimpsed these last few years, already seems to be disappearing. How have you experienced this trajectory?

—I've followed a certain path, and along the way my orientation hasn't changed. There was a period in my work, one which to my mind is inevitable for anyone who writes, of work on the ego. One must go through the ego to get to the other and to others. For one to personally become the world stage, one must be capable of ego effacement.

What matters to me is what is fragile. This is what seems to me to be the vocation of writing: to safeguard what is simultaneously necessary, rare, alive, and precarious. For me women are this precarious people, at once totally present and totally absent, one that can be forgotten at any moment, or remembered at any moment. With that I took a step further, that is, toward others, not only toward women, but not to the exclusion of women, toward others who are similarly threatened, and in this case, it was Cambodia that had all these characteristics: a people at once cultured, sensitive, and threatened with disappearance. I didn't sacrifice women, I tried to concern myself with an absolutely adorable people in danger of death at this moment, a people of great tenderness, the bearers of a strong femininity. I couldn't have worked on a virile people.

Françoise Collin[4]

QUESTION #1—First of all, it is writing in my own time, the only one given to me. . . . And it is true that today writing doubtless no longer commands center stage as it once did, that it can even seem archaic in a culture dominated by images and telematics. But the relationship to the archaic interests me: it seems to me to protect something essential. The archaic in that sense does not belong to the past. . . . Writing, in the twentieth century, makes it impossible for language (for words) to die.

QUESTION #2—Everything depends on what sort of writing you are talking about. If I am writing within a feminist framework, then yes, I situate myself as a woman among other women—which does not mean that I write in a style that is necessarily "feminine."

When I write fictional writing, I have no other place to stand in but the one imposed by what I am writing. Writing, then, consists of distancing everything that could stand as a screen, everything that could be normative in any way. The law I obey is an inexpressible, internal law. That my woman-being reappears is possible and even likely, but it is a being over which I have no say, that I do not predefine.

It seems to me that my fiction writing always sort of controls my theoretical and feminist texts, makes it impossible for them to become fixed as ideology or even as theory, and behaves with a sort of irony which makes "lying" impossible as well.

QUESTION #3—Creativity for me has nothing to do with the institution; creativity liberates one from the institution. However, the reception of texts, their critical understanding, their distribution, and therefore, as a boomerang effect, their confirmation, does happen thanks to editorial, newspaper, university, and media-related institutions. The presence of women in these institutions does mean that texts by women will have a greater chance of finding their legitimation. But, then again, the institutionalization of the feminine or of feminism very quickly creates a new norm.

QUESTION #4—The beginnings of feminism did in fact foster transdisciplinary thought where borders between categories were subverted. But it does not seem to me that what is happening today in feminist studies is faithful to that first movement. By inscribing itself in a university (and publishing) environment, feminist research has rediscovered those divisions—even if the borders are still somewhat porous. Current feminist work seems to be located within existing categories: feminist (literary) criticism, the renewal of history, sociological development, the revision of philosophy, etcetera. . . . Theory, moreover, has completely cut itself off from action, and more generally from the political even though the coupling of theory and practice had been one of the fundamental ambitions of its beginnings.

QUESTION #5—Is there a "canon" of the twentieth century? The notion of a canon is always retrospective: it enables literary historians to construct frameworks for reading after the fact. But these frameworks are modified from one era to another: the shape of the past changes with time.

I think that works that matter do not conform to any canon—or that they set up their own canon.

I never ask myself anything about the canon. I don't know if I belong to my time or not. By writing, I accomplish a task which is mine, a task whose origins are obscure, and I endeavor to remain faithful to them. As I write, of course I hope to be read, but I don't write what might be read, I don't write from the perspective of a probable reading. I would rather elicit the birth of new, male and female, readers. Of that, there is no guarantee.

QUESTION #6: You are a philosopher in a university, but also director of the independent, interdisciplinary journal *Cahiers du GRIF.* Could this double activity be the strategy that feminists have searched so hard for—to avoid the double pitfalls of recuperation and marginality?

—This question really made me laugh. Because my thought has some rigor, people immediately suppose that I belong to a university institution, as if the university were the guarantor of thought. In fact, I was excluded from teaching in the university, and while I owe a great deal to my philosophical training, the best work I have done I owe to my relative marginality—which, moreover, has cost me a lot. Having said this, belonging to an institution affords an enviable security, a social legitimacy, and the support of an environment that I do not underestimate. But does it not also sterilize the imaginary? It is difficult to be both on the inside and on the outside. That is the whole problem confronting young feminists who simultaneously denounce the institution and do everything they possibly can to belong to it. It is understandable that for previously excluded individuals—and this is the case of all minorities—entrance into the institution amounts to winning a certain sort of victory. But true victory is beyond that.

Marguerite Duras[5]

QUESTION #1—Writing. I've never asked myself what era I was living in. I've asked myself this question in relation to my child and his activity later on, or when wondering what would become of the working class, that is, in relation to political issues or political circumstances. But not in relation to writing. I think that writing is beyond everything.

QUESTION #2— . . . I'm still writing now. . . . I don't have any major problems anymore in terms of the reception of my books. The way men in society respond to me hasn't changed . . . misogyny still comes first. . . . But I know about safety valves, about how things are supposed to work. That is, from time to time I write theoretical articles, on criticism, and that frightens contemporary critics . . . and women too. It has to do with feminine writing [*écriture féminine*]. There are many women who side with men. . . .

QUESTION #3—I think that those women who can get beyond this feeling . . . of having to correct history . . . would save a lot of time. . . . All the women who are correcting history, who are trying to correct the injustice of which they have been victims, of which they still are victims—because nothing has changed, we have to remember that in men's heads it's all still the same— . . . these women who are attempting to correct man's nature, and that which has become his nature, call it whatever you like, are wasting their time. . . . I think that if a woman is free, alone, she can go ahead like that without barriers, that is how she will create fruitful work. . . . I don't care about men. I've given up on them. It's not a question of age, it's a question of intellectuality, of one's mental attitude. I've totally given up on trying to put men on a logical track, totally. . . . For women, the worst is behind them: they've already taken the biggest step. They've crossed over to the other side. All the successful books today are by women, the important films are women's films. The difference is fabulous. . . . One book, like *The Lover*, for example— which was a slap in the face for everyone, for men—is a giant leap forward for women, which is much more important. For a woman to command international attention is enough to make men sick. It just makes them sick. . . .

QUESTION #4—I don't know, it's dangerous. Because their criteria have been tested for a long time and they manipulate them with great skill and diplomacy. Men are not politicians, they're diplomats. That's even lower.

QUESTION #5—I don't know what it will be, and I don't know how it will be, or who will decide. The only thing that reassures me is the fact that I've become a bit of an international phenomenon now, and even a pretty big one. And what France won't do, other countries will. So I'm safe. But I have to speak in those terms. I am not safe in France. There my position is still shaky. . . . I got involved in men's business. First, I was involved in politics. I was in the Communist Party. I did things which are considered to be in bad taste for a woman. . . . The thing about my literary work is that I've never mixed political theory with literature. It never turns into rhetoric. Never. Even things like *The Sea Wall* remain a story. That is what saved me. . . .

QUESTION #6: We are asking you these questions about the future destiny of the work of contemporary women, when in fact your work seems to have been canonized already. Actually, you are one of the few people who not only have seen their work come out of an unfair obscurity into the limelight, but who have also seen it attain worldwide recognition. How has becoming a celebrity influenced a vision that was intentionally critical and other?

—You know, *The Lover* came late in my life. . . . I was accustomed to events like that which operate completely independently from you. It comes on you like lightning and takes place in inaccessible regions. You can't know why a book works when it works that well. . . . A tiny little book that's a worldwide hit—that's strange. So I was not at all a young girl in the face of those events. As for the end of your question—"a vision that was intentionally critical and other"— that has nothing to do with it. I understand the implication of your question that being famous somehow inhibits, intimidates. No, no, on the contrary. . . . That reminds me of something Robbe-Grillet told me one day: "When you and I are in the 500,000 copies range, that will mean we have nothing else to say." So I have nothing else to say, and he still has another book.

Claudine Herrmann[6]

QUESTION #1—Writing seems to me to be dangerous in a world where the very future of humanity is in jeopardy. I wonder sometimes if our descendants will know how to read and if books won't be a passing stage of the general evolution of things.

Writing should, in good logic, be what our editors think it is: addressing the present, at least, or, perhaps, the coming year. Still, things don't exactly happen that way for me. When I write, it seems to me (although I am willing to admit readily that this point of view is irrational), that I meet up with what escapes from time, with what is external to the entropy that surrounds me and possesses me. It is surely not that I imagine myself addressing posterity or that I am basking in excessive illusions about the durability of what I write, but the very act of writing displaces me inside and gives me the impression of communicating with what is invisible and what cannot be destroyed. In that respect I am probably much like other writers who came before me, the only difference being perhaps that I am not trying to place that feeling back into a system. Naturally, time is recaptured when the book appears and you have to deal face to face with what is now called "promotion." But that, too, is the twentieth century. . . .

QUESTION #2—Although the books that have shaped my thought were mostly books written by men, I know that today if there is anything in me that is personal and that is worth expressing, it is necessarily related to my experience and my woman's language [*langage de femme*], simply because I have no other. Even what is imaginary is transmitted through my own circuits and becomes feminized along the way. I became conscious of that with speech well before writing: in the speeches I gave as a young lawyer, I tried so hard to imitate the forms of discourse that were then in fashion. As I tried, however, to express in my own language what I really thought, the result would surprise me. That is what happens when I attempt to borrow a male concept: it becomes other. Sometimes I do an exercise that consists in narrating an essentially virile scene, a naval battle, for example. . . . You would be surprised to see how it turns out. . . .

QUESTION #3—I am wondering about the word *institution*. Just yesterday we still spoke of learning institutions, of legal institutions—so that I wonder to what institutions women belong today. . . . Are we talking about "society," as in an academic institution, or the official forces of labor, or have these two meanings become synonymous? Nearly all women who have written in the past held a position of importance in the society of their times. Today this position often takes the shape of a paid position, but I think that what is essential for a writer (but, when speaking about "works," is that about literary or scholarly works?) is to be in touch with the world, and for some women writers, who are not any less writers, that contact can be rather tenuous. I am thinking of Emily Dickinson.

QUESTION #4—I think personally that the production of *women*, to the extent that women will not be satisfied following in tow (or being in waiting), will be inscribed alongside men's productions, except in the exact sciences, if there are any left. . . .

QUESTION #5—I have absolutely no idea where my work, which I hope only to be able to complete, will stand. I wonder unsuccessfully about whether it will ever appear in a canon. That word for me has nasty connotations and I don't particularly care to be catapulted into the world of the official. I do nonetheless like having women and men readers and I do recognize that the usefulness of the canon lies in how it multiplies reading possibilities. I hope I am insulting no one by saying that this canon is a necessary evil. . . . Besides that, the future raises this question for me: there will certainly be more and more books and less and less time to teach them, because of the growth of other areas of knowledge, so, where do we cut back? I have no idea. Nevertheless, I hope that in this mythical canon, there will be proportionately more women than there are today.

QUESTION #6: In the United States, if there is a lively literary criticism, it is feminist criticism. Here in France, on the other hand, your book *The Tongue Snatchers* figures among the rare, serious contributions in this domain. Why has the meeting of literature and feminist theory inspired so few French women?

—Entrance into the French university system takes such a toll on everyone that it becomes difficult to attack it once one has entered its fortress: it has shaped your mind, submitted (or seduced) your intelligence and if you were not ready to be smitten, you would not have spent the best years of your life taking exhausting and competitive entrance exams. Today you can be critical of the impressive corpus of French literature only in accepted forms. Now, feminist criticism, as I see it, is radical and functions without courtesy like a lever. . . . What is more, to show yourself as culturally feminist offers the—justified—fear of displeasing those who will have to vote on your advancement. The French university is tied to its tradition and I can guarantee that it has no feminist tradition. . . . As for imagining that someone on the outside could launch into such a critical adventure, don't even think about it, for in France there is a solidly entrenched idea according to which, outside the university, there is no true knowledge. This reminds me, strangely, of the saying "Out of the Church, far from salvation" [*Hors de l'église, point de salut*]. It is, by the way, the Sorbonne that, a very long time ago, used to point out the dubious points of the faith. Today, it has got its hands on knowledge, for the better perhaps, but also for the worse. . . .

Jeanne Hyvrard[7]

QUESTION #1—I write in order to stay in touch with the sacred and culture. To overcome the antagonism of memory and of forgetfulness, of eternity and of time, of fusion and of separation. To attest to my belonging to a Western civilization that in this century, nevertheless, crushes me. To transmit the forms and the values of the European heritage I received. To accompany the revolution in cybernetics, in procreatics, and in geonomics (the overall management of the earth's resources). To forge the new tools that enable me to think the revolution and join it. In short, to survive. . . .

QUESTION #2— . . . As far as I'm concerned, for ten years I didn't write "as a woman" although my texts helped me to break with the imposed models. The pressures and discriminations that I have been subjected to as a woman writer have caused me to think about the imprisonment of French women in the literary arena, a cultivated version of knitting. . . . Having recognized this, I had to choose between being satisfied with the conceded territory ("write and keep quiet") and accepting the challenge of building on feminine networks to break through the dam. I tried to do that with *Canal de la Toussaint* by setting up philosophical tools to think through logarchy (a power system resting on the predominance of the logos) whose vehicles are Western males. It is indeed as a woman that I wrote *Canal de la Toussaint,* but the logarchy that is crossed is not uniquely masculine, just as the forged tools are not reserved for women. . . .

QUESTION #3— . . . Everyone knows that it isn't enough for a woman to be prime minister for politics to diverge from that of her masculine homolog. . . . What seems to be more worrisome is the integration of women into the masculine hierarchies based on the fiction that "women are men like all others." The cybernetics revolution can purely and simply make the notion of literary body and canon disappear. As for the bionomics (the management of "human capital": perception and economy of human beings leading to considering humans as stock parts that can be changed or thrown out according to profitability forecasts) in the process of taking shape, it could well render feminism itself obsolete. . . .

QUESTION #4— . . . One might think that the dam erected against women will erode in proportion to the accumulation of a body of writings that are not only feminine and feminist, but that grow out of woman-thought (sets of mental tools enabling thought about issues specific to women)—the sheer quantity would then make censorship impossible. This could lead at once to the establishment of women alongside men and to the disappearance of these categories. Woman-thought is not only destined for use by women but can also be used by men. . . .

QUESTION #5— . . . How can I know what will be said of me? That many of my contemporaries have already managed to present me as a typically West-Indian writer offers humorists all sorts of hope. But what kind of criticism will dare utter: "She was a housewife who dreamt of cooking up a chocolate Bavarian cream for her big family, but who was cornered, given the events that historically intervened in her life, into taking recourse in writing to emancipate herself and to rethink the world that was condemning her to death?"

QUESTION #6: "Although I was born and raised within the boundaries of France, and am white like all my ancestors, in everything from linguistics dissertations to the *Bordas Encyclopedia*, I am presented as a writer 'typically representative of West-Indian literature.'"[8] Instead of refusing this false impression, you retorted: "There is in my texts no exploded identity, but the anticipation of a new planetary identity." Does that transnational identity render the idea of a canon obsolete since one of the canon's major functions is to preserve a national culture through its language?

— . . . I am not really convinced that there exists a nation other than fantasmagorically. . . . History is constantly being rewritten by the victors and has a lot in common (this is not meant negatively) with mythology. We can wonder, then, whether the national culture's canon isn't itself a fantasy. . . . National cultures will not necessarily be rendered obsolete by the third culture (a transnational culture overarching Western and other cultures) that is being born. But their places, their meanings, their roles, and their value will be determined by the outcome of the struggle. . . . But we can also imagine that in an integrated world economy, the national fantasy will no longer be necessary and will relinquish its place to other ideologies born of communications and bionomics. We could begin to witness the emergence, for example, of the canon of a fusionary culture (dominating and dominated in the logarchy), that legitimates new values. . . .

Luce Irigaray[9]

QUESTION #2—I am a woman. I write with who I am. Why would that not be valid/of value, unless there were contempt for the value of women, or refusal of a culture in which the sexual/gendered[10] represented a dimension of subjectivity? But how could I be a woman on the one hand and write, on the other? This scission or split between the one who is a woman and the one who writes can only exist for those who confine themselves to verbal reflexes, taking on the protective coloring of already constituted meaning. My whole body is sexed/gendered. My sexuality is not limited to my sexual organs and to a few sexual acts. I think that the effects of repression and above all of the lack of a sexual culture—civil and religious—are still so powerful that it is possible to make statements as strange as these: "I am a woman" and "I don't write as a woman." These declarations also conceal an allegiance to the cultures of men-amongst-themselves. Indeed, alphabetical writing is historically linked to the civil and religious codification of patriarchal powers. Not to contribute toward giving a sex/gender to language and to its written forms is to perpetuate the pseudoneutrality of the laws of traditions which privilege masculine genealogies and their codes of logic.

QUESTION #4—The fluidity between disciplines and between different types of writing is not very great at the present time. The fact that branches of knowledge and new technologies are increasing in number means that the compartmentalization of knowledge is more watertight than it used to be in the past. In previous centuries, philosophers and scientists used to engage in dialogue. Nowadays, they are more often strangers to each other, because their languages have become mutually incommunicable.

Between certain disciplines such as philosophy, psychoanalysis, and literature, are there new possibilities for exchange to take place? This is a complex question. There are attempts to move from one field to another, but these attempts are not always sufficiently well informed to be pertinent. What we are witnessing is a modification in the use of language by certain philosophers who are turning back toward the origins of their culture. Thus Nietzsche and Heidegger, but also Hegel before them, interrogated their foundations in Ancient Greece and in religion; Levinas and Derrida are interrogating their relation to the texts of the Old Testament. Their gesture goes together with the use of a style which comes close to that of tragedy, poetry, the Platonic dialogues, the way in which myth, parables, and liturgies are expressed. This return looks back to the moment at which male identity constituted itself as patriarchal and phallocratic. Is it the fact that women have emerged from the privacy of the home, from silence, which has forced men to question themselves? All the philosophers I've mentioned—except Heidegger—are interested in feminine identity, and sometimes in their identity as feminine [*féminins*] or women. Does this lead to a confusion of categories? Which ones? In the name of what? Or whom? Why? I think that what you are calling categories refers to branches of knowledge, not the logical categories of discourse and truth. The installation of new logical forms and rules goes with the definition of a new subjective identity, new rules for determining meaning. That is a necessity too, in order for women to be able to situate themselves in cultural production, alongside and with men. Turning back toward the moment at which they seized sociocultural power(s), are men seeking a way to divest themselves of these powers? I hope so. Such a desire would imply that they are inviting women to share in the definition of truth and the exercising of it with them. Up to now, writing differently has not done much to affect the sex of political leaders or their civil and religious discourses.

Is it a question of patience? Is it our duty to be patient in the face of decisions which are made in our place and in our name? Certainly, I don't think that we have to resort to violence, but we do need to ask ourselves how to give an identity to scientific, religious, and political discourses, and how to situate ourselves in these discourses as subjects in our own right. Literature is all well and good. But how can we persuade the world of men to rule their peoples poetically, when they are interested above all in money, in competing for power, etcetera? And how can we as women run the world if we have not defined our identity, the rules of our genealogical relationships, our social, cultural, and linguistic order? For this task, psychoanalysis may be of great assistance to us, if we know how to use it in a way that is appropriate to our bodily and spiritual needs and desires. It can help us to free ourselves from our confinement in patriarchal culture, provided that we do not allow ourselves to be defined or seduced by the theories and problems of the world of masculine genealogy.

Sarah Kofman[11]

QUESTION #1—In your question what is most important for me is not the fact that I am in the twentieth century, but that I write. I write when I am not just translating a certain oral content, when I am not just aiming to defend certain ideas. In my writing activity, my referents—and in this respect I can belong only to the twentieth century—are the great thinkers on writing: Blanchot and Derrida. My own psychoanalysis also played a big part, although I wrote my first book, *The Childhood of Art*, before entering analysis. But it enabled me to introduce into myself and into my work a certain play, a certain irony that is but one with writing. . . .

QUESTION #2—Obviously one starts with the fact that I am a woman, and that I write as a woman. In fact, I write as a philosopher first. But I have shown—and I am not immune to this law—in my book on August Comte that even in a philosophical text that is presumably rational and systematic, independent of all empirical and pathological subjectivity, and therefore of sexuality, one cannot separate the text from the sexual position of the author . . . but the author's position is not to be identified with his or her anatomical sex. In other words, for me, one isn't a man or a woman: those categories are anatomical and social, and can be traced back to the metaphysical tradition that starts with Aristotle. . . . When you say to me, "Do you write as a woman?" I cannot accept this metaphysical formulation. . . .

QUESTION #3— . . . What is important is to know whether there are women in the twentieth century who are doing theoretical work that is significant enough for them to be integrated as authors in a curriculum. . . . I don't think, on this point, that women are excluded as women. I am not speaking about literature here, but about philosophy. Now, the fact is that, in this area, few women have accomplished sufficiently important and original work to merit a place in any curriculum. That does not mean that I think that the difference here stems from anatomy; it comes instead from the received education that results, in general, in women being far more submissive to what they read, more repetitive than innovative, and also more mimetic of a master whom they need to stimulate their research. . . .

QUESTION #4—From a philosophical point of view, I think [this parallelism] is extremely important; originally, however, there was not necessarily any parallel between the two problems. We owe to Nietzsche this idea that philosophy and literature are not separable. . . . This blurring of the boundaries between philosophy and literature is part of the system of crossing out, of putting under erasure all the metaphysical opposites, including, among others, this opposition between the feminine and the masculine. . . . I don't think that "women's" productions can lead in themselves to the blurring of these categories. It is nevertheless important that both women and men be able to produce in areas that have thus far been reserved for either one sex or the other, and in this way to blur the boundaries. . . .

QUESTION #5—It is rather difficult for a writer, and a bit pretentious, to say "My work will be included." And what is a "work"? I'm in *Who's Who.* So there are traces, and my books are traces. In addition, the feminist movement was such that any woman's work cannot be effaced. And those who compile *Who's Who,* far from excluding women, because there are few famous women, tend to include all of them. They are presented as women but perhaps not with all of the nuances that I give that expression. . . .

QUESTION #6: **As a philosopher and a Derridian, how would you go about discussing the notion of the canon?**

—It is rather amusing to see first of all that, while you seem to be aiming at questioning categories and metaphysical opposites, with this last question you are reintroducing a simple category: philosophy. Secondly, too, while your questionnaire seemed to me to want to stress the originality of women's work, you classified me from the outset as a Derridian and therefore as subordinate to a male philosopher. . . . I still want to keep the title of philosopher, but in quotation marks, for I believe that the specificity of philosophy is conceptual, rigorous reflection and I do want to claim that. On the other hand, I am troubled by your qualifier, "Derridian," not that I want to cover up my very strong ties to Derrida—a true encounter—but when I'm asked to think about the notion of a canon, that excludes classifying it in a genre. If I think, I can only think on my own. If I think "as a Derridian," then I am precisely no longer thinking. . . .

Julia Kristeva[12]

QUESTION #1—It means trying to keep things as personal as possible by avoiding every kind of pressure, whether it's from groups, the media, public opinion, or ideology. . . . It means preserving a margin of surprise and not-yet-known . . . because, contrary to appearances, I think we're beginning to see a uniformization of mentalities, information, and education. . . .

QUESTION #2—For me it's a requirement. But I feel that requirement is dependent upon . . . the need to write in my own name. It seems to me that helps protect the writer from the risk involved in writing "as a woman," for that can end up being a uniform of sorts: writing like all women. . . .

QUESTION #3— . . . Obviously the fact that women are now in institutions is a tremendous gain . . . but their position still has to be consolidated and improved. . . . And that does not mean the battle has been won once that's been attained. I think it's important to stay constantly vigilant. That's my practice in any case. . . . It is important to insist upon the fact that nothing can be taken for granted and that no one's situation is comfortable. Women must understand that the battle will never be over. . . .

QUESTION #4— . . . What struck me in your question . . . is the issue of blurring sexual difference. In the future sexual difference could fade away. . . . That's a fairly troubling problem to which there are two solutions. First, let's say that this really is going to happen: the difference between the sexes will no longer exist in the twenty-first century. Instead there'll be a kind of perpetual androgyny . . . and we'll see the end of desire and sexual pleasure. For after all, if you even out difference, given that it's what's different that's desirable and provokes sexual pleasure, then you could see a sexual anesthesia of sorts. . . . When we get to the point of sexual homeostasis, won't we see some sort of symbolic anesthesia and therefore little creativity? Or instead—since the types of societies and psychic life we've known up until now have not tolerated this homeostasis— won't new differences be created? . . .

QUESTION #5— . . . It seems to me the question you're asking is really about education and the transmission of information. I see this transmission as a TV with fifty to a hundred stations, each of which is very different and transmits different information—although they cancel each other out—but which give one the feeling they're all part of the same ideology or, in any case, of something not easily discernible but which is precisely a form of possible resistance to anything surprising or anything that could undermine the norm, and so on. In any event, it's my impression that [in the future] there won't be any canon in the current sense of the word given the plurality of infor-mation which the media has already started to carry and which the schools and universities are working against. . . .

QUESTION #6: In the diversity of your work, one always finds epistem-ological problems that have been posed across time examined from today's perspective. This perspective is a knowingly critical one and, since it is also that of a psychoanalyst, it has no choice but to take sexual difference into account. How is it possible to work in that way without at least appearing to repeat on a theoretical level the historical gesture of organizing knowledge by relegating women sub-jects and their texts to the background?

—I don't happen to agree with the position that, to the extent that the gesture that organizes knowledge is based on effacing sexual dif-ference in the name of an absolute or neutral subject, women must refuse that gesture. . . . Women must take their place inside the cul-tural field by trying to discover objects of knowledge men haven't. In doing this, do women respond as women? No doubt they do, espe-cially when one considers that we are always constituted bisexually and that a woman who makes her own that historical gesture of orga-nizing knowledge is exhibiting her phallic component. Now I don't see why women shouldn't exhibit that component. However, once women do exhibit that component . . . they are also uncovering their specificity which is not a phallic specificity. . . .

Eugénie Lemoine-Luccioni[13]

QUESTION #1— . . . It means strictly nothing at all. Because I don't see myself writing in any other century. . . . I started in the middle of the century, in the forties; it is so much a permanent function for me to write—I even started earlier. I started[14] my life as writer by writing short stories, with the distinct feeling of writing women's stories, as a woman, even if the "reciter's" first name often was "Michel." . . . If certain changes intervened, it's not an effect of the turn of the century. It's the result of my encounters. . . . I met Jacques Lacan. After several years of training (for I was an absolute novice), I started writing works of so-called psychoanalytic theory. I never went back to the short stories, even if regrets themselves often find their way back. . . .

QUESTION #2— . . . My first work, *The Dividing of Women's Lot*, was a woman's book. . . . In my latest book, which was first entitled *Le Lien social*, but now is called *Psychanalyse de la vie quotidienne*, I lay out how I place myself, as a writer and analyst, and as a woman, at one of the transmission links of psychoanalysis. . . .[15] [Is it valid to write as a woman?]. . . . The stakes are extremely important, and that has to do with the role of women in Lacanian theory. For Lacan, woman would be a symptom of man, insofar as she marks the place where there is nothing more to say. It is of course the man who has nothing else to say about what he encounters there as empty, an emptiness figured, as you know, organically. . . . So of course this, this is a phallic perspective, a man's perspective. So should woman shut up about herself, as unconscious? Of course not, because as far as that goes there's no such thing as men *and* women. There is a phallic function for women too, and to that extent she speaks, she's not just a hole. . . . What is true is that it puts women in a divided position (that I went over, in detail, in *The Dividing of Women's Lot*), a division which doubles the already divided subject. . . .

QUESTION #3— . . . It's difficult to predict, isn't it, what will become of women, because I think they are so transformed, and men, too, that these are problematics which will be left behind. . . . But really, women have occupied, without any difficulty whatsoever, whatever space they wanted on the psychoanalytic terrain. . . .

QUESTION #4— . . . The borders are shifting, as they are between the sexes; that does not mean that a difference shouldn't be maintained, but maintained in motion, not fixed. I prefer speaking about differentiation rather than difference—there is a differentiating function, it might be a moveable one, it might choose its own terrain, *I* don't know. That does not mean that soon we're just going to move into another whole new monstrous social configuration compared to ours, but it is true that we can imagine many, many profound transformations. It could all go as far as the suppression of engendering. . .

QUESTION #5— . . . A canon, that's not predictable, it emerges after the fact, it's a state of things, otherwise what would it be? Besides, would I, personally, conform to a canon? Look, I don't confer . . . a sure value on what I do at the level of theoretical invention. . . . I don't think women are gifted for theoretical invention. For instance I don't think it's accidental that Freud is a man, that Lacan is a man, that Einstein is a man, and I don't think, as many women do, that at the end of several centuries of feminist revolution, women will be capable of it. This is not modesty because I think they are capable of other things, and that what we write, men don't write. . . .

QUESTION #6: As a psychoanalyst and disciple of Lacan, how do you interpret our project on the canon?

— . . . I'm not interpreting at all; it's not a question of interpretation. You are trying, I think, to define something. I told you earlier how wary I am of definitions personally, but I don't interpret your desire to classify and define, nor even to predict. . . . This concern for having a place reveals [a] worry. It's probably a totally legitimate one. I would worry even more if I were a man about the place I would have in the twenty-first century. But about man as human being, you know . . . should humanity commit suicide, I wouldn't find it strange, provided I had the time to think.

Marcelle Marini [16]

QUESTION #1— . . . My writing is that of a critic. . . . It is not always or not often academic . . . and it does not respect university canons. This type of writing belongs to a genre called the essay. . . . Since it cannot be defined formally, it is, in my opinion, an important form for women to explore and inhabit . . . for it is one . . . that maintains its marginality in the face of any system that attempts to totalize. . . .

QUESTION #2— . . . I think that this aspect varies considerably at the time one is writing, when one is really inside writing. Fortunately one cannot always be mindful of what sex one belongs to. I believe it is very very important for women to come to the point where their specificity fades into the background and where they use their experience and what they have to say to communicate to everyone and not to play the role of a woman. . . .

QUESTION #3— . . . Women will only make their way into the twentieth-century canons if . . . they participate in the elaboration of these canons. Two things could hinder us. Either women will be marginalized . . . or else . . . their work will become part of some man's discourse. His text will be remembered instead of hers, and in it her ideas will be presented as his. . . . Men have taken everything they have to say about their feminine side from women. There's no reason to criticize them for this, for it's only natural that they should receive things from women. The problem is, men use what they've taken as their own . . . and are nourished by it, but they never acknowledge their indebtedness to women. . . . In times of crisis of the imaginary, or of theories or certitudes—because there is a crisis of certitudes and models now—women always have a chance. It's clear we're in one of those periods, but there have been many cases in History, especially in the field of literature . . . of phenomenally successful women who were unknown thirty years later. There is no guarantee . . . —women today could get caught in History's trap and be left behind when the tradition is established. . . . The only guarantee I know of is to be sure there are successive generations of women. . . .

QUESTION #4— . . . Predictions are difficult to make, it seems. One hopes, I believe one should hope—at least that's my personal position—for a blurring of these boundaries, I would even say a blurring of enunciations, so that identity and the way sexual identity is represented are transformed as well. . . .

QUESTION #5—I'm pessimistic about that. . . . I can only speak for my own narrow field of literary criticism. As far as I'm concerned, it does not even exist. It's not really a scientific field; it's a field of research, reflection, and writing, a crossroads of many other kinds of discourses. . . . My field is not a discipline in the scientific sense of the word, or in the way Foucault understood this term as having procedures that could be repeated. . . . I think that literary criticism has been tossing around a whole slew of discourses for the last twenty years and that it now must use them in a more conscious way. It has to . . . refuse to be a separate discipline and instead be a site of tension, meeting and confrontation. . . .

QUESTION #6: You are already trying to change things from inside the university by teaching women's writing from a feminist perspective. You're in a good position then to tell us about how the institution is reacting to this kind of action.

— . . . When I decided to write a book about Marguerite Duras, I wanted to write it without any kind of institutional constraint. So I had to make a choice: that is, I didn't write a dissertation, I wrote a book and had it published by a publishing firm. In other words, I went on my own to another institution instead of the one I was in. That wasn't a very smart thing to do strategically or tactically, since it meant I didn't get my Ph.D., but it was essential for me to do it.

That brings up a very important point—the price one pays. The only way to make progress is to be willing to pay the necessary price. . . . As for the university's reaction, it has varied because the university has changed. The fact that a lot of students from other universities and abroad come to my seminar has supported my efforts; the university stands to gain from their contributions. . . . That does not mean there isn't constant irony and more or less discrete questioning of "that feminist seminar" or things like it. . . . What I do is tolerated by the university, but is there any acknowledgement that my work is valuable and pertinent intellectually or culturally? It's considered work, but perhaps work done for nothing. . . .

Michèle Montrelay [17]

QUESTION #1—That means: 1) searching, and making a contribution through my work, so that the part of the human being known since the nineteenth century as the "unconscious" can be understood more and more rigorously, with its "laws," its structure, its dynamic, etcetera . . . 2) witnessing. A physicist does not have to prove the existence of matter (except perhaps to himself!). A biologist does not have to convince anyone that a cell is a reality, nor a historian that Louis XIV or Julius Caesar were in fact real human beings. Everything happens, instead, as if the reality of the object of my discipline, although acknowledged theoretically, needs to be proven again and again. The unconscious is the object of censorship and repression—that is its essence. That can be verified not only on an individual basis, but also on cultural and social levels. We acknowledge that the unconscious exists, but no one really believes in it. . . . Now, that object does indeed exist. The unconscious possesses laws and structures. . . . A science, ours among others, exists only on the condition that it enlarge, specify, and refine its models and its experimentation, as time goes by. I am trying to contribute to this. That work is also a political battle. . . . I am profoundly convinced that in our civilization, psychoanalysis, as theory and as treatment, is one of the most precious, highest, most symbolic forms of freedom. This practice, indeed, simultaneously recognizes the existence of violence, of homicidal desire, in every human being, and wagers that he won't be the same, that he will transform himself as soon as a place opens up where another can hear about it. These are fantastically high stakes for freedom, something totalitarian states understand well, judging from the extent to which psychoanalysis has been the object of persecution there. . . .

QUESTION #2—Never do I say to myself: "I write as a woman; I will be able to transmit this message better than a man, or less well." What is important, I repeat, is the unconscious, the female unconscious, or the male unconscious which I'm busy with these days. . . . Nonetheless, I have to note, after the fact, that I certainly would not have written the texts I can now reread, if I'd been a man. That's for sure! "Writing as a woman," that can also mean: writing to express, to defend points of view, truths, rights that belong to women. It can mean: to be a feminist writer. I never was one. . . .

QUESTION #3—That new space enables them [women] to acquire credibility, notoriety, a workplace, all more easily. As for the canon, history makes that decision. What will be the values which in the next centuries will decide to place this woman, and not that one, in the canon? I do not know, but I'm inclined to think that women will find a place there thanks to values that are foreign to institutions. Because these women will be recognized either as brilliant, or as pioneers and precursors.

QUESTION #4—Paradoxically, at this time, I feel that my work is better understood in interdisciplinary meetings than in psychoanalytic milieus, especially French milieus. I don't attribute that to my being female, but to the fact that in these meetings, each person is less threatened, more at ease. Questions of propriety and jealousy lose their immediacy, and do so regardless of gender.

QUESTION #5— . . . I would like for it to be said of my thought, that while being a woman's—I mean while being gendered feminine—it is rigorous and bold. . . . True rigor and logic must move through avenues where a writer's subjectivity, imagination, values, and anguish are put into play. . . .

QUESTION #6: In your work, *L'Ombre et le nom*, you explore the relationships between primary imagination and the feminine. You speak of this feminine in terms that one could qualify as traditional, such as the "shadow," [*ombre*], the "nonrepresentable," the "outside," [*dehors*], etcetera. Far from criticizing such a metaphoric description of femininity, you confer value on it by designating it as an essential supporting element of the culture, a support that shouldn't be endangered. What do we risk if women, in spite of everything, move out of the shadow to touch the male corpus of the canon?

—All women will not move out of the shadow. Only some will. Perhaps, during the course of this new generation, more will. But allow me to come back nevertheless to some of your formulations. It is not because more men than women have a place in the "canon" that it remains male for all that. What enters the canon is what lasts, therefore what matters, artistically and scientifically, what is a *work* in the strong sense of that word. And all human work worthy of the name is what, each time, in its own way, reconciles and unites the masculine and the feminine. . . .

Christiane Rochefort [18]

QUESTION #1— . . . It means I'm in that century. How do you expect me to think about what it would mean to be in any other one? . . . I've lived through several historical periods, some in my childhood which I remember, some good ones like the sixties, and now we're in a very frightening, terrifying period—the eighties. . . . I'm pretty up on history and contemporary history; I mean I'm like a sponge that soaks up what's going on. Well, that means I've got to deal with the century I live in. . . .

QUESTION #2—A lot of stupid things, especially in reference to biology, have been written about "writing as a woman." . . . Of course, people do have different experiences but writing as a woman is like writing as a black, a coal miner, a samurai, an Indian Buddhist, or the CEO of some huge corporation. What it means is that each person has a certain material that differs from that of the person next door. That's what it means to me—I have a certain material. It does not mean there's a specificity of writing. . . .

QUESTION #3— . . . There are a lot of people, men and women, who aren't in the canon but who are worthwhile. Having said that, there are a lot more worthwhile women who didn't make it into the canon because no one paid any attention to them. . . . I think that's been taken care of today now that we have an old-boy republic and an old-girl republic to boot. . . . Things are evening out, but within that old-boy, old-girl network. . . . There probably won't be as many women who disappear . . . completely. . . . So I think this equalizing business is a good thing. Well, that's more or less going to be the case in publishing for the simple reason that they can make more money if they publish women's books too. . . . It has nothing to do with being more liberal. . . .

QUESTION #4— . . . We're seeing far too much literary theory being written today considering literary theory isn't at all important. . . . First there was the terrible period when literature was theoretically analyzed by using autobiography and biography. . . . Now we're in the terrible period when literature is being analyzed by using— what? . . . Literature has nonetheless remained outside of all that. . . . It's a separate entity, except when every now and then a philosopher comes along who knows how to write. That happens sometimes, as with Nietzsche for instance. That changes everything but it's pretty rare, and by the way, only then is he a good philosopher. . . . It's a good idea to be interdisciplinary, whether the subject being studied is women or elephants. . . . [But] why talk about blurring category distinctions? I'm not so sure it blurs them. On the contrary, I think it should clarify them. . . . It's about time people were interdisciplinary. Classifying things is a result of the nineteenth century, so I don't see what women have to do with it. . . . Everybody needs to do it. . . .

QUESTION #5— . . . I couldn't really say. I'm already in the grade school . . . and high school books. I don't know if I'll go any higher than that though. . . . I am subject to a particular kind of ostracism. . . . It's not easy to classify me because I go by my own rules. . . I'm not part of any consensus, so to the extent that the words *canon* and *consensus* can be confused . . . my work doesn't stand much chance of being included. . . . To tell you the truth, I couldn't care less. I did have something happen to me once, though. A friend of mine told me about this friend of hers who was half-crazy—this guy had been sent to fight in the Algerian War even though he was of Berber descent. He deserted from the army . . . and lost his mind. . . . At some point someone lent him one of my books, *Les Petits Enfants du siècle.* It gave him back his courage and calmed him down. He was cured by it and felt better afterward. . . . Things don't happen in literary history or in literary anthologies; they happen in life. . . . Now *that's* immortality. . . .

QUESTION #6: People don't usually smile while they're reading a book that's supposed to be feminist, but they do when reading *Les Stances à Sophie* for example. Will this funny kind of marriage between criticism of masculine society and feminine-style humor help a body of work such as your own be included in the canon or will it act as an obstacle to inclusion?

—It's an obstacle because not everyone has a sense of humor. . . . I remember that in the beginning of the women's movement there were about fifteen of us . . . and a couple of us said, "We're not going to have any demonstration unless it's funny!" Without humor there can be no revolution or change. You can be sure you've got it wrong if it isn't funny. . . . We didn't win of course, humor never does. The truth is, humor is a minority too. . . .

Monique Wittig

QUESTION #1—If I were to answer this question from the point of view of literary history, I would remind us that our century has taught us more than once what the revolution of the novel is about. I am thinking of Stein, Proust, Joyce, Dos Passos, Faulkner, Woolf, Sarraute, etcetera. These are the giants of our century. I always keep them in mind, for they taught us that form is meaning. They taught us to tear off limb by limb a new literary reality from the literary landscape of the time. The accent on form is what is new to this century. And a writer's work today is on form. But to invent a form that is new and raw is difficult. We aren't here to make pretty things. We might ask who is writing the new American experimental novel today? Is it not our work as writers to experiment so as to fight the canon, to break it down? A writer never works in (or to be in) the canon. All of the above writers were fighting the canon.

QUESTION #2. . . . . .[19]

QUESTION #3—To say that writers have been excluded from the canon because they are women seems to me not only inexact, but the very idea proceeds from a trend toward theories of victimization. There are few great writers in any century. Each time there was one, not only was she welcome within the canon, but she was acclaimed, applauded, and praised in her time—sometimes *especially* because she was a woman. I'm thinking of Sand and Colette. I do not think that real innovators have been passed by. In the university, we ruin the purpose of what we do if we make a special category for women—

especially when teaching. When we do that as feminists, we ourselves turn the canon into a male edifice.

QUESTION #4—First of all, I do not think this process is specifically
linked to women. Secondly, I think the disciplines have on the contrary strengthened their boundaries.

QUESTION #5—That's a provocative question to which no writer with
any modesty can respond.

QUESTION #6: Deciding the content of the canon is a classification
process that is doubly complicated in your case.

First, given the positive way *The Opoponax*, with its stylistic
innovations, was received in France, one can imagine that a category will be proposed in order to include it in the canon. But when
one adds to this formal experimentation an even more radically
other exploration of sexuality, as in *Les Guérillères* and *The Lesbian Body*, one can expect to see a complete refusal of your work on
the part of the guardians of the dominant culture.

Secondly, to make this process even more problematic, especially
in relation to the questions we have asked you, you refuse the category of woman and declare that you are instead a lesbian. What do
you think about the fact that you have been so successful at discon-
certing these efforts at categorization?

—First, the question of the canon is a question for literary criticism,
not for fiction writers.

Secondly, there is confusion created when a purely sociological
matter is transported into literary criticism. For example, women
are a sociological group whose very existence vis-à-vis the sociological group of men is barely accepted. The fact that these two groups
exist in a conflictual political situation is not yet taken seriously so
it is important not to jump ahead, past this essential fact. Lesbians,
by their very existence, are fugitive women—people trying to escape
their class. It is true that the notion of woman is the ideological
aspect, the alienated representation of oneself which seems to em-
anate from the group but is in fact imported from outside. That is
to say: women exist as a class while woman is an imaginary formation (to use an expression by Guillaumin). These are sociological
issues. Now to return to the literary problem: I can no more say I am
a lesbian writer than I can say I am a woman writer. I am simply a
writer. Writing is what is important, not sociological categories. I
do think some changes of form are more open to history than others;

but working, writing—for the writer—is an individual process, never a collective one.

Notes

1. Translated by Anne M. Menke.
2. Translated by Deborah W. Carpenter.
3. The question is about Cixous' play *Histoire terrible mais inachevée de Norodom Sihanouk roi du Cambodge,* produced at the Théâtre du Soleil in 1985.
4. Translated by Patricia Baudoin.
5. Translated by Heidi Gilpin.
6. Translated by Patricia Baudoin.
7. Translated by Patricia Baudoin.
8. "Le français contrelangue," *Revue et corrigée* 18 (1985).
9. We have agreed with Luce Irigaray to publish the full answers to two of the questions instead of excerpts from each one. They were translated by Margaret Whitford.
10. Sexual/gendered translates *sexué.* (Translator's note)
11. Translated by Patricia Baudoin.
12. Translated by Anne M. Menke.
13. Translated by Patricia Baudoin.
14. The following passage, up to "Michel," is an excerpt from a letter to Alice Jardine and Anne Menke dated 18 May 1986.
15. Excerpt from letter dated 18 May 1986.
16. Translated by Anne M. Menke.
17. Translated by Patricia Baudoin.
18. Translated by Anne M. Menke.
19. Monique Wittig chose not to answer this question. Her remarks in "The Straight Mind" may help to explain her position. See *Feminist Issues* 1 (1980): 103–111.

15 PAOL KEINEG

Vains Ecrivains, Vaines Ecrivaines: Women Writers of Québec and the Canon

Six Interviews

A woman friend of mine, a native speaker of French, with whom I was discussing the *écrivaines* from Québec, protested my use of such an ugly word; besides, she said, it rhymes with *vaines*. Dumbfounded at first, I eventually retorted that, as *écrivains* rhymes with *vains*, I could not see her point. My friend's indignation reminded me of an official dinner in Québec City a few years ago at which I had a conversation with a famous French novelist. I told her of the Québécois efforts to "desexualize" the French language. When I added that as a matter of course I now use feminine nouns such as *écrivaine* or *auteure*, she nearly had a fit. She was determined to remain an *écrivain* and no one would dare call her otherwise. Over her dead body.

Québécois literature was born in and of the North American space. The necessary exploration and colonization of what was becoming Canada opened up a space within the emerging society that made it possible for women to take a major part in the construction of that literature. Indeed, if the familiar oppositions between public/masculine and private/feminine can be found there as elsewhere, the exclusion of women did not take the same form as in Europe. Women were active in intellectual life from the start, whether they belonged to religious orders (which offered a significant alternative to marriage and *galanterie* in the New World) or stayed at home, in charge of the family correspondence and the children's education, under the supervision of priests of course. Men were mostly gone to the woods to clear land for cultivation. Their absence, combined with an acute inferiority complex resulting from English colonization, empowered women in a way not possible in France at the time. A women's intellectual tradition was born, and that in part explains Québécois women writers' visibility today. As Madeleine Gagnon observes, not only were they not excluded from the canon, but they made a decisive contribution to the diffusion of Québécois literature, which a large number of people first discovered through its women writers.

Some of them, such as Anne Hébert and Marie-Claire Blais, are well known in France and elsewhere, but since the apparent demise of so-called French feminism in the early eighties, the younger female writers have been largely ignored. After a long period of noncommunication following the French Revolution, Québec embraced French literary currents and influences, and the two societies seemed to be growing closer: now it appears that on a certain level France and Québec are once again parting ways. On the one hand, Québec has made a considerable effort at standardizing its language (without reducing it to its European counterpart); on the other, the Québécois and above all the Québécoises, as Louky Bersianik points out, have undertaken a vast reform of one of the most sexist languages in the West, for instance by providing feminine forms for professions which had none. In France today the French will eventually welcome neologisms forged in Québec to replace technical English words, but they are unwilling to accept antisexist innovations coming from North America. They not only cringe at hearing *écrivaines*, but many women insist on being called Madame le Ministre, Madame le Directeur, etcetera.

The first three interviews that follow (Gagnon, Théoret, Dupré) were carried out in Montréal in May 1989. As a Breton poet, who had taken a keen interest in Québécois literature in the early sixties, I was thrilled at being offered the opportunity of meeting women writers who had initially emerged as part of the nationalist generation, but who had come to question forcefully many of that generation's assumptions (and of whom I could see no equivalent in France, and certainly not in Brittany). As a man, I was more than a little apprehensive. I shouldn't have been. All, including those who later sent me their answers by mail (Marchessault, Bersianik, Michaud), were extremely friendly and open. This attitude reflects, I think, something very appealing about Québec society as a whole.[1]

Madeleine Gagnon is probably the best known outside Québec, in part because of her collaboration with Hélène Cixous and Annie Leclerc in *La Venue à l'écriture*. She is the author of an important body of work that includes, *Lueur, Les Fleurs du catalpa, Autographie 1, Toute Écriture est amour (Autographie 2)*. She teaches comparative literature at the Université de Montréal and is a member of the Académie canadienne-française.

After teaching for nineteen years at the college level, France Théoret is now devoting all her energies to writing. She cofounded the feminist newspaper *Les Têtes de pioche* and was from 1981 to 1984 the editor of the important monthly *Spirale*. A poet and novelist, she has published eight books, including *Nécessairement putain* and *Nous parlerons comme on écrit*.

The youngest of the six, Louise Dupré has already published several books of poems, including *Chambres*, and *Bonheur*. She teaches literature at the Université de Montréal, and *Stratégies du regard*, her long study of the works of Nicole Brossard, Madeleine Gagnon, and France Théoret, has just appeared.

A novelist and playwright, Jovette Marchessault tries to make a living from her writing. Poverty is the price to pay, she says, but she is happy. She has written a trilogy consisting of *Comme un enfant de la terre, La Mère des herbes*, and *Des Cailloux blancs pour les forêts obscures*. Among her plays are *La Terre est trop courte, Violette Leduc*, and *Anaïs dans la queue de la comète*.

Louky Bersianik studied in France and traveled in Greece before returning to Québec, where she wrote for radio, TV, and the movies. In 1976, *L'Euguélionne*, the first feminist novel in Québec, became a best seller. She has since published another novel, *Pique-nique sur l'Acropole*, and several books of poems, including *Kerameikos*. She is also an essayist.

Of the six writers, Ginette Michaud is the only professional critic. She teaches literature at the Université de Montréal, although for the past three years she has been living on a Bourse du Canada as a research professor. She is the author of numerous articles and has published *Lire le fragment: Théorie et transfert de la lecture chez Roland Barthes*. She is a member of the editorial boards of *Spirale* and *Etudes françaises*.

Despite the prominence of women writers in Québec, it would be wrong to assume that patriarchy has vanished there into the mists of the past. Rather, patriarchy in Québec for historical reasons (the absence and/or humiliation of the male population by English rule) did not take the same form as in other societies. Therefore, the nationalist movement that emerged in the fifties and the sixties was never able to become an instrument for the emancipation of men only, as it did in other colonial societies. It is not surprising, then, in the international context of the seventies, to see women take advantage of the cracks and upheavals in society (of which the most striking manifestation has been the accelerated secularization of a land long in thrall to the Catholic Church) and demand their share of power. Language has always been at the center of Québécois pre-occupations ("Langagement," André Major said[2]), and women writers have posed, beyond the struggle for linguistic survival in North America, the question of to whom language belongs and what purposes and whose interests it serves. The road to equality will be a long one, but at least the Québécois canon has already decided that literature belongs to men *and* women. Even if it does not know it yet, the French-speaking world owes a lot to the women of Québec.

Perhaps such a revolution was possible only in a small nation like Québec. Speaking of the Jewish literature of his time, Franz Kafka wrote in his *Diaries:* "The liveliness of such a literature exceeds even that of one rich in talent, for, as it has no writer whose great gifts could silence at least the majority of cavilers, literary competition on the greatest scale has a real justification." With no apparent "genius" capable of stifling all others, Québécois literature of today has become a most dynamic, most vibrant force. For the Québécois, literature is a serious, vital matter. Kafka adds: "A small nation's memory is not smaller than the memory of a large one and so can digest the existing material more thoroughly."[3]

Interview Questions

QUESTION #1: What does it mean to you to write at the end of this century?

QUESTION #2: Could you describe your relationship to language today?

QUESTION #3: Unlike the case of women's writing in France, in Québécois literature women writers have always occupied a privileged position. To what do you attribute this difference?

QUESTION #4: In general, Québécois writers have to guard against both France and Anglophone America. Are there specific problems for Québécois women writers, particularly in these years of declining Québécois nationalism?

QUESTION #5: What is your relationship with Canadian and U.S. feminisms? And with French feminisms?

Madeleine Gagnon

QUESTION #1—End of the century, beginning of the century, that doesn't mean anything. I don't understand people who get upset because it's the end of the century, or even the end of a millennium. We should have a sense of the end of something, but for me the end of a century isn't the end of anything.

QUESTION #2—The older I get, the more I think about writing and speech—therefore about language—the more aware I become of how difficult it has been for us, as Québécois, to speak and to write in our own language. There was a feeling, not necessarily conscious, of being somehow at fault, because here in Québec the gap between spoken language and written language is much greater than in France, even though we learned almost the same language, read the same texts. It's as if, in French, we were from the beginning a bit bilingual. Maybe this is true in France too, in regions other than Paris, but it's less and less true. Here too this feeling of fault and of the gap is subsiding with uniformization. The French of Québec is being standardized, and then in the entire world, we all finally have the same problems with regard to a language which is English. But I can't say that it bothers me or wears me down, because I continue to read and write in French, while reading English too. I don't really feel that there's a threat, that we are going to let ourselves be smothered, swallowed, assimilated—I don't think so. I think that English will be the only esperanto to succeed.

The case of Ireland interests me. Politically, the Irish were not given the choice of sacrificing their language. But what is amazing is the point to which they came into English to open it up, to enrich it—all the great poets, writers, not only Joyce—what an extraordinary route! A completely different path from ours, Québécois, French Canadian, not better, not worse.

QUESTION #3—This could be explained by historical reasons: here in Québec women were better educated than men, except for the clerical elite in charge of education. The men, gone off to clear the land, didn't have a choice. The women stayed home, read, went to see the priest; and so they were responsible for the passing down of all of the moral, cultural, and, in part, intellectual values. Women played a big part, without it really showing, in literature as well.

QUESTION #4—To start, I wouldn't say that there are more problems for women than for men. Québécois writers should "guard against the others"? First of all, one shouldn't protect oneself against others; on the contrary, we have to open up. We were closed for too long, for historical reasons. There were two Indexes. First the Church's Index that was very very strong up through the 1950s and forbade us most of the important books from France, from the United States, and elsewhere. It was therefore a small culture very closed unto itself, very self-protective, very chauvinistic; but by force of circumstance it was not an arrogant chauvinism. Rather, it was a chauvinism of the colonized, about which Memmi spoke so well, a kind of closure toward the other that can be understood by the very condition of the Québécois as colonized. And there was also censorship by the English which is always discussed less. In the eighteenth century there was a period when all books coming by boat from France were diverted to London. We are in a period of openness. We should definitely not protect ourselves from other literatures. Just the contrary.

Are women writers treated less well than their male colleagues? Among the women of my generation, several have had greater success elsewhere (in English Canada, the United States, France, among others) because they were feminists. That there is machismo, phallocracy here in Québec, certainly; but that all the networks for reception of books are completely closed to a category of books because they are feminist, no. It would be rather the opposite.

QUESTION #5—I'll start with French feminism, with which I had quite close relations in the seventies. I used to go to France often; I knew all the groups fairly well. There was the book I did with Hélène Cixous and Annie Leclerc. And then, practically all my French friends left their respective groups, with horrible stories: there were power struggles; incredible hierarchical systems got set up. When they saw that the kind of power they had denounced so strongly elsewhere was being reproduced among women, they said to themselves that a gynecocracy was no better than a phallocracy—and my French friends would no longer call themselves feminists in the way they understood the term in the seventies. And when it's said that feminism in France is dead, it's true in a certain way. The feminism that became official is still alive, but for those who never wanted this officialized feminism, this feminism of power is death. The others, who were real feminists, at heart and in spirit, who really wanted to change fundamental things, in relations between the sexes for example, and in all the relations of domination and power, those women therefore who would be faithful to what we believed, that's to say to a world in which there would no longer be what Derrida calls phallogocentrism, those women no longer call themselves feminists. It's very paradoxical.

In U.S. and English Canadian feminisms, it's different. It's as if seeds have continued to bear fruit here and there on all sorts of small islands: women in the universities, for example, without it being a big movement as in France, with all the theoretical and political apparatus that founded it and made it official. Because of U.S. and English Canadian feminists in the universities, there was an opening onto what was happening in writing in Québec. First they started by reading women of my generation, then those of preceding generations, to understand where we came from. For them, it was a very promising outpouring of language, a new way of conceiving of and practising writing. They started to be interested in Québécois literature in general, and to interest their colleagues in it too, male and female, mostly in literature departments, to show them that there was a complex, varied, and quite fascinating movement of writing from the sixties on. In a certain way, it is through U.S. and English Canadian feminists in the universities that our literature began to circulate.

In the seventies, I was much closer to what was happening in France. It was perhaps like a more loving, even passionate relationship; I followed the debates there much more than in the United States and English Canada, not as a refusal of what was happening there, but by closeness. France is my second country; I studied there; I have natural affinities with it. I still have several friends there, and I continue to receive and read some beautiful books: Hélène Cixous's, especially her latest, more accomplished novels, and others—Annie Leclerc, Annie Cohen—some friends from the time of the big movement, who are no longer in what is called feminism.

France Théoret

QUESTION #1—To write. I'll give two answers to this question. About fifteen years ago I wagered that there existed a culture in the feminine [*une culture au féminin*] that is not dissociated from the culture in the masculine [*la culture au masculin*]; it was included in the great universal culture, but this culture in the feminine was repressed by patriarchal culture. I don't think that there are two parallel cultures, a masculine one and a feminine one, but rather that there is a single culture from which the feminine has been excluded.

And I write for more personal reasons. I learned a long time ago that there are, on the one hand, necessities, often of an economic order, and then there are what are called questions of conscience. And I write so as not to adopt all of the excuses for refusing to progress on the side of conscience. In the 1980s, there have been some good excuses: the economic recession, the return of sexual and familial norms, the instituting of new conformisms that present themselves as changes. And since adolescence, I have wanted to write. It's important to realize the desires of our adolescence.

QUESTION #2—Above all, writing is an art. My relationship to language passes through memory. I have kept in my memory everything that has to do with my learning of language, and with the way in which I learned to think about language. When I write I am constantly developing my knowledge of language.

I don't want to make politically engaged art; I don't have a utilitarian conception of language. I work with language to make expression count much more than communication.

In a story that will appear this fall entitled "The Man Who Painted Stalin," I denounce the kind of art that is all show.

QUESTION #3—Some Québécois women novelists, like Laure Conan, Germaine Guèvremont, Gabrielle Roy, and Anne Hébert, have written works that count. But the same cannot be said of poetry; it is men who have marked the history of Québécois poetry. There have always been more male than female writers, but certain women writers have written novels that are pivotal works in the history of our literature.

A recent book by Patricia Smart, *Ecrire dans la maison du père*, does just this analysis of works by women of the past as pivotal novels. She shows how institutions recognized these works, but also how they erased the inscription of the feminine. In Laure Conan, Germaine Guèvremont, Gabrielle Roy, Anne Hébert, we can read a contestation of patriarchal history and order. This is a new reading of their work.

QUESTION #4—*Reformulated Question:* In a way Québécois literature remains colonized by the French publishing industry. The distribution networks are held by French groups; French publishing houses buy Québécois publications. Is there a particular problem for women writers, especially with regard to French publishers who, in the image of the French literary world, don't pay much attention to women?

—Yes, our market is invaded by French publishing, just as the other media are: our newspapers, radio, television. And there is in fact a form of colonization by French publishing, and a kind of alienation on our part. I don't really understand why we don't denounce this situation. I don't understand how, individually, we would stand to lose anything as writers by denouncing the situation since French editors publish very few Québécois authors. And when they do publish them, it's not out of altruism, but again it's in order to exploit our market.

With regard to French publishers, it seems that our misfortune is that of writing in French. Because when I think of books by women, certain writing, certain problematics interest French publishers when they belong to a foreign culture. I'm thinking of Christa Wolf and Verena Stefan. If they had originally been written in French, I'm not sure that their works would have created as much interest.

QUESTION #5—In the United States, I'm in touch with some women in the universities who are interested in writing in the feminine [*l'écriture au féminin*]. I've had the opportunity to give talks and readings there. I feel at ease there; there have always been echoes of a feminism that I could develop in my books.

Otherwise, I don't have any ties to French feminism. I went to France quite recently. I always go there privately. I didn't try to make any contacts. It seems that feminism is outdated there. That's what I've been told for a while now.

Life has made me conscious of self-censorship. And so I write what I have to write; I write while thinking of those who will never read me.

Louise Dupré

QUESTION #1—I've thought about this problematic a long time, and the question I asked myself is this: would it be different for me if I were at the beginning of a century, in the middle of a century, if I were in a less turbulent time? At the end of a century, of a millennium, there's always a sense of urgency. I certainly have some of this sense of urgency now, but I think that, in my case, writing has more to do with finding a personal subjectivity than with an unconscious collective that would feel the approaching end. In my early works, I was more preoccupied by more collective thematics: the survival of the planet, problems concerning women. Now it could be said that my writing is becoming more interiorized, closer to me, to my fantasies, to my own imaginary. I am working much more on a kind of poetry invested with a consciousness and an unconscious that have something to do with childhood, memory, singularity.

But, at this century's end, with the arrival of feminism, many paths are opening for women: most women seem to be carried by a new breath of air. There are openings in employment, there is the presence of women in the social sphere, and there is new research (psychoanalysis has done a lot of work in that area), so that we feel enthusiastic. We have everything still to build, to invent, to say . . .

Québécois feminism has stayed alive because it was never an ideology. It has been a very fluctuating, changing movement, so that it felt less constraining than in France, less like an enclosure that could over time become reductive, a "superego." Here we lived it more as an opening up. I think that this fact comes from our territorial situation, between France and the United States, between European nationality, if you like, and U.S. pragmatism.

QUESTION #2—I can tell you what I attempt to do with language: I try to really work word by word, to open up the words. I don't at all conceive of writing as a linearity—I've always tried to break that. Having said that, I don't feel at all original; I'm aware enough to know that someone like Luce Irigaray in France has also sought to rethink language, to see how one could inscribe in language a subjectivity in the feminine. Hélène Cixous has tried to do the same thing. I don't have the impression of inventing everything, but I try to give back the musicality and the rhythm of language to the words, to language, that's to say, to give a sense, a resonance of the body that would represent my own relationship to my body. In *Bonheur*, for example, I worked on the word *happiness* in order to try to rethink it outside of binarity, to undo it from the connotations of advertising. Today we all know that you have to be happy, that it's a virtue, and that it's often linked to consumerism. I worked on the word *happiness* to show that it's not only tied to a rose-colored vision, but also to a darker vision. And in the book, I wrote that "happiness is not the other side of melancholy, but its wall of light." I think that the role of poets is to work on words, to make it so that words take on what I call a volume, a materiality.

QUESTION #3—There's a tendency to say that we have a matriarchy in Québec, and I think that's false. Women have never had any real social power; the men had that, but they were Anglophone men. Women only had power in the home, and that's not much power. They were caught between the Francophone clergy telling them what to do on the one side, and the businessmen, the Anglophone politicians on the other—Francophones were in the service of Anglophone power. Women had an advantage over the men because they could be better educated, and they were closer to the language. They were the ones who passed on education. In Québec, women are traditionally closer to intellectual work, to intellectual research. Among our grandmothers, among our mothers, it's not rare to find a woman who writes poetry, keeps a personal diary, sends letters. Very often the man was illiterate, and he started to work in the lumber camps very young. The men went off to clear the land, and the women gave themselves to "ladies' works." Unfortunately some of this has stayed in the literature. You have to see how hard it is to get boys from technical school to like literature!

Having said that, when there are literary myths in Québec, they're always about men: Nelligan and his madness, Gauvreau, Grandbois, Ducharme. . . . Women rarely become the object of myths. They are recognized, what they do is accepted as important, like Anne Hébert, Gabrielle Roy, but this isn't comparable to the myth of Nelligan. The women write until an advanced age, and then they die. . . .

QUESTION #4—That is the problem today. Since there is a decrease in nationalism, big problems arise in criticism. There's a tendency to see Québécois literature as a subliterature again, and I'm in a research group working on this very question. It is our main problem: getting the Québec public to accept that we have a worthwhile literature. At book conventions, foreign writers are always better received than Québécois writers. And then there's the whole appeal of the best seller, of an "accessible" literature: Stephen King, John Irving—people love that. This has to do with the tendency of "televisual" society, of mass media, with a need for the democratization of culture. I think it's always harder for the major Québécois newspapers to get people to admit that a Québécois book is good, whereas it will be said more quickly that a French book is a good book. Yes, there is a kind of new colonialism.

QUESTION #5—I consider myself in my personal life to be a feminist. I can go to demonstrations for abortion, for the recognition of women in the job market. . . . In writing fiction, it's more difficult. I prefer to say that I practice a writing in the feminine [une écriture au féminin] rather than a feminist writing, because, for all that, writing is driven by an unconscious—if there is a feminist consciousness, I don't think that it can be said that there is a feminist unconscious—so there's a tension in the writing, and you can't submit the writing to a superego. I practice a writing that is traversed by a feminist consciousness, but I don't consider it feminist writing.

Having said that, I continue to be very interested in women's thought. In France there's obviously Luce Irigaray whom I was talking to you about, and whose work is very motivating, very renewing. I very much liked what Hélène Cixous did. In Belgium I would mention Claire Lejeune. In the United States, I like Mary Daly's work a lot, I was very interested in Kate Millett, and I follow closely what women in the universities are doing, like Alice Jardine, Teresa de Lauretis. Ties are being established between Anglophone women in Québec and those in the rest of Canada, at the level of writing, reading, theoretical exchange. I feel very close to them, and I admire very much the work of Daphne Marlatt, Betsy Warland, Erin Mouré, Gail Scott, women who are working in modernity, who are ready to call into question the forms of fictionality.

The ties to the Anglophone women came about at the end of the seventies, beginning of the eighties, after the years of an all-enveloping Québécois nationalism when we really felt the desire to define an identity for ourselves. These ties came finally with feminism, when we understood that there wasn't only the question of nationalism, but that there were other interesting questions from which thought, writing, criticism, etcetera could benefit.

Jovette Marchessault

QUESTION #1—To write at the end of this century when the energy of intelligence can be engaged more than ever before on all continents to incite us to a more and more creative way of living, as much in the field of art as in that of our existence, is a privileged moment.

At the end of every century, new ideas appear that we accept and that we try to transform into ideals. The end of a century is a time when humanity is more sensitive than ever to new ideas. I also notice that among those men and women who write, many are making an effort to go beyond the present world and its state of crisis in order to penetrate into the distant universe of causes, and thereby to pass beyond the effects that keep us from seeing the past and the present in the right perspective. Writing at the end of this century is for me indissociable from reading. These past years, it seems to me that I hear more and more new voices in the distance of my mountains. I try to capture what is happening in the sky and the air of my time, and there are days when the waves are filled with radiant voices that come from afar. . . . But I also capture the disembodied voices that seem to come forth from the great body of the planet in distress, from this dear earth thirsting for appeasement and rest.

To write and to read answer the needs of my soul and my spirit. It allows me to seize the opportunity to serve, no matter the cost, in silence and moral solitude, the great family of the children of the earth.

QUESTION #2—Since I voluntarily decentered myself by leaving the Montréal literary scene and now spend my life in the Laurentian Mountains, my relationship to language has changed. I can't explain it, but I think that in this way I got closer to the language of my thinking activity, even if it is still the language of obscurity, sometimes crude and close to the abyss. I have the feeling that I am starting to grasp the property of language, of a language that is one of desire, that all languages come from desire and that all will end in desire. Each literary form, novel, poem, dramatic text takes its temporal form by reaping the grain of this desire in order to then return to its first place which is eternity. Everything that I write is unrefined, but I hope that one day I will manage to light the fires of desire in language, and that they will burn for a long time.

QUESTION #3—Yes, in Québec as in the rest of Canada, women who write occupy a privileged place. We are talking here about women novelists, about those who work in fiction. What is the reason for this? I can think of two important ones: our literature is young and these women, at least most of them, are our contemporaries. But what will the case be in fifty or one hundred years? Maybe they will in turn be hidden, forgotten.

When I think of all the women who made French literature, in particular of the *Salonnières* who influenced the development of all Western literature, I know that the worst can happen. Without women writers, French literature and Western literature are practically empty and it would take more than the imagination of men to fill them. Here, as in France, as elsewhere, anything is possible because one has succeeded in erasing them bit by bit, without fearing refutation on the part of these mortal women, in this way killing a second time that which had already perished.

QUESTION #4—Yes, we should be careful to safeguard our language. At birth we plunge into the civilization of a people, we place ourselves in a hereditary current. If it doesn't make for vanity or bad nationalism, I think that this love of our maternal language, which is a psychic and spiritual love, is compatible with cosmopolitanism and that it won't ever harm our sense of the universal. In these years of decrease in Québécois nationalism, I don't know anything about the future of our language, and it pains me when I see the way things are going in the domain of education and politics. They say that all that is born is destined to disappear. As soon as I try to understand the meaning of all these births and all these deaths, the greater the mystery grows, and the more I am struck by the tragic character of our civilizations. But I refuse to give myself up to the beatitude of renunciation. On the contrary, in my work, I intend to use every means at my disposal to continue the fight, to follow my development and that of our literature. Maybe one day, from the heart of infinite possibilities, a true answer will arise.

QUESTION #5—It's difficult for me to imagine my life and my work without this relationship with the international feminist movement. Without the feminist movement, my personal evolution would not have been the same. In a text written in the early 1940s, Simone Weil, a philosopher, one of the great minds of our time, analyzes the responsibility of writers in the misfortunes of our century in this way: "The essential character of the first half of the 20th century, is the weakening and almost the disappearance of the notion of value. Dadaism, surrealism are extreme cases. They expressed the drunkenness of total license. The surrealists built a model of non-oriented thought. Other writers of the time and earlier did not go as far, but almost all of them are touched by the same deficiency, the deficiency of the feeling of value. Words such as spontaneity, gratuity, richness, enrichment, words that imply an almost complete indifference to the opposition of values, appeared more often under their pen than words that contain a rapport with good and evil."

It seems to me that feminist writers, essayists, novelists, philosophers, make the notion of value and everything that is necessary for human life at all times of prime importance. And they haven't done it with sweeping slogans. Those that I especially like—Simone de Beauvoir, Christiane Rochefort, Barbara Deming, Adrienne Rich, Marie-Claire Blais, Mary Meigs, Gloria Orenstein, Kate Millett—have written about the meaning of good and evil in our civilization. They tell the horror, the sorrows, and the miseries in the most intimate part of the spirit of all women and children of the earth.

Louky Bersianik

QUESTION #1—Writing is timeless. For me, the gesture I perform in writing is the same as the one that occurred two thousand years ago, one hundred years ago or when I started making sentences out of words. However, this gesture is inscribed in the context of a certain time. Writing at the end of this century means making sentences with *fin-de-siècle* words, that is, with words burdened with the fall of their meaning, or, on the contrary, invested with new meanings. As a feminist, it is certain that my gesture in writing takes place in a cultural field unknown in our declining Judeo-Christian patriarchal civilization. According to my personal vision, this entirely new cultural field, with its absolutely subversive content, is capable of integrating the notion of a culture in the feminine in a perpetual state of becoming [*une culture au féminin en perpétuel devenir*], and of working in every possible way to make visible the specific *imaginary* of women and their *memory of the future.* To imagine a memory of the future is to have in one's memory a future that would not flow entirely out of the past—since a part of the past has not yet arrived. It is to *memorize the future,* the twenty-first century for example, and to use it to think and act in the present. This is an optimistic view of things because it supposes that women will belong to themselves totally, not only physically but symbolically and through all languages. This vision helps me live and it's in this vision that I find my inspiration for writing.

QUESTION #2—As I wrote in March 1987, in a text entitled *Langue étrangère en quête d'auteure,* for years I felt ill at ease with language [*longtemps je me suis sentie . . .*], which must be just as bad as [Marcel] having to go to bed early when everybody else is up having a good time. And still today I feel cramped by language. I have always had the strange feeling that my own language was foreign to me, ignorant of my existence and my identity. This feeling is stronger now than ever because I have had a lot of time to think about the question. And even though I cling stubbornly to the preservation of the French language in Québec, I am at the same time at daggers drawn with it. Western male writers are masters in their language, no matter which one, whereas women are born on the wrong side of grammar, of syntax, of semantics, so that all Western women writers have problems in their own language, with its obvious sexism, its non-neutrality, and its eminently symbolic character in which the feminine appears as a poor, silent, and often derided relation of the masculine. No specialist of modern linguistics or the philosophy of language has ever taken into account the terrible effects of the sexuation and sexism of language. Sexist because it is hierarchized according to the sexes in which one has a greater symbolic value than the other. This is why we are obliged to write "otherwise," to find linguistic strategies that assure our visibility and attest to our existence as well as to the emergence of our imaginary. This is one of the creative aspects of the culture in the feminine that I mentioned earlier.

QUESTION #3—In France, it's very clear that the long literary tradition is exclusively masculine since it has always rejected the very idea that a woman could be a writer. There were women who were exceptions, those of whom it was said that they "wrote like men." The others were quite simply ignored. I think that the act of writing for women, especially for those who came before us, has always been an act of transgression. A transgression of our condition as "minors" that was given us historically, a will to affirm ourselves as *subjects,* a quality previously granted only to men. "To transgress is to progress" says the Euguélionne. To transgress patriarchal symbolic law through literature is to progress along the path of self-determination. As women, we all write "in the house of the father," in Patricia Smart's expression, and self-censorship has dominated our creative act for a long time, otherwise our works were not published. Smart even suggests that women held no place at all in our literature (even though they continued to write) in the period from Laure Conan to Germaine Guèvremont, which represents a good sixty-odd years (1884–1945). The acceptance of a manuscript and the criticism of a book took place according to the only admissible aesthetic and moral criteria, that is, patriarchal. According to Smart, it took one century before any readings in the feminine [analyses au féminin] of Conan's work appeared (*Ecrire dans la maison du père*, 46). However, even when crushed by the hold of the masculine imaginary, the feminine imaginary was able from that time on to put forth more and more numerous shoots in their works, and their works were able to proliferate.

It's important to remember that the mother had an overwhelming importance in Québec, to the point that people have spoken, and incorrectly so, of a matriarchy. The mother was often better educated than the father; and in his absence he left the running of the household to her, a situation that has certainly marked the imagination of children, notably that of the girls who found it natural to take up the pen to express themselves. Today it's not uncommon to find that all that is remembered of women's writings is their subversive character to the detriment of a recognition of their literary qualities, so that we occupy no place of choice within literature on the whole. I would add that this so-called privileged position that women seem to have held in Québécois literature is perhaps more an appearance and a sham than a real quantitative recognition, since it only takes two or three women to succeed in a domain traditionally reserved for men for the men to feel invaded. Examples of this can be seen in politics and in the upper echelons of any organization or institution. When it was recently said that almost half of the Québécois ministerial cabinet was female, it was to be understood that one out of five ministers appointed was a woman. . . . I don't believe that there have been more women than men to hold a privileged place in Québécois literature. Quite the contrary. The women were only visible exceptions that confirmed the rule, and it was on these grounds that they were "chosen" to hold that position.

QUESTION #4—Certainly. For example, the problematic of the national language drowning in an Anglophone sea is really taken very seriously, both by writers, men or women, and by the government. There are laws that sanction the use of French in the public space. The presence of women in the professional sector does not overly preoccupy our leaders. There are certain encouraging measures to feminize titles, but the more profound work is done by women's supervisory committees in public sector institutions and by the unions. Otherwise, it's an understatement when I say that the specific problems of writing in the feminine while wrestling with a sexist language—problems that I mentioned earlier—are a major preoccupation of Québécois women writers, at least of those who are traversed by a feminist consciousness of the situation.

QUESTION #5—Recently my relationship with both English Canadian and U.S. feminisms has greatly improved. I am often invited to speak, sometimes in English, throughout Canada and the U.S. at conferences concerning literature in general, Québécois literature, or feminist literature in Québec. No matter the subject, I always give my feminist point of view on the topic. Last May, I went to Cincinnati to an important conference on the imaginary, the fantasm, and the dream in literature, and I addressed the audience in French; I spoke about the recalcitrant female characters in my novels. I just got back from the state of Washington, where there was a conference entitled "Focus Québec" at Pullman University; I gave my paper there in English (it was on the sexism of the English language), and I participated in a round-table discussion on the reemergence of Québécois nationalism. The week before, I was in Vancouver, where I spoke in English about sexism in the French language and in the humanities; that conference was organized by Women's Studies at the University of British Columbia. At the beginning of November, I'll take part in a colloquium in London, Ontario, on feminist postmodern writing in Québec; and the following week, I'll be at another colloquium in Edmonton, Alberta, on the theme of literature in the feminine and the literary institution. Everywhere the themes and the discussions seem to indicate that the preoccupations of feminist women professors in Canada and the U.S. either coincide with those of feminist women writers in Québec or acknowledge and study them. Otherwise, my ties to French feminisms are more or less nonexistent; there's no exchange on that side, except with one Belgian woman writer.

Ginette Michaud

QUESTION #3[4] —It is most important to note that the value of works by women writers was quickly recognized by the Québécois literary institution. During the contemporary period alone (from the end of the Second World War, which brought modernization to Québécois society, but maybe not a true intellectual modernity—that would only arrive with time), prestigious French literary prizes were awarded: the *Prix Fémina* to Gabrielle Roy for *Bonheur d'Occasion* (1945) (*The Tin Flute*); the *Prix Médicis* to Marie-Claire Blais for *Une Saison dans la vie d'Emmanuel* (1965) (*A Season in the Life of Emmanuel*); Anne Hébert is published in France (where she also lives, which perhaps takes the edge off this apparent breakthrough somewhat, and it must be noted that Jacques Godbout and Réjean Ducharme were published there too); and in *Le Survenant* (1945) (*The Outlanders*), Germaine Guèvremont created one of the most moving characters of Québécois literature. . . .

Should this rapid celebration and institutional recognition be seen as just so many isolated facts, justified by the quality alone of the respective works, or is there really something more significant here, that would be explained by some sociosymbolic configuration particular to the Québécois situation? To answer this question well would require marshaling data from historians, sociocritics, political scientists, and cultural sociologists, which is far beyond my capabilities. I will hazard instead a grossly oversimplified and global interpretation, limiting myself for now to emphasizing that the privileged position accorded to women in Québécois literature is somehow linked to the position generally occupied in Québécois society by the imaginary in regard to the symbolic, to use the Lacanian categories. (And this situation repeats itself in an interesting way in the case of key female characters, even in novels written by men. I'm thinking of Louis Hémon's *Maria Chapdelaine* of course, but also of Michel Tremblay's unforgettable *Belles-Soeurs*, of Réjean Ducharme's Bérénice Einberg in *L'Avalée des avalés* [*The Swallower Swallowed*], of Jacques Ferron's Tinamer de Portanqueue in *L'Amélanchier* [*The Juneberry Tree*], and of so many others.) We often lacked access to the symbolic (look at the figure of the absent and weak father, even in his reduced version as literary theme), notably by dint of our failure in the political domain. The space would then remain that much more open for free play of the imaginary. More concretely, to explain this greater openness on the part of the literary institution with regard to women writers would require going back much further in time and remembering that our distance from the great cultural *métropoles* perhaps did not have solely negative effects. For example, one only has to turn to the founding speeches occasioned by the inauguration of Montréal in 1642 to notice that women already played at that time a role of primary importance; and I'm not only thinking of the "heroines" (Jeanne Mance, Marguerite Bourgeois, Marie de l'Incarnation, etc.) who really give Montréal its first institutions, but also of those women who wrote and preserved the traces of this foundation, the writings of Sister Marie Morin, for example. This probably has to do with the fact that the women who decided to flee the rigidity of a society that was doing everything to reduce their field of action and, precisely, to keep them in *their* place—seventeenth-century France was structured by a fixed hierarchy—these women made their decision knowing full well what they were letting themselves in for. And afterward, they approached their lives as emancipated women, with remarkable strength of character and courage (that should also be seen in relation to their very strong attraction toward mysticism and the sublime). From the beginning, then, a certain tradition is created in Québec in which women place themselves from the outset as equals, if not also as conquerors and as explorers of this "New World." Their contribution to so-called personal literature [*la littérature intime*]—correspondence, diaries, memoirs, etcetera, domain of private life *par excellence*—is particularly rich, and even daring. I'm thinking of Elisabeth Bégon's *Lettres au cher fils*, of Laure Conan, of Henriette Dessaulles, who will all leave a considerable body of work, but whose example will especially serve as a model and inspiration much later for other women writers who, like Madeleine Gagnon, for example, will once again take up this heritage.

QUESTION #4—It's certain that in Québec in the seventies the problematic of feminist writing came, up to a certain point at least, to take up, if not take over altogether, the aesthetic questions which were largely based on nationalism. By that I mean the alliance of poetic and political discourses that started making itself felt in the sixties: notably, the theme of the "nation" [*"le pays"*] as it was exploited (in all the senses of the word) by the poets of L'Hexagone, an important publishing house, and by the writers linked to the revues *Liberté* and *Parti pris*. I would need more space than I have here to provide a nuanced account of the question of Québécois nationalism and the different forms in which it was taken up in literary and critical discourses. Suffice it to say that in the emergence of the Québécois collective subject there is also something slightly other than a strict nationalist ideology, which for good reason is often accompanied by rather negative connotations, and that in Québec's version of nationalism, it is also a case of a certain access to modernity. The subject that constructs and affirms itself there, if it does experience its own affirmation, self-recognition, a certain absolutization of self (that is, a form of sovereign assumption in which it narcissistically exalts its tiniest difference), this experience is also, and necessarily so—structurally one could say—one of impoverishment (Saint-Denys Garneau's "Le Mauvais Pauvre"), of dereliction (Miron), of loss and exile from self. In this sense, the fate, raised to the level of myth, of the Québécois writer or artist *par excellence*—let's mention the most spectacular figures: Nelligan, Aquin, Borduas—is not foreign to that experience of wandering, even if it is sometimes a wandering "sur place," that will be shared by many intellectuals and writers after the Second World War. For, between the fact of placing oneself as a subject by "singing" of the nation (remember that this is also the time in which poetry in the lyric mode reigned), and the apparently very different fact of celebrating the body, for example, as was done in a certain feminist discourse that privileges a "mixed" prose genre—between these two discourses of difference, which in some ways became equally dominant doxa, there is perhaps after all only a difference of degree. That is to say an inversion of points of view and of power relations that masks, under the guise of change (and precisely by shortchanging), a much more significant continuity.

How are the questions of nationalism, sexual gender, and genre related? How are these questions implicated with one another? In what ways do they respond to and exclude one another? Failing to approach this question in articulated (and therefore theoretical) terms, feminism will find itself more and more confined to a discursive space that will belong to it alone (the right to a "Room of One's Own" seems to have been established), but it will not cease to act as a troubling force affecting all of culture, just as it had earlier imagined this to be its most urgent task at the time of its teeming "heroic" beginnings.

QUESTION #5—Let me start by pointing out that a certain strongly ideologized attitude has long prevailed in Québécois intellectual circles concerning U.S. and French feminisms. According to this conception, which has the harshness of a caricature and allows for no nuances, U.S. feminism could only be perceived in opposition to French feminism, following the well-known paradigm of idealization and rejection that marks Québec's intellectual dealings with France and the United States. In this way, U.S. feminism was often seen as possessing, whether it liked it or not, certain qualities or traits typical of the American national psyche. That is: pragmatism, a tendency toward action (political activism), narcissistic and subjective outpourings, the inevitable return of "experience," the primary importance accorded to the body, the denegration of the unconscious and of its effects, etcetera. In counterpoint to this, French feminism was centered mainly in Québec around the names of Julia Kristeva, Luce Irigaray, Marguerite Duras (the object of a real cult), and especially Hélène Cixous (who came to teach in Québec in the early seventies), the Editions des Femmes publishing house, very alive at that time and run by Antoinette Fouque, the *Femmes en mouvement* publication, the "Psy et Po" movement, and the MLF (Women's Liberation Movement) in general that fought in favor of abortion rights for example (the famous Bobigny trial, and the cases defended by Gisèle Halimi, etc.). French feminism, therefore, appeared to be infinitely better articulated intellectually, more rigorous, and above all, it was a kind of magical in-word at that time, more theoretical, capable of performing previously unknown epistemological tricks. And it made no difference that this binary division—a caricatural one, let me repeat—was founded more in myth than in reality. Even at the time, when the generally unanimous denunciation that marked the discourses of the "heroic pioneer women" was already a bit out of fashion, I must admit that it was French feminism that interested me most then. This was because the task that it had set itself of criticizing the sociosymbolic order down to its foundations, and of rethinking the conditions necessary for a new conceptual configuration, was not incompatible (it even formed a kind of natural alliance) with deconstruction as it was being practiced by Derrida and Foucault, and also with the propositions concerning the theory of the Text, of the subject, and of reading found in Barthes and Kristeva. . . .

At this point, the current in feminism I am attracted to is what I would call critical feminism. It works slowly, is reflective and speculative, and its effects are only beginning to make themselves felt. It displays itself in a less spectacular manner perhaps, but it pays the greatest attention to all of the questions touching on representation, the inscription of the feminine subject, socially and historically situated, and its relationships to language. In this way, by a curious detour, it was in following the "deconstructive" path in the United States that I discovered this other critical feminism that ended up short-circuiting and bypassing the French feminism that I originally liked. When I look today for the finest articulation of the questions that interest me, I still turn to Kristeva and Judith Schlanger, but it is also more and more often on the American side that the newest, most stimulating elements are formulated . . .

And finally, regarding ties between French and English feminisms in Canada, although they are still relatively recent, it can be said that they are perhaps in the process of inventing a new manner of displacing the national question (the eternal image of the *Two Solitudes*) through the use of quite original practices of bilingual translation. One thinks for example of the alliance of Nicole Brossard with Daphne Marlatt, who cosign their texts, but also of that which is being elaborated in places such as the journal *Tessera*, the anthology *A Mazing Space*, the "Women and Words" conference, and in the work of someone like Gail Scott. . . . There is in these bridges, in these intersections, something relatively new for both Québec and English-speaking Canada, and that manages to go beyond geolinguistic borders, thanks to shared projects of writing and criticism. This is still completely unusual for the "vases non communicants" that these two communities generally remain, even with regard to literature. Feminism has played a primary role in the constitution of these collaborative networks, always fragile and to be rebuilt of course, but that have the possibility of becoming deeper and of developing because they are founded on a truly mutual communication, respectful of and attentive to the other.

All interviews were translated by Elizabeth A. Houlding.

Notes

1. On the day of my visit, France Théoret, with good reason, was still upset by the savage attack published against her and her fellow feminists in the Canadian literary magazine *Liberté* (no. 181, April 1989). There are obvious limits to conviviality. But in my opinion literary life still seems less nasty in Montréal than in Paris!

2. André Major, "Langagement (1960–1975)," *Voix et Images* 1, no. 1 (September 1975): 120–24.

3. *The Diaries of Franz Kafka*, ed. Max Brod, trans. Joseph Kresh (New York: Schocken Books, 1948), 192, 193.

4. Due to lack of space, we were unable to include answers to questions 1 and 2, and additional deletions have been marked by ellipses.

Contributors

Joan Dayan, whose *Fables of Mind: An Inquiry into Poe's Fiction* was published in 1987, teaches at Queens College and the Graduate Center, City University of New York. She is currently working on a book called *History and Poetic Language in the Caribbean*.

Joan DeJean teaches at the University of Pennsylvania. She is the author of several books on seventeenth- and eighteenth-century French prose fiction, including *Literary Fortification: Rousseau, Laclos, Sade*. Her *Fictions of Sappho, 1546–1937* has just appeared.

Elizabeth A. Houlding is a Ph. D. candidate in the Department of French and Romance Philology at Columbia University who is writing a dissertation on French women and the occupation of Paris.

Alice A. Jardine is professor of Romance languages and literatures at Harvard University. She is the author of *Gynesis: Configurations of Woman and Modernity;* and coeditor of *The Future of Difference* (with Hester Eisenstein), *Men in Feminism* (with Paul Smith), and *Shifting Scenes: Interviews on Women, Writing, and Politics in Post-68 France* (with Anne Menke). She is cotranslator of Julia Kristeva's *Desire in Language* and an editor of the journal of cultural criticism *Copyright*.

BARBARA JOHNSON is professor of English and comparative literatures at Harvard University. She is the author of *Défigurations du language poétique, The Critical Difference,* and *A World of Difference;* and translator of Jacques Derrida's *Dissemination.*

ANN ROSALIND JONES is professor of comparative literature at Smith College. Her book, *The Currency of Eros: Women's Love Lyric in Europe, 1540–1620,* was published in 1990. Her research interests also include women's writing in the twentieth century and contemporary literary theory.

PAOL KEINEG, a poet and a translator, has published twelve books, including *Lieux communs, Boudica, Taliesin, et autres poèmes,* and this year, both in Montreal and Paris, *Silva rerum.* He arrived in the United States in 1974 and is currently an adjunct associate professor at Duke University.

FRANÇOISE LIONNET teaches French and comparative literature and theory at Northwestern University. She is the author of *Autobiographical Voices: Race, Gender, Self-Portraiture* (1989).

ELAINE MARKS is Germaine Brée Professor of French and Women's Studies at the University of Wisconsin at Madison. She is the author of books on Colette (1960) and Simone de Beauvoir (1973); coeditor of *Homosexualities and French Literature* (1979) and *New French Feminisms* (1980); and editor of *Critical Essays on Simone de Beauvoir* (1987). She is currently working on "the Jewish question in French writing."

HELENE MATHIEU, agrégée de Lettres Modernes, teaches at the Ecole normale d'instituteurs and is a consultant to the Ministry of Culture.

ANNE M. MENKE is assistant professor of French at Swarthmore College. She is the coeditor (with Alice Jardine) of *Shifting Scenes: Interviews on Women, Writing, and Politics in Post-68 France;* and the translator of Julia Kristeva's *Language: The Unknown.*

NANCY K. MILLER is distinguished professor of English at Lehman College and the Graduate Center, City University of New York. She is the author of *The Heroine's Text: Readings in the*

French and English Novel, 1722–1782 and *Subject to Change: Reading Feminist Writing;* and editor of *The Poetics of Gender.*

STEPHEN G. NICHOLS is Edmund J. Kahn Professor of Humanities and associate dean for humanities at the University of Pennsylvania. He is the author of *Romanesque Signs: Early Medieval Narrative and Iconography;* and editor of *The Legitimacy of the Middle Ages.* He is completing a book called *Reading Images,* dealing with problems of text and image in medieval manuscripts.

MAUREEN QUILLIGAN is May Company Professor of English at the University of Pennsylvania. She is the author of *The Language of Allegory: Defining the Genre* and *Milton's Spenser: The Politics of Reading;* and coeditor (with Nancy J. Vickers and Margaret W. Ferguson) of *Rewriting the Renaissance: The Discourses of Sexual Difference in Early Modern Europe.* She has just completed a book on Christine de Pizan.

NAOMI SCHOR is William H. Wannamaker Professor of Romance Studies at Duke University. Her most recent books are *Breaking the Chain: Women, Theory, and French Realist Fiction* and *Reading in Detail: Aesthetics and the Feminine.* She is currently completing a study on George Sand.

ENGLISH SHOWALTER, JR. was executive director of the Modern Language Association from 1983 to 1985 and is currently distinguished professor of French at Rutgers University, Camden. He is the author of books and articles on the eighteenth-century novel and on Albert Camus. He is currently working on a nine-volume edition of the letters of Mme de Graffigny.

SUSAN RUBIN SULEIMAN is professor of Romance and comparative literatures at Harvard University. She is the author of *Subversive Intent: Gender, Politics, and the Avant-Garde* and *Authoritarian Fictions: The Ideological Novel as a Literary Genre;* coeditor (with Inge Crosman) of *The Reader in the Text: Essays on Audience and Interpretation;* and editor of *The Female Body in Western Culture: Contemporary Perspectives* and of *Writing Lives: Sartre, Beauvoir, and (Auto)Biography.* She has published numerous articles on modern French literature and on literary theory, and is currently working on problems of avant-garde writing.

ANNE-MARIE THIESSE, agrégée de Lettres Modernes, has been at the Centre national de la recherche scientifique since 1982. She writes on the sociology of contemporary French literature.

NANCY J. VICKERS is professor of comparative literature at the University of Southern California. She has written on Dante, Petrarch, and Shakespeare as well as on politics and patronage in the reign of François I.

Designed by Pat Crowder
Composed by A. W. Bennett, Inc., in Trump text and display
Printed by Thomson-Shore, Inc., on 50-lb Glatfelter paper